The Mis-Education of the Negro

and

The Education of the Negro

by

Carter G. Woodson

The Education of the Negro

Copyright © 2013
All Rights Reserved
Printed in the USA

Published through CreateSpace

The Education of the Negro

1. Introduction 5
2. Religion With Letters 12
3. Education as a Right of Man 26
4. Actual Education 35
5. Better Beginnings 45
6. Educating the Urban Negro 58
7. The Reaction 71
8. Religion without Letters 83
9. Learning in Spite of Opposition 94
10. Educating Negroes Transplanted to Free Soil 105
11. Higher Education 118
12. Vocational Training 130
13. Education at Public Expense 140

Appendix: Documents 152
Bibliography 183

The Mis-Education of the Negro
BEGINS ON PAGE 211

Preface

About two years ago the author decided to set forth in a small volume the leading facts of the development of Negro education, thinking that he would have to deal largely with the movement since the Civil War. In looking over documents for material to furnish a background for recent achievements in this field, he discovered that he would write a much more interesting book should he confine himself to the ante-bellum period. In fact, the accounts of the successful strivings of Negroes for enlightenment under most adverse circumstances read like beautiful romances of a people in an heroic age.

Interesting as is this phase of the history of the American Negro, it has as a field of profitable research attracted only M.B. Goodwin, who published in the Special Report of the United States Commissioner of Education of 1871 an exhaustive History of the Schools for the Colored Population in the District of Columbia. In that same document was included a survey of the Legal Status of the Colored Population in Respect to Schools and Education in the Different States. But although the author of the latter collected a mass of valuable material, his report is neither comprehensive nor thorough. Other publications touching this subject have dealt either with certain localities or special phases.

Yet evident as may be the failure of scholars to treat this neglected aspect of our history, the author of this dissertation is far from presuming that he has exhausted the subject. With the hope of vitally interesting some young master mind in this large task, the undersigned has endeavored to narrate in brief how benevolent teachers of both races strove to give the ante-bellum Negroes the education through which many of them gained freedom in its highest and best sense.

The author desires to acknowledge his indebtedness to Dr. J.E. Moorland, International Secretary of the Young Men's Christian Association, for valuable information concerning the Negroes of Ohio.

C.G. Woodson.
Washington, D.C. June 11, 1919.

Chapter 1

Introduction

Brought from the African wilds to constitute the laboring class of a pioneering society in the new world, the heathen slaves had to be trained to meet the needs of their environment. It required little argument to convince intelligent masters that slaves who had some conception of modern civilization and understood the language of their owners would be more valuable than rude men with whom one could not communicate. The questions, however, as to exactly what kind of training these Negroes should have, and how far it should go, were to the white race then as much a matter of perplexity as they are now. Yet, believing that slaves could not be enlightened without developing in them a longing for liberty, not a few masters maintained that the more brutish the bondmen the more pliant they become for purposes of exploitation. It was this class of slaveholders that finally won the majority of southerners to their way of thinking and determined that Negroes should not be educated.

The history of the education of the ante-bellum Negroes, therefore, falls into two periods. The first extends from the time of the introduction of slavery to the climax of the insurrectionary movement about 1835, when the majority of the people in this country answered in the affirmative the question whether or not it was prudent to educate their slaves. Then followed the second period, when the industrial revolution changed slavery from a patriarchal to an economic institution, and when intelligent Negroes, encouraged by abolitionists, made so many attempts to organize servile insurrections that the pendulum began to swing the other way. By this time most southern white people reached the conclusion that it was impossible to cultivate the minds of Negroes without arousing overmuch self-assertion.

The early advocates of the education of Negroes were of three classes: first, masters who desired to increase the economic efficiency of their labor supply; second, sympathetic persons who wished to help the oppressed; and third, zealous missionaries who, believing that the message of divine love came equally to all, taught slaves the English language that they might learn the principles of the Christian religion. Through the kindness of the first class, slaves had their best chance for mental improvement. Each slaveholder dealt with the situation to suit himself, regardless of public opinion. Later, when measures were passed to prohibit the education of slaves, some masters, always a law unto themselves, continued to teach their Negroes in defiance of the hostile legislation. Sympathetic persons were not able to accomplish much because they were usually reformers, who not only did not own slaves, but dwelt in practically free settlements far from the plantations on which the bondmen lived.

The Spanish and French missionaries, the first to face this problem, set an example which influenced the education of the Negroes throughout America. Some of these early heralds of Catholicism manifested more interest in the Indians than in the Negroes, and advocated the enslavement of the Africans rather than that of the Red Men. But being anxious to see the Negroes enlightened and brought into the Church, they courageously directed their attention to the teaching of their slaves, provided for the instruction of the numerous mixed-breed offspring, and granted freedmen the educational privileges of the highest classes. Put to shame by this noble example of the Catholics, the English colonists had to find a way to overcome the objections of those who, granting that the enlightenment of the slaves might not lead to servile insurrection, nevertheless feared that their conversion might work manumission. To meet this exigency the colonists secured, through legislation by their assemblies and formal declarations of the Bishop of London, the abrogation of the law that a Christian could not be held as a slave. Then allowed access to the bondmen, the missionaries of the Church of England, sent out by the Society for the Propagation of the Gospel among the Heathen in Foreign Parts, undertook to educate the slaves for the purpose of extensive proselyting.

Contemporaneous with these early workers of the Established Church of England were the liberal Puritans, who directed their attention to the conversion of the slaves long before this sect advocated abolition. Many of this connection justified slavery as established by the precedent of the Hebrews, but they felt that persons held to service should be instructed as were the servants of the household of Abraham. The progress of the cause was impeded, however, by the bigoted class of Puritans, who did not think well of the policy of incorporating undesirable persons into the Church so closely connected then with the state. The first settlers of the American colonies to offer Negroes the same educational and religious privileges they provided for persons of their own race, were the Quakers. Believing in the brotherhood of man and the fatherhood of God, they taught the colored people to read their own "instruction in the book of the law that they might be wise unto salvation."

Encouraging as was the aspect of things after these early efforts, the contemporary complaints about the neglect to instruct the slaves show that the cause lacked something to make the movement general. Then came the days when the struggle for the rights of man was arousing the civilized world. After 1760 the nascent social doctrine found response among the American colonists. They looked with opened eyes at the Negroes. A new day then dawned for the dark-skinned race. Men like Patrick Henry and James Otis, who demanded liberty for themselves, could not but concede that slaves were entitled at least to freedom of body. The frequent acts of manumission and emancipation which followed upon this change in attitude toward persons of color, turned loose upon society a large number of men whose chief needs were education and training in the duties of citizenship. To enlighten these freedmen schools, missions, and churches were established by benevolent and religious workers. These colaborers included at this time the Baptists and Methodists who, thanks to the spirit of toleration incident to the Revolution, were allowed access to Negroes bond and free.

With all of these new opportunities Negroes exhibited a rapid mental development. Intelligent colored men proved to be useful and trustworthy servants; they became much better laborers and artisans, and many of them showed administrative ability adequate to the management of business establishments and large plantations. Moreover, better rudimentary education served many ambitious persons of color as a stepping-stone to higher attainments. Negroes learned to appreciate and write poetry and contributed something to math-

Introduction

ematics, science, and philosophy. Furthermore, having disproved the theories of their mental inferiority, some of the race, in conformity with the suggestion of Cotton Mather, were employed to teach white children.

Observing these evidences of a general uplift of the Negroes, certain educators advocated the establishment of special colored schools. The founding of these institutions, however, must not be understood as a movement to separate the children of the races on account of caste prejudice. The dual system resulted from an effort to meet the needs peculiar to a people just emerging from bondage. It was easily seen that their education should no longer be dominated by religion. Keeping the past of the Negroes in mind, their friends tried to unite the benefits of practical and cultural education. The teachers of colored schools offered courses in the industries along with advanced work in literature, mathematics, and science. Girls who specialized in sewing took lessons in French.

So startling were the rapid strides made by the colored people in their mental development after the revolutionary era that certain southerners who had not seriously objected to the enlightenment of the Negroes began to favor the half reactionary policy of educating them only on the condition that they should be colonized. The colonization movement, however, was supported also by some white men who, seeing the educational progress of the colored people during the period of better beginnings, felt that they should be given an opportunity to be transplanted to a free country where they might develop without restriction.

Timorous southerners, however, soon had other reasons for their uncharitable attitude. During the first quarter of the nineteenth century two effective forces were rapidly increasing the number of reactionaries who by public opinion gradually prohibited the education of the colored people in all places except certain urban communities where progressive Negroes had been sufficiently enlightened to provide their own school facilities. The first of these forces was the worldwide industrial movement. It so revolutionized spinning and weaving that the resulting increased demand for cotton fiber gave rise to the plantation system of the South, which required a larger number of slaves. Becoming too numerous to be considered as included in the body politic as conceived by Locke, Montesquieu, and Blackstone, the slaves were generally doomed to live without any enlightenment whatever. Thereafter rich planters not only thought it unwise to educate men thus destined to live on a plane with beasts, but considered it more profitable to work a slave to death during seven years and buy another in his stead than to teach and humanize him with a view to increasing his efficiency.

The other force conducive to reaction was the circulation through intelligent Negroes of antislavery accounts of the wrongs to colored people and the well portrayed exploits of Toussaint L'Ouverture. Furthermore, refugees from Haiti settled in Baltimore, Norfolk, Charleston, and New Orleans, where they gave Negroes a first-hand story of how black men of the West Indies had righted their wrongs. At the same time certain abolitionists and not a few slaveholders were praising, in the presence of slaves, the bloody methods of the French Revolution. When this enlightenment became productive of such disorders that slaveholders lived in eternal dread of servile insurrection, Southern States adopted the thoroughly reactionary policy of making the education of Negroes impossible.

The prohibitive legislation extended over a period of more than a century, beginning with the act of South Carolina in 1740. But with the exception of the action of this State and that of Georgia the important measures which actually

The Education of the Negro

proscribed the teaching of Negroes were enacted during the first four decades of the nineteenth century. The States attacked the problem in various ways. Colored people beyond a certain number were not allowed to assemble for social or religious purposes, unless in the presence of certain "discreet" white men; slaves were deprived of the helpful contact of free persons of color by driving them out of some Southern States; masters who had employed their favorite blacks in positions which required a knowledge of bookkeeping, printing, and the like, were commanded by law to discontinue that custom; and private and public teachers were prohibited from assisting Negroes to acquire knowledge in any manner whatever.

The majority of the people of the South had by this time come to the conclusion that, as intellectual elevation unfits men for servitude and renders it impossible to retain them in this condition, it should be interdicted. In other words, the more you cultivate the minds of slaves, the more unserviceable you make them; you give them a higher relish for those privileges which they cannot attain and turn what you intend for a blessing into a curse. If they are to remain in slavery they should be kept in the lowest state of ignorance and degradation, and the nearer you bring them to the condition of brutes the better chance they have to retain their apathy. It had thus been brought to pass that the measures enacted to prevent the education of Negroes had not only forbidden association with their fellows for mutual help and closed up most colored schools in the South, but had in several States made it a crime for a Negro to teach his own children.

The contrast of conditions at the close of this period with those of former days is striking. Most slaves who were once counted as valuable, on account of their ability to read and write the English language, were thereafter considered unfit for service in the South and branded as objects of suspicion. Moreover, when within a generation or so the Negroes began to retrograde because they had been deprived of every elevating influence, the white people of the South resorted to their old habit of answering their critics with the bold assertion that the effort to enlighten the blacks would prove futile on account of their mental inferiority. The apathy which these bondmen, inured to hardships, consequently developed was referred to as adequate evidence that they were content with their lot, and that any effort to teach them to know their real condition would be productive of mischief both to the slaves and their masters.

The reactionary movement, however, was not confined to the South. The increased migration of fugitives and free Negroes to the asylum of Northern States, caused certain communities of that section to feel that they were about to be overrun by undesirable persons who could not be easily assimilated. The subsequent anti-abolition riots in the North made it difficult for friends of the Negroes to raise funds to educate them. Free persons of color were not allowed to open schools in some places, teachers of Negroes were driven from their stations, and colored schoolhouses were burned.

Ashamed to play the role of a Christian clergy guarding silence on the indispensable duty of saving the souls of the colored people, certain of the most influential southern ministers hit upon the scheme of teaching illiterate Negroes the principles of Christianity by memory training or the teaching of religion without letters. This the clergy were wont to call religious instruction. The word instruction, however, as used in various documents, is rather confusing. Before the reactionary period all instruction of the colored people included the

Introduction

teaching of the rudiments of education as a means to convey Christian thought. But with the exception of a few Christians the southerners thereafter used the word instruction to signify the mere memorizing of principles from the most simplified books. The sections of the South in which the word instruction was not used in this restricted sense were mainly the settlements of Quakers and Catholics who, in defiance of the law, persisted in teaching Negroes to read and write. Yet it was not uncommon to find others who, after having unsuccessfully used their influence against the enactment of these reactionary laws, boldly defied them by instructing the Negroes of their communities. Often opponents to this custom winked at it as an indulgence to the clerical profession. Many Scotch-Irish of the Appalachian Mountains and liberal Methodists and Baptists of the Western slave States did not materially change their attitude toward the enlightenment of the colored people during the reactionary period. The Negroes among these people continued to study books and hear religious instruction conveyed to maturing minds.

Yet little as seemed this enlightenment by means of verbal instruction, some slaveholders became sufficiently inhuman to object to it on the grounds that the teaching of religion would lead to the teaching of letters. In fact, by 1835 certain parts of the South reached the third stage in the development of the education of the Negroes. At first they were taught the common branches to enable them to understand the principles of Christianity; next the colored people as an enlightened class became such a menace to southern institutions that it was deemed unwise to allow them any instruction beyond that of memory training; and finally, when it was discovered that many ambitious blacks were still learning to stir up their fellows, it was decreed that they should not receive any instruction at all. Reduced thus to the plane of beasts, where they remained for generations, Negroes developed bad traits which since their emancipation have been removed only with great difficulty.

Dark as the future of the Negro students seemed, all hope was not yet gone. Certain white men in every southern community made it possible for many of them to learn in spite of opposition. Slaveholders were not long in discovering that a thorough execution of the law was impossible when Negroes were following practically all the higher pursuits of labor in the South. Masters who had children known to be teaching slaves protected their benevolent sons and daughters from the rigors of the law. Preachers, on finding out that the effort at verbal education could not convey Christian truths to an undeveloped mind, overcame the opposition in their localities and taught the colored people as before. Negroes themselves, regarding learning as forbidden fruit, stole away to secret places at night to study under the direction of friends. Some learned by intuition without having had the guidance of an instructor. The fact is that these drastic laws were not passed to restrain "discreet" southerners from doing whatever they desired for the betterment of their Negroes. The aim was to cut off their communication with northern teachers and abolitionists, whose activity had caused the South to believe that if such precaution were not taken these agents would teach their slaves principles subversive of southern institutions. Thereafter the documents which mention the teaching of Negroes to read and write seldom even state that the southern white teacher was so much as censured for his benevolence. In the rare cases of arrest of such instructors they were usually acquitted after receiving a reprimand.

The Education of the Negro

With this winking at the teaching of Negroes in defiance of the law a better day for their education brightened certain parts of the South about the middle of the nineteenth century. Believing that an enlightened laboring class might stop the decline of that section, some slaveholders changed their attitude toward the elevation of the colored people. Certain others came to think that the policy of keeping Negroes in ignorance to prevent servile insurrections was unwise. It was observed that the most loyal and subordinate slaves were those who could read the Bible and learn the truth for themselves. Private teachers of colored persons, therefore, were often left undisturbed, little effort was made to break up the Negroes' secret schools in different parts, and many influential white men took it upon themselves to instruct the blacks who were anxious to learn.

Other Negroes who had no such opportunities were then finding a way of escape through the philanthropy of those abolitionists who colonized some freedmen and fugitives in the Northwest Territory and promoted the migration of others to the East. These Negroes were often fortunate. Many of them settled where they could take up land and had access to schools and churches conducted by the best white people of the country. This migration, however, made matters worse for the Negroes who were left in the South. As only the most enlightened blacks left the slave States, the bondmen and the indigent free persons of color were thereby deprived of helpful contact. The preponderance of intelligent Negroes, therefore, was by 1840 on the side of the North. Thereafter the actual education of the colored people was largely confined to eastern cities and northern communities of transplanted freedmen. The pioneers of these groups organized churches and established and maintained a number of successful elementary schools.

In addition to providing for rudimentary instruction, the free Negroes of the North helped their friends to make possible what we now call higher education. During the second quarter of the nineteenth century the advanced training of the colored people was almost prohibited by the refusals of academies and colleges to admit persons of African blood. In consequence of these conditions, the long-put-forth efforts to found Negro colleges began to be crowned with success before the Civil War. Institutions of the North admitted Negroes later for various reasons. Some colleges endeavored to prepare them for service in Liberia, while others, proclaiming their conversion to the doctrine of democratic education, opened their doors to all.

The advocates of higher education, however, met with no little opposition. The concentration in northern communities of the crude fugitives driven from the South necessitated a readjustment of things. The training of Negroes in any manner whatever was then very unpopular in many parts of the North. When prejudice, however, lost some of its sting, the friends of the colored people did more than ever for their education. But in view of the changed conditions most of these philanthropists concluded that the Negroes were very much in need of practical education. Educators first attempted to provide such training by offering classical and vocational courses in what they called the "manual labor schools." When these failed to meet the emergency they advocated actual vocational training. To make this new system extensive the Negroes freely cooeperated with their benefactors, sharing no small part of the real burden. They were at the same time paying taxes to support public schools which they could not attend.

Introduction

This very condition was what enabled the abolitionists to see that they had erred in advocating the establishment of separate schools for Negroes. At first the segregation of pupils of African blood was, as stated above, intended as a special provision to bring the colored youth into contact with sympathetic teachers, who knew the needs of their students. When the public schools, however, developed at the expense of the state into a desirable system better equipped than private institutions, the antislavery organizations in many Northern States began to demand that the Negroes be admitted to the public schools. After extensive discussion certain States of New England finally decided the question in the affirmative, experiencing no great inconvenience from the change. In most other States of the North, however, separate schools for Negroes did not cease to exist until after the Civil War. It was the liberated Negroes themselves who, during the Reconstruction, gave the Southern States their first effective system of free public schools.

Chapter 2

Religion With Letters

The first real educators to take up the work of enlightening American Negroes were clergymen interested in the propagation of the gospel among the heathen of the new world. Addressing themselves to this task, the missionaries easily discovered that their first duty was to educate these crude elements to enable them not only to read the truth for themselves, but to appreciate the supremacy of the Christian religion. After some opposition slaves were given the opportunity to take over the Christian civilization largely because of the adverse criticism[1] which the apostles to the lowly heaped upon the planters who neglected the improvement of their Negroes. Made then a device for bringing the blacks into the Church, their education was at first too much dominated by the teaching of religion.

Many early advocates of slavery favored the enlightenment of the Africans. That it was an advantage to the Negroes to be brought within the light of the gospel was a common argument in favor of the slave trade.

[2] When the German Protestants from Salsburg had scruples about enslaving men, they were assured by a message from home stating that if they took slaves in faith and with the intention of conducting them to Christ, the action would not be a sin, but might prove a benediction.

[3] This was about the attitude of Spain. The missionary movement seemed so important to the king of that country that he at first allowed only Christian slaves to be brought to America, hoping that such persons might serve as apostles to the Indians.[4] The Spaniards adopted a different policy, however, when they ceased their wild search for an "El Dorado" and became permanently attached to the community. They soon made settlements and opened mines which they thought required the introduction of slavery. Thus becoming commercialized, these colonists experienced a greed which, disregarding the consequences of the future, urged the importation of all classes of slaves to meet the demand for cheap labor.[5] This request was granted by the King of Spain, but the masters of such bondmen were expressly ordered to have them indoctrinated in the principles of Christianity. It was the failure of certain Spaniards to live up to these regulations that caused the liberal-minded Jesuit, Alphonso Sandoval, to register the first protest against slavery in America.[6] In later years the change in the attitude of the Spaniards toward this problem was noted. In Mexico the ayuntamientos were under the most rigid responsibility to see that free children born of slaves received the best education that could be given them. They had to place them "for that purpose at the public schools and other places of instruction wherein they" might "become useful to society."[7]

In the French settlements of America the instruction of the Negroes did not early become a difficult problem. There were not many Negroes among the French. Their methods of colonization did not require many slaves. Nevertheless, whenever the French missionary came into contact with Negroes he considered

Religion With Letters

it his duty to enlighten the unfortunates and lead them to God. As early as 1634 Paul Le Jeune, a Jesuit missionary in Canada, rejoiced that he had again become a real preceptor in that he was teaching a little Negro the alphabet. Le Jeune hoped to baptize his pupil as soon as he learned sufficient to understand the Christian doctrine.[8] Moreover, evidence of a general interest in the improvement of Negroes appeared in the Code Noir which made it incumbent upon masters to enlighten their slaves that they might grasp the principles of the Christian religion.[9] To carry out this mandate slaves were sometimes called together with white settlers. The meeting was usually opened with prayer and the reading of some pious book, after which the French children were turned over to one catechist, and the slaves and Indians to another. If a large number of slaves were found in the community their special instruction was provided for in meetings of their own.[10]

After 1716, when Jesuits were taking over slaves in larger numbers, and especially after 1726, when Law's Company was importing many to meet the demand for laborers in Louisiana, we read of more instances of the instruction of Negroes by French Catholics.[11] Writing about this task in 1730, Le Petit spoke of being "settled to the instruction of the boarders, the girls who live without, and the Negro women."[12] In 1738 he said, "I instruct in Christian morals the slaves of our residence, who are Negroes, and as many others as I can get from their masters."[13] Years later Francois Philibert Watrum, seeing that some Jesuits had on their estates one hundred and thirty slaves, inquired why the instruction of the Indian and Negro serfs of the French did not give these missionaries sufficient to do.[14] Hoping to enable the slaves to elevate themselves, certain inhabitants of the French colonies requested of their king a decree protecting their title to property in such bondmen as they might send to France to be confirmed in their instruction and in the exercise of their religion, and to have them learn some art or trade from which the colonies might receive some benefit by their return from the mother country.

The education of Negroes was facilitated among the French and Spanish by their liberal attitude toward their slaves. Many of them were respected for their worth and given some of the privileges of freemen. Estevanecito, an enlightened slave sent by Niza, the Spanish adventurer, to explore Arizona, was a favored servant of this class.[15] The Latin custom of miscegenation proved to be a still more important factor in the education of Negroes in the colonies. As the French and Spanish came to America for the purpose of exploitation, leaving their wives behind, many of them, by cohabiting with and marrying colored women, gave rise to an element of mixed breeds. This was especially true of the Spanish settlements. They had more persons of this class than any other colonies in America. The Latins, in contradistinction to the English, generally liberated their mulatto offspring and sometimes recognized them as their equals. Such Negroes constituted a class of persons who, although they could not aspire to the best in the colony, had a decided advantage over other inhabitants of color. They often lived in luxury, and, of course, had a few social privileges. The Code Noir granted freedmen the same rights, privileges, and immunities as those enjoyed by persons born free, with the view that the accomplishment of acquired liberty should have on the former the same effect that the happiness of natural liberty caused in other subjects.[16] As these mixed breeds were later lost, so to speak, among the Latins, it is almost impossible to determine what their circumstances were, and what advantages of education they had.

The Education of the Negro

The Spanish and French were doing so much more than the English to enlighten their slaves that certain teachers and missionaries in the British colonies endeavored more than ever to arouse their countrymen to discharge their duty to those they held in bondage. These reformers hoped to do this by holding up to the members of the Anglican Church the praiseworthy example of the Catholics whom the British had for years denounced as enemies of Christ. The criticism had its effect. But to prosecute this work extensively the English had to overcome the difficulty found in the observance of the unwritten law that no Christian could be held a slave. Now, if the teaching of slaves enabled them to be converted and their Christianization led to manumission, the colonists had either to let the institution gradually pass away or close all avenues of information to the minds of their Negroes. The necessity of choosing either of these alternatives was obviated by the enactment of provincial statutes and formal declarations by the Bishop of London to the effect that conversion did not work manumission.[18] After the solution of this problem English missionaries urged more vigorously upon the colonies the duty of instructing the slaves. Among the active churchmen working for this cause were Rev. Morgan Goodwyn and Bishops Fleetwood, Lowth, and Sanderson.[19]

Complaints from men of this type led to systematic efforts to enlighten the blacks. The first successful scheme for this purpose came from the Society for the Propagation of the Gospel in Foreign Parts. It was organized by the members of the Established Church in London in 1701[20] to do missionary work among Indians and Negroes. To convert the heathen they sent out not only ministers but schoolmasters. They were required to instruct the children, to teach them to read the Scriptures and other poems and useful books, to ground them thoroughly in the Church catechism, and to repeat "morning and evening prayers and graces composed for their use at home."[21]

The first active schoolmaster of this class was Rev. Samuel Thomas of Goose Creek Parish in South Carolina. He took up this work there in 1695, and in 1705 could count among his communicants twenty Negroes, who with several others "well understanding the English tongue" could read and write.[22] Rev. Mr. Thomas said: "I have here presumed to give an account of one thousand slaves so far as they know of it and are desirous of Christian knowledge and seem willing to prepare themselves for it, in learning to read, for which they redeem the time from their labor. Many of them can read the Bible distinctly, and great numbers of them were learning when I left the province."[23] But not only had this worker enlightened many Negroes in his parish, but had enlisted in the work several ladies, among whom was Mrs. Haig Edwards. The Rev. Mr. Taylor, already interested in the cause, hoped that other masters and mistresses would follow the example of Mrs. Edwards.[24]

Through the efforts of the same society another school was opened in New York City in 1704 under Elias Neau.[25] This benefactor is commonly known as the first to begin such an institution for the education of Negroes; but the school in Goose Creek Parish, South Carolina, was in operation at least nine years earlier. At first Neau called the Negroes together after their daily toil was over and taught them at his house. By 1708 he was instructing thus as many as two hundred. Neau's school owes its importance to the fact that not long after its beginning certain Negroes who organized themselves to kill off their masters were accredited as students of this institution. For this reason it was immediately closed.[26] When upon investigating the causes of the insurrection, however, it was discovered that only one person connected with the institution had taken part in the struggle, the officials of the colony permitted Neau to continue his work and extended him their protection. After having been of invaluable service to the Negroes of New York this school was closed in 1722 by the death of its founder. The work of Neau, however, was taken up by Mr. Huddlestone. Rev. Mr. Wetmore entered the field in 1726. Later there appeared Rev. Mr. Colgan and Noxon, both of whom did much to promote the cause. In 1732 came Rev. Mr. Charlton who toiled in this field until 1747 when he was succeeded by Rev. Mr. Auchmutty. He had the cooeperation of Mr. Hildreth, the assistant of his predecessor. Much help was obtained from Rev. Mr. Barclay who, at the death of Mr. Vesey in 1764, became the rector of the parish supporting the school.[27]

The results obtained in the English colonies during the early period show that the agitation for the enlightenment of the Negroes spread not only wherever these unfortunates were found, but claimed the attention of the benevolent far away. Bishop Wilson of Sodor and Man, active in the cause during the first half of the eighteenth century, availed himself of the opportunity to aid those missionaries who were laboring in the colonies for the instruction of the Indians and Negroes. In 1740 he published a pamphlet written in 1699 on the Principles and Duties of Christianity in their Direct Bearing on the Uplift of the Heathen. To teach by example he further aided this movement by giving fifty pounds for the education of colored children in Talbot County, Maryland.[28]

After some opposition this work began to progress somewhat in Virginia. [29] The first school established in that colony was for Indians and Negroes. [30] In the course of time the custom of teaching the latter had legal sanction there. On binding out a "bastard or pauper child black or white," churchwardens specifically required that he should be taught "to read, write, and calculate as well as to follow some profitable form of labor."[31] Other Negroes also had an opportunity to learn. Reports of an increase in the number of colored communicants came from Accomac County where four or five hundred families were instructing their slaves at home, and had their children catechized on Sunday. Unusual interest in the cause at Lambeth, in the same colony, is attested by an interesting document, setting forth in 1724 a proposition for "Encouraging the Christian Education of Indian, Negro, and Mulatto Children." The author declares it to be the duty of masters and mistresses of America to endeavor to educate and instruct their heathen slaves in the Christian faith, and mentioned the fact that this work had been "earnestly recommended by his Majesty's instructions." To encourage the movement it was proposed that "every Indian, Negro and Mulatto child that should be baptized and afterward brought into the Church and publicly catechized by the minister, and should before the fourteenth year of his or her age give a distinct account of the creed, the Lord's Prayer, and the Ten Commandments," should receive from the minister a certificate which would entitle such children to exemption from paying all levies until the age of eighteen.[32] The neighboring colony of North Carolina also was moved by these efforts despite some difficulties which the missionaries there encountered.[33]

This favorable attitude toward the people of color, and the successful work among them, caused the opponents of this policy to speak out boldly against their enlightenment. Some asserted that the Negroes were such stubborn creatures that there could be no such close dealing with them, and that even when converted they became saucier than pious. Others maintained that these bondmen were so ignorant and indocile, so far gone in their wickedness, so confirmed in their habit of evil ways, that it was vain to undertake to teach them such knowledge. Less cruel slaveholders had thought of getting out of the difficulty by the excuse that the instruction of Negroes required more time and labor than masters could well spare from their business. Then there were others who frankly confessed that, being an ignorant and unlearned people themselves, they could not teach others.[34]

Seeing that many leading planters had been influenced by those opposed to the enlightenment of Negroes, Bishop Gibson of London issued an appeal in behalf of the bondmen, addressing the clergy and laymen in two letters[35] published in London in 1727. In one he exhorted masters and mistresses of families to encourage and promote the instruction of their Negroes in the Christian faith. In the other epistle he directed the missionaries of the colonies to give to this work whatever assistance they could. Writing to the slaveholders, he took the position that considering the greatness of the profit from the labor of the slaves it might be hoped that all masters, those especially who were possessed of considerable numbers, should be at some expense in providing for the instruction of those poor creatures. He thought that others who did not own so many should share in the expense of maintaining for them a common teacher.

Equally censorious of these neglectful masters was Reverend Thomas Bacon, the rector of the Parish Church in Talbot County, Maryland. In 1749 he set forth his protest in four sermons on "the great and indispensable duty of all Christian masters to bring up their slaves in the knowledge and fear of God."[36] Contending that slaves should enjoy rights like those of servants in the household of the patriarchs, Bacon insisted that next to one's children and brethren by blood, one's servants, and especially one's slaves, stood in the nearest relation to him, and that in return for their drudgery the master owed it to his bondmen to have them enlightened. He believed that the reading and explaining of the Holy Scriptures should be made a stated duty. In the course of time the place of catechist in each family might be supplied out of the intelligent slaves by choosing such among them as were best taught to instruct the rest.[37] He was of the opinion, too, that were some of the slaves taught to read, were they sent to school for that purpose when young, were they given the New Testament and other good books to be read at night to their fellow-servants, such a course would vastly increase their knowledge of God and direct their minds to a serious thought of futurity.[38]

With almost equal zeal did Bishops Williams and Butler plead the same cause.[39] They deplored the fact that because of their dark skins Negro slaves were treated as a species different from the rest of mankind. Denouncing the more cruel treatment of slaves as cattle, unfit for mental and moral improvement, these churchmen asserted that the highest property possible to be acquired in servants could not cancel the obligation to take care of the religious instruction of those who "despicable as they are in the eyes of man are nevertheless the creatures of God."[40]

On account of these appeals made during the seventeenth and eighteenth centuries a larger number of slaves of the English colonies were thereafter treated as human beings capable of mental, moral, and spiritual development. Some masters began to provide for the improvement of these unfortunates, not because they loved them, but because instruction would make them more useful to the community. A much more effective policy of Negro education was brought forward in 1741 by Bishop Secker.[41] He suggested the employment of young

Negroes prudently chosen to teach their countrymen. To carry out such a plan he had already sent a missionary to Africa. Besides instructing Negroes at his post of duty, this apostle sent three African natives to England where they were educated for the work.[42] It was doubtless the sentiment of these leaders that caused Dr. Brearcroft to allude to this project in a discourse before the Society for the Propagation of the Gospel in Foreign Parts in 1741.[43]

This organization hit upon the plan of purchasing two Negroes named Harry and Andrew, and of qualifying them by thorough instruction in the principles of Christianity and the fundamentals of education, to serve as schoolmasters to their people. Under the direction of Rev. Mr. Garden, the missionary who had directed the training of these young men, a building costing about three hundred and eight pounds was erected in Charleston, South Carolina. In the school which opened in this building in 1744 Harry and Andrew served as teachers.[44] In the beginning the school had about sixty young students, and had a very good daily attendance for a number of years. The directors of the institution planned to send out annually between thirty and forty youths "well instructed in religion and capable of reading their Bibles to carry home and diffuse the same knowledge to their fellow slaves."[45] It is highly probable that after 1740 this school was attended only by free persons of color. Because the progress of Negro education had been rather rapid, South Carolina enacted that year a law prohibiting any person from teaching or causing a slave to be taught, or from employing or using a slave as a scribe in any manner of writing.

In 1764 the Charleston school was closed for reasons which it is difficult to determine. From one source we learn that one of the teachers died, and the other having turned out profligate, no instructors could be found to continue the work. It does not seem that the sentiment against the education of free Negroes had by that time become sufficiently strong to cause the school to be discontinued.[46] It is evident, however, that with the assistance of influential persons of different communities the instruction of slaves continued in that colony. Writing about the middle of the eighteenth century, Eliza Lucas, a lady of South Carolina, who afterward married Justice Pinckney, mentions a parcel of little Negroes whom she had undertaken to teach to read.[47]

The work of the Society for the Propagation of the Gospel in Foreign Parts was also effective in communities of the North in which the established Church of England had some standing. In 1751 Reverend Hugh Neill, once a Presbyterian minister of New Jersey, became a missionary of this organization to the Negroes of Pennsylvania. He worked among them fifteen years. Dr. Smith, Provost of the College of Philadelphia, devoted a part of his time to the work, and at the death of Neill in 1766 enlisted as a regular missionary of the Society.[48] It seems, however, that prior to the eighteenth century not much had been done to enlighten the slaves of that colony, although free persons of color had been instructed. Rev. Mr. Wayman, another missionary to Pennsylvania about the middle of the eighteenth century, asserted that "neither" was "there anywhere care taken for the instruction of Negro slaves," the duty to whom he had "pressed upon masters with little effect."[49]

To meet this need the Society set the example of maintaining catechetical lectures for Negroes in St. Peter's and Christ Church of Philadelphia, during the incumbency of Dr. Jennings from 1742 to 1762. William Sturgeon, a student of Yale, selected to do this work, was sent to London for ordination and placed in charge in 1747.[50] In this position Rev. Mr. Sturgeon remained nineteen years, rendering such satisfactory services in the teaching of Negroes that he deserves to be recorded as one of the first benefactors of the Negro race.

Antedating this movement in Pennsylvania were the efforts of Reverend Dr. Thomas Bray. In 1696 he was sent to Maryland by the Bishop of London on an ecclesiastical mission to do what he could toward the conversion of adult Negroes and the education of their children.[51] Bray's most influential supporter was M. D'Alone, the private secretary of King William. D'Alone gave for the maintenance of the cause a fund, the proceeds of which were first used for the employment of colored catechists, and later for the support of the Thomas Bray Mission after the catechists had failed to give satisfaction. At the death of this missionary the task was taken up by certain followers of the good man, known as the "Associates of Doctor Bray."[52] They extended their work beyond the confines of Maryland. In 1760 two schools for the education of Negroes were maintained in Philadelphia by these benefactors. It was the aid obtained from the Dr. Bray fund that enabled the abolitionists to establish in that city a permanent school which continued for almost a hundred years.[53] About the close of the French and Indian War, Rev. Mr. Stewart, a missionary in North Carolina, found there a school for the education of Indians and free Negroes, conducted by Dr. Bray's Associates. The example of these men appealing to him as a wise policy, he directed to it the attention of the clergy at home.[54]

Not many slaves were found among the Puritans, but the number sufficed to bring the question of their instruction before these colonists almost as prominently as we have observed it was brought in the case of the members of the Established Church of England. Despite the fact that the Puritans developed from the Calvinists, believers in the doctrine of election which swept away all class distinction, this sect did not, like the Quakers, attack slavery as an institution. Yet if the Quakers were the first of the Protestants to protest against the buying and selling of souls, New England divines were among the first to devote attention to the mental, moral, and spiritual development of Negroes. [55] In 1675 John Eliot objected to the Indian slave trade, not because of the social degradation, but for the reason that he desired that his countrymen "should follow Christ his Designe in this matter to promote the free passage of Religion" among them. He further said: "For to sell Souls for Money seemeth to me to be dangerous Merchandise, to sell away from all Means of Grace whom Christ hath provided Means of Grace for you is the Way for us to be active in destroying their Souls when they are highly obliged to seek their Conversion and Salvation." Eliot bore it grievously that the souls of the slaves were "exposed by their Masters to a destroying Ignorance meerly for the Fear of thereby losing the Benefit of their Vassalage."[56]

Further interest in the work was manifested by Cotton Mather. He showed his liberality in his professions published in 1693 in a set of Rules for the Society of Negroes, intended to present the claims of the despised race to the benefits of religious instruction.[57] Mather believed that servants were in a sense like one's children, and that their masters should train and furnish them with Bibles and other religious books for which they should be given time to read. He maintained that servants should be admitted to the religious exercises of the family and was willing to employ such of them as were competent to teach his children lessons of piety. Coming directly to the issue of the day, Mather deplored the fact that the several plantations which lived upon the labor of their Negroes were guilty of the "prodigious Wickedness of deriding, neglecting, and opposing all due Means of bringing the poor Negroes unto God." He hoped that the masters, of whom God would one day require the souls of slaves committed to their care, would see to it that like Abraham they have catechised servants. They were not to imagine that the "Almighty God made so many thousands reasonable Creatures for nothing but only to serve the Lusts of Epicures, or the Gains of Mammonists."[58]

The sentiment of the clergy of this epoch was more directly expressed by Richard Baxter, the noted Nonconformist, in his "Directions to Masters in Foreign Plantations," incorporated as rules into the Christian Directory.[59] Baxter believed in natural liberty and the equality of man, and justified slavery only on the ground of "necessitated consent" or captivity in lawful war. For these reasons he felt that they that buy slaves and "use them as Beasts for their meer Commodity, and betray, or destroy or neglect their Souls are fitter to be called incarnate Devils than Christians, though they be no Christians whom they so abuse."[60] His aim here, however, is not to abolish the institution of slavery but to enlighten the Africans and bring them into the Church.[61] Exactly what effect Baxter had on this movement cannot be accurately figured out. The fact, however, that his creed was extensively adhered to by the Protestant colonists among whom his works were widely read, leads us to think that he influenced some masters to change their attitude toward their slaves.

The next Puritan of prominence who enlisted among the helpers of the African slaves was Chief Justice Sewall, of Massachusetts. In 1701 he stirred his section by publishing his Selling of Joseph, a distinctly anti-slavery pamphlet, based on the natural and inalienable right of every man to be free.[62] The appearance of this publication marked an epoch in the history of the Negroes. It was the first direct attack on slavery in New England. The Puritan clergy had formerly winked at the continuation of the institution, provided the masters were willing to give the slaves religious instruction. In the Selling of Joseph Sewall had little to say about their mental and moral improvement, but in the Athenian Oracle, which expressed his sentiments so well that he had it republished in 1705,[63] he met more directly the problem of elevating the Negro race. Taking up this question, Sewall said: "There's yet less doubt that those who are of Age to answer for themselves would soon learn the Principles of our Faith, and might be taught the Obligation of the Vow they made in Baptism, and there's little Doubt but Abraham instructed his Heathen Servants who were of Age to learn, the Nature of Circumcision before he circumcised them; nor can we conclude much less from God's own noble Testimony of him, 'I know him that he will command his Children and his Household, and they shall keep the Way of the Lord.'"[64] Sewall believed that the emancipation of the slaves should be promoted to encourage Negroes to become Christians. He could not understand how any Christian could hinder or discourage them from learning the principles of the Christian religion and embracing the faith.

This interest shown in the Negro race was in no sense general among the Puritans of that day. Many of their sect could not favor such proselyting,[65] which, according to their system of government, would have meant the extension to the slaves of social and political privileges. It was not until the French provided that masters should take their slaves to church and have them indoctrinated in the Catholic faith, that the proposition was seriously considered by many of the Puritans. They, like the Anglicans, felt sufficient compunction of conscience to take steps to Christianize the slaves, lest the Catholics, whom they had derided

The Education of the Negro

as undesirable churchmen, should put the Protestants to shame.[66] The publication of the Code Noir probably influenced the instructions sent out from England to his Majesty's governors requiring them "with the assistance of our council to find out the best means to facilitate and encourage the conversion of Negroes and Indians to the Christian Religion." Everly subsequently mentions in his diary the passing of a resolution by the Council Board at Windsor or Whitehall, recommending that the blacks in plantations be baptized, and meting out severe censure to those who opposed this policy.[67]

More effective than the efforts of other sects in the enlightenment of the Negroes was the work of the Quakers, despite the fact that they were not free to extend their operations throughout the colonies. Just as the colored people are indebted to the Quakers for registering in 1688 the first protest against slavery in Protestant America, so are they indebted to this denomination for the earliest permanent and well-developed schools devoted to the education of their race. As the Quakers believed in the freedom of the will, human brotherhood, and equality before God, they did not, like the Puritans, find difficulties in solving the problem of enlightening the Negroes. While certain Puritans were afraid that conversion might lead to the destruction of caste and the incorporation of undesirable persons into the "Body Politick," the Quakers proceeded on the principle that all men are brethren and, being equal before God, should be considered equal before the law. On account of unduly emphasizing the relation of man to God the Puritans "atrophied their social humanitarian instinct" and developed into a race of self-conscious saints. Believing in human nature and laying stress upon the relation between man and man the Quakers became the friends of all humanity.

Far from the idea of getting rid of an undesirable element by merely destroying the institution which supplied it, the Quakers endeavored to teach the Negro to be a man capable of discharging the duties of citizenship. As early as 1672 their attention was directed to this important matter by George Fox.[68] In 1679 he spoke out more boldly, entreating his sect to instruct and teach their Indians and Negroes "how that Christ, by the Grace of God, tasted death for every man."[69] Other Quakers of prominence did not fail to drive home this thought. In 1693 George Keith, a leading Quaker of his day, came forward as a promoter of the religious training of the slaves as a preparation for emancipation.[70] William Penn advocated the emancipation of slaves,[71] that they might have every opportunity for improvement. In 1696 the Quakers, while protesting against the slave trade, denounced also the policy of neglecting their moral and spiritual welfare.[72] The growing interest of this sect in the Negroes was shown later by the development in 1713 of a definite scheme for freeing and returning them to Africa after having been educated and trained to serve as missionaries on that continent.[73]

The inevitable result of this liberal attitude toward the Negroes was that the Quakers of those colonies where other settlers were so neglectful of the enlightenment of the colored race, soon found themselves at war with the leaders of the time. In slaveholding communities the Quakers were persecuted, not necessarily because they adhered to a peculiar faith, not primarily because they had manners and customs unacceptable to the colonists, but because in answering the call of duty to help all men they incurred the ill will of the masters who denounced them as undesirable persons, bringing into America spurious doctrines subversive of the institutions of the aristocratic settlements.

Religion With Letters

Their experience in the colony of Virginia is a good example of how this worked out. Seeing the unchristian attitude of the preachers in most parts of that colony, the Quakers inquired of them, "Who made you ministers of the Gospel to white people only, and not to the tawny and blacks also?"[74] To show the nakedness of the neglectful clergy there some of this faith manifested such zeal in teaching and preaching to the Negroes that their enemies demanded legislation to prevent them from gaining ascendancy over the minds of the slaves. Accordingly, to make the colored people of that colony inaccessible to these workers it was deemed wise in 1672 to enact a law prohibiting members of that sect from taking Negroes to their meetings. In 1678 the colony enacted another measure excluding Quakers from the teaching profession by providing that no person should be allowed to keep a school in Virginia unless he had taken the oath of allegiance and supremacy.[75] Of course, it was inconsistent with the spirit and creed of the Quakers to take this oath.

The settlers of North Carolina followed the same procedure to check the influence of Quakers, who spoke there in behalf of the man of color as fearlessly as they had in Virginia. The apprehension of the dominating element was such that Governor Tryon had to be instructed to prohibit from teaching in that colony any person who had not a license from the Bishop of London.[76] Although this order was seemingly intended to protect the faith and doctrine of the Anglican Church, rather than to prevent the education of Negroes, it operated to lessen their chances for enlightenment, since missionaries from the Established Church did not reach all parts of the colony.[77] The Quakers of North Carolina, however, had local schools and actually taught slaves. Some of these could read and write as early as 1731. Thereafter, household servants were generally given the rudiments of an English education.

It was in the settlements of New Jersey, Pennsylvania, and New York that the Quakers encountered less opposition in carrying out their policy of cultivating the minds of colored people. Among these Friends the education of Negroes became the handmaiden of the emancipation movement. While John Hepburn, William Burling, Elihu Coleman, and Ralph Sandiford largely confined their attacks to the injustice of keeping slaves, Benjamin Lay was working for their improvement as a prerequisite of emancipation.[78] Lay entreated the Friends to "bring up the Negroes to some Learning, Reading and Writing and" to "endeavor to the utmost of their Power in the sweet love of Truth to instruct and teach 'em the Principles of Truth and Religiousness, and learn some Honest Trade or Imployment and then set them free. And," says he, "all the time Friends are teaching of them let them know that they intend to let them go free in a very reasonable Time; and that our Religious Principles will not allow of such Severity, as to keep them in everlasting Bondage and Slavery."[79]

The struggle of the Northern Quakers to enlighten the colored people had important local results. A strong moral force operated in the minds of most of this sect to impel them to follow the example of certain leaders who emancipated their slaves.[80] Efforts in this direction were redoubled about the middle of the eighteenth century when Anthony Benezet,[81] addressing himself with unwonted zeal to the uplift of these unfortunates, obtained the assistance of Clarkson and others, who solidified the antislavery sentiment of the Quakers and influenced them to give their time and means to the more effective education of the blacks. After this period the Quakers were also concerned with the improvement of the colored people's condition in other settlements.[82]

The Education of the Negro

What the other sects did for the enlightenment of Negroes during this period, was not of much importance. As the Presbyterians, Methodists, and Baptists did not proselyte extensively in this country prior to the middle of the eighteenth century, these denominations had little to do with Negro education before the liberalism and spirit of toleration, developed during the revolutionary era, made it possible for these sects to reach the people. The Methodists, however, confined at first largely to the South, where most of the slaves were found, had to take up this problem earlier. Something looking like an attempt to elevate the Negroes came from Wesley's contemporary, George Whitefield,[83] who, strange to say, was regarded by the Negro race as its enemy for having favored the introduction of slavery. He was primarily interested in the conversion of the colored people. Without denying that "liberty is sweet to those who are born free," he advocated the importation of slaves into Georgia "to bring them within the reach of those means of grace which would make them partake of a liberty far more precious than the freedom of body."[84] While on a visit to this country in 1740 he purchased a large tract of land at Nazareth, Pennsylvania, for the purpose of founding a school for the education of Negroes.[85] Deciding later to go south, he sold the site to the Moravian brethren who had undertaken to establish a mission for Negroes at Bethlehem in 1738.[86] Some writers have accepted the statement that Whitefield commenced the erection of a schoolhouse at Nazareth; others maintain that he failed to accomplish anything.[87] Be that as it may, accessible facts are sufficient to show that, unwise as was his policy of importing slaves, his intention was to improve their condition. It was because of this sentiment in Georgia in 1747, when slavery was finally introduced there, that the people through their representatives in convention recommended that masters should educate their young slaves, and do whatever they could to make religious impressions upon the minds of the aged. This favorable attitude of early Methodists toward Negroes caused them to consider the new churchmen their friends and made it easy for this sect to proselyte the race.

[1: Bourne, Spain in America, p. 241; and The Penn. Mag. of History, xii., 265.]
[2: Proslavery Argument; and Lecky, History of England, vol. ii., p. 17.]
[3: Faust, German Element in United States, vol. i., pp. 242-43.]
[4: Bancroft, History of United States, vol. i., p. 124.]
[5: Herrera, Historia General, dec. iv., libro ii.; dec. v., libro ii.; dec. vii., libro iv.]
[6: Bourne, Spain in America, p. 241.]
[7: Special Report U.S. Com. of Ed., 1871, p. 389.]
[8: Jesuit Relations, vol. v., p. 63.]
[9: Code Noir, p. 107.]
[10: Jesuit Relations, vol. v., p. 62.]
[11: Ibid., vol. lxvii., pp. 259 and 343.]
[12: Ibid., vol. lxviii., p. 201.]
[13: Ibid., vol. lxix., p. 31.]
[14: Ibid., vol. lxx., p. 245.]
[16: Bancroft, Arizona and New Mexico, pp. 27-32.]
[17: The Code Noir obliged every planter to have his Negroes instructed and baptized. It allowed the slave for instruction, worship, and rest not only every Sunday, but every festival usually observed by the Roman Catholic Church. It did not permit any market to be held on Sundays or holidays. It prohibited, under severe penalties, all masters and managers from corrupting their female

slaves. It did not allow the Negro husband, wife, or infant children to be sold separately. It forbade them the use of torture, or immoderate and inhuman punishments. It obliged the owners to maintain their old and decrepit slaves. If the Negroes were not fed and clothed as the law prescribed, or if they were in any way cruelly treated, they might apply to the Procureur, who was obliged by his office to protect them. See Code Noir, pp. 99-100.]

[18: Special Report of the U.S. Com. of Ed., 1871, p. 352.]

[19: On observing that laws had been passed in Virginia to prevent slaves from attending the meetings of Quakers for purposes of being instructed, Morgan Goodwyn registered a most earnest protest. He felt that prompt attention should be given to the instruction of the slaves to prevent the Church from falling into discredit, and to obviate the causes for blasphemy on the part of the enemies of the Church who would not fail to point out that ministers sent to the remotest parts had failed to convert the heathen. Therefore, he preached in Westminster Abbey in 1685 a sermon "to stir up and provoke" his "Majesty's subjects abroad, and even at home, to use endeavors for the propagation of Christianity among their domestic slaves and vassals." He referred to the spreading of mammonism and irreligion by which efforts to instruct and Christianize the heathen were paralyzed. He deplored the fact that the slaves who were the subjects of such instruction became the victims of still greater cruelty, while the missionaries who endeavored to enlighten them were neglected and even persecuted by the masters. They considered the instruction of the Negroes an impracticable and needless work of popish superstition, and a policy subversive of the interests of slaveholders. Bishop Sanderson found it necessary to oppose this policy of Virginia which had met the denunciation of Goodwyn. In strongly emphasizing this duty of masters, Bishop Fleetwood moved the hearts of many planters of North Carolina to allow missionaries access to their slaves. Many of them were thereafter instructed and baptized. See Goodwyn, The Negroes and Indians' Advocate; Hart, History Told by Contemporaries, vol. i., No. 86; Special Rep. U.S. Com. of Ed., 1871, p. 363; An Account of the Endeavors of the Soc., etc., p. 14.]

[20: Pascoe, Classified Digest of the Records of the Society for the Propagation of the Gospel in Foreign Parts, p. 24.]

[21: Dalcho, An Historical Account of the Protestant Episcopal Church in South Carolina, p. 39; Special Rep. U.S. Com. of Ed., 1871, p. 362.]

[22: Meriwether, Education in South Carolina, p. 123].

[23: Special Rep. U.S. Com. of Ed., 1871, p. 362.]

[24: An Account of the Endeavors Used by the Society for the Propagation of the Gospel in Foreign Parts, pp. 13-14.]

[25: An Account of the Endeavors Used by the Society for the Propagation of the Gospel in Foreign Parts, pp. 6-12.]

[26: Ibid., p. 9.]

[27: Special Report U.S. Com. of Ed., 1871, p. 362.]

[28: Ibid., 1871, p. 364.]

[29: Meade, Old Families and Churches in Virginia, p. 264; Plumer, Thoughts on the Religious Instruction of Negroes, pp. 11-12.]

[30: Monroe, Cyclopaedia of Education, vol. iv., p. 406.]

[31: Russell, The Free Negro in Virginia, in J.H.U. Studies, Series xxxi., No. 3, p. 107.]

[32: Meade, Old Families and Churches in Virginia, pp. 264-65.]

[33: Ashe, History of North Carolina, pp. 389-90.]

[34: For a summary of this argument see Meade, Four Sermons of Reverend Bacon, pp. 81-97; also, A Letter to an American Planter from his Friend in London, p. 5.]
[35: An Account of the Endeavors Used by the Society for the Propagation of the Gospel in Foreign Parts, pp. 16, 21, and 32; and Dalcho, An Historical Account, etc., pp. 104 et seq.]
[36: Meade, Sermons of Thomas Bacon, pp. 31 et seq.]
[37: Meade, Sermons of Thomas Bacon, pp. 116 et seq.]
[38: Ibid., p. 118.]
[39: Special Report of the U.S. Com. of Ed., 1871, p. 363.]
[40: Special Report of the U.S. Com. of Ed., 1871, p. 363.]
[41: Secker, Works, vol. v., p. 88.]
[42: Ibid., vol. vi., p. 467.]
[43: An Account of the Endeavors Used by the Society for the Propagation of the Gospel in Foreign Parts, p.6.]
[44: Meriwether, Education in South Carolina, p. 123; McCrady, South Carolina, etc., p. 246; Dalcho, An Historical Account of the Protestant Episcopal Church in South Carolina, pp. 156, 157, 164.]
[45: Ibid., pp. 157 and 164.]
[46: An Account of the Endeavors Used by the Society for the Propagation of the Gospel in Foreign Parts, p. 15.]
[47: Bourne, Spain in America, p. 241.]
[48: Special Report of the U.S. Com. of Ed., 1871, p. 362.]
[49: Wickersham, History of Education in Pennsylvania, p. 248.]
[50: Ibid., p. 241.]
[51: Ibid., p. 252; Smyth, Works of Franklin, vol. iv., p. 23; and vol. v., p. 431.]
[52: Smyth, Works of Franklin, vol. v., p. 431.]
[53: Wickersham, History of Education in Pennsylvania, p. 249.]
[54: Bassett, Slavery and Servitude in North Carolina, Johns Hopkins University Studies, vol. xv., p. 226.]
[55: Pennsylvania Magazine of History, vol. xiii., p. 265.]
[56: Locke, Anti-slavery Before 1808, p. 15; Mather, Life of John Eliot, p. 14; New Plymouth Colony Records, vol. x., p. 452.]
[57: Locke, Anti-slavery, etc., p. 15.]
[58: Meade, Sermons of Thomas Bacon, p. 137 et seq.]
[59: Baxter, Practical Works, vol. i., p. 438.]
[60: Baxter, Practical Works, vol. i., p. 438-40.]
[61: Ibid., p. 440.]
[62: Moore, Notes on Slavery in Massachusetts, p. 91.]
[63: Moore, Notes on Slavery in Massachusetts, p. 92; Locke, Anti-slavery, etc., p. 31.]
[64: Moore, Notes on Slavery, etc., p. 91; The Athenian Oracle, vol. ii., pp. 460 et seq.]
[65: Moore, Notes on Slavery, etc., p. 79.]
[66: This good example of the Catholics was in later years often referred to by Bishop Porteus. Works of Bishop Porteus, vol. vi, pp. 168, 173, 177, 178, 401; Moore, Notes on Slavery, etc., p. 96.]
[67: Ibid., p. 96.]
[68: Quaker Pamphlet, p. 8; Moore, Anti-slavery, etc., p. 79.]
[69: Ibid., p. 79.]

[70: Special Report of the U.S. Com. of Ed., p. 376.]
[71: Rhodes, History of the United States, vol. i., p. 6; Bancroft, History of the United States, vol. ii., p. 401.]
[72: Locke, Anti-slavery, p. 32.]
[73: Ibid., p. 30.]
[74: Quaker Pamphlet, p. 9.]
[75: Hening, Statutes at Large, vol. i., 532; ii., 48, 165, 166, 180, 198, and 204. Special Report of the U.S. Com. of Ed., 1871, p. 391.]
[76: Ashe, History of North Carolina, vol. i., p. 389. The same instructions were given to Governor Francis Nicholson.]
[77: Ibid., pp. 389, 390.]
[78: Locke, Anti-slavery, etc., p. 31.]
[79: Ibid., p. 32.]
[80: Dr. DuBois gives a good account of these efforts in his Suppression of the African Slave Trade.]
[81: Benezet was a French Protestant. Persecuted on account of their religion, his parents moved from France to England and later to Philadelphia. He became a teacher in that city in 1742. Thirteen years later he was teaching a school established for the education of the daughters of the most distinguished families in Philadelphia. He was then using his own spelling-book, primer, and grammar, some of the first text-books published in America. Known to persecution himself, Benezet always sympathized with the oppressed. Accordingly, he connected himself with the Quakers, who at that time had before them the double task of fighting for religious equality and the amelioration of the condition of the Negroes. Becoming interested in the welfare of the colored race, Benezet first attacked the slave trade, so exposing it in his speeches and writings that Clarkson entered the field as an earnest advocate of the suppression of the iniquitous traffic. See Benezet, Observations, p. 30, and the African Repository, vol. iv., p. 61.]
[82: Quaker Pamphlet, p. 31.]
[83: Special Report of the U.S. Com. of Ed., 1871, p. 374.]
[84: Ibid., p. 374.]
[85: Turner, The Negro in Pennsylvania, p. 128.]
[86: Equally interested in the Negroes were the Moravians who settled in the uplands of Pennsylvania and roamed over the hills of the Appalachian region as far south as Carolina. A painting of a group of their converts prior to 1747 shows among others two Negroes, Johannes of South Carolina and Jupiter of New York. See Hamilton, History of the Church known as the Moravian, p. 80; Plumer, Thoughts on the Religious Instruction of Negroes, p. 3; Reichel, The Moravians in North Carolina, p. 139.]
[87: Special Report of the U.S. Com. of Ed., 1869, p. 374.]

Chapter 3

Education as a Right of Man

In addition to the mere diffusion of knowledge as a means to teach religion there was a need of another factor to make the education of the Negroes thorough. This required force was supplied by the response of the colonists to the nascent social doctrine of the eighteenth century. During the French and Indian War there were set to work certain forces which hastened the social and political upheaval called the American Revolution. "Bigoted saints" of the more highly favored sects condescended to grant the rising denominations toleration, the aristocratic elements of colonial society deigned to look more favorably upon those of lower estate, and a large number of leaders began to think that the Negro should be educated and freed. To acquaint themselves with the claims of the underman Americans thereafter prosecuted more seriously the study of Coke, Milton, Locke, and Blackstone. The last of these was then read more extensively in the colonies than in Great Britain. Getting from these writers strange ideas of individual liberty and the social compact theory of man's making in a state of nature government deriving its power from the consent of the governed, the colonists contended more boldly than ever for religious freedom, industrial liberty, and political equality. Given impetus by the diffusion of these ideas, the revolutionary movement became productive of the spirit of universal benevolence. Hearing the contention for natural and inalienable rights, Nathaniel Appleton[1] and John Woolman,[2] were emboldened to carry these theories to their logical conclusion. They attacked not only the oppressors of the colonists but censured also those who denied the Negro race freedom of body and freedom of mind. When John Adams heard James Otis basing his argument against the writs of assistance on the British constitution "founded in the laws of nature," he "shuddered at the doctrine taught and the consequences that might be derived from such premises."[3]

So effective was the attack on the institution of slavery and its attendant evils that interest in the question leaped the boundaries of religious organizations and became the concern of fair-minded men throughout the country. Not only did Northern men of the type of John Adams and James Otis express their opposition to this tyranny of men's bodies and minds, but Laurens, Henry, Wythe, Mason, and Washington pointed out the injustice of such a policy. Accordingly we find arrayed against the aristocratic masters almost all the leaders of the American Revolution.[4] They favored the policy, first, of suppressing the slave trade, next of emancipating the Negroes in bondage, and finally of educating them for a life of freedom.[2] While students of government were exposing the inconsistency of slaveholding among a people contending for political liberty, and men like Samuel Webster, James Swan, and Samuel Hopkins attacked the institution on economic grounds;[5] Jonathan Boucher,[6] Dr. Rush,[7] and Benjamin Franklin[8] were devising plans to educate slaves for freedom; and

Education as a Right of Man

Isaac Tatem[9] and Anthony Benezet[10] were actually in the schoolroom endeavoring to enlighten their black brethren.

The aim of these workers was not merely to enable the Negroes to take over sufficient of Western civilization to become nominal Christians, not primarily to increase their economic efficiency, but to enlighten them because they are men. To strengthen their position these defendants of the education of the blacks cited the customs of the Greeks and Romans, who enslaved not the minds and wills, but only the bodies of men. Nor did these benefactors fail to mention the cases of ancient slaves, who, having the advantages of education, became poets, teachers, and philosophers, instrumental in the diffusion of knowledge among the higher classes. There was still the idea of Cotton Mather, who was willing to treat his servants as part of the family, and to employ such of them as were competent to teach his children lessons of piety.[12]

[12: Meade, Sermons of Thomas Bacon, appendix.]

The chief objection of these reformers to slavery was that its victims had no opportunity for mental improvement. "Othello," a free person of color, contributing to the American Museum in 1788, made the institution responsible for the intellectual rudeness of the Negroes who, though "naturally possessed of strong sagacity and lively parts," were by law and custom prohibited from being instructed in any kind of learning.[13] He styled this policy an effort to bolster up an institution that extinguished the "divine spark of the slave, crushed the bud of his genius, and kept him unacquainted with the world." Dr. McLeod denounced slavery because it "debases a part of the human race" and tends "to destroy their intellectual powers."[14] "The slave from his infancy," continued he, "is obliged implicitly to obey the will of another. There is no circumstance which can stimulate him to exercise his intellectual powers." In his arraignment of this system Rev. David Rice complained that it was in the power of the master to deprive the slaves of all education, that they had not the opportunity for instructing conversation, that it was put out of their power to learn to read, and that their masters kept them from other means of information.[15] Slavery, therefore, must be abolished because it infringes upon the natural right of men to be enlightened.

During this period religion as a factor in the educational progress of the Negroes was not eliminated. In fact, representative churchmen of the various sects still took the lead in advocating the enlightenment of the colored people. These protagonists, however, ceased to claim this boon merely as a divine right and demanded it as a social privilege. Some of the clergy then interested had not at first seriously objected to the enslavement of the African race, believing that the lot of these people would not be worse in this country where they might have an opportunity for enlightenment. But when this result failed to follow, and when the slavery of the Africans' bodies turned out to be the slavery of their minds, the philanthropic and religious proclaimed also the doctrine of enlightenment as a right of man. Desiring to see Negroes enjoy this privilege, Jonathan Boucher,[16] one of the most influential of the colonial clergymen, urged his hearers at the celebration of the Peace of 1763 to improve and emancipate their slaves that they might "participate in the general joy." With the hope of inducing men to discharge the same duty, Bishop Warburton[17] boldly asserted a few years later that slaves are "rational creatures endowed with all our qualities except that of color, and our brethren both by nature and grace." John Woolman,[18] a Quaker minister, influenced by the philosophy of John Locke, began to preach that liberty is the right of all men, and that slaves, being the fellow-creatures of their masters, had a natural right to be elevated.

Thus following the theories of the revolutionary leaders these liberal-minded men promulgated along with the doctrine of individual liberty that of the freedom of the mind. The best expression of this advanced idea came from the Methodist Episcopal Church, which reached the acme of antislavery sentiment in 1784. This sect then boldly declared: "We view it as contrary to the golden law of God and the prophets, and the inalienable rights of mankind as well as every principle of the Revolution to hold in deepest abasement, in a more abject slavery than is perhaps to be found in any part of the world, except America, so many souls that are capable of the image of God."[19]

Frequently in contact with men who were advocating the right of the Negroes to be educated, statesmen as well as churchmen could not easily evade the question. Washington did not have much to say about it and did little more than to provide for the ultimate liberation of his slaves and the teaching of their children to read.[20] Less aid to this movement came from John Adams, although he detested slavery to the extent that he never owned a bondman, preferring to hire freemen at extra cost to do his work.[21] Adams made it clear that he favored gradual emancipation. But he neither delivered any inflammatory speeches against slaveholders neglectful of the instruction of their slaves, nor devised any scheme for their enjoyment of freedom. So was it with Hamilton who, as an advocate of the natural rights of man, opposed the institution of slavery, but, with the exception of what assistance he gave the New York African Free Schools[22] said and did little to promote the actual education of the colored people.

Madison in stating his position on this question was a little more definite than some of his contemporaries. Speaking of the necessary preparation of the colored people for emancipation he thought it was possible to determine the proper course of instruction. He believed, however, that, since the Negroes were to continue in a state of bondage during the preparatory period and to be within the jurisdiction of commonwealths recognizing ample authority over them, "a competent discipline" could not be impracticable. He said further that the "degree in which this discipline" would "enforce the needed labor and in which a voluntary industry" would "supply the defect of compulsory labor, were vital points on which it" might "not be safe to be very positive without some light from actual experiment."[23] Evidently he was of the opinion that the training of slaves to discharge later the duties of freemen was a difficult task but, if well planned and directed, could be made a success.

No one of the great statesmen of this time was more interested in the enlightenment of the Negro than Benjamin Franklin.[24] He was for a long time associated with the friends of the colored people and turned out from his press such fiery anti-slavery pamphlets as those of Lay and Sandiford. Franklin also became one of the "Associates of Dr. Bray." Always interested in the colored schools of Philadelphia, the philosopher was, while in London, connected with the English "gentlemen concerned with the pious design,"[25] serving as chairman of the organization for the year 1760. He was a firm supporter of Anthony Benezet,[26] and was made president of the Abolition Society of Philadelphia which in 1774 founded a successful colored school.[27] This school was so well planned and maintained that it continued about a hundred years.

Education as a Right of Man

John Jay kept up his interest in the Negro race.[28] In the Convention of 1787 he cooeperated with Gouverneur Morris, advocating the abolition of the slave trade and the rejection of the Federal ratio. His efforts in behalf of the colored people were actuated by his early conviction that the national character of this country could be retrieved only by abolishing the iniquitous traffic in human souls and improving the Negroes.[29] Showing his pity for the downtrodden people of color around him, Jay helped to promote the cause of the abolitionists of New York who established and supported several colored schools in that city. Such care was exercised in providing for the attendance, maintenance, and supervision of these schools that they soon took rank among the best in the United States.

More interesting than the views of any other man of this epoch on the subject of Negro education were those of Thomas Jefferson. Born of pioneer parentage in the mountains of Virginia, Jefferson never lost his frontier democratic ideals which made him an advocate of simplicity, equality, and universal freedom. Having in mind when he wrote the Declaration of Independence the rights of the blacks as well as those of whites, this disciple of John Locke, could not but feel that the slaves of his day had a natural right to education and freedom. Jefferson said so much more on these important questions than his contemporaries that he would have been considered an abolitionist, had he lived in 1840.

Giving his views on the enlightenment of the Negroes he asserted that the minds of the masters should be "apprized by reflection and strengthened by the energies of conscience against the obstacles of self-interest to an acquiescence in the rights of others." The owners would then permit their slaves to be "prepared by instruction and habit" for self-government, the honest pursuit of industry, and social duty.[30] In his scheme for a modern system of public schools Jefferson included the training of the slaves in industrial and agricultural branches to equip them for a higher station in life, else he thought they should be removed from the country when liberated.[31] Capable of mental development, as he had found certain men of color to be, the Sage of Monticello doubted at times that they could be made the intellectual equals of white men,[32] and did not actually advocate their incorporation into the body politic.

So much progress in the improvement of slaves was effected with all of these workers in the field that conservative southerners in the midst of the antislavery agitation contented themselves with the thought that radical action was not necessary, as the institution would of itself soon pass away. Legislatures passed laws facilitating manumission,[33] many southerners emancipated their slaves to give them a better chance to improve their condition, regulations unfavorable to the assembly of Negroes for the dissemination of information almost fell into desuetude, a larger number of masters began to instruct their bondmen, and persons especially interested in these unfortunates found the objects of their piety more accessible.[34]

Not all slaveholders, however, were thus induced to respect this new right claimed for the colored people. Georgia and South Carolina were exceptional in that they were not sufficiently stirred by the revolutionary movement to have much compassion for this degraded class. The attitude of the people of Georgia, however, was then more favorable than that of the South Carolinians.[35] Nevertheless, the Georgia planters near the frontier were not long in learning that the general enlightenment of the Negroes would endanger the institution of slavery. Accordingly, in 1770, at the very time when radical reformers were clamoring for the rights of man, Georgia, following in the wake of South Carolina, reenacted its act of 1740 which imposed a penalty on any one who should teach or cause slaves to be taught or employ them "in any manner of writing whatever."[36] The penalty, however, was less than that imposed in South Carolina.[37] The same measure terminated the helpful mingling of slaves by providing for their dispersion when assembled for the old-time "love feast" emphasized so much among the rising Methodists of the South.

Those advocating the imposition of restraints upon Negroes acquiring knowledge were not, however, confined to South Carolina and Georgia where the malevolent happened to be in the majority. The other States had not seen the last of the generation of those who doubted that education would fit the slaves for the exalted position of citizens. The retrogressives made much of the assertion that adult slaves lately imported, were, on account of their attachment to heathen practices and idolatrous rites, loath to take over the Teutonic civilization, and would at best learn to speak the English language imperfectly only.[38] The reformers, who at times admitted this, maintained that the alleged difficulties encountered in teaching the crudest element of the slaves could not be adduced as an argument against the religious instruction of free Negroes and the education of the American born colored children.[39] This problem, however, was not a serious one in most Northern States, for the reason that the small number of slaves in that section obviated the necessity for much apprehension as to what kind of education the blacks should have, and whether they should be enlightened before or after emancipation. Although the Northern people believed that the education of the race should be definitely planned, and had much to say about industrial education, most of them were of the opinion that ordinary training in the fundamentals of useful knowledge and in the principles of Christian religion, was sufficient to meet the needs of those designated for freedom.

On the other hand, most southerners who conceded the right of the Negro to be educated did not openly aid the movement except with the understanding that the enlightened ones should be taken from their fellows and colonized in some remote part of the United States or in their native land.[40] The idea of colonization, however, was not confined to the southern slaveholders, for Thornton, Fothergill, and Granville Sharp had long looked to Africa as the proper place for enlightened people of color.[41] Feeling that it would be wrong to expatriate them, Benezet and Branagan[42] advocated the colonization of such Negroes on the public lands west of the Alleghanies. There was some talk of giving slaves training in the elements of agriculture and then dividing plantations among them to develop a small class of tenants. Jefferson, a member of a committee appointed in 1779 by the General Assembly of that commonwealth to revise its laws, reported a plan providing for the instruction of its slaves in agriculture and the handicrafts to prepare them for liberation and colonization under the supervision of the home government until they could take care of themselves.[43]

Without resorting to the subterfuge of colonization, not a few slaveholders were still wise enough to show why the improvement of the Negroes should be neglected altogether. Vanquished by the logic of Daniel Davis[44] and Benjamin Rush,[45] those who had theretofore justified slavery on the ground that it gave the bondmen a chance to be enlightened, fell back on the theory of African racial inferiority. This they said was so well exhibited by the Negroes' lack of wisdom and of goodness that continued heathenism of the race was justifiable.[46] Answering these inconsistent persons, John Wesley inquired: "Allowing them to be as stupid as you say, to whom is that stupidity owing? Without doubt it lies altogether at the door of the inhuman masters who give them no opportunity for improving their understanding and indeed leave them no motive, either from hope or fear to attempt any such thing." Wesley asserted, too, that the Africans were in no way remarkable for their stupidity while they remained in their own country, and that where they had equal motives and equal means of improvement, the Negroes were not only not inferior to the better inhabitants of Europe, but superior to some of them.[47]

William Pinkney, the antislavery leader of Maryland, believed also that Negroes are no worse than white people under similar conditions, and that all the colored people needed to disprove their so-called inferiority was an equal chance with the more favored race.[48] Others like George Buchanan referred to the Negroes' talent for the fine arts and to their achievements in literature, mathematics, and philosophy. Buchanan informed these merciless aristocrats "that the Africans whom you despise, whom you inhumanly treat as brutes and whom you unlawfully subject to slavery with tyrannizing hands of despots are equally capable of improvement with yourselves."[49]

Franklin considered the idea of the natural inferiority of the Negro as a silly excuse. He conceded that most of the blacks were improvident and poor, but believed that their condition was not due to deficient understanding but to their lack of education. He was very much impressed with their achievements in music.[50] So disgusting was this notion of inferiority to Abbe Gregoire of Paris that he wrote an interesting essay on "Negro Literature" to prove that people of color have unusual intellectual power.[51] He sent copies of this pamphlet to leading men where slavery existed. Another writer discussing Jefferson's equivocal position on this question said that one would have thought that "modern philosophy himself" would not have the face to expect that the wretch, who is driven out to labor at the dawn of day, and who toils until evening with a whip over his head, ought to be a poet. Benezet, who had actually taught Negroes, declared "with truth and sincerity" that he had found among them as great variety of talents as among a like number of white persons. He boldly asserted that the notion entertained by some that the blacks were inferior in their capacities was a vulgar prejudice founded on the pride or ignorance of their lordly masters who had kept their slaves at such a distance as to be unable to form a right judgment of them.[52]

[1: Locke, Anti-slavery, etc., p. 19, 20, 23.]
[2: Works of John Woolman in two parts, pp. 58 and 73; Moore, Notes on Slavery in Mass., p. 71.]
[3: Adams, Works of John Adams, vol. x., p. 315; Moore, Notes on Slavery in Mass., p. 71.]
[4: Cobb, Slavery, etc., p. 82.]
[5: Madison, Works of, vol. iii., p. 496; Smyth, Works of Franklin, vol. v., p. 431; Washington, Works of Jefferson, vol. ix., p. 163; Brissot de Warville, New Travels, vol. i., p. 227; Proceedings of the American Convention of Abolition Societies, 1794, 1795, 1797.]

[6: Webster, A Sermon Preached before the Honorable Council, etc.; Webster, Earnest Address to My Country on Slavery; Swan, A Dissuasion to Great Britain and the Colonies; Hopkins, Dialogue Concerning Slavery.]

[7: Boucher, A View of the Causes and Consequences of the American Revolution, p. 39.]

[8: Rush, An Address to the Inhabitants of, etc., p. 16.]

[9: Smyth, Works of Franklin, vol. iv., p. 23; vol. v., p. 431.]

[10: Wickersham, History of Ed. in Pa., p. 249.]

[11: Ibid., p. 250; Special Report of the U.S. Com. of Ed., 1869, p. 375; African Repository, vol. iv., p. 61; Benezet, Observations; Benezet, A Serious Address to the Rulers of America.]

[13: The American Museum, vol. iv., pp. 415 and 511.]

[14: McLeod, Negro Slavery, p. 16.]

[15: Rice, Speech in the Constitutional Convention of Kentucky, p. 5.]

[16: Jonathan Boucher was a rector of the Established Church in Maryland. Though not a promoter of the movement for the political rights of the colonists, Boucher was, however, so moved by the spirit of uplift of the downtrodden that he takes front rank among those who, in emphasizing the rights of servants, caused a decided change in the attitude of white men toward the improvement of Negroes. Boucher was not an immediate abolitionist. He abhorred slavery, however, to the extent that he asserted that if ever the colonies would be improved to their utmost capacity, an essential part of that amelioration had to be the abolition of slavery. His chief concern then was the cultivation of the minds in order to make amends for the drudgery to their bodies. See Boucher, Causes, etc., p. 39.]

[17: Special Report of the U.S. Com. of Ed., 1871, p. 363.]

[18: An influential minister of the Society of Friends and an extensive traveler through the colonies, Woolman had an opportunity to do much good in attacking the policy of those who kept their Negroes in deplorable ignorance, and in commending the good example of those who instructed their slaves in reading. In his Considerations on the Keeping of Slaves he took occasion to praise the Friends of North Carolina for the unusual interest they manifested in the cause at their meetings during his travels in that colony about the year 1760. With such workers as Woolman in the field it is little wonder that Quakers thereafter treated slaves as brethren, alleviated their burdens, enlightened their minds, emancipated and cared for them until they could provide for themselves. See Works of John Woolman in two parts, pp. 58 and 73.]

[19: Matlack, History of American Slavery and Methodism, pp. 29 et seq.; McTyeire, History of Methodism, p. 28.]

[20: Lossing, Life of George Washington, vol. iii., p. 537.]

[21: Adams, Works of John Adams, vol. viii., p. 379; vol. ix., p. 92; vol. x., p. 380.]

[22: Andrews, History of the New York African Free Schools, p. 57.]

[23: Madison, Works of, vol. iii., p. 496.]

[24: Smyth, Works of Benjamin Franklin, vol. v., p. 431.]

[25: Ibid., vol. iv., p. 23.]

[26: Smyth, Works of Benjamin Franklin, vol. v., p. 431.]

[27: Ibid., vol. x., p. 127; and Wickersham, History of Education in Pennsylvania, p. 253.]

[28: Jay, Works of John Jay, vol. i., p. 136; vol. iii, p. 331.]

Education as a Right of Man

[29: Ibid., vol. iii., p. 343.]

[30: Washington, Works of Jefferson, vol. vi., p. 456.]

[31: Ibid., vol. viii., p. 380; and Mayo, Educational Movement in the South, p. 37.]

[32: As to what Jefferson thought of the Negro intellect we are still in doubt. Writing in 1791 to Banneker, the Negro mathematician and astronomer, he said that nobody wished to see more than he such proofs as Banneker exhibited that nature has given to our black brethren talents equal to those of men of other colors, and that the appearance of a lack of such native ability was owing only to their degraded condition in Africa and America. Jefferson expressed himself as being ardently desirous of seeing a good system commenced for raising the condition both of the body and the mind of the slaves to what it ought to be as fast as the "imbecility" of their then existence and other circumstances, which could not be neglected, would admit. Replying to Gregoire of Paris, who wrote an interesting essay on the Literature of Negroes, showing the power of their intellect, Jefferson assured him that no person living wished more sincerely than he to see a complete refutation of the doubts he himself had entertained and expressed on the grade of understanding allotted to them by nature and to find that in this respect they are on a par with white men. These doubts, he said, were the result of personal observations in the limited sphere of his own State where "the opportunities for the development of their genius were not favorable, and those of exercising it still less so." He said that he had expressed them with great hesitation; but "whatever be the degree of their talent, it is no measure of their rights. Because Sir Isaac Newton was superior to others in understanding, he was not therefore lord of the person or property of others." In this respect he believed they were gaining daily in the opinions of nations, and hopeful advances were being made toward their reestablishment on an equal footing with other colors of the human family. He prayed, therefore, that God might accept his thanks for enabling him to observe the "many instances of respectable intelligence in that race of men, which could not fail to have effect in hastening the day of their relief." Yet a few days later when writing to Joel Barlow, Jefferson referred to Bishop Gregoire's essay and expressed his doubt that this pamphlet was weighty evidence of the intellect of the Negro. He said that the whole did not amount in point of evidence to what they themselves knew of Banneker. He conceded that Banneker had spherical knowledge enough to make almanacs, but not without the suspicion of aid from Ellicott who was his neighbor and friend, and never missed an opportunity of puffing him. Referring to the letter he received from Banneker, he said it showed the writer to have a mind of very common stature indeed. See Washington, Works of Jefferson, vol. v., pp. 429 and 503.]

[33: Locke, Anti-slavery, etc., p. 14.]

[34: Brissot de Warville, New Travels, vol. i., p. 220; Johann Schoepf, Travels in the Confederation, p. 149.]

[35: The laws of Georgia were not so harsh as those of South Carolina. A larger number of intelligent persons of color were found in the rural districts of Georgia. Charleston, however, was exceptional in that its Negroes had unusual educational advantages.]

[36: Marbury and Crawford, Digest of the Laws of the State of Georgia, p. 438.]

[37: Brevard, Digest of the Public Statutes of South Carolina, vol. ii., p. 243.]

[38: Meade, Sermons of Thomas Bacon, pp. 81-87.]

[39: Porteus, Works of, vol. vi., p. 177; Warburton, A Sermon, etc., pp. 25 and 27.]

[40: Writings of James Monroe, vol. iii., pp. 261, 266, 292, 295, 321, 322, 336, 338, 349, 351, 352, 353, 378.]

[41: Brissot de Warville, Travels, vol. i., p. 262.]

[42: Tyrannical Libertymen, pp. 10-11; Locke, Anti-slavery, etc., pp. 31-32; Branagan, Serious Remonstrance, p. 18.]

[43: Washington, Works of Jefferson, vol. iii., p. 296; vol. iv., p. 291 and vol. viii., p. 380.]

[44: Davis was a logical antislavery agitator. He believed that if the slaves had had the means of education, if they had been treated with humanity, making slaves of them had been no more than doing evil that good might come. He thought that Christianity and humanity would have rather dictated the sending of books and teachers into Africa and endeavors for their salvation.]

[45: Benjamin Rush was a Philadelphia physician of Quaker parentage. He was educated at the College of New Jersey and at the Medical School of Edinburgh, where he came into contact with some of the most enlightened men of his time. Holding to the ideals of his youth, Dr. Rush was soon associated with the friends of the Negroes on his return to Philadelphia. He not only worked for the abolition of the slave trade but fearlessly advocated the right of the Negroes to be educated. He pointed out that an inquiry into the methods of converting Negroes to Christianity would show that the means were ill suited to the end proposed. "In many cases," said he, "Sunday is appropriated to work for themselves. Reading and writing are discouraged among them. A belief is inculcated among some that they have no souls. In a word, every attempt to instruct or convert them has been constantly opposed by their masters." See Rush, An Address to the Inhabitants, etc., p. 16.]

[46: Meade, Sermons of Rev. Thomas Bacon, pp. 81-97.]

[47: Wesley, Thoughts upon Slavery, p. 92.]

[48: Pinkney, Speech in Maryland House of Delegates, p. 6.]

[49: Buchanan, An Oration on the Moral and Political Evil of Slavery, p. 10.]

[50: Smyth, Works of Franklin, vol. vi., p. 222.]

[51: Gregoire, La Litterature des Negres.]

[52: Special Report of the U.S. Com. of Ed., 1871, p. 375.]

Chapter 4

Actual Education

Would these professions of interest in the mental development of the blacks be translated into action? What these reformers would do to raise the standard of Negro education above the plane of rudimentary training incidental to religious instruction, was yet to be seen. Would they secure to Negroes the educational privileges guaranteed other elements of society? The answer, if not affirmative, was decidedly encouraging. The idea uppermost in the minds of these workers was that the people of color could and should be educated as other races of men.

In the lead of this movement were the antislavery agitators. Recognizing the Negroes' need of preparation for citizenship, the abolitionists proclaimed as a common purpose of their organizations the education of the colored people with a view to developing in them self-respect, self-support, and usefulness in the community.[1]

The proposition to cultivate the minds of the slaves came as a happy solution of what had been a perplexing problem. Many Americans who considered slavery an evil had found no way out of the difficulty when the alternative was to turn loose upon society so many uncivilized men without the ability to discharge the duties of citizenship.[2] Assured then that the efforts at emancipation would be tested by experience, a larger number of men advocated abolition. These leaders recommended gradual emancipation for States having a large slave population, that those designated for freedom might first be instructed in the value and meaning of liberty to render them comfortable in the use of it.[3] The number of slaves in the States adopting the policy of immediate emancipation was not considered a menace to society, for the schools already open to colored people could exert a restraining influence on those lately given the boon of freedom. For these reasons the antislavery societies had in their constitutions a provision for a committee of education to influence Negroes to attend school, superintend their instruction, and emphasize the cultivation of the mind as the necessary preparation for "that state in society upon which depends our political happiness."[4] Much stress was laid upon this point by the American Convention of Abolition Societies in 1794 and 1795 when the organization expressed the hope that freedmen might participate in civil rights as fast as they qualified by education.[5]

This work was organized by the abolitionists but was generally maintained by members of the various sects which did more for the enlightenment of the people of color through the antislavery organizations than through their own.[6] The support of the clergy, however, did not mean that the education of the Negroes would continue incidental to the teaching of religion. The blacks were to be accepted as brethren and trained to be useful citizens. For better education the colored people could then look to the more liberal sects, the Quakers, Baptists, Methodists, and Presbyterians, who prior to the Revolution had been restrained by intolerance from extensive proselyting. Upon the attainment of

The Education of the Negro

religious liberty they were free to win over the slaveholders who came into the Methodist and Baptist churches in large numbers, bringing their slaves with them.[7] The freedom of these "regenerated" churches made possible the rise of Negro exhorters and preachers, who to exercise their gifts managed in some way to learn to read and write. Schools for the training of such leaders were not to be found, but to encourage ambitious blacks to qualify themselves white ministers often employed such candidates as attendants, allowing them time to observe, to study, and even to address their audiences.[8]

It must be observed, however, that the interest of these benevolent men was no longer manifested in the mere traditional teaching of individual slaves. The movement ceased to be the concern of separate philanthropists. Men really interested in the uplift of the colored people organized to raise funds, open schools, and supervise their education.[9] In the course of time their efforts became more systematic and consequently more successful. These educators adopted the threefold policy of instructing Negroes in the principles of the Christian religion, giving them the fundamentals of the common branches, and teaching them the most useful handicrafts.[10] The indoctrination of the colored people, to be sure, was still an important concern to their teachers, but the accession to their ranks of a militant secular element caused the emphasis to shift to other phases of education. Seeing the Negroes' need of mental development, the Presbyterian Synod of New York and Pennsylvania urged the members of that denomination in 1787 to give their slaves "such good education as to prepare them for a better enjoyment of freedom."[11] In reply to the inquiry as to what could be done to teach the poor black and white children to read, the Methodist Conference of 1790 recommended the establishment of Sunday schools and the appointment of persons to teach gratis "all that will attend and have a capacity to learn."[12] The Conference recommended that the Church publish a special text-book to teach these children learning as well as piety.[13] Men in the political world were also active. In 1788 the State of New Jersey passed an act preliminary to emancipation, making the teaching of slaves to read compulsory under a penalty of five pounds.[14]

With such influence brought to bear on persons in the various walks of life, the movement for the effective education of the colored people became more extensive. Voicing the sentiment of the different local organizations, the American Convention of Abolition Societies of 1794 urged the branches to have the children of free Negroes and slaves instructed in "common literature."[15] Two years later the Abolition Society of the State of Maryland proposed to establish an academy to offer this kind of instruction. To execute this scheme the American Convention thought that it was expedient to employ regular tutors, to form private associations of their members or other well-disposed persons for the purpose of instructing the people of color in the most simple branches of education.[16]

The regular tutors referred to above were largely indentured servants who then constituted probably the majority of the teachers of the colonies.[17] In 1773 Jonathan Boucher said that two thirds of the teachers of Maryland belonged to this class.[18] The contact of Negroes with these servants is significant. In the absence of rigid caste distinctions they associated with the slaves and the barrier between them was so inconsiderable that laws had to be passed to prevent the miscegenation of the races. The blacks acquired much useful knowledge from servant teachers and sometimes assisted them.

Actual Education

Attention was directed also to the fact that neither literary nor religious education prepared the Negroes for a life of usefulness. Heeding the advice of Kosciuszko, Madison and Jefferson, the advocates of the education of the Negroes endeavored to give them such practical training as their peculiar needs demanded. In the agricultural sections the first duty of the teacher of the blacks was to show them how to get their living from the soil. This was the final test of their preparation for emancipation. Accordingly, on large plantations where much supervision was necessary, trustworthy Negroes were trained as managers. Many of those who showed aptitude were liberated and encouraged to produce for themselves. Slaves designated for freedom were often given small parcels of land for the cultivation of which they were allowed some of their time. An important result of this agricultural training was that many of the slaves thus favored amassed considerable wealth by using their spare time in cultivating crops of their own.[19]

The advocates of useful education for the degraded race had more to say about training in the mechanic arts. Such instruction, however, was not then a new thing to the blacks of the South, for they had from time immemorial been the trustworthy artisans of that section. The aim then was to give them such education as would make them intelligent workmen and develop in them the power to plan for themselves. In the North, where the Negroes had been largely menial servants, adequate industrial education was deemed necessary for those who were to be liberated.[20] Almost every Northern colored school of any consequence then offered courses in the handicrafts. In 1784 the Quakers of Philadelphia employed Sarah Dwight to teach the colored girls sewing.[21] Anthony Benezet provided in his will that in the school to be established by his benefaction the girls should be taught needlework.[22] The teachers who took upon themselves the improvement of the free people of color of New York City regarded industrial training as one of their important tasks.[23]

None urged this duty upon the directors of these schools more persistently than the antislavery organizations. In 1794 the American Convention of Abolition Societies recommended that Negroes be instructed in "those mechanic arts which will keep them most constantly employed and, of course, which will less subject them to idleness and debauchery, and thus prepare them for becoming good citizens of the United States."[24] Speaking repeatedly on this wise the Convention requested the colored people to let it be their special care to have their children not only to work at useful trades but also to till the soil.[25] The early abolitionists believed that this was the only way the freedmen could learn to support themselves.[26] In connection with their schools the antislavery leaders had an Indenturing Committee to find positions for colored students who had the advantages of industrial education.[27] In some communities slaves were prepared for emancipation by binding them out as apprentices to machinists and artisans until they learned a trade.

Two early efforts to carry out this policy are worthy of notice here. These were the endeavors of Anthony Benezet and Thaddeus Kosciuszko. Benezet was typical of those men, who, having the courage of their conviction, not only taught colored people, but gladly appropriated property to their education. Benezet died in 1784, leaving considerable wealth to be devoted to the purpose of educating Indians and Negroes. His will provided that as the estate on the death of his wife would not be sufficient entirely to support a school, the Overseers of the Public Schools of Philadelphia should join with a committee appointed by the

The Education of the Negro

Society of Friends, and other benevolent persons, in the care and maintenance of an institution such as he had planned. Finally in 1787 the efforts of Benezet reached their culmination in the construction of a schoolhouse, with additional funds obtained from David Barclay of London and Thomas Sidney, a colored man of Philadelphia. The pupils of this school were to study reading, writing, arithmetic, plain accounts, and sewing.[28]

With respect to conceding the Negroes' claim to a better education, Thaddeus Kosciuszko, the Polish general, was not unlike Benezet. None of the revolutionary leaders were more moved with compassion for the colored people than this warrior. He saw in education the powerful leverage which would place them in position to enjoy the newly won rights of man. While assisting us in gaining our independence, Kosciuszko acquired here valuable property which he endeavored to devote to the enlightenment of the slaves. He authorized Thomas Jefferson, his executor, to employ the whole thereof in purchasing Negroes and liberating them in the name of Kosciuszko, "in giving them an education in trades or otherwise, and in having them instructed for their new condition in the duties of morality." The instructors were to provide for them such training as would make them "good neighbors, good mothers or fathers, good husbands or wives, teaching them the duties of citizenship, teaching them to be defenders of their liberty and country, and of the good order of society, and whatsoever might make them useful and happy."[29] Clearly as this was set forth the executor failed to discharge this duty enjoined upon him. The heirs of the donor instituted proceedings to obtain possession of the estate, which, so far as the author knows, was never used for the purpose for which it was intended.

In view of these numerous strivings we are compelled to inquire exactly what these educators accomplished. Although it is impossible to measure the results of their early efforts, various records of the eighteenth century prove that there was lessening objection to the instruction of slaves and practically none to the enlightenment of freedmen. Negroes in considerable numbers were becoming well grounded in the rudiments of education. They had reached the point of constituting the majority of the mechanics in slaveholding communities; they were qualified to be tradesmen, trustworthy helpers, and attendants of distinguished men, and a few were serving as clerks, overseers, and managers.[30] Many who were favorably circumstanced learned more than mere reading and writing. In exceptional cases, some were employed not only as teachers and preachers to their people, but as instructors of the white race.[31]

A more accurate estimate of how far the enlightenment of the Negroes had progressed before the close of the eighteenth century, is better obtained from the reports of teachers and missionaries who were working among them. Appealing to the Negroes of Virginia about 1755, Benjamin Fawcett addressed them as intelligent people, commanding them to read and study the Bible for themselves and consider "how the Papists do all they can to hide it from their fellowmen." "Be particularly thankful," said he, "for the Ministers of Christ around you, who are faithfully laboring to teach the truth as it is in Jesus."[32] Rev. Mr. Davies, then a member of the Society for Promoting the Gospel among the Poor, reported that there were multitudes of Negroes in different parts of Virginia who were "willingly, eagerly desirous to be instructed and embraced every opportunity of acquainting themselves with the Doctrine of the Gospel," and though they had generally very little help to learn to read, yet to his surprise many of them by dint of application had made such progress that they could "intelligently read a plain author and especially their Bible." Pity it was, he thought, that any of them should be without necessary books. Negroes were wont to come to him with such moving accounts of their needs in this respect that he could not help supplying them.[33] On Saturday evenings and Sundays his home was crowded with numbers of those "whose very Countenances still carry the air of importunate Petitioners" for the same favors with those who came before them. Complaining that his stock was exhausted, and that he had to turn away many disappointed, he urged his friends to send him other suitable books, for nothing else, thought he, could be a greater inducement to their industry to learn to read.

Still more reliable testimony may be obtained, not from persons particularly interested in the uplift of the blacks, but from slaveholders. Their advertisements in the colonial newspapers furnish unconscious evidence of the intellectual progress of the Negroes during the eighteenth century. "He's an 'artful,'"[34] "plausible,"[35] "smart,"[36] or "sensible fellow,"[37] "delights much in traffic,"[38] and "plays on the fife extremely well,"[39] are some of the statements found in the descriptions of fugitive slaves. Other fugitives were speaking "plainly,"[40] "talking indifferent English,"[41] "remarkably good English,"[42] and "exceedingly good English."[43] In some advertisements we observe such expressions as "he speaks a little French,"[44] "Creole French,"[45] "a few words of High-Dutch,"[46] and "tolerable German."[47] Writing about a fugitive a master would often state that "he can read print,"[48] "can read writing,"[49] "can read and also write a little,"[50] "can read and write,"[51] "can write a pretty hand and has probably forged a pass."[52] These conditions obtained especially in Charleston, South Carolina, where were advertised various fugitives, one of whom spoke French and English fluently, and passed for a doctor among his people,[53] another who spoke Spanish and French intelligibly,[54] and a third who could read, write, and speak both French and Spanish very well.[55]

Equally convincing as to the educational progress of the colored race were the high attainments of those Negroes who, despite the fact that they had little opportunity, surpassed in intellect a large number of white men of their time. Negroes were serving as salesmen, keeping accounts, managing plantations, teaching and preaching, and had intellectually advanced to the extent that fifteen or twenty per cent of their adults could then at least read. Most of this talented class became preachers, as this was the only calling even conditionally open to persons of African blood. Among these clergymen was George Leile,[56] who won distinction as a preacher in Georgia in 1782, and then went to Jamaica where he founded the first Baptist church of that colony. The competent and indefatigable Andrew Bryan[57] proved to be a worthy successor of George Leile in Georgia. From 1770 to 1790 Negro preachers were in charge of congregations in Charles City, Petersburg, and Allen's Creek in Lunenburg County, Virginia.[58] In 1801 Gowan Pamphlet of that State was the pastor of a progressive Baptist church, some members of which could read, write, and keep accounts.[59] Lemuel Haynes was then widely known as a well-educated minister of the Protestant Episcopal Church. John Gloucester, who had been trained under Gideon Blackburn of Tennessee, distinguished himself in Philadelphia where he founded the African Presbyterian Church.[60] One of the most interesting of these preachers was Josiah Bishop. By 1791 he had made such a record in his profession that he was called to the pastorate of the First Baptist Church (white) of Portsmouth, Virginia.[61] After serving his white brethren a number of years he preached some time in Baltimore and then went to New York to take charge of the Abyssinian Baptist Church.[62] This favorable condition of affairs could not long exist after the aristocratic element in the country began to recover some of the ground it had lost during the social upheaval of the revolutionary era. It was the objection to treating Negroes as members on a plane of equality with all, that led to the establishment of colored Baptist churches and to the secession of the Negro Methodists under the leadership of Richard Allen in 1794. The importance of this movement to the student of education lies in the fact that a larger number of Negroes had to be educated to carry on the work of the new churches.

The intellectual progress of the colored people of that day, however, was not restricted to their clergymen. Other Negroes were learning to excel in various walks of life. Two such persons were found in North Carolina. One of these was known as Caesar, the author of a collection of poems, which, when published in that State, attained a popularity equal to that of Bloomfield's.[63] Those who had the pleasure of reading the poems stated that they were characterized by "simplicity, purity, and natural grace."[64] The other noted Negro of North Carolina was mentioned in 1799 by Buchan in his Domestic Medicine as the discoverer of a remedy for the bite of the rattlesnake. Buchan learned from Dr. Brooks that, in view of the benefits resulting from the discovery of this slave, the General Assembly of North Carolina purchased his freedom and settled upon him a hundred pounds per annum.[65]

To this class of bright Negroes belonged Thomas Fuller, a native African, who resided near Alexandria, Virginia, where he startled the students of his time by his unusual attainments in mathematics, despite the fact that he could neither read nor write. Once acquainted with the power of numbers, he commenced his education by counting the hairs of the tail of the horse with which he worked the fields. He soon devised processes for shortening his modes of calculation, attaining such skill and accuracy as to solve the most difficult problems. Depending upon his own system of mental arithmetic he learned to obtain accurate results just as quickly as Mr. Zerah Colburn, a noted calculator of that day, who tested the Negro mathematician.[66] The most abstruse questions in relation to time, distance, and space were no task for his miraculous memory, which, when the mathematician was interrupted in the midst of a long and tedious calculation, enabled him to take up some other work and later resume his calculation where he left off.[67] One of the questions propounded him, was how many seconds of time had elapsed since the birth of an individual who had lived seventy years, seven months, and as many days. Fuller was able to answer the question in a minute and a half.

Another Negro of this type was James Durham, a native slave of the city of Philadelphia. Durham was purchased by Dr. Dove, a physician in New Orleans, who, seeing the divine spark in the slave, gave him a chance for mental development. It was fortunate that he was thrown upon his own resources in this environment, where the miscegenation of the races since the early French settlement, had given rise to a thrifty and progressive class of mixed breeds, many of whom at that time had the privileges and immunities of freemen. Durham was not long in acquiring a rudimentary education, and soon learned several modern languages, speaking English, French, and Spanish fluently. Beginning his medical education early in his career, he finished his course, and by the time he was twenty-one years of age became one of the most distinguished physicians[68] of New Orleans. Dr. Benjamin Rush, the noted physician of Philadelphia, who was educated at the Edinburgh Medical College, once deigned to converse professionally with Dr. Durham. "I learned more from him than he could expect from me," was the comment of the Philadelphian upon a conversation in which he had thought to appear as instructor of the younger physician.[69]

Most prominent among these brainy persons of color were Phyllis Wheatley and Benjamin Banneker. The former was a slave girl brought from Africa in 1761 and put to service in the household of John Wheatley of Boston. There, without any training but that which she obtained from her master's family, she learned in sixteen months to speak the English language fluently, and to read the most difficult parts of sacred writings. She had a great inclination for Latin and made some progress in the study of that language. Led to writing by curiosity, she was by 1765 possessed of a style which enabled her to count among her correspondents some of the most influential men of her time. Phyllis Wheatley's title to fame, however, rested not on her general attainments as a scholar but rather on her ability to write poetry. Her poems seemed to have such rare merit that men marveled that a slave could possess such a productive imagination, enlightened mind, and poetical genius. The publishers were so much surprised that they sought reassurance as to the authenticity of the poems from such persons as James Bowdoin, Harrison Gray, and John Hancock.[70] Glancing at her works, the modern critic would readily say that she was not a poetess, just as the student of political economy would dub Adam Smith a failure as an economist. A bright college freshman who has studied introductory economics can write a treatise as scientific as the Wealth of Nations. The student of history, however, must not "despise the day of small things." Judged according to the standards of her time, Phyllis Wheatley was an exceptionally intellectual person.

The other distinguished Negro, Benjamin Banneker, was born in Baltimore County, Maryland, November 9, 1731, near the village of Ellicott Mills. Banneker was sent to school in the neighborhood, where he learned reading, writing, and arithmetic. Determined to acquire knowledge while toiling, he applied his mind to things intellectual, cultivated the power of observation, and developed a retentive memory. These acquirements finally made him tower above all other American scientists of his time with the possible exception of Benjamin Franklin. In conformity with his desire to do and create, his tendency was toward mathematics. Although he had never seen a clock, watches being the only timepieces in the vicinity, he made in 1770 the first clock manufactured in the United States,[71] thereby attracting the attention of the scientific world. Learning these things, the owner of Ellicott Mills became very much interested in this man of inventive genius, lent him books, and encouraged him in his chosen field. Among these volumes were treatises on astronomy, which Banneker soon mastered without any instruction.[72] Soon he could calculate eclipses of sun and moon and the rising of each star with an accuracy almost unknown to Americans. Despite his limited means, he secured through Goddard and Angell of Baltimore the publication of the first almanac produced in this country. Jefferson received from Banneker a copy, for which he wrote the author a letter of thanks. It appears that Jefferson had some doubts about the man's genius, but the fact that the philosopher invited Banneker to visit him at Monticello in 1803, indicates that the increasing reputation of the Negro must have caused Jefferson to change his opinion as to the extent of Banneker's attainments and the value of his contributions to mathematics and science.[73]

The Education of the Negro

So favorable did the aspect of things become as a result of this movement to elevate the Negroes, that persons observing the conditions then obtaining in this country thought that the victory for the despised race had been won. Traveling in 1783 in the colony of Virginia, where the slave trade had been abolished and schools for the education of freedmen established, Johann Schoepf felt that the institution was doomed.[74] After touring Pennsylvania five years later, Brissot de Warville reported that there existed then a country where the blacks were allowed to have souls, and to be endowed with an understanding capable of being formed to virtue and useful knowledge, and where they were not regarded as beasts of burden in order that their masters might have the privilege of treating them as such. He was pleased that the colored people by their virtue and understanding belied the calumnies which their tyrants elsewhere lavished against them, and that in that community one perceived no difference between "the memory of a black head whose hair is craped by nature, and that of the white one craped by art."[75]

[1: Smyth, Works of Benjamin Franklin, vol. x., p. 127; Torrey, Portraiture of Slavery, p. 21. See also constitution of almost any antislavery society organized during this period.]
[2: Washington, Works of Jefferson, vol. vi., p. 456; vol. viii., p. 379; Madison, Works of, vol. iii., p. 496; Monroe, Writings of, vol. iii., pp. 321, 336, 349, 378; Adams, Works of John Adams, vol. ix., p. 92 and vol. x., p. 380.]
[3: Proceedings of the American Convention, etc., 1797, address.]
[4: The constitution of almost any antislavery society of that time provided for this work. See Proc. of Am. Conv., etc., 1795, address.]
[5: Proceedings of the American Convention of Abolition Societies, 1794, p. 21; and 1795, p. 17; and Rise and Progress of the Testimony of Friends, etc., p. 27.]
[6: The antislavery societies were at first the uniting influence among all persons interested in the uplift of the Negroes. The agitation had not then become violent, for men considered the institution not a sin but merely an evil.]
[7: Coke, Journal, etc., p. 114; Lambert, Travels, p. 175; Baird, A Collection, etc., pp. 381, 387 and 816; James, Documentary, etc., p. 35; Foote, Sketches of Virginia, p. 31; Matlack, History of American Slavery and Methodism, p. 31; Semple, History of the Rise and Progress of the Baptists in Virginia, p. 222.]
[8: Ibid., and Coke, Journal, etc., pp. 16-18.]
[9: Proceedings of the American Convention of Abolition Societies, 1797.]
[10: Proceedings of the American Convention of Abolition Societies, 1797.]
[11: Locke, Anti-slavery, etc., p. 44.]
[12: Washington, Story of the Negro, vol. ii, p. 121.]
[13: Ibid., p. 121.]
[14: Laws of New Jersey, 1788.]
[15: Proceedings of the American Convention of Abolition Societies, 1796, p. 18.]
[16: Ibid., 1797, p. 41.]
[17: See the descriptions of indentured servants in the advertisements of colonial newspapers referred to on pages 82-84; and Boucher, A View of the Causes, etc., p. 39.]
[18: Ibid., pp. 39 and 40.]
[19: Special Report of the U.S. Com. of Ed., 1871, p. 196.]

[20: See the Address of the Am. Conv. of Abolition Societies, 1794; ibid., 1795; ibid., 1797 et passim.]

[21: Wickersham, History of Ed. in Pa., p. 249.]

[22: Special Report of the U.S. Com. of Ed., 1869, p. 375.]

[23: Andrews, History of the New York African Free Schools, p. 20.]

[24: Proceedings of the American Convention, 1794, p. 14.]

[25: Ibid., 1795, p. 29; ibid., 1797, pp. 12, 13, and 31.]

[26: Ibid., 1797, p. 31.]

[27: Ibid., 1818, p. 9.]

[28: Special Report of the U.S. Com. of Ed., 1871, p. 375.]

[29: African Repository, vol. xi., pp. 294-295.]

[30: Georgia and South Carolina had to pass laws to prevent Negroes from following these occupations for fear that they might thereby become too well informed. See Brevard, Digest of Public Statute Laws of S.C., vol. ii., p. 243; and Marbury and Crawford, Digest of the Laws of the State of Georgia, p. 438.]

[31: Bassett, Slavery in North Carolina, p. 74; manuscripts relating to the condition of the colored people of North Carolina, Ohio, and Tennessee now in the hands of Dr. J.E. Moorland.]

[32: Fawcett, Compassionate Address, etc., p. 33.]

[33: Fawcett, Compassionate Address, etc., p. 33.]

[34: Virginia Herald (Fredericksburg), Jan. 21, 1800; The Maryland Gazette, Feb. 27, 1755; Dunlop's Maryland Gazette and Baltimore Advertiser, July 23, 1776; The State Gazette of South Carolina, May 18, 1786; The State Gazette of North Carolina, July 2, 1789.]

[35: The City Gazette and Daily Advertiser (Charleston, S.C.), Sept. 26, 1797, and The Carolina Gazette, June 3, 1802.]

[36: The Charleston Courier, June 1, 1804; The State Gazette of South Carolina, Feb. 20, and 27, 1786; and The Maryland Journal and Baltimore Advertiser, Feb. 19, 1793.]

[37: South Carolina Weekly Advertiser, Feb. 19 and April 2, 1783; State Gazette of South Carolina, Feb. 20 and May 18, 1786.]

[38: The Maryland Journal and Baltimore Advocate, Oct. 17, 1780.]

[39: The Virginia Herald (Fredericksburg), Jan. 21, 1800; and The Norfolk and Portsmouth Chronicle, April 24, 1790.]

[40: The City Gazette and Daily Advertiser, Jan. 20 and March 1, 1800; and The South Carolina Weekly Gazette, Oct. 24 to 31, 1759.]

[41: The City Gaz. and Daily Adv., Jan. 20 and March 1, 1800; and S.C. Weekly Gaz., Oct. 24 to 31, 1759.]

[42: The Newbern Gazette, May 23 and Aug. 15, 1800; The Maryland Journal and Baltimore Advertiser, Feb. 19, 1793; The City Gazette and Daily Advertiser (Charleston, S.C.), Sept. 26, 1797; Oct. 5, 1798; Aug. 23 and Sept. 9, 1799; Aug. 18 and Oct. 3, 1800; and March 7, 1801; and Maryland Gazette, Dec. 30, 1746; and April 4, 1754; South Carolina Weekly Advertiser, Oct. 24 to 31, 1759; and Feb. 19, 1783; The Gazette of the State of South Carolina, Sept. 13 and Nov. 1, 1784; and The Carolina Gazette, Aug. 12, 1802.]

[43: The City Gazette and Daily Advertiser, Sept. 26, 1797; May 15, 1799; and Oct. 3, 1800; The State Gazette of South Carolina, Aug. 21, 1786; The Gazette of the State of South Carolina, Aug. 26, 1784; The Maryland Gazette, Aug. 1, 1754; Oct. 28, 1773; and Aug. 19, 1784; and The Columbian Herald, April 30, 1789.]

[44: The City Gazette and Daily Advertiser, Oct. 5, 1798; Aug. 18 and Sept. 18, 1800; The Gazette of the State of South Carolina, Aug. 16, 1784.]

[45: The City Gazette and Daily Advertiser, Oct. 5, 1798.]

[46: The Maryland Gazette, Aug. 19, 1784.]

[47: The State Gazette of South Carolina, Feb. 20 and 27, 1780.]

[48: The Maryland Journal and Baltimore Advertiser, Oct. 17, 1780. Dunlop's Maryland Gazette and Baltimore Advertiser, July 23, 1776.]

[49: The Maryland Gazette, May 21, 1795.]

[50: The Maryland Journal and Baltimore Advertiser, Oct. 17, 1780; and Sept. 20, 1785; and The Maryland Gazette, May 21, 1795; and January 4, 1798; The Carolina Gazette, June 3, 1802; and The Charleston Courier, June 29, 1803. The Norfolk and Portsmouth Chronicle, March 19, 1791.]

[51: The Maryland Gazette, Feb. 27, 1755; and Oct. 27, 1768; The Maryland Journal and Baltimore Advertiser, Oct. 1, 1793; The Virginia Herald (Fredericksburg), Jan. 21, 1800.]

[52: The Maryland Gazette, Feb. 1, 1755 and Feb. 1, 1798; The State Gazette of North Carolina, April 30, 1789; The Norfolk and Portsmouth Chronicle, April 24, 1790; The City Gazette and Daily Advertiser (Charleston, South Carolina), Jan. 5, 1799; and March 7, 1801; The Carolina Gazette, Feb. 4, 1802; and The Virginia Herald (Fredericksburg), Jan. 21, 1800.]

[53: The City Gazette and Daily Advertiser, Jan. 5, 1799; and March 5, 1800; The Gazette of the State of South Carolina, Aug. 16, 1784; and The Maryland Journal and Baltimore Advertiser, Sept. 20, 1793.]

[54: The City Gazette of South Carolina, Jan. 5, 1799.]

[55: The City Gazette and Daily Advertiser (Charleston, South Carolina), June 22 and Aug. 8, 1797; April 1 and May 15, 1799.]

[56: He was sometimes called George Sharp. See Benedict, History of the Baptists, etc., p. 189.]

[57: Ibid., p. 189.]

[58: Semple, History of the Baptists, etc., p. 112.]

[59: Ibid., p. 114.]

[60: Baird, A Collection, etc., p. 817.]

[61: Semple, History of the Baptists, etc., p. 355.]

[62: Ibid., p. 356.]

[63: Baldwin, Observations, etc., p. 20.]

[64: Ibid., p. 21.]

[65: Smyth, A Tour in the U.S., p. 109; and Baldwin, Observations, p. 20.]

[66: Baldwin, Observations, p. 21.]

[67: Needles, An Historical Memoir, etc., p. 32.]

[68: Brissot de Warville, New Travels, vol. i., p. 223.]

[69: Baldwin, Observations, etc., p. 17.]

[70: Baldwin, Observations, etc., p. 18; Wright, Poems of Phyllis Wheatley, Introduction.]

[71: Washington, Jefferson's Works, vol. v., p. 429.]

[72: Baldwin, Observations, etc., p. 16.]

[73: Washington, Jefferson's Works, vol. v., p. 429.]

[74: Schoepf, Travels in the Confederation, p. 149.]

[75: Brissot de Warville, New Travels, vol. I., p. 220.]

Chapter 5

Better Beginnings

Sketching the second half of the eighteenth century, we have observed how the struggle for the rights of man in directing attention to those of low estate, and sweeping away the impediments to religious freedom, made the free blacks more accessible to helpful sects and organizations. We have also learned that this upheaval left the slaves the objects of piety for the sympathetic, the concern of workers in behalf of social uplift, a class offered instruction as a prerequisite to emancipation. The private teaching of Negroes became tolerable, benevolent persons volunteered to instruct them, and some schools maintained for the education of white students were thrown open to those of African blood. It was the day of better beginnings. In fact, it was the heyday of victory for the ante-bellum Negro. Never had his position been so advantageous; never was it thus again until the whole race was emancipated. Now the question which naturally arises here is, to what extent were such efforts general? Were these beginnings sufficiently extensive to secure adequate enlightenment to a large number of colored people? Was interest in the education of this class so widely manifested thereafter as to cause the movement to endure? A brief account of these efforts in the various States will answer these questions.

In the Northern and Middle States an increasing number of educational advantages for the white race made germane the question as to what consideration should be shown to the colored people.[1] A general admission of Negroes to the schools of these progressive communities was undesirable, not because of the prejudice against the race, but on account of the feeling that the past of the colored people having been different from that of the white race, their training should be in keeping with their situation. To meet their peculiar needs many communities thought it best to provide for them "special," "individual," or "unclassified" schools adapted to their condition.[2] In most cases, however, the movement for separate schools originated not with the white race, but with the people of color themselves.

In New England, Negroes had almost from the beginning of their enslavement some chance for mental, moral, and spiritual improvement, but the revolutionary movement was followed in that section by a general effort to elevate the people of color through the influence of the school and church. In 1770 the Rhode Island Quakers were endeavoring to give young Negroes such an education as becomes Christians. In 1773 Newport had a colored school, maintained by a society of benevolent clergymen of the Church of England, with a handsome fund for a mistress to teach thirty children reading and writing. Providence did not exhibit such activity until the nineteenth century. Having a larger black population than any other city in New England, Boston was the center of these endeavors. In 1798 a separate school for colored children, under the charge of Elisha Sylvester, a white man, was established in that city in the house of Primus Hall, a Negro of very good standing.[3] Two years later sixty-six free blacks of that city petitioned the school committee for a separate school, but the citizens in a special town meeting called to consider the question refused to grant this request.[4] Undaunted by this refusal, the patrons of the special school established in the house of Primus Hall, employed Brown and Hall of Harvard College as instructors, until 1806.[5] The school was then moved to the African Meeting House in Belknap Street where it remained until 1835 when, with funds contributed by Abiel Smith, a building was erected. An epoch in the history of Negro education in New England was marked in 1820, when the city of Boston opened its first primary school for the education of colored children.[6]

Generally speaking, we can say that while the movement for special colored schools met with some opposition in certain portions of New England, in other parts of the Northeastern States the religious organizations and abolition societies, which were espousing the cause of the Negro, yielded to this demand. These schools were sometimes found in churches of the North, as in the cases of the schools in the African Church of Boston, and the Sunday-school in the African Improved Church of New Haven. In 1828 there was in that city another such school supported by public-school money; three in Boston; one in Salem; and one in Portland, Maine.[7]

Outside of the city of New York, not so much interest was shown in the education of Negroes as in the States which had a larger colored population.[8] Those who were scattered through the State were allowed to attend white schools, which did not "meet their special needs."[9] In the metropolis, where the blacks constituted one-tenth of the inhabitants in 1800, however, the mental improvement of the dark race could not be neglected. The liberalism of the revolutionary era led to the organization in New York of the "Society for Promoting the Manumission of Slaves and Protecting such of them as have been or may be liberated." This Society ushered in a new day for the free persons of color of that city in organizing in 1787 the New York African Free School.[10] Among those interested in this organization and its enterprises were Melancthon Smith, John Bleecker, James Cogswell, Jacob Seaman, White Matlock, Matthew Clarkson, Nathaniel Lawrence, and John Murray, Jr.[11] The school opened in 1790 with Cornelius Davis as a teacher of forty pupils. In 1791 a lady was employed to instruct the girls in needle-work.[12] The expected advantage of this industrial training was soon realized.

Despite the support of certain distinguished members of the community, the larger portion of the population was so prejudiced against the school that often the means available for its maintenance were inadequate. The struggle was continued for about fifteen years with an attendance of from forty to sixty pupils.[13] About 1801 the community began to take more interest in the institution, and the Negroes "became more generally impressed with a sense of the advantages and importance of education, and more disposed to avail themselves of the privileges offered them."[14] At this time one hundred and thirty pupils of both sexes attended this school, paying their instructor, a "discreet man of color," according to their ability and inclination.[15] Many more colored children were then able to attend as there had been a considerable increase in the number of colored freeholders. As a result of the introduction of the Lancastrian and monitorial systems of instruction the enrollment was further increased and the general tone of the school was improved. Another impetus was given the work in 1810.[16] Having in mind the preparation of slaves for freedom, the legislature of the State of New York, made it compulsory for masters to teach all minors born of slaves to read the Scriptures.[17]

Decided improvement was noted after 1814. The directors then purchased a lot on which they constructed a building the following year.[18] The nucleus then took the name of the New York "African Free Schools." These schools grew so rapidly that it was soon necessary to rent additional quarters to accommodate the department of sewing. This work had been made popular by the efforts of Misses Turpen, Eliza J. Cox, Ann Cox, and Caroline Roe.[19] The subsequent growth of the classes was such that in 1820 the Manumission Society had to erect a building large enough to accommodate five hundred pupils.[20] The instructors were then not only teaching the elementary branches of reading, writing, arithmetic, and geography, but also astronomy, navigation, advanced composition, plain sewing, knitting, and marking.[21] Knowing the importance of industrial training, the Manumission Society then had an Indenturing Committee find employment in trades for colored children, and had recommended for some of them the pursuit of agriculture.[22] The comptrollers desired no better way of measuring the success of the system in shaping the character of its students than to be able to boast that no pupils educated there had ever been convicted of crime.[23] Lafayette, a promoter of the emancipation and improvement of the colored people, and a member of the New York Manumission Society, visited these schools in 1824 on his return to the United States. He was bidden welcome by an eleven-year-old pupil in well-chosen and significant words. After spending the afternoon inspecting the schools the General pronounced them the "best disciplined and the most interesting schools of children" he had ever seen.[24]

The outlook for the education of Negroes in New Jersey was unusually bright. Carrying out the recommendations of the Haddonfield Quarterly Meeting in 1777, the Quakers of Salem raised funds for the education of the blacks, secured books, and placed the colored children of the community at school. The delegates sent from that State, to the Convention of the Abolition Societies in 1801, reported that there had been schools in Burlington, Salem, and Trenton for the education of the Negro race, but that they had been closed.[25] It seemed that not much attention had been given to this work there, but that the interest was increasing. These delegates stated that they did not then know of any schools among them exclusively for Negroes. In most parts of the State, and most commonly in the northern division, however, they were incorporated with the white children in the various small schools scattered over the State.[26] There was then in the city of Burlington a free school for the education of poor children supported by the profits of an estate left for that particular purpose, and made equally accessible to the children of both races. Conditions were just as favorable in Gloucester. An account from its antislavery society shows that the local friends of the indigent had funds of about one thousand pounds established for schooling poor children, white and black, without distinction. Many of the black children, who were placed by their masters under the care of white instructors, received as good moral and school education as the lower class of whites.[27] Later reports from this State show the same tendency toward democratic education.

The efforts made in this direction in Delaware, were encouraging. The Abolition Society of Wilmington had not greatly promoted the special education of "the Blacks and the people of color." In 1801, however, a school was kept the first day of the week by one of the members of the Society, who instructed them gratis in reading, writing, and arithmetic. About twenty pupils generally attended and by their assiduity and progress showed themselves as "capable as white persons laboring under similar disadvantages."[28] In 1802 plans for the extension of this system were laid and bore good fruit the following year.[29] Seven years later, however, after personal and pecuniary aid had for some time been extended, the workers had still to lament that beneficial effects had not been more generally experienced, and that there was little disposition to aid them in their friendly endeavors.[30] In 1816 more important results had been obtained. Through a society formed a few years prior to this date for the express purpose of educating colored children, a school had been established under a Negro teacher. He had a fair attendance of bright children, who "by the facility with which they took in instruction were silently but certainly undermining the prejudice"[31] against their education. A library of religious and moral publications had been secured for this institution. In addition to the school in Wilmington there was a large academy for young colored women, gratuitously taught by a society of young ladies. The course of instruction covered reading, writing, and sewing. The work in sewing proved to be a great advantage to the colored girls, many of whom through the instrumentality of that society were provided with good positions.[32]

In Pennsylvania the interest of the large Quaker element caused the question of educating Negroes to be a matter of more concern to that colony than it was to the others. Thanks to the arduous labors of the antislavery movement, emancipation was provided for in 1780. The Quakers were then especially anxious to see masters give their "weighty and solid attention" to qualifying slaves for the liberty intended. By the favorable legislation of the State the poor were by 1780 allowed the chance to secure the rudiments of education.[33] Despite this favorable appearance of things, however, friends of the despised race had to keep up the agitation for such a construction of the law as would secure to the Negroes of the State the educational benefits extended to the indigent. The colored youth of Pennsylvania thereafter had the right to attend the schools provided for white children, and exercised it when persons interested in the blacks directed their attention to the importance of mental improvement.[34] But as neither they nor their defenders were numerous outside of Philadelphia and Columbia, not many pupils of color in other parts of the State attended school during this period. Whatever special effort was made to arouse them to embrace their opportunities came chiefly from the Quakers.

Not content with the schools which were already opened to Negroes, the friends of the race continued to agitate and raise funds to extend their philanthropic operations. With the donation of Anthony Benezet the Quakers were able to enlarge their building and increase the scope of the work. They added a female department in which Sarah Dwight[35] was teaching the girls spelling, reading, and sewing in 1784. The work done in Philadelphia was so successful that the place became the rallying center for the Quakers throughout the country,[36] and was of so much concern to certain members of this sect in London that in 1787 they contributed five hundred pounds toward the support of this school.[37] In 1789 the Quakers organized "The Society for the Free Instruction of the Orderly Blacks and People of Color." Taking into consideration the "many disadvantages which many well-disposed blacks and people of color labored under from not being able to read, write, or cast accounts, which would qualify them to act for themselves or provide for their families," this society in connection with other organizations established evening schools for the education of adults of African blood.[38] It is evident then that with the exception of the school of the Abolition Society organized in 1774, and the efforts of a few other persons generally cooeperating like the anti-slavery leaders with the Quakers, practically all of the useful education of the colored people of this State was accomplished in their schools. Philadelphia had seven colored schools in 1797.[39]

The next decade was of larger undertakings.[40] The report of the Pennsylvania Abolition Society of 1801 shows that there had been an increasing interest in Negro education. For this purpose the society had raised funds to the amount of $530.50 per annum for three years.[41] In 1803 certain other friends of the cause left for this purpose two liberal benefactions, one amounting to one thousand dollars, and the other to one thousand pounds.[42] With these contributions the Quakers and Abolitionists erected in 1809 a handsome building valued at four thousand dollars. They named it Clarkson Hall in honor of the great friend of the Negro race.[43] In 1807 the Quakers met the needs of the increasing population of the city by founding an additional institution of learning known as the Adelphi School.[44]

After the first decade of the nineteenth century the movement for the uplift of the Negroes around Philadelphia was checked a little by the migration to that city of many freedmen who had been lately liberated. The majority of them did not "exhibit that industry, economy, and temperance" which were "expected by many and wished by all."[45] Not deterred, however, by this seemingly discouraging development, the friends of the race toiled on as before. In 1810 certain Quaker women who had attempted to establish a school for colored girls in 1795 apparently succeeded.[46] The institution, however, did not last many years. But the Clarkson Hall schools maintained by the Abolition Society were then making such progress that the management was satisfied that they furnished a decided refutation of the charge that the "mental endowments of the descendants of the African race are inferior to those possessed by their white brethren."[47] They asserted without fear of contradiction that the pupils of that seminary would sustain a fair comparison with those of any other institution in which the same elementary branches were taught. In 1815 these schools were offering free instruction to three hundred boys and girls, and to a number of adults attending evening schools. These victories had been achieved despite the fact that in regard to some of the objects of the Society for the Abolition of the Slave Trade "a tide of prejudice, popular and legislative, set strongly against them."[48] After 1818, however, help was obtained from the State to educate the colored children of Columbia and Philadelphia.

The assistance obtained from the State, however, was not taken as a pretext for the cessation of the labors on the part of those who had borne the burden for more than a century. The faithful friends of the colored race remained as active as ever. In 1822 the Quakers in the Northern Liberties organized the Female Association which maintained one or more schools.[49] That same year the Union Society founded in 1810 for the support of schools and domestic manufactures for the benefit of the "African race and people of color" was conducting three schools for adults.[50] The Infant School Society of Philadelphia was also doing good work in looking after the education of small colored children.[51] In the course of time crowded conditions in the colored schools necessitated the opening of additional evening classes and the erection of larger buildings.

The Education of the Negro

At this time Maryland was not raising any serious objection to the instruction of slaves, and public sentiment there did not seem to interfere with the education of free persons of color. Maryland was long noted for her favorable attitude toward her Negroes. We have already observed how Banneker, though living in a small place, was permitted to attend school, and how Ellicott became interested in this man of genius and furnished him with books. Other Negroes of that State were enjoying the same privilege. The abolition delegates from Maryland reported in 1797 that several children of the Africans and other people of color were under a course of instruction, and that an academy and qualified teachers for them would be provided.[52] These Negroes were then getting light from another source. Having more freedom in this State than in some others, the Quakers were allowed to teach colored people.

Most interest in the cause in Maryland was manifested near the cities of Georgetown and Baltimore.[53] Long active in the cause of elevating the colored people, the influence of the revolutionary movement was hardly necessary to arouse the Catholics to discharge their duty of enlightening the blacks. Wherever they had the opportunity to give slaves religious instruction, they generally taught the unfortunates everything that would broaden their horizon and help them to understand life. The abolitionists and Protestant churches were also in the field, but the work of the early fathers in these cities was more effective. These forces at work in Georgetown made it, by the time of its incorporation into the District of Columbia, a center sending out teachers to carry on the instruction of Negroes. So liberal were the white people of this town that colored children were sent to school there with white boys and girls who seemed to raise no objection.[54] Later in the nineteenth century the efforts made to educate the Negroes of the rural districts of Maryland were eclipsed by the better work accomplished by the free blacks in Baltimore and the District of Columbia.

Having a number of antislavery men among the various sects buoyant with religious freedom, Virginia easily continued to look with favor upon the uplift of the colored people. The records of the Quakers of that day show special effort in this direction there about 1764, 1773, and 1785. In 1797 the abolitionists of Alexandria, some of whom were Quakers, had been doing effective work among the Negroes of that section. They had established a school with one Benjamin Davis as a teacher. He reported an attendance of one hundred and eight pupils, four of whom "could write a very legible hand," "read the Scriptures with tolerable facility," and had commenced arithmetic. Eight others had learned to read, but had made very little progress in writing. Among his less progressive pupils fifteen could spell words of three or four syllables and read easy lessons, some had begun to write, while the others were chiefly engaged in learning the alphabet and spelling monosyllables.[55] It is significant that colored children of Alexandria, just as in the case of Georgetown, attended schools established for the whites.[56] Their coeducation extended not only to Sabbath schools but to other institutions of learning, which some Negroes attended during the week.[57] Mrs. Maria Hall, one of the early teachers of the District of Columbia, obtained her education in a mixed school of Alexandria.[58] Controlled then by aristocratic people who did not neglect the people of color, Alexandria also became a sort of center for the uplift of the blacks in Northern Virginia.

Schools for the education of Negroes were established in Richmond, Petersburg, and Norfolk. An extensive miscegenation of the races in these cities had given rise to a very intelligent class of slaves and a considerable number of thrifty free persons of color, in whom the best people early learned to show much interest.[59] Of the schools organized for them in the central part of the commonwealth, those about Richmond seemed to be less prosperous. The abolitionists of Virginia, reporting for that city in 1798, said that considerable progress had been made in the education of the blacks, and that they contemplated the establishment of a school for the instruction of Negroes and other persons. They were apprehensive, however, that their funds would be scarcely sufficient for this purpose.[60] In 1801, one year after Gabriel's Insurrection, the abolitionists of Richmond reported that the cause had been hindered by the "rapacious disposition which emboldened many tyrants" among them "to trample upon the rights of colored people even in the violation of the laws of the State." For this reason the complainants felt that, although they could not but unite in the opinion with the American Convention of Abolition Societies as to the importance of educating the slaves for living as freedmen, they were compelled on account of a "domineering spirit of power and usurpation"[61] to direct attention to the Negroes' bodily comfort.

This situation, however, was not sufficiently alarming to deter all the promoters of Negro education in Virginia. It is remarkable how Robert Pleasants, a Quaker of that State who emancipated his slaves at his death in 1801, had united with other members of his sect to establish a school for colored people. In 1782 they circulated a pamphlet entitled "Proposals for Establishing a Free School for the Instruction of Children of Blacks and People of Color."[62] They recommended to the humane and benevolent of all denominations cheerfully to contribute to an institution "calculated to promote the spiritual and temporal interests of that unfortunate part of our fellow creatures in forming their minds in the principles of virtue and religion, and in common or useful literature, writing, ciphering, and mechanic arts, as the most likely means to render so numerous a people fit for freedom, and to become useful citizens." Pleasants proposed to establish a school on a three-hundred-and-fifty-acre tract of his own land at Gravelly Hills near Four-Mile Creek, Henrico County. The whole revenue of the land was to go toward the support of the institution, or, in the event the school should be established elsewhere, he would give it one hundred pounds. Ebenezer Maule, another friend, subscribed fifty pounds for the same purpose.[63] Exactly what the outcome was, no one knows; but the memorial on the life of Pleasants shows that he appropriated the rent of the three-hundred-and-fifty-acre tract and ten pounds per annum to the establishment of a free school for Negroes, and that a few years after his death such an institution was in operation under a Friend at Gravelly Run.[64]

Such philanthropy, however, did not become general in Virginia. The progress of Negro education there was decidedly checked by the rapid development of discontent among Negroes ambitious to emulate the example of Toussaint L'Ouverture. During the first quarter of the nineteenth century that commonwealth tolerated much less enlightenment of the colored people than the benevolent element allowed them in the other border States. The custom of teaching colored pauper children apprenticed by church-wardens was prohibited by statute immediately after Gabriel's Insurrection in 1800.[65] Negroes eager to learn were thereafter largely restricted to private tutoring and instruction offered in Sabbath-schools. Furthermore, as Virginia developed few urban communities there were not sufficient persons of color in any one place to cooeperate in enlightening themselves even as much as public sentiment allowed. After 1838 Virginia Negroes had practically no chance to educate themselves.

North Carolina, not unlike the border States in their good treatment of free persons of color, placed such little restriction on the improvement of the colored people that they early attained rank among the most enlightened ante-bellum Negroes. This interest, largely on account of the zeal of the antislavery leaders and Quakers,[66] continued unabated from 1780, the time of their greatest activity, to the period of the intense abolition agitation and the servile insurrections. In 1815 the Quakers were still exhorting their members to establish schools for the literary and religious instruction of Negroes.[67] The following year a school for Negroes was opened for two days in a week.[68] So successful was the work done by the Quakers during this period that they could report in 1817 that most colored minors in the Western Quarter had been "put in a way to get a portion of school learning."[69] In 1819 some of them could spell and a few could write. The plan of these workers was to extend the instruction until males could "read, write, and cipher," and until the females could "read and write."[70]

In the course of time, however, these philanthropists met with some discouragement. In 1821 certain masters were sending their slaves to a Sunday-school opened by Levi Coffin and his son Vestal. Before the slaves had learned more than to spell words of two or three syllables other masters became unduly alarmed, thinking that such instruction would make the slaves discontented. [71] The timorous element threatened the teachers with the terrors of the law, induced the benevolent slaveholders to prohibit the attendance of their Negroes, and had the school closed.[72] Moreover, it became more difficult to obtain aid for this cause. Between 1815 and 1825 the North Carolina Manumission Societies were redoubling their efforts to raise funds for this purpose. By 1819 they had collected $47.00 but had not increased this amount more than $2.62 two years later.[73]

The work done by the various workers in North Carolina did not affect the general improvement of the slaves, but thanks to the humanitarian movement, they were not entirely neglected. In 1830 the General Association of the Manumission Societies of that commonwealth complained that the laws made no provision for the moral improvement of the slaves.[74] Though learning was in a very small degree diffused among the colored people of a few sections, it was almost unknown to the slaves. They pointed out, too, that the little instruction some of the slaves had received, and by which a few had been taught to spell, or perhaps to read in "easy places," was not due to any legal provision, but solely to the charity "which endureth all things" and is willing to suffer reproach for the sake of being instrumental in "delivering the poor that cry" and "directing the wanderer in the right way."[75] To ameliorate these conditions the association recommended among other things the enactment of a law providing for the instruction of slaves in the elementary principles of language at least so far as to enable them to read the Holy Scriptures.[76] The reaction culminated, however, before this plan could be properly presented to the people of that commonwealth.

During these years an exceptionally bright Negro was serving as a teacher not of his own race but of the most aristocratic white people of North Carolina. This educator was a freeman named John Chavis. He was born probably near Oxford, Granville County, about 1763. Chavis was a full-blooded Negro of dark brown color. Early attracting the attention of his white neighbors, he was sent to Princeton "to see if a Negro would take a collegiate education." His rapid advancement under Dr. Witherspoon "soon convinced his friends that the experiment would issue favorable."[77] There he took rank as a good Latin and a fair Greek scholar.

From Princeton he went to Virginia to preach to his own people. In 1801 he served at the Hanover Presbytery as a "riding missionary under the direction of the General Assembly."[78] He was then reported also as a regularly commissioned preacher to his people in Lexington. In 1805 he returned to North Carolina where he often preached to various congregations.[79] His career as a clergyman was brought to a close in 1831 by the law enacted to prevent Negroes from preaching.[80] Thereafter he confined himself to teaching, which was by far his most important work. He opened a classical school for white persons, "teaching in Granville, Wake, and Chatham Counties."[81] The best people of the community patronized this school. Chavis counted among his students W.P. Mangum, afterwards United States Senator, P.H. Mangum, his brother, Archibald and John Henderson, sons of Chief Justice Henderson, Charles Manly, afterwards Governor of that commonwealth, and Dr. James L. Wortham of Oxford, North Carolina.[82]

We have no evidence of any such favorable conditions in South Carolina. There was not much public education of the Negroes of that State even during the revolutionary epoch. Regarding education as a matter of concern to persons immediately interested South Carolinians had long since learned to depend on private instruction for the training of their youth. Colored schools were not thought of outside of Charleston. Yet although South Carolina prohibited the education of the slaves in 1740[83] and seemingly that of other Negroes in 1800,[84] these measures were not considered a direct attack on the instruction of free persons of color. Furthermore, the law in regard to the teaching of the blacks was ignored by sympathetic masters. Colored persons serving in families and attending traveling men shared with white children the advantage of being taught at home. Free persons of color remaining accessible to teachers and missionaries interested in the propagation of the gospel among the poor still had the opportunity to make intellectual advancement.[85]

In the territory known as Louisiana the good treatment of the mixed breeds and the slaves by the French assured for years the privilege to attend school. Rev. James Flint, of Salem, Massachusetts, received letters from a friend in Louisiana, who, in pointing out conditions around him, said: "In the regions where I live masters allow entire liberty to the slaves to attend public worship, and as far as my knowledge extends, it is generally the case in Louisiana. We have," said he, "regular meetings of the blacks in the building where I attend public worship. I have in the past years devoted myself assiduously, every Sabbath morning, to the labor of learning them to read. I found them quick of apprehension, and capable of grasping the rudiments of learning more rapidly than the whites."[88]

Later the problem of educating Negroes in this section became more difficult. The trouble was that contrary to the stipulation in the treaty of purchase that the inhabitants of the territory of Louisiana should be admitted to all the rights and immunities of citizens of the United States, the State legislation, subsequent to the transfer of jurisdiction, denied the right of education to a large class of mixed breeds.[89] Many of these, thanks to the liberality of the French, had been freed, and constituted an important element of society. Not

The Education of the Negro

a few of them had educated themselves, accumulated wealth, and ranked with white men of refinement and culture.[90]

Considering the few Negroes found in the West, the interest shown there in their mental uplift was considerable. Because of the scarcity of slaves in that section they came into helpful contact with their masters. Besides, the Kentucky and Tennessee abolitionists, being much longer active than those in most slave States, continued to emphasize the education of the blacks as a correlative to emancipation. Furthermore, the Western Baptists, Methodists, and Scotch-Irish Presbyterians early took a stand against slavery, and urged the masters to give their servants all the proper advantages for acquiring the knowledge of their duty both to man and God. In the large towns of Tennessee Negroes were permitted to attend private schools, and in Louisville and Lexington there were several well-regulated colored schools.

Two institutions for the education of slaves in the West are mentioned during these years. In October, 1825, there appeared an advertisement for eight or ten Negro slaves with their families to form a community of this kind under the direction of an "Emancipating Labor Society" of the State of Kentucky. In the same year Frances Wright suggested a school on a similar basis. She advertised in the "Genius of Universal Emancipation" an establishment to educate freed blacks and mulattoes in West Tennessee. This was supported by a goodly number of persons, including George Fowler and, it was said, Lafayette. A letter from a Presbyterian clergyman in South Carolina says that the first slave for this institution went from York District of that State. The enterprise, however, was not well supported, and little was heard of it in later years. Some asserted it was a money-making scheme for the proprietor, and that the Negroes taught there were in reality slaves; others went to the press to defend it as a benevolent effort. Both sides so muddled the affair that it is difficult to determine exactly what the intentions of the founders were.[91]

[1: Niles's Register, vol. xvi., pp. 241-243 and vol. xxiii., p. 23.]
[2: See The Proceedings of the Am. Conv. of Abolition Societies.]
[3: Special Report of U.S. Com. of Ed., 1871, p. 357.]
[4: Ibid., p. 357.]
[5: Next to be instructor of this institution was Prince Saunders, who was brought to Boston by Dr. Channing and Caleb Bingham in 1809. Brought up in the family of a Vermont lawyer, and experienced as a diplomatic official of Emperor Christopher of Hayti, Prince Saunders was able to do much for the advancement of this work. Among others who taught in this school was John B. Russworm, a graduate of Bowdoin College, and, later, Governor of the Colony of Cape Palmas in Southern Liberia. See Special Report of the U.S. Com. of Ed., 1871, p. 357; and African Repository, vol. ii., p. 271.]
[6: Special Rep. of the U.S. Com. of Ed., 1871, p. 357.]
[7: Adams, Anti-slavery, p. 142.]
[8: La Rochefoucauld-Liancourt, Travels, etc., p. 233.]
[9: Am. Conv., 1798, p. 7.]
[10: Andrews, History of the New York African Free Schools, p. 14.]
[11: Ibid., pp. 14 and 15.]
[12: Ibid., p. 16.]
[13: Ibid., p. 17.]

[14: Proceedings of the American Convention of Abolition Societies, 1801, p. 6.]
[15: Ibid., 1801, Report from New York.]
[16: Andrews, History of the New York African Free Schools, p. 20.]
[17: Proceedings of the American Convention of Abolition Societies, 1812, p. 7.]
[18: Andrews, History of the New York African Free Schools, p. 18.]
[19: Andrews, History of the New York African Free Schools, p. 17.]
[20: Ibid., p. 18.]
[21: Ibid., p. 19.]
[22: Proceedings of the Am. Convention of Abolition Soc., 1818, P. 9; Adams, Anti-slavery, p. 142.]
[23: Proceedings of the American Convention, etc., 1820.]
[24: Andrews, History of the New York African Free Schools, p. 20.]
[25: Proceedings of the American Convention, etc., 1801, p. 12.]
[26: Ibid., p. 12, and Quaker Pamphlet, p. 40.]
[27: Proceedings of the American Conv., etc., 1801, p. 12.]
[28: Ibid., p. 20.]
[29: Ibid., 1802, p. 17.]
[30: Proceedings of the American Convention, etc., 1809, p. 20.]
[31: Ibid., 1816, p. 20.]
[32: Ibid., 1821, p. 18.]
[33: A.M.E. Church Review, vol. xv., p. 625.]
[34: Wickersham, History of Education in Pa., p. 253.]
[35: Ibid., p. 251.]
[36: Quaker Pamphlet, p. 42.]
[37: Wickersham, History of Ed. in Pa., p. 252.]
[38: Ibid., p. 251.]
[39: Turner, The Negro in Pa., p. 128.]
[40: Parish, Remarks on the Slavery, etc., p. 43.]
[41: Proceedings of the American Conv., 1802, p. 18.]
[42: Ibid., 1803, p. 13.]
[43: Statistical Inquiry into the Condition of the Colored People of Philadelphia, p. 19.]
[44: Ibid., p. 20.]
[45: Proceedings of the American Conv., 1809, p. 16, and 1812, p. 16.]
[46: Wickersham, History of Ed. in Pa., p. 252.]
[47: Proceedings of the American Convention, etc., 1812, Report from Philadelphia.]
[48: Ibid., 1815, Report from Phila.]
[49: Wickersham, History of Education in Pa., p. 252.]
[50: One of these was at the Sessions House of the Third Presbyterian Church; one at Clarkston Schoolhouse, Cherry Street; one in the Academy on Locust Street. See Statistical Inquiry into the Condition of the Colored People of Philadelphia, p. 19; and Wickersham, Education in Pa., p. 253.]
[51: Statistical Inquiry, etc., p. 19.]
[52: Proceedings of the American Convention, etc., 1797, p. 16.]
[53: Special Report of the U.S. Com. of Ed., pp. 195 et seq., and pp. 352-353.]
[54: Ibid., p. 353.]
[55: Proceedings of the Am. Conv., etc., 1797, p. 35.]

[56: Ibid., 1797, p. 36.]
[57: Proceedings of the Am. Conv., p. 17; ibid., 1827, p. 53.]
[58: Special Report of U.S. Com. of Ed., 1871, p. 198.]
[59: Ibid., p. 393.]
[60: Proceedings of the Am. Conv., etc., 1798, p. 16.]
[61: Proceedings of the Am. Conv., 1801, p. 15.]
[62: Weeks, Southern Quakers, p. 215.]
[63: Weeks, Southern Quakers, p. 216.]
[64: Ibid., p. 216.]
[65: Hening, Statutes at Large, vol. xvi., p. 124.]
[66: Weeks, Southern Quakers, p. 231; Levi Coffin, Reminiscences, pp. 69-71; Bassett, Slavery in North Carolina, p. 66.]
[67: Weeks, Southern Quakers, p. 232.]
[68: Thwaites, Early Travels, vol. ii., p. 66.]
[69: Weeks, Southern Quakers, p. 232.]
[70: Ibid., 232.]
[71: Coffin, Reminiscences, p. 69.]
[72: Ibid., p. 70.]
[73: Weeks, Southern Quakers, p. 241.]
[74: An Address to the People of North Carolina on the Evils of Slavery by the Friends of Liberty and Equality, passim.]
[75: Ibid.]
[76: Ibid.]
[77: Bassett, Slavery in North Carolina, p. 73.]
[78: Ibid., p. 74; and Baird, A Collection, etc., pp. 816-817.]
[79: Paul C. Cameron, a son of Judge Duncan of North Carolina, said: "In my boyhood life at my father's home I often saw John Chavis, a venerable old negro man, recognized as a freeman and as a preacher or clergyman of the Presbyterian Church. As such he was received by my father and treated with kindness and consideration, and respected as a man of education, good sense and most estimable character." Mr. George Wortham, a lawyer of Granville County, said: "I have heard him read and explain the Scriptures to my father's family repeatedly. His English was remarkably pure, containing no 'negroisms'; his manner was impressive, his explanations clear and concise, and his views, as I then thought and still think, entirely orthodox. He was said to have been an acceptable preacher, his sermons abounding in strong common sense views and happy illustrations, without any effort at oratory or sensational appeals to the passions of his hearers." See Bassett, Slavery in N.C., pp. 74-75.]
[80: See Chapter VII.]
[81: Bassett, Slavery in North Carolina, p. 74.]
[82: John S. Bassett, Professor of History at Trinity College, North Carolina, learned from a source of great respectability that Chavis not only taught the children of these distinguished families, but "was received as an equal socially and asked to table by the most respectable people of the neighborhood." See Bassett, Slavery in North Carolina, p. 75.]
[83: Brevard, Digest of the Public Statute Law of South Carolina, vol. ii., p. 243.]
[84: Ibid., p. 243.]
[85: Laws of 1740 and 1800, and Simmons, Men of Mark, p. 1078.]

Although not as reactionary as South Carolina, little could be expected of Georgia where slavery had such a firm hold. Unfavorable as conditions in that State were, however, they were not intolerable. It was still lawful for a slave to learn to read, and free persons of color had the privilege of acquiring any knowledge whatsoever.[86] The chief incentive to the education of Negroes in that State came from the rising Methodists and Baptists who, bringing a simple message to plain people, instilled into their minds as never before the idea that the Bible being the revelation of God, all men should be taught to read that book.[87]

[86: Marbury and Crawford, Digest of the Laws of the State of Georgia, p. 438.]

[87: Orr, Education in the South.]

[88: Flint, Recollections of the Last Ten Years, p. 345.]

[89: Laws of Louisiana.]

[90: Alliot, Collections Historiques, p. 85; and Thwaites, Early Western Travels, vol. iv., pp. 320 and 321; vol. xii., p. 69; and vol. xix., p. 126.]

[91: Adams, Anti-slavery, p. 152.]

Chapter 6

Understanding the Urban Negro

Such an impetus was given Negro education during the period of better beginnings that some of the colored city schools then established have existed even until to-day. Negroes learned from their white friends to educate themselves. In the Middle and Southern States, however, much of the sentiment in favor of developing the intellect of the Negro passed away during the early part of the nineteenth century. This reform, like many others of that day, suffered when Americans forgot the struggle for the rights of man. Recovering from the social upheaval of the Revolution, caste soon began to claim its own. To discourage the education of the lowest class was natural to the aristocrats who on coming to power established governments based on the representation of interests, restriction of suffrage, and the ineligibility of the poor to office. After this period the work of enlightening the blacks in the southern and border States was largely confined to a few towns and cities where the concentration of the colored population continued.

The rise of the American city made possible the contact of the colored people with the world, affording them a chance to observe what the white man was doing, and to develop the power to care for themselves. The Negroes who had this opportunity to take over the western civilization were servants belonging to the families for which they worked; slaves hired out by their owners to wait upon persons; and watermen, embracing fishermen, boatmen, and sailors. Not a few slaves in cities were mechanics, clerks, and overseers. In most of these employments the rudiments of an education were necessary, and what the master did not seem disposed to teach the slaves so situated, they usually learned by contact with their fellowmen who were better informed. Such persons were the mulattoes resulting from miscegenation, and therefore protected from the rigors of the slave code; house servants, rewarded with unusual privileges for fidelity and for manifesting considerable interest in things contributing to the economic good of their masters; and slaves who were purchasing their freedom. [1] Before the close of the first quarter of the nineteenth century not much was said about what these classes learned or taught. It was then the difference in circumstances, employment, and opportunities for improvement that made the urban Negro more intelligent than those who had to toil in the fields. Yet, the proportion did not differ very much from that of the previous period, as the first Negroes were not chiefly field hands but to a considerable extent house servants, whom masters often taught to read and write.

Urban Negroes had another important advantage in their opportunity to attend well-regulated Sunday-schools. These were extensively organized in the towns and cities of this country during the first decades of the last century. The "Sabbath-school" constituted an important factor in Negro education. Although cloaked with the purpose of bringing the blacks to God by giving them religious instruction the institution permitted its workers to teach them reading and writing when they were not allowed to study such in other institutions.[2] Even the radical slaveholder was slow to object to a policy which was intended to facilitate the conversion of men's souls. All friends especially interested in the mental and spiritual uplift of the race hailed this movement as marking an epoch in the elevation of the colored people.

In the course of time racial difficulties caused the development of the colored "Sabbath-school" to be very much like that of the American Negro Church. It began as an establishment in the white churches, then moved to the colored chapels, where white persons assisted as teachers, and finally became an organization composed entirely of Negroes. But the separation here, as in the case of the church, was productive of some good. The "Sabbath-schools," which at first depended on white teachers to direct their work, were thereafter carried on by Negroes, who studied and prepared themselves to perform the task given up by their former friends. This change was easily made in certain towns and cities where Negroes already had churches of their own. Before 1815 there was a Methodist church in Charleston, South Carolina, with a membership of eighteen hundred, more than one thousand of whom were persons of color. About this time, Williamsburg and Augusta had one each, and Savannah three colored Baptist churches. By 1822 the Negroes of Petersburg had in addition to two churches of this denomination, a flourishing African Missionary Society.[3] In Washington, Baltimore, Philadelphia, New York, and Boston the free blacks had experienced such a rapid religious development that colored churches in these cities were no longer considered unusual.

The increase in the population of cities brought a larger number of these unfortunates into helpful contact with the urban element of white people who, having few Negroes, often opposed the institution of slavery. But thrown among colored people brought in their crude state into sections of culture, the antislavery men of towns and cities developed from theorists, discussing a problem of concern to persons far away, into actual workers striving by means of education to pave the way for universal freedom.[4] Large as the number of abolitionists became and bright as the future of their cause seemed, the more the antislavery men saw of the freedmen in congested districts, the more inclined the reformers were to think that instant abolition was an event which they "could not reasonably expect, and perhaps could not desire." Being in a state of deplorable ignorance, the slaves did not possess sufficient information "to render their immediate emancipation a blessing either to themselves or to society."[5]

Yet in the same proportion that antislavery men convinced masters of the wisdom of the policy of gradual emancipation, they increased their own burden of providing extra facilities of education, for liberated Negroes generally made their way from the South to urban communities of the Northern and Middle States. The friends of the colored people, however, met this exigency by establishing additional schools and repeatedly entreating these migrating freedmen to avail themselves of their opportunities. The address of the American Convention of Abolition Societies in 1819 is typical of these appeals.[6] They requested free persons of color to endeavor as much as possible to use economy in their expenses, to save something from their earnings for the education of their children ... and "let all those who by attending to this admonition have acquired means, send their children to school as soon as they are old enough, where their morals will be an object of attention as well as their improvement in school learning." Then followed some advice which would now seem strange. They said, "Encourage, also, those among you who are qualified as teachers of schools, and when you are able to pay, never send your children to free schools; for this may be considered as robbing the poor of their opportunities which are intended for them alone."[7]

The concentration of the colored population in cities and towns where they had better educational advantages tended to make colored city schools self-supporting. There developed a class of self-educating Negroes who were able to provide for their own enlightenment. This condition, however, did not obtain throughout the South. Being a proslavery farming section of few large towns and cities, that part of the country did not see much development of the self-sufficient class. What enlightenment most urban blacks of the South experienced resulted mainly from private teaching and religious instruction. There were some notable exceptions, however. A colored "Santo Dominican" named Julian Troumontaine taught openly in Savannah up to 1829 when such an act was prohibited by law. He taught clandestinely thereafter, however, until 1844.[8] In New Orleans, where the Creoles and freedmen counted early in the nineteenth century as a substantial element in society, persons of color had secured to themselves better facilities of education. The people of this city did not then regard it as a crime for Negroes to acquire an education, their white instructors felt that they were not condescending in teaching them, and children of Caucasian blood raised no objection to attending special and parochial schools accessible to both races. The educational privileges which the colored people there enjoyed, however, were largely paid for by the progressive freedmen themselves.[9] Some of them educated their children in France.

Charleston, South Carolina, furnished a good example of a center of unusual activity and rapid strides of self-educating urban Negroes. Driven to the point of doing for themselves, the free people of color of this city organized in 1810 the "Minor Society" to secure to their orphan children the benefits of education.[10] Bishop Payne, who studied later under Thomas Bonneau, attended the school founded by this organization. Other colored schools were doing successful work. Enjoying these unusual advantages the Negroes of Charleston were early in the nineteenth century ranked by some as economically and intellectually superior to any other such persons in the United States. A large portion of the leading mechanics, fashionable tailors, shoe manufacturers, and mantua-makers were free blacks, who enjoyed "a consideration in the community far more than that enjoyed by any of the colored population in the Northern cities."[11] As such positions required considerable skill and intelligence, these laborers had of necessity acquired a large share of useful knowledge. The favorable circumstances of the Negroes in certain liberal southern cities like Charleston were the cause of their return from the North to the South, where they often had a better opportunity for mental as well as economic improvement.[12] The return of certain Negroes from Philadelphia to Petersburg, Virginia, during the first decade of the nineteenth century, is a case in evidence.[13]

The successful strivings of the race in the District of Columbia furnish us with striking examples of Negroes making educational progress. When two white teachers, Henry Potter and Mrs. Haley, invited black children to study with their white pupils, the colored people gladly availed themselves of this opportunity.[14] Mrs. Maria Billings, the first to establish a real school for Negroes in Georgetown, soon discovered that she had their hearty support.

She had pupils from all parts of the District of Columbia, and from as far as Bladensburg, Maryland. The tuition fee in some of these schools was a little high, but many free blacks of the District of Columbia were sufficiently well established to meet these demands. The rapid progress made by the Bell and Browning families during this period was of much encouragement to the ambitious colored people, who were laboring to educate their children.[15]

The city Negroes, however, were learning to do more than merely attend accessible elementary schools. In 1807 George Bell, Nicholas Franklin, and Moses Liverpool, former slaves, built the first colored schoolhouse in the District of Columbia. Just emerging from bondage, these men could not teach themselves, but employed a white man to take charge of the school.[16] It was not a success. Pupils of color thereafter attended the school of Anne Maria Hall, a teacher from Prince George County, Maryland, and those of teachers who instructed white children.[17] The ambitious Negroes of the District of Columbia, however, were not discouraged by the first failure to provide their own educational facilities. The Bell School which had been closed and used as a dwelling, opened again in 1818 under the auspices of an association of free people of color of the city of Washington called the "Resolute Beneficial Society." The school was declared open then "for the reception of free people of color and others that ladies and gentlemen may think proper to send to be instructed in reading, writing, arithmetic, English grammar, or other branches of education apposite to their capacities, by steady, active and experienced teachers, whose attention is wholly devoted to the purpose described." The founders presumed that free colored families would embrace the advantages thus presented to them either by subscription to the funds of the Society or by sending their children to the school. Since the improvement of the intellect and the morals of the colored youth were the objects of the institution, the patronage of benevolent ladies and gentlemen was solicited. They declared, too, that "to avoid disagreeable occurrences no writing was to be done by the teacher for a slave, neither directly nor indirectly to serve the purpose of a slave on any account whatever."[18] This school was continued until 1822 under Mr. Pierpont, of Massachusetts, a relative of the poet. He was succeeded two years later by John Adams, a shoemaker, who was known as the first Negro to teach in the District of Columbia.[19]

Of equal importance was the colored seminary established by Henry Smothers, a pupil of Mrs. Billings. Like her, he taught first in Georgetown. He began his advanced work near the Treasury building, having an attendance of probably one hundred and fifty pupils, generally paying tuition. The fee, however, was not compulsory. Smothers taught for about two years, and then was succeeded by John Prout, a colored man of rare talents, who later did much in opposition to the scheme of transporting Negroes to Africa before they had the benefits of education.[20] The school was then called the "Columbian Institute." Prout was later assisted by Mrs. Anne Maria Hall.[21]

Of this self-educative work of Negroes some of the best was accomplished by colored women. With the assistance of Father Vanlomen, the benevolent priest then in charge of the Holy Trinity Church, Maria Becraft, the most capable colored woman in the District of Columbia at that time, established there the first seminary for the education of colored girls. She had begun to teach in a less desirable section, but impressed with the unusual beauty and strong character of this girl, Father Vanlomen had her school transferred to a larger building on Fayette Street where she taught until 1831. She then turned over her seminary to girls she had trained, and became a teacher in a convent at Baltimore as a Sister of Providence.[22] Other good results were obtained by Louisa Parke Costin, a member of one of the oldest colored families in the District of Columbia. Desiring to diffuse the knowledge she acquired from white teachers in the early mixed schools of the District, she decided to teach. She opened her school just about the time that Henry Smothers was making his reputation as an educator. She died in 1831, after years of successful work had crowned her efforts. Her task was then taken up by her sister, Martha, who had been trained in the Convent Seminary of Baltimore.[23]

Equally helpful was the work of Arabella Jones. Educated at the St. Frances Academy at Baltimore, she was well grounded in the English branches and fluent in French. She taught on the "Island," calling her school "The St. Agnes Academy."[24] Another worker of this class was Mary Wormley, once a student in the Colored Female Seminary of Philadelphia under Sarah Douglass. This lady began teaching about 1830, getting some assistance from Mr. Calvert, an Englishman.[25] The institution passed later into the hands of Thomas Lee, during the incumbency of whom the school was closed by the "Snow Riot." This was an attempt on the part of the white people to get rid of the progressive Negroes of the District of Columbia. Their excuse for such drastic action was that Benjamin Snow, a colored man running a restaurant in the city, had made unbecoming remarks about the wives of the white mechanics.[26] John F. Cook, one of the most influential educators produced in the District of Columbia, was driven out of the city by this mob. He then taught at Lancaster, Pa.

While the colored schools of the District of Columbia suffered as a result of this disturbance, the Negroes then in charge of them were too ambitious, too well-educated to discontinue their work. The situation, however, was in no sense encouraging. With the exception of the churches of the Catholics and Quakers who vied with each other in maintaining a benevolent attitude toward the education of the colored people,[27] the churches of the District of Columbia, in the Sabbath schools of which Negroes once sat in the same seats with white persons, were on account of this riot closed to the darker race. [2] This expulsion however, was not an unmixed evil, for the colored people themselves thereafter established and directed a larger number of institutions of learning.[3]

[28: The Catholics admitted the colored people to their churches on equal footing with others when they were driven to the galleries of the Protestant churches. Furthermore, they continued to admit them to their parochial schools. The Sisters of Georgetown trained colored girls, and the parochial school of the Aloysius Church at one time had as many as two hundred and fifty pupils of color. Many of the first colored teachers of the District of Columbia obtained their education in these schools. See Special Report of U.S. Com. of Ed., 1871, p. 218 et. seq.]

The colored schools of the District of Columbia soon resumed their growth recovering most of the ground they had lost and exhibiting evidences of more systematic work. These schools ceased to be elementary classes, offering merely courses in reading and writing, but developed into institutions of higher grade supplied with competent teachers. Among other useful schools then flourishing in this vicinity were those of Alfred H. Parry, Nancy Grant, Benjamin McCoy, John Thomas Johnson, James Enoch Ambush, and Dr. John H. Fleet.[29] John

F. Cook returned from Pennsylvania and reopened his seminary.[30] About this time there flourished a school established by Fannie Hampton. After her death the work was carried on by Margaret Thompson until 1846. She then married Charles Middleton and became his assistant teacher. He was a free Negro who had been educated in Savannah, Georgia, while attending school with white and colored children. He founded a successful school about the time that Fleet and Johnson[31] retired. Middleton's school, however, owes its importance to the fact that it was connected with the movement for free colored public schools started by Jesse E. Dow, an official of the city, and supported by Rev. Doctor Wayman, then pastor of the Bethel Church.[32] Other colaborers with these teachers were Alexander Cornish, Richard Stokes, and Margaret Hill.[33]

Then came another effort on a large scale. This was the school of Alexander Hays, an emancipated slave of the Fowler family of Maryland. Hays succeeded his wife as a teacher. He soon had the support of such prominent men as Rev. Doctor Sampson, William Winston Seaton and R.S. Coxe. Joseph T. and Thomas H. Mason and Mr. and Mrs. Fletcher were Hays's contemporaries. The last two were teachers from England. On account of the feeling then developing against white persons instructing Negroes, these philanthropists saw their schoolhouses burned, themselves expelled from the white churches, and finally driven from the city in 1858.[34] Other white men and women were teaching colored children during these years. The most prominent of these were Thomas Tabbs, an erratic philanthropist, Mr. Nutall, an Englishman; Mr. Talbot, a successful tutor stationed near the present site of the Franklin School; and Mrs. George Ford, a Virginian, conducting a school on New Jersey Avenue between K and L Streets.[35] The efforts of Miss Myrtilla Miner, their contemporary, will be mentioned elsewhere.[36]

The Negroes of Baltimore were almost as self-educating as those of the District of Columbia. The coming of the refugees and French Fathers from Santo Domingo to Baltimore to escape the revolution[37] marked an epoch in the intellectual progress of the colored people of that city. Thereafter their intellectual class had access to an increasing black population, anxious to be enlightened. Given this better working basis, they secured from the ranks of the Catholics additional catechists and teachers to give a larger number of illiterates the fundamentals of education. Their untiring co-worker in furnishing these facilities, was the Most Reverend Ambrose Marechal, Archbishop of Baltimore from 1817 to 1828.[38] These schools were such an improvement over those formerly opened to Negroes that colored youths of other towns and cities thereafter came to Baltimore for higher training.[39]

The coming of these refugees to Baltimore had a direct bearing on the education of colored girls. Their condition excited the sympathy of the immigrating colored women. These ladies had been educated both in the Island of Santo Domingo and in Paris. At once interested in the uplift of this sex, they soon constituted the nucleus of the society that finally formed the St. Frances Academy for girls in connection with the Oblate Sisters of Providence Convent in Baltimore, June 5, 1829.[40] This step was sanctioned by the Reverend James Whitefield, the successor of Archbishop Marechal, and was later approved by the Holy See. The institution was located on Richmond Street in a building which on account of the rapid growth of the school soon gave way to larger quarters. The aim of the institution was to train girls, all of whom "would become mothers or household servants, in such solid virtues and religious and moral principles as modesty, honesty, and integrity."[41] To reach this end they endeavored to supply the school with cultivated and capable teachers. Students were offered courses in all the branches of "refined and useful education, including all that is regularly taught in well regulated female seminaries."[42] This school was so well maintained that it survived all reactionary attacks and became a center of enlightenment for colored women.

At the same time there were other persons and organizations in the field. Prominent among the first of these workers was Daniel Coker, known to fame as a colored Methodist missionary, who was sent to Liberia. Prior to 1812 he had in Baltimore an academy which certain students from Washington attended when they had no good schools of their own, and when white persons began to object to the co-education of the races. Because of these conditions two daughters of George Bell, the builder of the first colored schoolhouse in the District of Columbia, went to Baltimore to study under Coker.[43] An adult Negro school in this city had 180 pupils in 1820. There were then in the Baltimore Sunday-schools about 600 Negroes. They had formed themselves into a Bible association which had been received into the connection of the Baltimore Bible Society.[44] In 1825 the Negroes there had a day and a night school, giving courses in Latin and French. Four years later there appeared an "African Free School" with an attendance of from 150 to 175 every Sunday.[45]

By 1830 the Negroes of Baltimore had several special schools of their own. [46] In 1835 there was behind the African Methodist Church in Sharp Street a school of seventy pupils in charge of William Watkins.[47] W. Livingston, an ordained clergyman of the Episcopal Church, had then a colored school of eighty pupils in the African Church at the corner of Saratoga and Ninth Streets.[48] A third school of this kind was kept by John Fortie at the Methodist Bethel Church in Fish Street. Five or six other schools of some consequence were maintained by free women of color, who owed their education to the Convent of the Oblate Sisters of Providence.[49] Observing these conditions, an interested person thought that much more would have been accomplished in that community, if the friends of the colored people had been able to find workers acceptable to the masters and at the same time competent to teach the slaves.[50] Yet another observer felt that the Negroes of Baltimore had more opportunities than they embraced.[51]

These conditions, however, were so favorable in 1835 that when Professor E.A. Andrews came to Baltimore to introduce the work of the American Union for the Relief and Improvement of the Colored People,[52] he was informed that the education of the Negroes of that city was fairly well provided for. Evidently the need was that the "systematic and sustained exertions" of the workers should spring from a more nearly perfect organization "to give efficiency to their philanthropic labors."[53] He was informed that as his society was of New England, it would on account of its origin in the wrong quarter, be productive of mischief.[54] The leading people of Baltimore thought that it would be better to accomplish this task through the Colonization Society, a southern organization carrying out the very policy which the American Union proposed to pursue.[55]

The instruction of ambitious blacks in this city was not confined to mere rudimentary training. The opportunity for advanced study was offered colored girls in the Convent of the Oblate Sisters of Providence. These Negroes, however, early learned to help themselves. In 1835 considerable assistance came from

Nelson Wells, one of their own color. He left to properly appointed trustees the sum of $10,000, the income of which was to be appropriated to the education of free colored children.[56] With this benefaction the trustees concerned established in 1835 what they called the Wells School. It offered Negroes free instruction long after the Civil War.

In seeking to show how these good results were obtained by the Negroes' cooperative power and ability to supply their own needs, we are not unmindful of the assistance which they received. To say that the colored people of Baltimore, themselves, provided all these facilities of education would do injustice to the benevolent element of that city. Among its white people were found so much toleration of opinion on slavery and so much sympathy with the efforts for its removal, that they not only permitted the establishment of Negro churches, but opened successful colored schools in which white men and women assisted personally in teaching. Great praise is due philanthropists of the type of John Breckenridge and Daniel Raymond, who contributed their time and means to the cause and enlisted the efforts of others. Still greater credit should be given to William Crane, who for forty years was known as an "ardent, liberal, and wise friend of the black man." At the cost of $20,000 he erected in the central part of the city an edifice exclusively for the benefit of the colored people. In this building was an auditorium, several large schoolrooms, and a hall for entertainments and lectures. The institution employed a pastor and two teachers [57] and it was often mentioned as a high school.

In northern cities like Philadelphia and New York, where benevolent organizations provided an adequate number of colored schools, the free blacks did not develop so much of the power to educate themselves. The Negroes of these cities, however, cannot be considered exceptions to the rule. Many of those of Philadelphia were of the most ambitious kind, men who had purchased their freedom or had developed sufficient intelligence to delude their would-be captors and conquer the institution of slavery. Settled in this community, the thrifty class accumulated wealth which they often used, not only to defray the expenses of educating their own children, but to provide educational facilities for the poor children of color.

Gradually developing the power to help themselves, the free people of color organized a society which in 1804 opened a school with John Trumbull as teacher.[58] About the same time the African Episcopalians founded a colored school at their church.[59] A colored man gave three hundred pounds of the required funds to build the first colored schoolhouse in Philadelphia.[60] In 1830 one fourth of the twelve hundred colored children in the schools of that city paid for their instruction, whereas only two hundred and fifty were attending the public schools in 1825.[61] The fact that some of the Negroes were able and willing to share the responsibility of enlightening their people caused a larger number of philanthropists to come to the rescue of those who had to depend on charity. Furthermore, of the many achievements claimed for the colored schools of Philadelphia none were considered more significant than that they produced teachers qualified to carry on this work. Eleven of the sixteen colored schools in Philadelphia in 1822 were taught by teachers of African descent. In 1830 the system was practically in the hands of Negroes.[62]

The statistics of later years show how successful these early efforts had been. By 1849 the colored schools of Philadelphia had developed to the extent that they seemed like a system. According to the Statistical Inquiry into the Condition of

Colored People in and about Philadelphia, published that year, there were 1643 children of color attending well-regulated schools. The larger institutions were mainly supported by State and charitable organizations of which the Society of Friends and the Pennsylvania Abolition Society were the most important. Besides supporting these institutions, however, the intelligent colored men of Philadelphia had maintained smaller schools and organized a system of lyceums and debating clubs, one of which had a library of 1400 volumes. Moreover, there were then teaching in the colored families and industrial schools of Philadelphia many men and women of both races.[63] Although these instructors restricted their work to the teaching of the rudiments of education, they did much to help the more advanced schools to enlighten the Negroes who came to that city in large numbers when conditions became intolerable for the free people of color in the slave States. The statistics of the following decade show unusual progress. In the year 1859 there were in the colored public schools of Philadelphia, 1031 pupils; in the charity schools, 748; in the benevolent schools, 211; in private schools, 331; in all, 2321, whereas in 1849 there were only 1643.[64]

Situated like those of Philadelphia, the free blacks of New York City did not have to maintain their own schools. This was especially true after 1832 when the colored people had qualified themselves to take over the schools of the New York Manumission Society. They then got rid of all the white teachers, even Andrews, the principal, who had for years directed this system. Besides, the economic progress of certain Negroes there made possible the employment of the increasing number of colored teachers, who had availed themselves of the opportunities afforded by the benevolent schools. The stigma then attached to one receiving seeming charity through free schools stimulated thrifty Negroes to have their children instructed either in private institutions kept by friendly white teachers or by teachers of their own color.[65] In 1812 a society of the free people of color was organized to raise a fund, the interest of which was to sustain a free school for orphan children.[66] This society succeeded later in establishing and maintaining two schools. At this time there were in New York City three other colored schools, the teachers of which received their compensation from those who patronized them.[67]

Whether from lack of interest in their welfare on the part of the public, or from the desire of the Negroes to share their own burdens, the colored people of Rhode Island were endeavoring to provide for the education of their children during the first decades of the last century. The Newport Mercury of March 26, 1808, announced that the African Benevolent Society had opened there a school kept by Newport Gardner, who was to instruct all colored people "inclined to attend." The records of the place show that this school was in operation eight years later.[68]

In Boston, where were found more Negroes than in most New England communities, the colored people themselves maintained a separate school after the revolutionary era. In the towns of Salem, Nantucket, New Bedford, and Lowell the colored schools failed to make much progress after the first quarter of the nineteenth century on account of the more liberal construction of the laws which provided for democratic education. This the free blacks were forced to advocate for the reason that the seeming onerous task of supporting a dual system often caused the neglect, and sometimes the extinction of the separate schools. Furthermore, either the Negroes of some of these towns were too scarce or the movement to furnish them special facilities of education started too late to escape the attacks of the abolitionists. Seeing their mistake of first establishing separate schools, they began to attack caste in public education.

In the eastern cities where colored school systems thereafter continued, the work was not always successful. The influx of fugitives in the rough sometimes jeopardized their chances for education by menacing liberal communities with the trouble of caring for an undesirable class. The friends of the Negroes, however, received more encouragement during the two decades immediately preceding the Civil War. There was a change in the attitude of northern cities toward the uplift of the colored refugees. Catholics, Protestants, and abolitionists often united their means to make provision for the education of accessible Negroes, although these friends of the oppressed could not always agree on other important schemes. Even the colonizationists, the object of attack from the ardent antislavery element, considerably aided the cause. They educated for work in Liberia a number of youths, who, given the opportunity to attend good schools, demonstrated the capacity of the colored people. More important factors than the colonizationists were the free people of color. Brought into the rapidly growing urban communities, these Negroes began to accumulate sufficient wealth to provide permanent schools of their own. Many of these were later assimilated by the systems of northern cities when their separate schools were disestablished.

[1: Jones, Religious Instruction, p. 117.]
[2: See the reports of almost any abolition society of the first quarter of the nineteenth century. Special Report of the U.S. Com. of Ed., 1871, p. 200; and Plumer, Thoughts on the Religious Instruction of Negroes.]
[3: Adams, Anti-slavery, etc., pp. 73 and 74.]
[4: As some masters regarded the ignorance of the slaves as an argument against their emancipation, the antislavery men's problem became the education of the master as well as that of the slave. Believing that intellectual and moral improvement is a "safe and permanent basis on which the arch of freedom could be erected," Jesse Torrey, harking back to Jefferson's proposition, recommended that it begin by instructing the slaveholders, overseers, their sons and daughters, hitherto deprived of the blessing of education. Then he thought that such enlightened masters should see to it that every slave less than thirty years of age should be taught the art of reading sufficiently for receiving moral and religious instruction from books in the English language. In presenting this scheme Torrey had the idea of most of the antislavery men of that day, who advocated the education of slaves because they believed that, whenever the slaves should become qualified by intelligence and moral cultivation for the rational enjoyment of liberty and the performance of the various social duties, enlightened legislators would listen to the voice of reason and justice and the spirit of the social organization, and permit the release of the slave without banishing him as a traitor from his native land. See Torrey's Portraiture of Domestic Slavery, p. 21.]
[5: Sidney, An Oration Commemorative of the Abolition of the Slave Trade in the United States, p. 5; and Adams, Anti-slavery, etc., pp. 40, 43, 65, and 66.]
[6: Proceedings of the American Convention, etc., 1819, p. 21.]
[7: Proceedings of the American Convention, etc., 1819, p. 22.]
[8: Wright, Negro Education in Georgia, p. 20.]
[9: Many of the mixed breeds of New Orleans were leading business men.]

[10: Simmons, Men of Mark, p. 1078.]
[11: Niles Register, vol. xlix., p. 40.]
[12: Notions of the Americans, p. 26.]
[13: Wright, Views of Society and Manners in America, p. 73.]
[14: Special Report of the U.S. Com. of Ed., 1871, pp. 195 et seq.]
[15: Special Report of the U.S. Com. of Ed., 1871, p. 195.]
[16: Ibid., 196.]
[17: Ibid., 197.]
[18: Daily National Intelligencer, August 29, 1818.]
[19: Special Report of the U.S. Com. of Ed., 1871, p. 198.]
[20: Ibid., 1871, p. 199.]
[21: Other schools of importance were springing up from year to year. As early as 1824 Mrs. Mary Wall, a member of the Society of Friends, had opened a school for Negroes and received so many applications that many had to be refused. From this school came many well-prepared colored men, among whom were James Wormley and John Thomas Johnson. Another school was established by Thomas Tabbs, who received "a polished education from the distinguished Maryland family to which he belonged." Mr. Tabbs came to Washington before the War of 1812 and began teaching those who came to him when he had a schoolhouse, and when he had none he went from house to house, stopping even under the trees to teach wherever he found pupils who were interested. See Special Report of the U.S. Com. of Ed., 1871, pp. 212, 213, and 214.]
[22: Ibid., p. 204.]
[23: Special Report of the U.S. Com. of Ed., 1871, p. 203.]
[24: Ibid., p. 211.]
[25: Ibid., p. 211.]
[26: Special Report of the U.S. Com. of Ed., p. 201.]
[27: Sp. Report, etc. 187, pp. 217, 218, 219, 220, 221.]
[28: Ibid., pp. 220-222.]
[29: Special Report of the U.S. Com. of Ed., 1871, pp. 212, 213, and 283.]
[30: Ibid., p. 200.]
[31: Compelled to leave Washington in 1838 because of the persecution of free persons of color, Johnson stopped in Pittsburg where he entered a competitive teacher examination with two white aspirants and won the coveted position. He taught in Pittsburg several years, worked on the Mississippi a while, returned later to Washington, and in 1843 constructed a building in which he opened another school. It was attended by from 150 to 200 students, most of whom belonged to the most prominent colored families of the District of Columbia. See Special Report of the U.S. Com. of Ed., 1871, p. 214.]
[32: Ibid., p. 215.]
[33: Ibid., pp. 214-215.]
[34: Besides the classes taught by these workers there was the Eliza Ann Cook private school; Miss Washington's school; a select primary school; a free Catholic school maintained by the St. Vincent de Paul Society, an association of colored Catholics in connection with St. Matthew's Church. This institution was organized by the benevolent Father Walter at the Smothers School. Then there were teachers like Elizabeth Smith, Isabella Briscoe, Charlotte Beams, James Shorter, Charlotte Gordon, and David Brown. Furthermore, various churches, parochial, and Sunday-schools were then sharing the burden of educating the

Negro population of the District of Columbia. See Special Report of the U.S. Com. of Ed., 1871, pp. 214, 215, 216, 217, 218 et seq.]

[35: Ibid., p. 214.]
[36: O'Connor, Myrtilla Miner, p. 80.]
[37: Drewery, Slave Insurrections in Virginia, p. 121.]
[38: Special Report of the U.S. Com. of Ed., 1871, p. 205.]
[39: Ibid., p. 205.]
[40: Ibid., p. 205.]
[41: Ibid., p. 206.]
[42: Special Report of the U.S. Com. of Ed., p. 206.]
[40: Ibid., p. 196.]
[41: Adams, Anti-slavery, etc., p. 14.]
[42: Adams, Anti-Slavery, etc., pp. 14 and 15.]
[43: Ibid., p. 196.]
[44: Adams, Anti-slavery, etc., p. 14.]
[45: Adams, Anti-Slavery, etc., pp. 14 and 15.]
[46: Buckingham, America, Historical, etc., vol. i., p. 438.]
[47: Ibid., p. 438; Andrews, Slavery and the Domestic Slave Trade, pp. 54, 55, and 56; and Varle, A Complete View of Baltimore, p. 33.]
[48: Varle, A Complete View of Baltimore, p. 33; and Andrews, Slavery and the Domestic Slave Trade, pp. 85 and 92.]
[49: Ibid., p. 33.]
[50: Ibid., p. 54.]
[51: Ibid., p. 37.]
[52: On January 14, 1835, a convention of more than one hundred gentlemen from ten different States assembled in Boston and organized the "American Union for the Relief and Improvement of the Colored Race." Among these workers were William Reed, Daniel Noyes, J.W. Chickering, J.W. Putnam, Baron Stow, B.B. Edwards, E.A. Andrews, Charles Scudder, Joseph Tracy, Samuel Worcester, and Charles Tappan. The gentlemen were neither antagonistic to the antislavery nor to the colonization societies. They aimed to do that which had been neglected in giving the Negroes proper preparation for freedom. Knowing that the actual emancipation of an oppressed race cannot be effected by legislation, they hoped to provide religious and literary instruction for all colored children that they might "ameliorate their economic condition" and prepare themselves for higher usefulness. See the Exposition of the Object and Plans of the American Union, pp. 11-14.]
[53: Andrews, Slavery and the Domestic Slave Trade, p. 57.]
[54: Ibid., p. 188.]
[55: Andrews, Slavery, etc., p. 56.]
[56: Special Report of the U.S. Com. of Ed., 1871, p. 353.]
[57: A contributor to the Christian Chronicle found in this institution a pastor, a principal of the school, and an assistant, all of superior qualifications. The classes which this reporter heard recite grammar and geography convinced him of the thoroughness of the work and the unusual readiness of the colored people to learn. See The African Repository, vol. xxxii., p. 91.]
[58: Turner, The Negro in Pennsylvania, p. 129.]
[59: Ibid., p. 130.]
[60: Special Report of the U.S. Com. of Ed., 1871, p. 377.]
[61: Proceedings of the American Convention, etc., 1825, p. 13.]

The Education of the Negro

[62: Proceedings of the Am. Convention, etc., 1830, p.8; and Wickersham, History of Education in Pennsylvania, p. 253.]

[63: About the middle of the nineteenth century colored schools of various kinds arose in Philadelphia. With a view to giving Negroes industrial training their friends opened "The School for the Destitute" at the House of Industry in 1848. Three years later Sarah Luciana was teaching a school of seventy youths at this House of Industry, and the Sheppard School, another industrial institution, was in operation in 1850 in a building bearing the same name. In 1849 arose the "Corn Street Unclassified School" of forty-seven children in charge of Sarah L. Peltz. "The Holmesburg Unclassified School" was organized in 1854. Other institutions of various purposes were "The House of Refuge," "The Orphans' Shelter," and "The Home for Colored Children." See Bacon, Statistics of the Colored People of Philadelphia, 1859. Among those then teaching in private schools of Philadelphia were Solomon Clarkson, Robert George, John Marshall, John Ross, Jonathan Tudas, and David Ware. Ann Bishop, Virginia Blake, Amelia Bogle, Anne E. Carey, Sarah Ann Douglass, Rebecca Hailstock, Emma Hall, Emmeline Higgins, Margaret Johnson, Martha Richards, Dinah Smith, Mary Still, and one Peterson were teaching in families. See Statistical Inquiry, etc., 1849, p. 19; and Bacon, Statistics of the Colored People of Philadelphia, 1859.]

[64: Statistical Inquiry into the Condition of the Colored People of Philadelphia, in 1859.]

[65: See the Address of the American Convention, 1819.]

[66: Proceedings of the Am. Convention, etc., 1812, p. 7.

Certain colored women were then organized to procure and make for destitute persons of color. See Andrews, History of the New York African Free Schools, p. 58.]

[67: Ibid., p. 58.]

[68: Stockwell, History of Ed. in R.I., p. 30.]

Chapter 7

The Reaction

Encouraging as had been the movement to enlighten the Negroes, there had always been at work certain reactionary forces which impeded the intellectual progress of the colored people. The effort to enlighten them that they might be emancipated to enjoy the political rights given white men, failed to meet with success in those sections where slaves were found in large numbers. Feeling that the body politic, as conceived by Locke and Montesquieu, did not include the slaves, many citizens opposed their education on the ground that their mental improvement was inconsistent with their position as persons held to service. For this reason there was never put forward any systematic effort to elevate the slaves. Every master believed that he had a divine right to deal with the situation as he chose. Moreover, even before the policy of mental and moral improvement of the slaves could be given a trial, some colonists, anticipating the "evils of the scheme," sought to obviate them by legislation. Such we have observed was the case in Virginia,[1] South Carolina,[2] and Georgia.[3] To control the assemblies of slaves, North Carolina,[4] Delaware,[5] and Maryland[6] early passed strict regulations for their inspection.

The actual opposition of the masters to the mental improvement of Negroes, however, did not assume sufficiently large proportions to prevent the intellectual progress of that race, until two forces then at work had had time to become effective in arousing southern planters to the realization of what a danger enlightened colored men would be to the institution of slavery. These forces were the industrial revolution and the development of an insurrectionary spirit among slaves, accelerated by the rapid spreading of the abolition agitation. The industrial revolution was effected by the multiplication of mechanical appliances for spinning and weaving which so influenced the institution of slavery as seemingly to doom the Negroes to heathenism. These inventions were the spinning jenny, the steam engine, the power loom, the wool-combing machine, and the cotton gin. They augmented the output of spinning mills, and in cheapening cloth, increased the demand by bringing it within the reach of the poor. The result was that a revolution was brought about not only in Europe, but also in the United States to which the world looked for this larger supply of cotton fiber. [7] This demand led to the extension of the plantation system on a larger scale. It was unfortunate, however, that many of the planters thus enriched, believed that the slightest amount of education, merely teaching slaves to read, impaired their value because it instantly destroyed their contentedness. Since they did not contemplate changing their condition, it was surely doing them an ill service to destroy their acquiescence in it. This revolution then had brought it to pass that slaves who were, during the eighteenth century advertised as valuable on account of having been enlightened, were in the nineteenth century considered more dangerous than useful.

The Education of the Negro

With the rise of this system, and the attendant increased importation of slaves, came the end of the helpful contact of servants with their masters. Slavery was thereby changed from a patriarchal to an economic institution. Thereafter most owners of extensive estates abandoned the idea that the mental improvement of slaves made them better servants. Doomed then to be half-fed, poorly clad, and driven to death in this cotton kingdom, what need had the slaves for education? Some planters hit upon the seemingly more profitable scheme of working newly imported slaves to death during seven years and buying another supply rather than attempt to humanize them.[8] Deprived thus of helpful advice and instruction, the slaves became the object of pity not only to abolitionists of the North but also to some southerners. Not a few of these reformers, therefore, favored the extermination of the institution. Others advocated the expansion of slavery not to extend the influence of the South, but to disperse the slaves with a view to bringing about a closer contact between them and their masters.[9] This policy was duly emphasized during the debate on the admission of the State of Missouri.

Seeking to direct the attention of the world to the slavery of men's bodies and minds the abolitionists spread broadcast through the South newspapers, tracts, and pamphlets which, whether or not they had much effect in inducing masters to improve the condition of their slaves, certainly moved Negroes themselves. It hardly required enlightenment to convince slaves that they would be better off as freemen than as dependents whose very wills were subject to those of their masters. Accordingly even in the seventeenth century there developed in the minds of bondmen the spirit of resistance. The white settlers of the colonies held out successfully in putting down the early riots of Negroes. When the increasing intelligent Negroes of the South, however, observed in the abolition literature how the condition of the American slaves differed from that of the ancient servants and even from what it once had been in the United States; when they fully realized their intolerable condition compared with that of white men, who were clamoring for liberty and equality, there rankled in the bosom of slaves that insurrectionary passion productive of the daring uprisings which made the chances for the enlightenment of colored people poorer than they had ever been in the history of this country.

The more alarming insurrections of the first quarter of the nineteenth century were the immediate cause of the most reactionary measures. It was easily observed that these movements were due to the mental improvement of the colored people during the struggle for the rights of man. Not only had Negroes heard from the lips of their masters warm words of praise for the leaders of the French Revolution but had developed sufficient intelligence themselves to read the story of the heroes of the world, who were then emboldened to refresh the tree of liberty "with the blood of patriots and tyrants."[10] The insurrectionary passion among the colored people was kindled, too, around Baltimore, Norfolk, Charleston, and New Orleans by certain Negroes who to escape the horrors of the political upheaval in Santo Domingo,[11] immigrated into this country in 1793. The education of the colored race had paved the way for the dissemination of their ideas of liberty and equality. Enlightened bondmen persistently made trouble for the white people in these vicinities. Negroes who could not read, learned from others the story of Toussaint L'Ouverture, whose example colored men were then ambitious to emulate.

The Reaction

The insurrection of Gabriel in Virginia and that of South Carolina in the year 1800 are cases in evidence. Unwilling to concede that slaves could have so well planned such a daring attack, the press of the time insisted that two Frenchmen were the promoters of the affair in Virginia.[12] James Monroe said there was no evidence that any white man was connected with it.[13] It was believed that the general tendency of the Negroes toward an uprising had resulted from French ideas which had come to the slaves through intelligent colored men.[14] Observing that many Negroes were sufficiently enlightened to see things as other men, the editor of the Aurora asserted that in negotiating with the "Black Republic" the United States and Great Britain had set the seal of approval upon servile insurrection.[15] Others referred to inflammatory handbills which Negroes extensively read.[16] Discussing the Gabriel plot in 1800, Judge St. George Tucker said: "Our sole security then consists in their ignorance of this power (doing us mischief) and their means of using it--a security which we have lately found is not to be relied on, and which, small as it is, every day diminishes. Every year adds to the number of those who can read and write; and the increase in knowledge is the principal agent in evolving the spirit we have to fear."[17]

Camden was disturbed by an insurrection in 1816 and Charleston in 1822 by a formidable plot which the officials believed was due to the "sinister" influences of enlightened Negroes.[18] The moving spirit of this organization was Denmark Vesey. He had learned to read and write, had accumulated an estate worth $8000, and had purchased his freedom in 1800[19] Jack Purcell, an accomplice of Vesey, weakened in the crisis and confessed. He said that Vesey was in the habit of reading to him all the passages in the newspapers, that related to Santo Domingo and apparently every accessible pamphlet that had any connection with slavery.[20] One day he read to Purcell the speeches of Mr. King on the subject of slavery and told Purcell how this friend of the Negro race declared he would continue to speak, write, and publish pamphlets against slavery "the longest day he lived," until the Southern States consented to emancipate their slaves.[21]

The statement of the Governor of South Carolina also shows the influence of the educated Negro. This official felt that Monday, the slave of Mr. Gill, was the most daring conspirator. Being able to read and write he "attained an extraordinary and dangerous influence over his fellows." "Permitted by his owner to occupy a house in the central part of this city, he was afforded hourly opportunities for the exercise of his skill on those who were attracted to his shop by business or favor." "Materials were abundantly furnished in the seditious pamphlets brought into the State by equally culpable incendiaries, while the speeches of the oppositionists in Congress to the admission of Missouri gave a serious and imposing effect to his machinations."[22] It was thus brought home to the South that the enlightened Negro was having his heart fired with the spirit of liberty by his perusal of the accounts of servile insurrections and the congressional debate on slavery.

Southerners of all types thereafter attacked the policy of educating Negroes. [23] Men who had expressed themselves neither one way nor the other changed their attitude when it became evident that abolition literature in the hands of slaves would not only make them dissatisfied, but cause them to take drastic measures to secure liberty. Those who had emphasized the education of the Negroes to increase their economic efficiency were largely converted. The clergy who had insisted that the bondmen were entitled to, at least, sufficient training to enable them to understand the principles of the Christian religion, were thereafter willing to forego the benefits of their salvation rather than see them destroy the institution of slavery.

In consequence of this tendency, State after State enacted more stringent laws to control the situation. Missouri passed in 1817 an act so to regulate the traveling and assembly of slaves as to make them ineffective in making headway against the white people by insurrection. Of course, in so doing the reactionaries deprived them of the opportunities of helpful associations and of attending schools.[24] By 1819 much dissatisfaction had arisen from the seeming danger of the various colored schools in Virginia. The General Assembly, therefore, passed a law providing that there should be no more assemblages of slaves, or free Negroes, or mulattoes, mixing or associating with such slaves for teaching them reading and writing.[25] The opposition here seemed to be for the reasons that Negroes were being generally enlightened in the towns of the State and that white persons as teachers in these institutions were largely instrumental in accomplishing this result. Mississippi even as a Territory had tried to meet the problem of unlawful assemblies. In the year 1823 it was declared unlawful for Negroes above the number of five to meet for educational purposes.[26] Only with the permission of their masters could slaves attend religious worship conducted by a recognized white minister or attended by "two discreet and reputable persons."[27]

The problem in Louisiana was first to keep out intelligent persons who might so inform the slaves as to cause them to rise. Accordingly in 1814[28] the State passed a law prohibiting the immigration of free persons of color into that commonwealth. This precaution, however, was not deemed sufficient after the insurrectionary Negroes of New Berne, Tarborough, and Hillsborough, North Carolina,[29] had risen, and David Walker of Massachusetts had published to the slaves his fiery appeal to arms.[30] In 1830, therefore, Louisiana enacted another measure, providing that whoever should write, print, publish, or distribute anything having the tendency to produce discontent among the slaves, should on conviction thereof be imprisoned at hard labor for life or suffer death at the discretion of the court. It was provided, too, that whoever used any language or became instrumental in bringing into the State any paper, book, or pamphlet inducing this discontent should suffer practically the same penalty. All persons who should teach, or permit or cause to be taught, any slave to read or write, should be imprisoned not less than one month nor more than twelve.[31]

Yielding to the demand of slaveholders, Georgia passed a year later a law providing that any Negro who should teach another to read or write should be punished by fine and whipping. If a white person should so offend, he should be punished with a fine not exceeding $500 and with imprisonment in the common jail at the discretion of the committing magistrate.[32]

In Virginia where the prohibition did not then extend to freedmen, there was enacted in 1831 a law providing that any meeting of free Negroes or mulattoes for teaching them reading or writing should be considered an unlawful assembly. To break up assemblies for this purpose any judge or justice of the peace could issue a warrant to apprehend such persons and inflict corporal punishment not exceeding twenty lashes. White persons convicted of teaching Negroes to read or write were to be fined fifty dollars and might be imprisoned

The Reaction

two months. For imparting such information to a slave the offender was subject to a fine of not less than ten nor more than one hundred dollars.[33]

The whole country was again disturbed by the insurrection in Southampton County, Virginia, in 1831. The slave States then had a striking example of what the intelligent Negroes of the South might eventually do. The leader of this uprising was Nat Turner. Precocious as a youth he had learned to read so easily that he did not remember when he first had that attainment.[34] Given unusual social and intellectual advantages, he developed into a man of considerable "mental ability and wide information." His education was chiefly acquired in the Sunday-schools in which "the text-books for the small children were the ordinary speller and reader, and that for the older Negroes the Bible."[35] He had received instruction also from his parents and his indulgent young master, J.C. Turner.

When Nat Turner appeared, the education of the Negro had made the way somewhat easier for him than it was for his predecessors. Negroes who could read and write had before them the revolutionary ideas of the French, the daring deeds of Toussaint L'Ouverture, the bold attempt of General Gabriel, and the far-reaching plans of Denmark Vesey. These were sometimes written up in the abolition literature, the circulation of which was so extensive among the slaves that it became a national question.[36]

The aim of the subsequent reactionary legislation of the South was to complete the work of preventing the dissemination of information among Negroes and their reading of abolition literature. This they endeavored to do by prohibiting the communication of the slaves with one another, with the better informed free persons of color, and with the liberal white people; and by closing all the schools theretofore opened to Negroes. The States passed laws providing for a more stringent regulation of passes, defining unlawful assemblies, and fixing penalties for the same. Other statutes prohibited religious worship, or brought it under direct supervision of the owners of the slaves concerned, and proscribed the private teaching of slaves in any manner whatever.

Mississippi, which already had a law to prevent the mental improvement of the slaves, enacted in 1831 another measure to remove from them the more enlightened members of their race. All free colored persons were to leave the State in ninety days. The same law provided, too, that no Negro should preach in that State unless to the slaves of his plantation and with the permission of the owner.[39] Delaware saw fit to take a bold step in this direction. The act of 1831 provided that no congregation or meeting of free Negroes or mulattoes of more than twelve persons should be held later than twelve o'clock at night, except under the direction of three respectable white persons who were to attend the meeting. It further provided that no free Negro should attempt to call a meeting for religious worship, to exhort or preach, unless he was authorized to do so by a judge or justice of the peace, upon the recommendation of five "respectable and judicious citizens." [40] This measure tended only to prevent the dissemination of information among Negroes by making it impossible for them to assemble. It was not until 1863 that the State of Delaware finally passed a positive measure to prevent the assemblages of colored persons for instruction and all other meetings except for religious worship and the burial of the dead. [41] Following the example of Delaware in 1832, Florida passed a law prohibiting all meetings of Negroes except those for divine worship at a church or place attended by white persons.[42] Florida made the same regulations more stringent in 1846 when she enjoyed the freedom of a State.[43]

Alabama had some difficulty in getting a satisfactory law. In 1832 this commonwealth enacted a law imposing a fine of from $250 to $500 on persons who should attempt to educate any Negro whatsoever. The act also prohibited the usual unlawful assemblies and the preaching or exhorting of Negroes except in the presence of five "respectable slaveholders" or unless the officiating minister was licensed by some regular church of which the persons thus exhorted were members.[44] It soon developed that the State had gone too far. It had infringed upon the rights and privileges of certain creoles, who, being residents of the Louisiana Territory when it was purchased in 1803, had been guaranteed the rights of citizens of the United States. Accordingly in 1833 the Mayor and the Aldermen of Mobile were authorized by law to grant licenses to such persons as they might deem suitable to instruct for limited periods, in that city and the counties of Mobile and Baldwin, the free colored children, who were descendants of colored creoles residing in the district in 1803.[45]

Another difficulty of certain commonwealths had to be overcome. Apparently Georgia had already incorporated into its laws provisions adequate to the prevention of the mental improvement of Negroes. But it was discovered that employed as they had been in various positions either requiring knowledge, or affording its acquirement, Negroes would pick up the rudiments of education, despite the fact that they had no access to schools. The State then passed a law imposing a penalty not exceeding one hundred dollars for the employment of any slave or free person of color "in setting up type or other labor about a printing office requiring a knowledge of reading and writing."[46] In 1834 South Carolina saw the same danger. In addition to enacting a more stringent law for the prevention of the teaching of Negroes by white or colored friends, and for the destruction of their schools, it provided that persons of African blood should not be employed as clerks or salesmen in or about any shop or store or house used for trading.[47]

North Carolina was among the last States to take such drastic measures for the protection of the white race. In this commonwealth the whites and blacks had lived on liberal terms. Negroes had up to this time enjoyed the right of suffrage there. Some attended schools open to both races. A few even taught white children.[48]

The intense feeling against Negroes engendered by the frequency of insurrections, however, sufficed to swing the State into the reactionary column by 1835. An act passed by the Legislature that year prohibited the public instruction of Negroes, making it impossible for youth of African descent to get any more education than what they could in their own family circle.[49] The public school system established thereafter specifically provided that its benefits should not extend to any descendant from Negro ancestors to the fourth generation inclusive.[50] Bearing so grievously this loss of their social status after they had toiled up from poverty, many ambitious free persons of color, left the State for more congenial communities.

The States of the West did not have to deal so severely with their slaves as was deemed necessary in Southern States. Missouri found it advisable in 1833 to amend the law of 1817[51] so as to regulate more rigorously the traveling and the assembling of slaves. It was not until 1847, however, that this commonwealth specifically provided that no one should keep or teach any school for the education of Negroes.[52] Tennessee had as early as 1803 a law governing the movement of slaves but exhibited a little more reactionary spirit in 1836 in providing that there should be no circulation of seditious books or pamphlets which might lead to insurrection or rebellion among Negroes.[53] Tennessee, however, did not positively forbid the education of colored people. Kentucky had a system of regulating the egress and regress of slaves but never passed any law prohibiting their instruction. Yet statistics show that although the education of Negroes was not penalized, it was in many places made impossible by public sentiment. So was it in the State of Maryland, which did not expressly forbid the instruction of anyone.

These reactionary results were not obtained without some opposition. The governing element of some States divided on the question. The opinions of this class were well expressed in the discussion between Chancellor Harper and J.B. O'Neal of the South Carolina bar. The former said that of the many Negroes whom he had known to be capable of reading, he had never seen one read anything but the Bible. He thought that they imposed this task upon themselves as a matter of duty. Because of the Negroes' "defective comprehension and the laborious nature of this employment to them"[54] he considered such reading an inefficient method of religious instruction. He, therefore, supported the oppressive measures of the South. The other member of the bar maintained that men could not reflect as Christians and justify the position that slaves should not be permitted to read the Bible. "It is in vain," added he, "to say there is danger in it. The best slaves of the State are those who can and do read the Scriptures. Again, who is it that teaches your slaves to read? It is generally done by the children of the owners. Who would tolerate an indictment against his son or daughter for teaching a slave to read? Such laws look to me as rather cowardly."[55] This attorney was almost of the opinion of many others who believed that the argument that to Christianize and educate the colored people of a slave commonwealth had a tendency to elevate them above their masters and to destroy the "legitimate distinctions" of the community, could be admitted only where the people themselves were degraded.

After these laws had been passed, American slavery extended not as that of the ancients, only to the body, but also to the mind. Education was thereafter regarded as positively inconsistent with the institution. The precaution taken to prevent the dissemination of information was declared indispensable to the system. The situation in many parts of the South was just as Berry portrayed it in the Virginia House of Delegates in 1832. He said: "We have as far as possible closed every avenue by which light may enter their [the slaves'] minds. If we could extinguish the capacity to see the light, our work would be completed; they would then be on a level with the beasts of the field and we should be safe! I am not certain that we would not do it, if we could find out the process, and that on the plea of necessity."[56]

The reactionary tendency was in no sense confined to the Southern States. Laws were passed in the North to prevent the migration of Negroes to that section. Their education at certain places was discouraged. In fact, in the proportion that the conditions in the South made it necessary for free blacks to flee from oppression, the people of the North grew less tolerant on account of the large number of those who crowded the towns and cities of the free States near the border. The antislavery societies at one time found it necessary to devote their time to the amelioration of the economic condition of the refugees to make them acceptable to the white people rather than to direct their attention to mere education.[58] Not a few northerners, dreading an influx of free Negroes, drove them even from communities to which they had learned to, repair for education.

The best example of this intolerance was the opposition encountered by Prudence Crandall, a well-educated young Quaker lady, who had established a boarding-school at Canterbury, Connecticut. Trouble arose when Sarah Harris, a colored girl, asked admission to this institution.[59] For many reasons Miss Crandall hesitated to admit her but finally yielded. Only a few days thereafter the parents of the white girls called on Miss Crandall to offer their objections to sending their children to school with a "nigger."[60] Miss Crandall stood firm, the white girls withdrew, and the teacher advertised for young women of color. The determination to continue the school on this basis incited the townsmen to hold an indignation meeting. They passed resolutions to protest through a committee of local officials against the establishment of a school of this kind in that community. At this meeting Andrew T. Judson denounced the policy of Miss Crandall, while the Rev. Samuel J. May ably defended it. Judson was not only opposed to the establishment of such a school in Canterbury but in any part of the State. He believed that colored people, who could never rise from their menial condition in the United States, should not to be encouraged to expect to elevate themselves in Connecticut. He considered them inferior servants who should not be treated as equals of the Caucasians, but should be sent back to Africa to improve themselves and Christianize the natives.[61] On the contrary, Mr. May thought that there would never be fewer colored people in this country than were found here then and that it would be unjust to exile them. He asserted that white people should grant Negroes their rights or lose their own and that since education is the primal, fundamental right of all men, Connecticut was the last place where this should be denied.[62]

Miss Crandall and her pupils were threatened with violence. Accommodation at the local stores was denied her. The pupils were insulted. The house was besmeared and damaged. An effort was made to invoke the law by which the selectmen might warn any person not an inhabitant of the State to depart under penalty of paying $1.67 for every week he remained after receiving such notice.[65] This failed, but Judson and his followers were still determined that the "nigger school" should never be allowed in Canterbury nor any town of the State. They appealed to the legislature. Setting forth in its preamble that the evil to be obviated was the increase of the black population of the commonwealth, that body passed a law providing that no person should establish a school for the instruction of colored people who were not inhabitants of the State of Connecticut, nor should any one harbor or board students brought to the State for this purpose without first obtaining, in writing, the consent of a majority of the civil authority and of the selectmen of the town.[66]

The enactment of this law caused Canterbury to go wild with joy. Miss Crandall was arrested on the 27th of June, and committed to await her trial at the next session of the Supreme Court. She and her friends refused to give bond that the officials might go the limit in imprisoning her. Miss Crandall was placed in a murderer's cell. Mr. May, who had stood by her, said when he saw the door locked and the key taken out, "The deed is done, completely done. It cannot be recalled. It has passed into the history of our nation and age." Miss Crandall was tried the 23d of August, 1833, at Brooklyn, the county seat of the county of Windham. The jury failed to agree upon a verdict, doubtless because Joseph Eaton, who presided, had given it as his opinion that the law was probably unconstitutional. At the second trial before Judge Dagget of the Supreme Court, who was an advocate of the law, Miss Crandall was convicted. Her counsel, however, filed a bill of exceptions and took an appeal to the Court of Errors. The case came up on the 22d of July, 1834. The nature of the law was ably discussed by W.W. Ellsworth and Calvin Goddard, who maintained that it was unconstitutional, and by A.T. Judson and C.F. Cleveland, who undertook to prove its constitutionality. The court reserved its decision, which was never given. Finding that there were defects in the information prepared by the attorney for the State, the indictment was quashed. Because of subsequent attempts to destroy the building, Mr. May and Miss Crandall decided to abandon the school.[67]

It resulted then that even in those States to which free blacks had long looked for sympathy, the fear excited by fugitives from the more reactionary commonwealths had caused northerners so to yield to the prejudices of the South that they opposed insuperable obstacles to the education of Negroes for service in the United States. The colored people, as we shall see elsewhere, were not allowed to locate their manual labor college at New Haven[68] and the principal of the Noyes Academy at Canaan, New Hampshire, saw his institution destroyed because he decided to admit colored students.[69] These fastidious persons, however, raised no objection to the establishment of schools to prepare Negroes to expatriate themselves under the direction of the American Colonization Society.[70]

Observing these conditions the friends of the colored people could not be silent. The abolitionists led by Caruthers, May, and Garrison hurled their weapons at the reactionaries, branding them as inconsistent schemers. After having advanced the argument of the mental inferiority of the colored race they had adopted the policy of educating Negroes on the condition that they be removed from the country.[71] Considering education one of the rights of man, the abolitionists persistently rebuked the North and South for their inhuman policy. On every opportune occasion they appealed to the world in behalf of the oppressed race, which the hostile laws had removed from humanizing influences, reduced to the plane of beasts, and made to die in heathenism.

In reply to the abolitionists the protagonists of the reactionaries said that but for the "intrusive and intriguing interference of pragmatical fanatics"[72] such precautionary enactments would never have been necessary. There was some truth in this statement; for in certain districts these measures operated not to prevent the aristocratic people of the South from enlightening the Negroes, but to keep away from them what they considered undesirable instructors. The southerners regarded the abolitionists as foes in the field, industriously scattering the seeds of insurrection which could then be prevented only by blocking every avenue through which they could operate upon the minds of the slaves. A writer of this period expressed it thus: "It became necessary to check or turn aside the stream which instead of flowing healthfully upon the Negro is polluted and poisoned by the abolitionists and rendered the source of discontent and excitement."[73] He believed that education thus perverted would become equally dangerous to the master and the slave, and that while fanaticism continued its war upon the South the measures of necessary precaution and defense had to be continued. He asserted, however, that education would not only unfit the Negro for his station in life and prepare him for insurrection, but would prove wholly impracticable in the performance of the duties of a laborer.[74] The South has not yet learned that an educated man is a better laborer than an ignorant one.

[1: Special Report of the U.S. Com. of Ed., 1871, p. 391.]
[2: Brevard, Digest of the Public Statute Law of S.C., vol. ii., p.243.]
[3: Marbury and Crawford, Digest of Laws of the State of Georgia, p. 438.]
[4: Laws of North Carolina, vol. i., pp. 126, 563, and 741.]
[5: Special Report of the U.S. Com. of Ed., 1871, p. 335.]
[6: Ibid., p. 352.]
[7: Turner, The Rise of the New West, pp. 45, 46, 47, 48, and 49; and Hammond, Cotton Industry, chaps. i. and ii.]
[8: Rhodes, History of the United States, vol. i., p. 32; Kemble, Journal, p. 28; Martineau, Society in America, vol. i., p. 308; Weld, Slavery, etc., p. 41.]
[9: Annals of Congress, First Session, vol. i., pp. 996 et seq. and 1296 et seq.]
[10: Washington, Works of Jefferson, vol. iv., p. 467.]
[11: Drewery, Insurrections in Virginia, p. 121.]
[12: The New York Daily Advertiser, Sept. 22, 1800; and The Richmond Enquirer, Oct. 21, 1831.]
[13: Writings of James Monroe, vol. iii., p. 217.]
[14: Educated Negroes then constituted an alarming element in Massachusetts, Virginia, and South Carolina. See The New York Daily Advertiser, Sept. 22, 1800.]
[15: See The New York Daily Advertiser, Sept. 22, 1800.]
[16: Ibid., Oct. 7, 1800.]
[17: Letter of St. George Tucker in Joshua Coffin's Slave Insurrections.]
[18: The City Gazette and Commercial Daily Advertiser (Charleston, South Carolina), August 21, 1822.]
[19: Ibid., August 21, 1822.]
[20: The City Gazette and Commercial Daily Advertiser, August 21, 1822.]
[21: Ibid., August 21, 1822.]
[22: The Norfolk and Portsmouth Herald, Aug. 30, 1822.]
[23: Hodgson, Whitney's Remarks during a Journey through North America, p. 184.]
[24: Laws of Missouri Territory, etc., p. 498.]
[25: Tate, Digest of the Laws of Virginia, pp. 849-850.]
[26: Poindexter, Revised Code of the Laws of Mississippi, p. 390.]
[27: Ibid., p. 390.]
[28: Bullard and Curry, A New Digest of the Statute Laws of the State of Louisiana, p. 161.]
[29: Coffin, Slave Insurrections, p. 22.]
[30: Walker mentioned "our wretchedness in consequence of slavery, our wretchedness in consequence of ignorance, our wretchedness in consequence of the preachers of the religion of Jesus Christ, and our wretchedness in consequence of the colonization plan." See Walker's Appeal.]
[31: Acts passed at the Ninth Session of the Legislature of Louisiana, p. 96.]
[32] Dawson, A Compilation of the Laws of the State of Georgia, etc., p. 413.
[33]Laws of Virginia, 1830-1831, p. 108, Sections 5 and 6.
[34] Drewery, Insurrections in Virginia, p. 27.
[35: Drewery, Insurrections in Virginia, p. 28.]

The Reaction

[36: These organs were The Albany Evening Journal, The New York Free Press, The Genius of Universal Emancipation, and The Boston Liberator. See The Richmond Enquirer, Oct. 21, 1831.]

Trying to account for this insurrection the Governor of the State lays it to the charge of the Negro preachers who were in position to foment much disorder on account of having acquired "great ascendancy over the minds" of discontented slaves. He believed that these ministers were in direct contact with the agents of abolition, who were using colored leaders as a means to destroy the institutions of the South. The Governor was cognizant of the fact that not only was the sentiment of the incendiary pamphlets read but often the words.[37] To prevent the "enemies" in other States from communicating with the slaves of that section he requested that the laws regulating the assembly of Negroes be more rigidly enforced and that colored preachers be silenced. The General Assembly complied with this request.[38]

[37: The Richmond Enquirer, Oct. 21, 1831.]
[38: The Laws of Virginia, 1831-1832, p. 20.]
[39] Hutchinson, Code of Mississippi, p. 533.
[40] Laws of Delaware, 1832, pp. 181-182.
[41] Ibid., 1863, p. 330 et seq.
[42: Acts of the Legislative Council of the Territory of Florida, 1832, p. 145.]
[43: Acts of Florida, 1846, ch. 87, sec. 9.]
[44 Clay, Digest of the Laws of the State of Alabama, p. 543.]
[45: Special Report of the U.S. Com. of Ed., 1871, p. 323.]
[46: Cobb, Digest of the Laws of Georgia, p. 555; and Prince, Digest of the Laws of Georgia, p. 658.]
[47: Laws of South Carolina, 1834.]
[48: Bassett, Slavery in North Carolina, p. 74; and testimonies of various ex-slaves.]
[49: Revised Statutes of North Carolina, 578.]
[50: Laws of North Carolina, 1835, C.6, S.2.]
[51: Laws of the Territory of Missouri, p. 498.]
[52: Laws of the State of Missouri, 1847, pp. 103 and 104.]
[53: Public Acts passed at the First Session of the General Assembly of the State of Tennessee, p. 145, chap. 44.]
[54: DeBow, The Industrial Resources of the Southern and Western States, vol. ii., p. 269.]
[55: DeBow, The Industrial Resources of the Southern and Western States, vol. ii., p. 279.]
[56: Coffin, Slave Insurrections, p. 23; and Goodell, Slave Code, p. 323.]

It had then come to pass that in the South, where once were found a considerable number of intelligent Negroes, they had become exceedingly scarce or disappeared from certain sections altogether. On plantations of hundreds of slaves it was common to discover that not one of them had the mere rudiments of education. In some large districts it was considered almost a phenomenon to find a Negro who could read the Bible or sign his name.[57]

[57:Ibid., pp. 323-324.]
[58: Proceedings of the American Convention.]
[61: Jay, An Inquiry, etc., p. 30.]
[62: Ibid., pp. 32 et seq.]

[63: Jay, An Inquiry, etc., p. 33; and Special Report of the U.S. Com. of Ed., pp. 328 et seq.]

[64: Jay, An Inquiry, etc., p. 33.]

[65: Special Report of the U.S. Com. of Ed., 1871, p. 331; and May, Letters to A.T. Judson, Esq., and Others, p. 5.]

[66: Ibid., p. 5.]

[67: Jay, An Inquiry, etc., p. 26.]

[68: Proceedings of the Third Annual Convention for the Improvement of the Free People of Color, p. 14.]

[69: Fourth Annual Report of the American Antislavery Society, p. 34.]

[70: Alexander, A History of Colonization on the Western Continent, p. 348.]

[71: Jay, An Inquiry, etc., p. 26; Johns Hopkins University Studies, Series xvi., p. 319; and Proceedings of the New York State Colonization Society, 1831, p. 6.]

[72: Hodgkin, An Inquiry into the Merits of the Am. Col. Soc., p. 31; and The South Vindicated from the Treason and Fanaticism of the Abolitionists, p. 68.]

[73: Ibid., p. 69.]

[74: The South Vindicated from the Treason and Fanaticism of the Abolitionists, p. 69.]

Chapter 8

Religion Without Letters

Stung by the effective charge of the abolitionists that the reactionary legislation of the South consigned the Negroes to heathenism, slaveholders considering themselves Christians, felt that some semblance of the religious instruction of these degraded people should be devised. It was difficult, however, to figure out exactly how the teaching of religion to slaves could be made successful and at the same time square with the prohibitory measures of the South. For this reason many masters made no effort to find a way out of the predicament. Others with a higher sense of duty brought forward a scheme of oral instruction in Christian truth or of religion without letters. The word instruction thereafter signified among the southerners a procedure quite different from what the term meant in the seventeenth and eighteenth centuries, when Negroes were taught to read and write that they might learn the truth for themselves.

Being aristocratic in its bearing, the Episcopal Church in the South early receded from the position of cultivating the minds of the colored people. As the richest slaveholders were Episcopalians, the clergy of that denomination could hardly carry out a policy which might prove prejudicial to the interests of their parishioners. Moreover, in their propaganda there was then nothing which required the training of Negroes to instruct themselves. As the qualifications of Episcopal ministers were rather high even for the education of the whites of that time, the blacks could not hope to be active churchmen. This Church, therefore, soon limited its work among the Negroes of the South to the mere verbal instruction of those who belonged to the local parishes. Furthermore, because this Church was not exceedingly militant, and certainly not missionary, it failed to grow rapidly. In most parts it suffered from the rise of the more popular Methodists and Baptists into the folds of which slaves followed their masters during the eighteenth century.

The adjustment of the Methodist and Baptist churches in the South to the new work among the darker people, however, was after the first quarter of the nineteenth century practically easy. Each of these denominations had once strenuously opposed slavery, the Methodists holding out longer than the Baptists. But the particularizing force of the institution soon became such that southern churches of these connections withdrew most of their objections to the system and, of course, did not find it difficult to abandon the idea of teaching Negroes to read.[1] Moreover, only so far as it was necessary to prepare men to preach and exhort was there an urgent need for literary education among these plain and unassuming missionaries. They came, not emphasizing the observance of forms which required so much development of the intellect, but laying stress upon the quickening of man's conscience and the regeneration of his soul. In the States, however, where the prohibitory laws were not so rigidly enforced, the instruction received in various ways from workers of these denominations often turned out to be more than religion without letters.[2]

The Education of the Negro

The Presbyterians found it more difficult to yield on this point. For decades they had been interested in the Negro race and had in 1818 reached the acme of antislavery sentiment.[3] Synod after synod denounced the attitude of cruel masters toward their slaves and took steps to do legally all they could to provide religious instruction for the colored people.[4] When public sentiment and reactionary legislation made the instruction of the Negroes of the South impracticable the Presbyterians of New York and New Jersey were active in devising schemes for the education of the colored people at points in the North.[5] Then came the crisis of the prolonged abolition agitation which kept the Presbyterian Church in an excited state from 1818 to 1830 and resulted in the recession of that denomination from the position it had formerly taken against slavery.[6] Yielding to the reactionaries in 1835, this noble sect which had established schools for Negroes, trained ambitious colored men for usefulness, and endeavored to fit them for the best civil and religious emoluments, thereafter became divided. The southern connection lost much of its interest in the dark race, and fell back on the policy of the verbal instruction and memory training of the blacks that they might never become thoroughly enlightened as to their condition.

Despite the fact that southern Methodists and Presbyterians generally ceased to have much anti-slavery ardor, there continued still in the western slave States and in the mountains of Virginia and North Carolina, a goodly number of these churchmen, who suffered no diminution of interest in the enlightenment of Negroes. In the States of Kentucky and Tennessee friends of the race were often left free to instruct them as they wished. Many of the people who settled those States came from the Scotch-Irish stock of the Appalachian Mountains, where early in the nineteenth century the blacks were in some cases treated as equals of the whites.[7]

The Quakers, and many Catholics, however, were as effective as the mountaineers in elevating Negroes. They had for centuries labored to promote religion and education among their colored brethren. So earnest were these sects in working for the uplift of the Negro race that the reactionary movement failed to swerve them from their course. When the other churches adopted the policy of mere verbal training, the Quakers and Catholics adhered to their idea that the Negroes should be educated to grasp the meaning of the Christian religion just as they had been during the seventeenth and eighteenth centuries.[8] This favorable situation did not mean so much, however, since with the exception of the Catholics in Maryland and Louisiana and the Quakers in Pennsylvania, not many members of these sects lived in communities of a large colored population. Furthermore, they were denied access to the Negroes in most southern communities, even when they volunteered to work as missionaries among the colored people.[9]

How difficult it was for these churchmen to carry out their policy of religion without letters may be best observed by viewing the conditions then obtaining. In most Southern States in which Negro preachers could not be deterred from their mission by public sentiment, they were prohibited by law from exhorting their fellows. The ground for such action was usually said to be incompetency and liability to abuse their office and influence to the injury of the laws and peace of the country. The elimination of the Christian teachers of the Negro race, and the prevention of the immigration of workers from the Northern States rendered the blacks helpless and dependent upon a few benevolent white ministers of the slave communities. During this period of unusual proselyting among the whites, these preachers could not minister to the needs of their own race.[10] Besides, even when there was found a white clergyman who was willing to labor among these lowly people, he often knew little about the inner workings of their minds, and failing to enlighten their understanding, left them the victims of sinful habits, incident to the institution of slavery.

To a civilized man the result was alarming. The Church as an institution had ceased to be the means by which the Negroes of the South could be enlightened. The Sabbath-schools in which so many colored people there had learned to read and write had by 1834 restricted their work to oral instruction.[11] In places where the blacks once had the privilege of getting an elementary education, only an inconceivable fraction of them could rise above illiteracy. Most of these were freedmen found in towns and cities. With the exception of a few slaves who were allowed the benefits of religious instruction, these despised beings were generally neglected and left to die like heathen. In 1840 there were in the South only fifteen colored Sabbath-schools, with an attendance of about 1459.

There had never been any regular daily instruction in Christian truths, but after this period only a few masters allowed field hands to attend family prayers. Some sections went beyond this point, prohibiting by public sentiment any and all kinds of religious instruction.[12] In South Carolina a formal remonstrance signed by over 300 planters and citizens was presented to a Methodist preacher chosen by a conference of that State as a "cautious and discreet person"[13] especially qualified to preach to slaves, and pledged to confine himself to verbal instruction. In Falmouth, Virginia, several white ladies began to meet on Sunday afternoons to teach Negro children the principles of the Christian religion. They were unable to continue their work a month before the local officials stopped them, although these women openly avowed that they did not intend to teach reading and writing.[14] Thus the development of the religious education of the Negroes in certain parts of the South had been from literary instruction as a means of imparting Christian truth to the policy of oral indoctrination, and from this purely memory teaching to no education at all.

Thereafter the chief privilege allowed the slaves was to congregate for evening prayers conducted by themselves under the surveillance of a number of "discreet persons." The leader chosen to conduct the services, would in some cases read a passage from the Scriptures and "line a hymn," which the slaves took up in their turn and sang in a tune of their own suitable to the meter. In case they had present no one who could read, or the law forbade such an exercise, some exhorter among the slaves would be given an opportunity to address the people, basing his remarks as far as his intelligence allowed him on some memorized portion of the Bible. The rest of the evening would be devoted to individual prayers and the singing of favorite hymns, developed largely from the experience of slaves, who while bearing their burdens in the heat of the day had learned to sing away their troubles.

For this untenable position the slave States were so severely criticized by southern and northern friends of the colored people that the ministers of that section had to construct a more progressive policy. Yet whatever might be the arguments of the critics of the South to prove that the enlightenment of Negroes was not a danger, it was clear after the Southampton insurrection in 1831 that two factors in Negro education would for some time continue generally eliminated. These were reading matter and colored preachers.

The Education of the Negro

Prominent among the southerners who endeavored to readjust their policy of enlightening the black population, were Bishop William Meade,[15] Bishop William Capers,[16] and Rev. C.C. Jones.[17] Bishop Meade was a native of Virginia, long noted for its large element of benevolent slaveholders who never lost interest in their Negroes. He was fortunate in finishing his education at Princeton, so productive then of leaders who fought the institution of slavery. [18] Immediately after his ordination in the Protestant Episcopal Church, Bishop Meade assumed the role of a reformer. He took up the cause of the colored people, devoting no little of his time to them when he was in Alexandria and Frederick in 1813 and 1814.[19] He began by preaching to the Negroes on fifteen plantations, meeting them twice a day, and in one year reported the baptism of forty-eight colored children.[20] Early a champion of the colonization of the Negroes, he was sent on a successful mission to Georgia in 1818 to secure the release of certain recaptured Africans who were about to be sold. Going and returning from the South he was active in establishing auxiliaries of the American Colonization Society. He helped to extend its sphere also into the Middle States and New-England.[21]

Bishop Meade was a representative of certain of his fellow-churchmen who were passing through the transitory stage from the position of advocating the thorough education of Negroes to that of recommending mere verbal instruction. Agreeing at first with Rev. Thomas Bacon, Bishop Meade favored the literary training of Negroes, and advocated the extermination of slavery. [22] Later in life he failed to urge his followers to emancipate their slaves, and did not entreat his congregation to teach them to read. He was then committed to the policy of only lessening their burden as much as possible without doing anything to destroy the institution. Thereafter he advocated the education and emancipation of the slaves only in connection with the scheme of colonization, to which he looked for a solution of these problems.[23]

Wishing to give his views on the religious instruction of Negroes, the Bishop found in Rev. Thomas Bacon's sermons that "every argument which was likely to convince and persuade was so forcibly exerted, and that every objection that could possibly be made, so fully answered, and in fine everything that ought to be said so well said, and the same things so happily confirmed ..." that it was deemed "best to refer the reader for the true nature and object of the book to the book itself."[24] Bishop Meade had uppermost in his mind Bacon's logical arraignment of those who neglected to teach their Negroes the Christian religion. Looking beyond the narrow circle of his own sect, the bishop invited the attention of all denominations to this subject in which they were "equally concerned." He especially besought "the ministers of the gospel to take it into serious consideration as a matter for which they also will have to give an account. Did not Christ," said he, "die for these poor creatures as well as for any other, and is it not given in charge of the minister to gather his sheep into the fold?"[25]

Another worker in this field was Bishop William Capers of the Methodist Episcopal Church of South Carolina. A southerner to the manner born, he did not share the zeal of the antislavery men who would educate Negroes as a preparation for manumission.[26] Regarding the subject of abolition as one belonging to the State and entirely inappropriate to the Church, he denounced the principles of the religious abolitionists as originating in false philosophy. Capers endeavored to prove that the relation of slave and master is authorized by the Holy Scriptures. He was of the opinion, however, that certain abuses which might ensue, were immoralities to be prevented or punished by all proper means, both by the Church discipline and the civil law.[27] Believing that the neglect of the spiritual needs of the slaves was a reflection on the slaveholders, he set out early in the thirties to stir up South Carolina to the duty of removing this stigma.

His plan of enlightening the blacks did not include literary instruction. His aim was to adapt the teaching of Christian truth to the condition of persons having a "humble intellect and a limited range of knowledge by means of constant and patient reiteration."[28] The old Negroes were to look to preachers for the exposition of these principles while the children were to be turned over to catechists who would avail themselves of the opportunity of imparting these fundamentals to the young at the time their minds were in the plastic state. Yet all instructors and preachers to Negroes had to be careful to inculcate the performance of the duty of obedience to their masters as southerners found them stated in the Holy Scriptures. Any one who would hesitate to teach these principles of southern religion should not be employed to instruct slaves. The bishop was certain that such a one could not then be found among the preachers of the Methodist Episcopal Church of South Carolina.[29]

Bishop Capers was the leading spirit in the movement instituted in that commonwealth about 1829 to establish missions to the slaves. So generally did he arouse the people to the performance of this duty that they not only allowed preachers access to their Negroes but requested that missionaries be sent to their plantations. Such petitions came from C.C. Pinckney, Charles Boring, and Lewis Morris.[30] Two stations were established in 1829 and two additional ones in 1833. Thereafter the Church founded one or two others every year until 1847 when there were seventeen missions conducted by twenty-five preachers. At the death of Bishop Capers in 1855 the Methodists of South Carolina had twenty-six such establishments, which employed thirty-two preachers, ministering to 11,546 communicants of color. The missionary revenue raised by the local conference had increased from $300 to $25,000 a year.[31]

The most striking example of this class of workers was the Rev. C.C. Jones, a minister of the Presbyterian Church. Educated at Princeton with men actually interested in the cause of the Negroes, and located in Georgia where he could study the situation as it was, Jones became not a theorist but a worker. He did not share the discussion of the question as to how to get rid of slavery. Accepting the institution as a fact, he endeavored to alleviate the sufferings of the unfortunates by the spiritual cultivation of their minds. He aimed, too, not to take into his scheme the solution of the whole problem but to appeal to a special class of slaves, those of the plantations who were left in the depths of ignorance as to the benefits of right living. In this respect he was like two of his contemporaries, Rev. Josiah Law[32] of Georgia and Bishop Polk of Louisiana. [33] Denouncing the policy of getting all one could out of the slaves and of giving back as little as possible, Jones undertook to show how their spiritual improvement would exterminate their ignorance, vulgarity, idleness, improvidence, and irreligion; Jones thought that if the circumstances of the Negroes were changed, they would equal, if not excel, the rest of the human family "in majesty of intellect, elegance of manners, purity of morals, and ardor of piety."[34] He feared that white men might cherish a contempt for Negroes that would cause them to sink lower in the scale of intelligence, morality, and religion. Emphasizing the fact that as one class of society rises so will the other, Jones advocated the mingling of the classes together in churches, to create kindlier feelings among them, increase the tendency of the blacks to subordination, and promote in a higher degree their mental and religious improvement. He was sure that these benefits could never result from independent church organization.[35]

Meeting the argument of those who feared the insubordination of Negroes, Jones thought that the gospel would do more for the obedience of slaves and the peace of the community than weapons of war. He asserted that the very effort of the masters to instruct their slaves created a strong bond of union between them and their masters.[36] History, he believed, showed that the direct way of exposing the slaves to acts of insubordination was to leave them in ignorance and superstition to the care of their own religion.[37] To disprove the falsity of the charge that literary instruction given in Neau's school in New York was the cause of a rising of slaves in 1709, he produced evidence that it was due to their opposition to becoming Christians. The rebellions in South Carolina from 1730 to 1739, he maintained, were fomented by the Spaniards in St. Augustine. The upheaval in New York in 1741 was not due to any plot resulting from the instruction of Negroes in religion, but rather to a delusion on the part of the whites. The rebellions in Camden in 1816 and in Charleston in 1822 were not exceptions to the rule. He conceded that the Southampton Insurrection in Virginia in 1831 originated under the color of religion. It was pointed out, however, that this very act itself was a proof that Negroes left to work out their own salvation, had fallen victims to "ignorant and misguided teachers" like Nat Turner. Such undesirable leaders, thought he, would never have had the opportunity to do mischief, if the masters had taken it upon themselves to instruct their slaves.[38] He asserted that no large number of slaves well instructed in the Christian religion and taken into the churches directed by white men had ever been found guilty of taking part in servile insurrections.[39]

To meet the arguments of these reformers the slaveholders found among laymen and preachers able champions to defend the reactionary policy. Southerners who had not gone to the extreme in the prohibition of the instruction of Negroes felt more inclined to answer the critics of their radical neighbors. One of these defenders thought that the slaves should have some enlightenment but believed that the domestic element of the system of slavery in the Southern States afforded "adequate means" for the improvement, adapted to their condition and the circumstances of the country; and furnished "the natural, safe, and effectual means"[40] of the intellectual and moral elevation of the Negro race. Another speaking more explicitly, said that the fact that the Negro is such per se carried with it the "inference or the necessity that his education--the cultivation of his faculties, or the development of his intelligence, must be in harmony with itself." In other words, "his instruction must be an entirely different thing from the training of the Caucasian," in regard to whom "the term education had widely different significations." For this reason these defenders believed that instead of giving the Negro systematic instruction he should be placed in the best position possible for the development of his imitative powers--"to call into action that peculiar capacity for copying the habits, mental and moral, of the superior race."[41] They referred to the facts that slaves still had plantation prayers and preaching by numerous members of their own race, some of whom could read and write, that they were frequently favored by their masters with services expressly for their instruction, that Sabbath-schools had been established for the benefit of the young, and finally that slaves were received into the churches which permitted them to hear the same gospel and praise the same God.[42]

Seeing even in the policy of religious instruction nothing but danger to the position of the slave States, certain southerners opposed it under all circumstances. Some masters feared that verbal instruction would increase the desire of slaves to learn. Such teaching might develop into a progressive system of improvement, which, without any special effort in that direction, would follow in the natural order of things.[43] Timorous persons believed that slaves thus favored would neglect their duties and embrace seasons of religious worship for originating and executing plans for insubordination and villainy. They thought, too, that missionaries from the free States would thereby be afforded an opportunity to come South and inculcate doctrines subversive of the interests and safety of that section.[44] It would then be only a matter of time before the movement would receive such an impetus that it would dissolve the relations of society as then constituted and revolutionize the civil institutions of the South.

The black population of certain sections, however, was not reduced to heathenism. Although often threatening to execute the reactionary laws, many of which were never intended to be rigidly enforced, the southerners did not at once eliminate the Negro as a religious instructor.[45] It was fortunate that a few Negroes who had learned the importance of early Christian training, organized among themselves local associations. These often appointed an old woman of the plantation to teach children too young to work in the fields, to say prayers, repeat a little catechism, and memorize a few hymns.[46] But this looked too much like systematic instruction. In some States it was regarded as productive of evils destructive to southern society and was, therefore, discouraged or prohibited.[47] To local associations organized by kindly slaveholders there was less opposition because the chief aim always was to restrain strangers and undesirable persons from coming South to incite the Negroes to servile insurrection. Two good examples of these local organizations were the ones found in Liberty and McIntosh counties, Georgia. The constitutions of these bodies provided that the instruction should be altogether oral, embracing the general principles of the Christian religion as understood by orthodox Christians.[48]

Directing their efforts thereafter toward mere verbal teaching, religious workers depended upon the memory of the slave to retain sufficient of the truths and principles expounded to effect his conversion. Pamphlets, hymn books, and catechisms especially adapted to the work were written by churchmen, and placed in the hands of discreet missionaries acceptable to the slaveholders. Among other publications of this kind were Dr. Capers's Short Catechism for the Use of Colored Members on Trial in the Methodist Episcopal Church in South Carolina; A Catechism to be Used by Teachers in the Religious Instruction of Persons of Color in the Episcopal Church of South Carolina; Dr. Palmer's Cathechism; Rev. John Mine's Catechism; and C.C. Jones's Catechism of Scripture, Doctrine and Practice Designed for the Original Instruction of Colored People. Bishop Meade was once engaged in collecting such literature addressed particularly to slaves in their stations. These extracts were to be read to them on proper occasions by any member of the family.[49]

Yet on the whole it can be safely stated that there were few societies formed in the South to give the Negroes religious and moral instruction. Only a few missionaries were exclusively devoted to work among them. In fact, after the reactionary period no propaganda of any southern church included anything which could be designated as systematic instruction of the Negroes.[50] Even owners, who took care to feed, clothe, and lodge their slaves well and treated them humanely, often neglected to do anything to enlighten their understanding as to their responsibility to God.

Observing closely these conditions one would wonder little that many Negroes became low and degraded. The very institution of slavery itself produced shiftless, undependable beings, seeking relief whenever possible by giving the least and getting the most from their masters. When the slaves were cut off from the light of the gospel by the large plantation system, they began to exhibit such undesirable traits as insensibility of heart, lasciviousness, stealing, and lying. The cruelty of the "Christian" master to the slaves made the latter feel that such a practice was not altogether inhuman. Just as the white slave drivers developed into hopeless brutes by having human beings to abuse, so it turned out with certain Negroes in their treatment of animals and their fellow-creatures in bondage. If some Negroes were commanded not to commit adultery, such a prohibition did not extend to the slave women forced to have illicit relations with masters who sold their mulatto offspring as goods and chattels. If the bondmen were taught not to steal the aim was to protect the supplies of the local plantation. Few masters raised any serious objection to the act of their half-starved slaves who at night crossed over to some neighboring plantation to secure food. Many white men made it their business to dispose of property stolen by Negroes.

In the strait in which most slaves were, they had to lie for protection. Living in an environment where the actions of almost any colored man were suspected as insurrectionary, Negroes were frequently called upon to tell what they knew and were sometimes forced to say what they did not know. Furthermore, to prevent the slaves from cooeperating to rise against their masters, they were often taught to mistreat and malign each other to keep alive a feeling of hatred. The bad traits of the American Negroes resulted then not from an instinct common to the natives of Africa, but from the institutions of the South and from the actual teaching of the slaves to be low and depraved that they might never develop sufficient strength to become a powerful element in society.

As this system operated to make the Negroes either nominal Christians or heathen, the anti-slavery men could not be silent.[51] James G. Birney said that the slaveholding churches like indifferent observers, had watched the abasement of the Negroes to a plane of beasts without remonstrating with legislatures against the iniquitous measures.[52] Moreover, because there was neither literary nor systematic oral instruction of the colored members of southern congregations, uniting with the Church made no change in the condition of the slaves. They were thrown back just as before among their old associates, subjected to corrupting influences, allowed to forego attendance at public worship on Sundays, and rarely encouraged to attend family prayers.[53] In view of this state of affairs Birney was not surprised that it was only here and there that one could find a few slaves who had an intelligent view of Christianity or of a future life.

William E. Charming expressed his deep regret that the whole lot of the slave was fitted to keep his mind in childhood and bondage. To Channing it seemed shameful that, although the slave lived in a land of light, few beams found their way to his benighted understanding. He was given no books to excite his curiosity. His master provided for him no teacher but the driver who broke him almost in childhood to the servile tasks which were to fill up his life.

Channing complained that when benevolence would approach the slave with instruction it was repelled. Not being allowed to be taught, the "voice which would speak to him as a man was put to silence." For the lack of the privilege to learn the truth "his immortal spirit was systematically crushed despite the mandate of God to bring all men unto Him."[54]

Discussing the report that slaves were taught religion, Channing rejoiced that any portion of them heard of that truth "which gives inward freedom."[55] He thought, however, that this number was very small. Channing was certain that most slaves were still buried in heathen ignorance. But extensive as was this so-called religious instruction, he did not see how the teaching of the slave to be obedient to his master could exert much power in raising one to the divinity of man. How slavery which tends to debase the mind of the bondman could prepare it for spiritual truth, or how he could comprehend the essential principles of love on hearing it from the lips of his selfish and unjust owner, were questions which no defender of the system ever answered satisfactorily for Channing. Seeing then no hope for the elevation of the Negro as a slave, he became a more determined abolitionist.

William Jay, a son of the first Chief Justice of the United States, and an abolition preacher of the ardent type, later directed his attention to these conditions. The keeping of human beings in heathen ignorance by a people professing to reverence the obligation of Christianity seemed to him an unpardonable sin. He believed that the natural result of this "compromise of principle, this suppression of truth, this sacrifice to unanimity," had been the adoption of expediency as a standard of right and wrong in the place of the revealed will of God. [56] "Thus," continued he, "good men and good Christians have been tempted by their zeal for the American Colonization Society to countenance opinions and practices inconsistent with justice and humanity."[57] Jay charged to this disastrous policy of neglect the result that in 1835 only 245,000 of the 2,245,144 slaves had a saving knowledge of the religion of Christ. He deplored the fact that unhappily the evil influence of the reactionaries had not been confined to their own circles but had to a lamentable extent "vitiated the moral sense" of other communities. The proslavery leaders, he said, had reconciled public opinion to the continuance of slavery, and had aggravated those sinful prejudices which subjected the free blacks to insult and persecution and denied them the blessings of education and religious instruction.[58]

Among the most daring of those who censured the South for its reactionary policy was Rev. John G. Fee, an abolition minister of the gospel of Kentucky. Seeing the inevitable result in States where public opinion and positive laws had made the education of Negroes impossible, Fee asserted that in preventing them from reading God's Word and at the same time incorporating them into the Church as nominal Christians, the South had weakened the institution. Without the means to learn the principles of religion it was impossible for such an ignorant class to become efficient and useful members.[59] Excoriating those who had kept their servants in ignorance to secure the perpetuity of the institution of slavery, Fee maintained that sealing up the mind of the slave, lest he should see his wrongs, was tantamount to cutting off the hand or foot in order to prevent his escape from forced and unwilling servitude.[60] "If by our practice, our silence, or our sloth," said he, "we perpetuate a system which paralyzes our hands when we attempt to convey to them the bread of life, and which inevitably consigns the great mass of them to unending perdition, can we be guiltless in the sight of Him who hath made us stewards of His grace? This is sinful. Said the Saviour: 'Woe unto you lawyers! for ye have taken away the key of knowledge: ye entered not in yourselves, and them that were entering in ye hindered.'"[60]

[1: Matlack, History of Methodism, etc., p. 132; Benedict, History of the Baptists, p. 212.]
[2: Adams, South-side View, p. 59.]
[3: Baird, Collections, etc., pp. 814-817.]
[4: Ibid., p. 815.]
[5: Enormity of the Slave Trade, etc. p. 67.]
[6: Baird, Collections, etc., pp. 816, 817.]
[7: Fourth Annual Report of the American Antislavery Society, New York, 1837, P. 31; The New England Antislavery Almanac, 1841, p. 31; and The African Repository, vol. xxxii., p. 16.]
[8: Special Report of the U.S. Com. of Ed., 1871, pp. 217-221.]
[9: In several Southern States special laws were enacted to prevent the influx of such Christian workers.]
[10: Jones, Religious Instruction, p. 175.]
[11: Goodell, Slave Code, p. 324.]
[12: The cause of this drastic policy was not so much race hatred as the fear that any kind of instruction might cause the Negroes to assert themselves.]
[13: Olmsted, Back Country, pp. 105, 108.]
[14: Conway, Testimonies Concerning Slavery, p. 5.]
[15: Goodloe, Southern Platform, pp. 64-65.]
[16: Wightman, Life of Bishop William Capers, p. 294.]
[17: Jones, Religious Instruction, Introductory Chapter.]
[18: Goodloe, Southern Platform, p. 64.]
[19: Ibid., p. 65.]
[20: Ibid., p. 66.]
[21: Niles Register, vol. xvi., pp. 165-166.]
[22: Meade, Sermons of Rev. Thos. Bacon, p. 2; and Goodell, The Southern Platform, pp. 64, 65.]
[23: Ibid., p. 65.]
[24: Meade, Sermons of Rev. Thos. Bacon, pp. 31, 32, 81, 90, 93, 95, 104, and 105.]
[25: Ibid., p. 104.]
[26: Wightman, Life of William Capers, p. 295.]
[27: Wightman, Life of William Capers, p. 296.]
[28: Ibid., p. 298.]
[29: Ibid., p. 296.]
[30: Wightman, Life of William Capers, p. 296.]
[31; African Repository, vol. xxiv., p. 157.]
[32: Rev. Josiah Law was almost as successful as Jones in carrying the gospel to the neglected Negroes. His life is a large chapter in the history of Christianity among the slaves of that commonwealth. See Wright, Negro Education in Georgia, p. 19.]
[33: Rhodes, History of the U.S., vol. i., p. 331.]
[34: Jones, Religious Instruction, p. 103.]
[35: Jones, Religious Instruction, pp. 106, 217.]

[36: Ibid., pp. 212, 274.]
[37: Ibid., p. 215.]
[38: Jones, Religious Instruction, etc., p. 212.]
[39: Plumer, Thoughts, etc., p. 4.]
[40: Smith, Lectures on the Philosophy and Practice of Slavery, pp. 228 et seq.]
[41: Van Evrie, Negroes and Negro Slavery, p. 215.]
[42: Smith, Lectures on the Philosophy of Slavery, p. 228.]
[43: Jones, Religious Instruction, p. 192; Olmsted, Back Country, pp. 106-108.]
[44: Ibid., p. 106.]
[45: This statement is based on the testimonies of ex-slaves.]
[46: Jones, Religious Instruction, pp. 114, 117.]
[47: While the laws in certain places were not so drastic as to prohibit religious assemblies, the same was effected by patrols and mobs.]
[48: The Constitution of the Liberty County Association for the Religious Instruction of Negroes, Article IV.]
[49: Meade, Sermons of Rev. Thomas Bacon, p. 2.]
[50: Madison's Works, vol. in., p. 314; Olmsted, Back Country, p. 107; Birney, The American Churches, etc., p. 6; and Jones, Religious Instruction, etc., p. 100.]
[51: Tower, Slavery Unmasked, p. 394.]
[52: Birney, American Churches, p. 6.]
[53: Ibid., p. 7.]
[54: Channing, Slavery, p. 77.]
[55: Ibid., p. 78.]
[56: Jay, An Inquiry, etc., p. 24.]
[57: Ibid., p. 25.]
[58: Jay, An Inquiry, etc., p. 26.]
[60: Fee, Antislavery Manual, p. 147.]
[61: Ibid., p. 148.]
[62: Fee, Antislavery Manual, p. 149.]

Chapter 9

Learning In Spite of Opposition

Discouraging as these conditions seemed, the situation was not entirely hopeless. The education of the colored people as a public effort had been prohibited south of the border States, but there was still some chance for Negroes of that section to acquire knowledge. Furthermore, the liberal white people of that section considered these enactments, as we have stated above, not applicable to southerners interested in the improvement of their slaves but to mischievous abolitionists. The truth is that thereafter some citizens disregarded the laws of their States and taught worthy slaves whom they desired to reward or use in business requiring an elementary education. As these prohibitions in slave States were not equally stringent, white and colored teachers of free blacks were not always disturbed. In fact, just before the middle of the nineteenth century there was so much winking at the violation of the reactionary laws that it looked as if some Southern States might recede from their radical position and let Negroes be educated as they had been in the eighteenth century.

The ways in which slaves thereafter acquired knowledge are significant. Many picked it up here and there, some followed occupations which were in themselves enlightening, and others learned from slaves whose attainments were unknown to their masters. Often influential white men taught Negroes not only the rudiments of education but almost anything they wanted to learn. Not a few slaves were instructed by the white children whom they accompanied to school. While attending ministers and officials whose work often lay open to their servants, many of the race learned by contact and observation. Shrewd Negroes sometimes slipped stealthily into back streets, where they studied under a private teacher, or attended a school hidden from the zealous execution of the law.

The instances of Negroes struggling to obtain an education read like the beautiful romances of a people in an heroic age. Sometimes Negroes of the type of Lott Carey[1] educated themselves. James Redpath discovered in Savannah that in spite of the law great numbers of slaves had learned to read well. Many of them had acquired a rudimentary knowledge of arithmetic. "But," said he, "blazon it to the shame of the South, the knowledge thus acquired has been snatched from the spare records of leisure in spite of their owners' wishes and watchfulness."[2] C.G. Parsons was informed that although poor masters did not venture to teach their slaves, occasionally one with a thirst for knowledge secretly learned the rudiments of education without any instruction.[3] While on a tour through parts of Georgia, E.P. Burke observed that, notwithstanding the great precaution which was taken to prevent the mental improvement of the slaves, many of them "stole knowledge enough to enable them to read and write with ease."[4] Robert Smalls[5] of South Carolina and Alfred T. Jones[6] of Kentucky began their education in this manner.

Learning In Spite of Opposition

Probably the best example of this class was Harrison Ellis of Alabama. At the age of thirty-five he had acquired a liberal education by his own exertions. Upon examination he proved himself a good Latin and Hebrew scholar and showed still greater proficiency in Greek. His attainments in theology were highly satisfactory. The Eufaula Shield, a newspaper of that State, praised him as a man courteous in manners, polite in conversation, and manly in demeanor. Knowing how useful Ellis would be in a free country, the Presbyterian Synod of Alabama purchased him and his family in 1847 at a cost of $2500 that he might use his talents in elevating his own people in Liberia.[7]

Intelligent Negroes secretly communicated to their fellow men what they knew. Henry Banks of Stafford County, Virginia, was taught by his brother-in-law to read, but not write.[8] The father of Benedict Duncan, a slave in Maryland, taught his son the alphabet.[9] M.W. Taylor of Kentucky received his first instruction from his mother. H.O. Wagoner learned from his parents the first principles of the common branches.[10] A mulatto of Richmond taught John H. Smythe when he was between the ages of five and seven.[11] The mother of Dr. C.H. Payne of West Virginia taught him to read at such an early age that he does not remember when he first developed that power.[12] Dr. E.C. Morris, President of the National Baptist Convention, belonged to a Georgia family, all of whom were well instructed by his father.[13]

The white parents of Negroes often secured to them the educational facilities then afforded the superior race. The indulgent teacher of J. Morris of North Carolina was his white father, his master.[14] W.J. White acquired his education from his mother, who was a white woman.[15] Martha Martin, a daughter of her master, a Scotch-Irishman of Georgia, was permitted to go to Cincinnati to be educated, while her sister was sent to a southern town to learn the milliner's trade.[16] Then there were cases like that of Josiah Settle's white father. After the passage of the law forbidding free Negroes to remain in the State of Tennessee, he took his children to Hamilton, Ohio, to be educated and there married his actual wife, their colored mother.[17]

The very employment of slaves in business establishments accelerated their mental development. Negroes working in stores often acquired a fair education by assisting clerks. Some slaves were clerks themselves. Under the observation of E.P. Burke came the notable case of a young man belonging to one of the best families of Savannah. He could read, write, cipher, and transact business so intelligently that his master often committed important trusts to his care.[18] B.K. Bruce, while still a slave, educated himself when he was working at the printer's trade in Brunswick, Missouri. Even farther south where slavery assumed its worst form, we find that this condition obtained. Addressing to the New Orleans Commercial Bulletin a letter on African colonization, John McDonogh stated that the work imposed on his slaves required some education for which he willingly provided. In 1842 he had had no white man over his slaves for twenty years. He had assigned this task to his intelligent colored manager who did his work so well that the master did not go in person once in six months to see what his slaves were doing. He says, "They were, besides, my men of business, enjoyed my confidence, were my clerks, transacted all my affairs, made purchases of materials, collected my rents, leased my houses, took care of my property and effects of every kind, and that with an honesty and fidelity which was proof against every temptation."[19] Traveling in Mississippi in 1852, Olmsted found another such group of slaves all of whom could read, whereas the master himself was entirely illiterate. He took much pride, however, in praising his loyal, capable, and intelligent Negroes.[20]

White persons deeply interested in Negroes taught them regardless of public opinion and the law. Dr. Alexander T. Augusta of Virginia learned to read while serving white men as a barber.[21] A prominent white man of Memphis taught Mrs. Mary Church Terrell's mother French and English. The father of Judge R.H. Terrell was well-grounded in reading by his overseer during the absence of his master from Virginia.[22] A fugitive slave from Essex County of the same State was not allowed to go to school publicly, but had an opportunity to learn from white persons privately.[23] The master of Charles Henry Green, a slave of Delaware, denied him all instruction, but he was permitted to study among the people to whom he was hired.[24] M.W. Taylor of Kentucky studied under attorneys J.B. Kinkaid and John W. Barr, whom he served as messenger.[25] Ignoring his master's orders against frequenting a night school, Henry Morehead of Louisville learned to spell and read sufficiently well to cause his owner to have the school unceremoniously closed.[26]

The educational experiences of President Scarborough and of Bishop Turner show that some white persons were willing to make unusual sacrifices to enlighten Negroes. President Scarborough began to attend school in his native home in Bibb County, Georgia, at the age of six years. He went out ostensibly to play, keeping his books concealed under his arm, but spent six or eight hours each day in school until he could read well and had mastered the first principles of geography, grammar, and arithmetic. At the age of ten he took regular lessons in writing under an old South Carolinian, J.C. Thomas, a rebel of the bitterest type. Like Frederick Douglass, President Scarborough received much instruction from his white playmates.[27]

Bishop Turner of Newberry Court House, in South Carolina, purchased a spelling book and secured the services of an old white lady and a white boy, who in violation of the State law taught him to spell as far as two syllables.[28] The white boy's brother stopped him from teaching this lad of color, pointing out that such an instructor was liable to arrest. For some time he obtained help from an old colored gentleman, a prodigy in sounds. At the age of thirteen his mother employed a white lady to teach him on Sundays, but she was soon stopped by indignant white persons of the community. When he attained the age of fifteen he was employed by a number of lawyers in whose favor he ingratiated himself by his unusual power to please people. Thereafter these men in defiance of the law taught him to read and write and explained anything he wanted to know about arithmetic, geography, and astronomy.[29]

Often favorite slaves were taught by white children. By hiding books in a hayloft and getting the white children to teach him, James W. Sumler of Norfolk, Virginia, obtained an elementary education.[30] While serving as overseer for his Scotch-Irish master, Daniel J. Lockhart of the same commonwealth learned to read under the instruction of his owner's boys. They were not interrupted in their benevolent work.[31] In the same manner John Warren, a slave of Tennessee, acquired a knowledge of the common branches.[32] John Baptist Snowden of Maryland was secretly instructed by his owner's children.[33] Uncle Cephas, a slave of Parson Winslow of Tennessee, reported that the white children taught him on the sly when they came to see Dinah, who was a very good cook. He was never without books during his stay with his master.[34] One of the Grimke Sisters taught her little maid to read while brushing her

Learning In Spite of Opposition

young mistress's locks.[35] Robert Harlan, who was brought up in the family of Honorable J.M. Harlan, acquired the fundamentals of the common branches from Harlan's older sons.[36] The young mistress of Mrs. Ann Woodson of Virginia instructed her until she could read in the first reader.[37] Abdy observed in 1834 that slaves of Kentucky had been thus taught to read. He believed that they were about as well off as they would have been, had they been free.[38] Giving her experiences on a Mississippi plantation, Susan Dabney Smedes stated that the white children delighted in teaching the house servants. One night she was formally invited with the master, mistress, governess, and guests by a twelve-year-old school mistress to hear her dozen pupils recite poetry. One of the guests was quite astonished to see his servant recite a piece of poetry which he had learned for this occasion.[39] Confining his operations to the kitchen, another such teacher of this plantation was unusually successful in instructing the adult male slaves. Five of these Negroes experienced such enlightenment that they became preachers.[40]

Planters themselves sometimes saw to the education of their slaves. Ephraim Waterford was bound out in Virginia until he was twenty-one on the condition that the man to whom he was hired should teach him to read.[41] Mrs. Isaac Riley and Henry Williamson, of Maryland, did not attend school but were taught by their master to spell and read but not to write.[42] The master and mistress of Williamson Pease, of Hardman County, Tennessee, were his teachers. [43] Francis Fredric began his studies under his master in Virginia. Frederick Douglass was indebted to his kind mistress for his first instruction.[44] Mrs. Thomas Payne, a slave in what is now West Virginia, was fortunate in having a master who was equally benevolent.[45] Honorable I.T. Montgomery, now the Mayor of Mound Bayou, Mississippi, was, while a slave of Jefferson Davis's brother, instructed in the common branches and trained to be the confidential accountant of his master's plantation.[46] While on a tour among the planters of East Georgia, C.G. Parsons discovered that about 5000 of the 400,000 slaves there had been taught to read and write. He remarked, too, that such slaves were generally owned by the wealthy slaveholders, who had them schooled when the enlightenment of the bondmen served the purposes of their masters.[47]

The enlightenment of the Negroes, however, was not limited to what could be accomplished by individual efforts. In many southern communities colored schools were maintained in defiance of public opinion or in violation of the law. Patrick Snead of Savannah was sent to a private institution until he could spell quite well and then to a Sunday-school for colored children.[48] Richard M. Hancock wrote of studying in a private school in Newbern, North Carolina;[49] John S. Leary went to one in Fayetteville eight years;[50] and W.A. Pettiford of this State enjoyed similar advantages in Granville County during the fifties. He then moved with his parents to Preston County where he again had the opportunity to attend a special school.[51] About 1840, J.F. Boulder was a student in a mixed school of white and colored pupils in Delaware.[52] Bishop J.M. Brown, a native of the same commonwealth, attended a private school taught by a friendly woman of the Quaker sect.[53] John A. Hunter, of Maryland, was sent to a school for white children kept by the sister of his mistress, but his second master said that Hunter should not have been allowed to study and stopped his attendance.[54] Francis L. Cardozo of Charleston, South Carolina, entered school there in 1842 and continued his studies until he was twelve years of age.[55] During the fifties J.W. Morris of the same city

The Education of the Negro

attended a school conducted by the then distinguished Simeon Beard.[56] In the same way T. McCants Stewart[57] and the Grimke brothers [58] were able to begin their education there prior to emancipation.

More schools for slaves existed than white men knew of, for it was difficult to find them. Fredrika Bremer heard of secret schools for slaves during her visit to Charleston, but she had extreme difficulty in finding such an institution. When she finally located one and gained admission into its quiet chamber, she noticed in a wretched dark hole a "half-dozen poor children, some of whom had an aspect that testified great stupidity and mere animal life."[59] She was informed, too, that there were in Georgia and Florida planters who had established schools for the education of the children of their slaves with the intention of preparing them for living as "good free human beings."[60] Frances Anne Kemble noted such instances in her diary.[61] The most interesting of these cases was discovered by the Union Army on its march through Georgia. Unsuspected by the slave power and undeterred by the terrors of the law, a colored woman by the name of Deveaux had for thirty years conducted a Negro school in the city of Savannah.[62]

The city Negroes of Virginia continued to maintain schools despite the fact that the fear of servile insurrection caused the State to exercise due vigilance in the execution of the laws. The father of Richard De Baptiste of Fredericksburg made his own residence a school with his children and a few of those of his relatives as pupils. The work was begun by a Negro and continued by an educated Scotch-Irishman, who had followed the profession of teaching in his native land. Becoming suspicious that a school of this kind was maintained at the home of De Baptiste, the police watched the place but failed to find sufficient evidence to close the institution before it had done its work.[63]

In 1854 there was found in Norfolk, Virginia, what the radically proslavery people considered a dangerous white woman. It was discovered that one Mrs. Douglass and her daughter had for three years been teaching a school maintained for the education of Negroes.[64] It was evident that this institution had not been run so clandestinely but that the opposition to the education of Negroes in that city had probably been too weak to bring about the close of the school at an earlier date. Mrs. Douglass and her pupils were arrested and brought before the court, where she was charged with violating the laws of the State. The defendant acknowledged her guilt, but, pleading ignorance of the law, was discharged on the condition that she would not commit the same "crime" again. Censuring the court for this liberal decision the Richmond Examiner referred to it as offering "a very convenient way of getting out of the scrape." The editor emphasized the fact that the law of Virginia imposed on such offenders the penalty of one hundred dollars fine and imprisonment for six months, and that its positive terms "allowed no discretion in the community magistrate."[65]

All such schools, however, were not secretly kept. Writing from Charleston in 1851 Fredrika Bremer made mention of two colored schools. One of these was a school for free Negroes kept with open doors by a white master. Their books which she examined were the same as those used in American schools for white children.[66] The Negroes of Lexington, Kentucky, had in 1830 a school in which thirty colored children were taught by a white man from Tennessee. [67] This gentleman had pledged himself to devote the rest of his life to the uplift of his "black brethren."[68] Travelers noted that colored schools were found also in Richmond, Maysville, Danville, and Louisville decades before the Civil

War.[69] William H. Gibson, a native of Baltimore, was after 1847 teaching at Louisville in a day and night school with an enrollment of one hundred pupils, many of whom were slaves with written permits from their masters to attend.[70] Some years later W.H. Stewart of that city attended the schools of Henry Adams, W.H. Gibson, and R.T.W. James. Robert Taylor began his studies there in Robert Lane's school and took writing from Henry Adams.[71] Negroes had schools in Tennessee also. R.L. Perry was during these years attending a school at Nashville.[72] An uncle of Dr. J.E. Moorland spent some time studying medicine in that city.

Many of these opportunities were made possible by the desire to teach slaves religion. In fact the instruction of Negroes after the enactment of prohibitory laws resembled somewhat the teaching of religion with letters during the seventeenth and eighteenth centuries. Thousands of Negroes like Edward Patterson and Nat Turner learned to read and write in Sabbath-schools. White men who diffused such information ran the gauntlet of mobs, but like a Baptist preacher of South Carolina who was threatened with expulsion from his church, if he did not desist, they worked on and overcame the local prejudice. When preachers themselves dared not undertake this task it was often done by their children, whose benevolent work was winked at as an indulgence to the clerical profession. This charity, however, was not restricted to the narrow circle of the clergy. Believing with churchmen that the Bible is the revelation of God, many laymen contended that no man should be restrained from knowing his Maker directly.[73] Negroes, therefore, almost worshiped the Bible, and their anxiety to read it was their greatest incentive to learn. Many southerners braved the terrors of public opinion and taught their Negroes to read the Scriptures. To this extent General Coxe of Fluvanna County, Virginia, taught about one hundred of his adult slaves.[74] While serving as a professor of the Military Institute at Lexington, Stonewall Jackson taught a class of Negroes in a Sunday-school.[75]

Further interest in the cause was shown by the Evangelical Society of the Synods of North Carolina and Virginia in 1834.[76] Later Presbyterians of Alabama and Georgia urged masters to enlighten their slaves.[77] The attitude of many mountaineers of Kentucky was well set forth in the address of the Synod of 1836, proposing a plan for the instruction and emancipation of the slaves.[78] They complained that throughout the land, so far as they could learn, there was but one school in which slaves could be taught during the week. The light of three or four Sabbath-schools was seen "glittering through the darkness" of the black population of the whole State. Here and there one found a family where humanity impelled the master, mistress, or children, to the laborious task of private instruction. In consequence of these undesirable conditions the Synod recommended that "slaves be instructed in the common elementary branches of education."[79]

Some of the objects of such charity turned out to be interesting characters. Samuel Lowry of Tennessee worked and studied privately under Rev. Mr. Talbot of Franklin College, and at the age of sixteen was sufficiently advanced to teach with success. He united with the Church of the Disciples and preached in that connection until 1859.[80] In some cases colored preachers were judged sufficiently informed, not only to minister to the needs of their own congregations, but to preach to white churches. There was a Negro thus engaged in the State of Florida.[81] Another colored man of unusual intelligence and much prominence worked his way to the front in Giles County, Tennessee. In 1859 he was the pastor of a Hard-shell Baptist Church, the membership of which was composed of the best white people in the community. He was so well prepared for his work that out of a four days' argument on baptism with a white minister he emerged victor. From this appreciative congregation he received a salary of from six to seven hundred dollars a year.[82]

Statistics of this period show that the proportionately largest number of Negroes who learned in spite of opposition were found among the Scotch-Irish of Kentucky and Tennessee. Possessing few slaves, and having no permanent attachment to the institution, those mountaineers did not yield to the reactionaries who were determined to keep the Negroes in heathendom. Kentucky and Tennessee did not expressly forbid the education of the colored people.[83] Conditions were probably better in Kentucky than in Tennessee. Traveling in Kentucky about this time, Abdy was favorably impressed with that class of Negroes who though originally slaves saved sufficient from their earnings to purchase their freedom and provide for the education of their children.[84]

[83: In 1830 one-twelfth of the population of Lexington consisted of free persons of color, who since 1822 had had a Baptist church served by a member of their own race and a school in which thirty-two of their children were taught by a white man from Tennessee. He had pledged himself to devote the rest of his life to the uplift of his colored brethren. One of these free Negroes in Lexington had accumulated wealth to the amount of $20,000. In Louisville, also a center of free colored population, efforts were being made to educate ambitious Negroes. Travelers noted that colored schools were found there generations before the Civil War and mentioned the intelligent and properly speaking colored preachers, who were bought and supported by their congregations. Charles Dabney, another traveler through this State in 1837, observed that the slaves of this commonwealth were taught to read and believed that they were about as well off as they would have been had they been free. See Dabney, Journal of a Tour through the U.S. and Canada, p. 185.]

It was the desire to train up white men to carry on the work of their liberal fathers that led John G. Fee and his colaborers to establish Berea College in Kentucky. In the charter of this institution was incorporated the declaration that "God has made of one blood all nations that dwell upon the face of the earth." No Negroes were admitted to this institution before the Civil War, but they came in soon thereafter, some being accepted while returning home wearing their uniforms.[85] The State has since prohibited the co-education of the two races.

The centers of this interest in the mountains of Tennessee were Maryville and Knoxville. Around these towns were found a goodly number of white persons interested in the elevation of the colored people. There developed such an antislavery sentiment in the former town that half of the students of the Maryville Theological Seminary became abolitionists by 1841.[86] They were then advocating the social uplift of Negroes through the local organ, the Maryville Intelligencer. From this nucleus of antislavery men developed a community with ideals not unlike those of Berea.[2]

The Knoxville people who advocated the enlightenment of the Negroes expressed their sentiment through the Presbyterian Witness. The editor felt that there was not a solitary argument that might be urged in favor of teaching a white man that might not as properly be urged in favor of enlightening a man of color. "If one has a soul that will never die," said he, "so has the other. Has one susceptibilities of improvement, mentally, socially, and morally? So has the other. Is one bound by the laws of God to improve the talents he has received from the Creator's hands? So is the other. Is one embraced in the command 'Search the Scriptures'? So is the other."[87] He maintained that unless masters could lawfully degrade their slaves to the condition of beasts, they were just as much bound to teach them to read the Bible as to teach any other class of their population.

But great as was the interest of the religious element, the movement for the education of the Negroes of the South did not again become a scheme merely for bringing them into the church. Masters had more than one reason for favoring the enlightenment of the slaves. Georgia slaveholders of the more liberal class came forward about the middle of the nineteenth century, advocating the education of Negroes as a means to increase their economic value, and to attach them to their masters. This subject was taken up in the Agricultural Convention at Macon in 1850, and was discussed again in a similar assembly the following year. After some opposition the Convention passed a resolution calling on the legislature to enact a law authorizing the education of slaves. The petition was presented by Mr. Harlston, who introduced the bill embodying this idea, piloted it through the lower house, but failed by two or three votes to secure the sanction of the senate.[88] In 1855 certain influential citizens of North Carolina[89] memorialized their legislature asking among other things that the slaves be taught to read. This petition provoked some discussion, but did not receive as much attention as that of Georgia.

In view of this renewed interest in the education of the Negroes of the South we are anxious to know exactly what proportion of the colored population had risen above the plane of illiteracy. Unfortunately this cannot be accurately determined. In the first place, it was difficult to find out whether or not a slave could read or write when such a disclosure would often cause him to be dreadfully punished or sold to some cruel master of the lower South. Moreover, statistics of this kind are scarce and travelers who undertook to answer this question made conflicting statements. Some persons of that day left records which indicate that only a few slaves succeeded in acquiring an imperfect knowledge of the common branches, whereas others noted a larger number of intelligent servants. Arfwedson remarked that the slaves seldom learned to read; yet elsewhere he stated that he sometimes found some who had that ability.[90] Abolitionists like May, Jay, and Garrison would make it seem that the conditions in the South were such that it was almost impossible for a slave to develop intellectual power.[91] Rev. C.C. Jones[92] believed that only an inconsiderable fraction of the slaves could read. Witnesses to the contrary, however, are numerous. Abdy, Smedes, Andrews, Bremer, and Olmsted found during their stay in the South many slaves who had experienced unusual spiritual and mental development.[93] Nehemiah Adams, giving the southern view of slavery in 1854, said that large numbers of the slaves could read and were furnished with the Scriptures.[94] Amos Dresser, who traveled extensively in the Southwest, believed that one out of every fifty could read and write.[95] C.G. Parsons thought that five thousand out of the four hundred thousand slaves of Georgia had these attainments.[96] These figures, of course, would run much higher were the free people of color included in the estimates. Combining the two it is safe to say that ten per cent. of the adult Negroes had the rudiments of education in 1860, but the proportion was much less than it was near the close of the era of better beginnings about 1825.

[1: Mott, Biographical Sketches, p. 87.]
[2: Redpath, Roving Editor, etc., p. 161.]
[3: Parsons, Inside View, etc., p. 248.]
[4: Burke, Reminiscences of Georgia, p. 85.]
[5: Simmons, Men of Mark, p. 126.]
[6: Drew, Refugee, p. 152.]
[7: Niles Register, vol. lxxi., p. 296.]
[8: Drew, Refugee, etc., p. 72.]
[9: Ibid., p. 110.]
[10: Simmons, Men of Mark, p. 679.]
[11: Ibid., p. 873.]
[12: Ibid., p. 368.]
[13: This is his own statement.]
[14: This is based on an account given by his son.]
[15: The Crisis, vol. v., p. 119.]
[16: Drew, Refugee, p. 143.]
[17: Simmons, Men of Mark, p. 539.]
[18: Burke, Reminiscences of Georgia, p. 86. Frances Anne Kemble gives in her journal an interesting account of her observations in Georgia. She says: "I must tell you that I have been delighted, surprised, and the very least perplexed, by the sudden petition on the part of our young waiter, Aleck, that I will teach him to read. He is a very intelligent lad of about sixteen, and preferred his request with urgent humility that was very touching. I will do it; and yet, it is simply breaking the laws of the government under which I am living. Unrighteous laws are made to be broken--perhaps--but then you see, I am a woman, and Mr.---- stands between me and the penalty--. I certainly intend to teach Aleck to read; and I'll teach every other creature that wants to learn." See Kemble, Journal, p. 34.]
[19: McDonogh, "Letter on African Colonization."]
[20: Olmsted, Cotton Kingdom, vol. ii., p. 70.]
[21: Special Report of the U.S. Com. of Ed., 1871, p. 258.]
[22: This is based on the statements of Judge and Mrs. Terrell.]
[23: Drew, Refugee, p. 335.]
[24: Ibid., p. 96.]
[25: Simmons, Men of Mark, p. 933.]
[26: Drew, Refugee, p. 180.]
[27: Simmons, Men of Mark, p. 410.]
[28: Bishop Turner says that when he started to learn there were among his acquaintances three colored men who had learned to read the Bible in Charleston. See Simmons, Men of Mark, p. 806.]
[29: Ibid., p. 806.]
[30: Drew, Refugee, p. 97.]
[31: Ibid., p. 45.]
[32: Ibid., p. 185.]
[33: Snowden, Autobiography, p. 23.]
[37: Albert, The House of Bondage, p. 125.]
[35: Birney, The Grimke Sisters, p. 11.]
[36: Simmons, Men of Mark, p. 613.]
[37: This fact is stated in one of her letters.]

[38: Abdy, Journal of a Residence and Tour in U.S.A., 1833-1834. P. 346.]
[39: Smedes, A Southern Planter, pp. 79-80.]
[40: Ibid., p. 80.]
[41: Drew, A North-Side View of Slavery, p. 373.]
[42: Ibid., p. 133.]
[43: Ibid., p. 123.]
[44: Lee, Slave Life in Virginia and Kentucky, p. x.]
[45: Simmons, Men of Mark, p. 368.]
[46: This is his own statement.]
[47: Parsons, Inside View, etc., p. 248.]
[48: Drew, Refugee, p. 99.]
[49: Simmons, Men of Mark, p. 406.]
[50: Ibid., p. 432.]
[51: Ibid., p. 469]
[52: Ibid., p. 708.]
[53: Ibid., 930.]
[54: Drew, Refugee, p. 114.]
[55: Simmons, Men of Mark, 428]
[56: Ibid., p. 162]
[57: Ibid., p. 1052]
[58: This is their own statement.]
[59: Bremer, The Homes of the New World, vol. ii., p. 499.]
[60: Ibid., p. 491; Burke, Reminiscences of Georgia, p. 85.]
[61: Kemble, Journal, etc., p. 34.]
[62: Special Report of the U.S. Com. of Ed., 1871, p. 340.]
[63: Simmons, Men of Mark, p. 352.]
[64: Parsons, Inside View of Slavery, p. 251; and Lyman, Leaven for Doughfaces, p. 43.]
[65: 13th Annual Report of the American and Foreign Antislavery Societies, 1853, p. 143.]
[66: Bremer, The Homes of the New World, vol. ii., p. 499.]
[67: Abdy, Journal of a Residence and Tour in U.S.A., 1833-34, p. 346.]
[68: Ibid., pp. 346-348.]
[69: Tower, Slavery Unmasked; Dabney, Journal of a Tour through the U.S. and Canada, p. 185; Niles Register, vol. lxxii., p. 322; and Simmons, Men of Mark, p. 631.]
[70: Simmons, Men of Mark, p. 603.]
[71: Simmons, Men of Mark, p. 629.]
[72: Ibid., p. 620.]
[73: Orr, "An Address on the Need of Education in the South, 1879."]
[74: This statement is made by several of General Coxe's slaves who are still living.]
[75: School Journal, vol. lxxx., p. 332.]
[76: African Repository, vol. x., pp. 174, 205, and 245.]
[77: Ibid., vol. xi., pp. 140 and 268.]
[78: Goodell, Slave Code, pp. 323-324.]
[79: The Enormity of the Slave Trade, etc., p. 74.]
[80: Simmons, Men of Mark, p. 144.]
[81: Bremer, Homes of the New World, vol. ii., pp. 488-491.]

[82: The Richmond Enquirer, July, 1859; and Afr. Repository, vol. xxxv., p. 255.]

[84: Abdy, Journal of a Tour, etc., 1833-1834, pp. 346-348.]

[85: Catalogue of Berea College, 1896-1897.]

[86: Some of the liberal-mindedness of the people of Kentucky and Tennessee was found in the State of Missouri. The question of slavery there, however, was so ardently discussed and prominently kept before the people that while little was done to help the Negroes, much was done to reduce them to the plane of beasts. There was not so much of the tendency to wink at the violation of the law on the part of masters in teaching their slaves. But little could be accomplished by private teachers in the dissemination of information among Negroes after the free persons of color had been excluded from the State. Fourth Annual Report of the American Antislavery Society, New York, 1837, p. 48; and the New England Antislavery Almanac for 1841, p. 31.]

[87: African Repository, vol. xxxii., p. 16.]

[88: Special Report of the U.S. Com. of Ed., p. 339]

[89: African Repository, vol. xxxi., pp. 117-118.]

[90: Arfwedson, The United States and Canada, p. 331.]

[91: See their pamphlets, addresses, and books referred to elsewhere.]

[92: Jones, Religious Instruction of Negroes, p. 115.]

[93: Redpath, The Roving Editor, p. 161.]

[94: Adams, South-Side View of Slavery, pp. 52 and 59.]

[95: Dresser, The Narrative of Amos Dresser, p. 27; Dabney, Journal of a Tour through the United States and Canada, p. 185.]

[96: Parsons, Inside View of Slavery, p. 248.]

Chapter 10
Educating Negroes Transplanted to Free Soil

While the Negroes of the South were struggling against odds to acquire knowledge, the more ambitious ones were for various reasons making their way to centers of light in the North. Many fugitive slaves dreaded being sold to planters of the lower South, the free blacks of some of the commonwealths were forced out by hostile legislation, and not a few others migrated to ameliorate their condition. The transplanting of these people to the Northwest took place largely between 1815 and 1850. They were directed mainly to Columbia and Philadelphia, Pennsylvania; Greenwich, New Jersey; and Boston, Massachusetts, in the East; and to favorable towns and colored communities in the Northwest. [1] The fugitives found ready helpers in Elmira, Rochester, Buffalo, New York; Pittsburgh, Pennsylvania; Gallipolis, Portsmouth, Akron, and Cincinnati, Ohio; and Detroit, Michigan.[2] Colored settlements which proved attractive to these wanderers had been established in Ohio, Indiana, and Canada. That most of the bondmen in quest of freedom and opportunity should seek the Northwest had long been the opinion of those actually interested in their enlightenment. The attention of the colored people had been early directed to this section as a more suitable place for their elevation than the jungles of Africa selected by the American Colonization Society. The advocates of Western colonization believed that a race thus degraded could be elevated only in a salubrious climate under the influences of institutions developed by Western nations.

The role played by the Negroes in this migration exhibited the development of sufficient mental ability to appreciate this truth. It was chiefly through their intelligent fellows that prior to the reaction ambitious slaves learned to consider the Northwest Territory the land of opportunity. Furthermore, restless freedmen, denied political privileges and prohibited from teaching their children, did not always choose to go to Africa. Many of them went north of the Ohio River and took up land on the public domain. Observing this longing for opportunity, benevolent southerners, who saw themselves hindered in carrying out their plan for educating the blacks for citizenship, disposed of their holdings and formed free colonies of their slaves in the same section. White men of this type thus made possible a new era of uplift for the colored race by coming north in time to aid the abolitionists, who had for years constituted a small minority advocating a seemingly hopeless cause.

A detailed description of these settlements has no place in this dissertation save as it has a bearing on the development of education among the colored people. These settlements, however, are important here in that they furnish the key to the location of many of the early colored churches and schools of the North and West. Philanthropists established a number of Negroes near Sandy Lake in Northwestern Pennsylvania.[3] There was a colored settlement near Berlin Crossroads, Ohio.[4] Another group of pioneering Negroes emigrating to this State found homes in the Van Buren township of Shelby County.

The Education of the Negro

Edward Coles, a Virginian, who in 1818 emigrated to Illinois, of which he later became Governor, made a settlement on a larger scale. He brought his slaves to Edwardsville, where they constituted a community known as "Coles' Negroes."[5] The settlement made by Samuel Gist, an Englishman possessing extensive plantations in Hanover, Amherst, and Henrico Counties, Virginia, was still more significant. He provided in his will that his slaves should be freed and sent to the North. It was further directed "that the revenue from his plantation the last year of his life be applied in building schoolhouses and churches for their accommodation," and "that all money coming to him in Virginia be set aside for the employment of ministers and teachers to instruct them."[6] In 1818, Wickham, the executor of this estate, purchased land and established these Negroes in what was called the Upper and Lower Camps of Brown County, Ohio.

Augustus Wattles, a native of Connecticut, made a settlement of Negroes in Mercer County early in the nineteenth century.[7] About the year 1834 many of the freedmen, then concentrating at Cincinnati, were induced to take up 30,000 acres of land in the same vicinity.[8] John Harper of North Carolina manumitted his slaves in 1850 and had them sent to this community.[9] John Randolph of Roanoke freed his slaves at his death, and provided for the purchase of farms for them in Mercer County.[10] The Germans, however, would not allow them to take possession of these lands. Driven later from Shelby County[11] also, these freedmen finally found homes in Miami County.[12] Then there was one Saunders, a slaveholder of Cabell County, now West Virginia, who liberated his slaves and furnished them homes in free territory. They finally made their way to Cass County, Michigan, where philanthropists had established a prosperous colored settlement and supplied it with missionaries and teachers. The slaves of Theodoric H. Gregg of Dinwiddie County, Virginia, were liberated in 1854 and sent to Ohio,[13] where some of them were educated.

Many free persons of color of Virginia and Kentucky went north about the middle of the nineteenth century. The immediate cause in Virginia was the enactment in 1838 of a law prohibiting the return of such colored students as had been accustomed to go north to attend school after they were denied this privilege in that State.[14] Prominent among these seekers of better opportunities were the parents of Richard De Baptiste. His father was a popular mechanic of Fredericksburg, where he for years maintained a secret school.[15] A public opinion proscribing the teaching of Negroes was then rendering the effort to enlighten them as unpopular in Kentucky as it was in Virginia. Thanks to a benevolent Kentuckian, however, an important colored settlement near Xenia, Greene County, Ohio, was then taking shape. The nucleus of this group was furnished about 1856 by Noah Spears, who secured small farms there for sixteen of his former bondmen.[16] The settlement was not only sought by fugitive slaves and free Negroes, but was selected as the site for Wilberforce University.[17]

During the same period, and especially from 1820 to 1835, a more continuous and effective migration of southern Negroes was being promoted by the Quakers of Virginia and North Carolina.[18] One of their purposes was educational. Convinced that the "buying, selling, and holding of men in slavery" is a sin, these Quakers with a view to future manumission had been "careful of the moral and intellectual training of such as they held in servitude."[19] To elevate their slaves to the plane of men, southern Quakers early hit upon the scheme of establishing in the Northwest such Negroes as they had by education been able to equip for living as citizens. When the reaction in the South made it impossible for the Quakers to continue their policy of enlightening the colored people, these philanthropists promoted the migration of the blacks to the Northwest Territory with still greater zeal. Most of these settlements were made in Hamilton, Howard, Wayne, Randolph, Vigo, Gibson, Grant, Rush, and Tipton Counties, Indiana, and in Darke County, Ohio.[20] Prominent among these promoters was Levi Coffin, the Quaker Abolitionist of North Carolina, and reputed President of the Underground Railroad. He left his State and settled among Negroes at Newport, Indiana.[21] Associated with these leaders also were Benjamin Lundy of Tennessee and James G. Birney, once a slaveholder of Huntsville, Alabama. The latter manumitted his slaves and apprenticed and educated some of them in Ohio.[22]

The importance of this movement to the student of education lies in the fact that it effected an unequal distribution of intelligent Negroes. The most ambitious and enlightened ones were fleeing to free territory. As late as 1840 there were more intelligent blacks in the South than in the North.[23] The number of southern colored people who could read was then decidedly larger than that of such persons found in the free States. The continued migration of Negroes to the North, despite the operation of the Fugitive Slave Law of 1850, made this distribution more unequal. While the free colored population of the slave States increased only 23,736 from 1850 to 1860, that of the free States increased 29,839. In the South only Delaware, Georgia, Maryland, and North Carolina showed a noticeable increase in the number of free persons of color during the decade immediately preceding the Civil War. This element of the population had only slightly increased in Alabama, Kentucky, Missouri, Tennessee, Virginia, Louisiana, South Carolina, and the District of Columbia. The number of free Negroes of Florida remained practically constant. Those of Arkansas, Mississippi, and Texas diminished. In the North, of course, the tendency was in the other direction. With the exception of Maine, New Hampshire, Vermont, and New York, which had about the same free colored population in 1860 as they had in 1850, there was a general increase in the number of Negroes in the free States. Ohio led in this respect having had during this period an increase of 11,394.[24]

On comparing the educational statistics of these sections this truth becomes more apparent. In 1850 there were 4,354 colored children attending school in the South, but by 1860 this number had dropped to 3,651. Slight increases were noted only in Alabama, Missouri, Delaware, South Carolina, and the District of Columbia. Georgia and Mississippi had then practically deprived all Negroes of this privilege. The former, which reported one colored child as attending school in 1850, had just seven in 1860; the latter had none in 1850 and only two in 1860. In all other slave States the number of pupils of African blood had materially decreased.[25] In the free States there were 22,107 colored children in school in 1850, and 28,978 in 1860. Most of these were in New Jersey, Ohio, New York, and Pennsylvania, which in 1860 had 2,741; 5,671; 5,694; and 7,573, respectively.[26]

The report on illiteracy shows further the differences resulting from the divergent educational policies of the two sections. In 1850 there were in the slave States 58,444 adult free Negroes who could not read, and in 1860 this number had reached 59,832. In all such commonwealths except Arkansas, Louisiana, Florida, and Mississippi there was an increase in illiteracy among the free blacks. These States, however, were hardly exceptional, because Arkansas and Mississippi had suffered a decrease in their free colored population, that of Florida had remained the same, and the difference in the case of Louisiana was very slight. The statistics of the Northern States indicate just the opposite trend. Notwithstanding the increase of persons of color resulting from the influx of the migrating element, there was in all free States exclusive of California, Illinois, Minnesota, Michigan, Ohio, and Pennsylvania a decrease in the illiteracy of Negroes. But these States hardly constitute exceptions; for California, Wisconsin, and Minnesota had very few colored inhabitants in 1850, and the others had during this decade received so many fugitives in the rough that race prejudice and its concomitant drastic legislation impeded the educational progress of their transplanted freedmen.[27] In the Northern States where this condition did not obtain, the benevolent whites had, in cooeperation with the Negroes, done much to reduce illiteracy among them during these years.

How the problem of educating these people on free soil was solved can be understood only by keeping in mind the factors of the migration. Some of these Negroes had unusual capabilities. Many of them had in slavery either acquired the rudiments of education or developed sufficient skill to outwit the most determined pursuers. Owing so much to mental power, no man was more effective than the successful fugitive in instilling into the minds of his people the value of education. Not a few of this type readily added to their attainments to equip themselves for the best service. Some of them, like Reverend Josiah Henson, William Wells Brown, and Frederick Douglass, became leaders, devoting their time not only to the cause of abolition, but also to the enlightenment of the colored people. Moreover, the free Negroes migrating to the North were even more effective than the fugitive slaves in advancing the cause of education.[28] A larger number of the former had picked up useful knowledge. In fact, the prohibition of the education of the free people of color in the South was one of the reasons they could so readily leave their native homes.[29] The free blacks then going to the Northwest Territory proved to be decidedly helpful to their benefactors in providing colored churches and schools with educated workers, who otherwise would have been brought from the East at much expense.

On perusing this sketch the educator naturally wonders exactly what intellectual progress was made by these groups on free soil. This question cannot be fully answered for the reason that extant records give no detailed account of many colored settlements which underwent upheaval or failed to endure. In some cases we learn simply that a social center flourished and was then destroyed. On "Black Friday," January 1, 1830, eighty Negroes were driven out of Portsmouth, Ohio, at the request of one or two hundred white citizens, set forth in an urgent memorial.[30] After the passage of the Fugitive Slave Law of 1850 the colored population of Columbia, Pennsylvania, dropped from nine hundred and forty-three to four hundred and eighty-seven.[31] The Negro community in the northwestern part of that State was broken up entirely.[32] The African Methodist and Baptist churches of Buffalo lost many communicants. Out of a membership of one hundred and fourteen, the colored Baptist church of Rochester lost one hundred and twelve, including its pastor. About the same time eighty-four members of the African Baptist church of Detroit crossed into Canada.[33] The break-up of these churches meant the end of the day and Sunday-schools which were maintained in them. Moreover, the migration of these Negroes aroused such bitter feeling against them that their schoolhouses were frequently burned. It often seemed that it was just as unpopular to educate the blacks in the North as in the South. Ohio, Illinois, and Oregon enacted laws to prevent them from coming into those commonwealths.

We have, however, sufficient evidence of large undertakings to educate the colored people then finding homes in less turbulent parts beyond the Ohio. In the first place, almost every settlement made by the Quakers was a center to which Negroes repaired for enlightenment. In other groups where there was no such opportunity, they had the cooeperation of certain philanthropists in providing facilities for their mental and moral development. As a result, the free blacks had access to schools and churches in Hamilton, Howard, Randolph, Vigo, Gibson, Rush, Tipton, Grant, and Wayne counties, Indiana,[34] and Madison, Monroe, and St. Clair counties, Illinois. There were colored schools and churches in Logan, Clark, Columbiana, Guernsey, Jefferson, Highland, Brown, Darke, Shelby, Green, Miami, Warren, Scioto, Gallia, Ross, and Muskingum counties, Ohio.[35] Augustus Wattles said that with the assistance of abolitionists he organized twenty-five such schools in Ohio counties after 1833.[36] Brown County alone had six. Not many years later a Negro settlement in Gallia County, Ohio, was paying a teacher fifty dollars a quarter.[37]

Still better colored schools were established in Pittsburgh, Pennsylvania, and in Springfield, Columbus, and Cincinnati, Ohio. While the enlightenment of the few Negroes in Pittsburgh did not require the systematic efforts put forth to elevate the race elsewhere, much was done to provide them educational facilities in that city. Children of color first attended the white schools there just as they did throughout the State of Pennsylvania.[38] But when larger numbers of them collected in this gateway to the Northwest, either race feeling or the pressing needs of the migrating freedmen brought about the establishment of schools especially adapted to their instruction. Such efforts were frequent after 1830.[39] John Thomas Johnson, a teacher of the District of Columbia, moved to Pittsburgh in 1838 and became an instructor in a colored school of that city.[40] Cleveland had an "African School" as early as 1832. John Malvin, the moving spirit of the enterprise in that city, organized about that time "The School Fund Society" which established other colored schools in Cincinnati, Columbus, and Springfield.[41]

The concentration of the freedmen and fugitives at Cincinnati was followed by efforts to train them for higher service. The Negroes themselves endeavored to provide their own educational facilities in opening in 1820 the first colored school in that city. This school did not continue long, but another was established the same year. Thereafter one Mr. Wing, who kept a private institution, admitted persons of color to his evening classes. On account of a lack of means, however, the Negroes of Cincinnati did not receive any systematic instruction before 1834. After that year the tide turned in favor of the free blacks of that section, bringing to their assistance a number of daring abolitionists, who helped them to educate themselves. Friends of the race, consisting largely of the students of Lane Seminary, had then organized colored Sunday and evening schools, and provided for them scientific and literary lectures twice a week. There was a permanent colored school in Cincinnati in 1834. In 1835 the Negroes of that city contributed $150 of the $1000 expended for their education. Four years later, however, they raised $889.03 for this purpose, and thanks to their economic progress, this sacrifice was less taxing than that of 1835.[42] In 1844 Rev. Hiram Gilmore opened there a high school which among other students attracted P.B.S. Pinchback, later Governor of Louisiana. Mary E. Miles, a graduate of the Normal School at Albany, New York, served as an assistant of Gilmore after having worked among her people in Massachusetts and Pennsylvania.[43]

The educational advantages given these people were in no sense despised. Although the Negroes of the Northwest did not always keep pace with their neighbors in things industrial they did not permit the white people to outstrip them much in education. The freedmen so earnestly seized their opportunity to acquire knowledge and accomplished so much in a short period that their educational progress served to disabuse the minds of indifferent whites of the idea that the blacks were not capable of high mental development.[44] The educational work of these centers, too, tended not only to produce men capable of ministering to the needs of their environment, but to serve as a training center for those who would later be leaders of their people. Lewis Woodson owed it to friends in Pittsburgh that he became an influential teacher. Jeremiah H. Brown, T. Morris Chester, James T. Bradford, M.R. Delany, and Bishop Benjamin T. Tanner obtained much of their elementary education in the early colored schools of that city.[45] J.C. Corbin, a prominent educator before and after the Civil War, acquired sufficient knowledge at Chillicothe, Ohio, to qualify in 1848 as an assistant in Rev. Henry Adams's school in Louisville.[46] John M. Langston was for a while one of Corbin's fellow-students at Chillicothe before the former entered Oberlin. United States Senator Hiram Revels of Mississippi spent some time in a Quaker seminary in Union County, Indiana.[47] Rev. J.T. White, one of the leading spirits of Arkansas during the Reconstruction, was born and educated in Clark County in that State.[48] Fannie Richards, still a teacher at Detroit, Michigan, is another example of the professional Negro equipped for service in the Northwest before the Rebellion.[49] From other communities of that section came such useful men as Rev. J.W. Malone, an influential minister of Iowa; Rev. D.R. Roberts, a very successful pastor of Chicago; Bishop C.T. Shaffer of the African Methodist Episcopal Church; Rev. John G. Mitchell, for many years the Dean of the Theological Department of Wilberforce University; and President S.T. Mitchell, once the head of the same institution.[50]

In the colored settlements of Canada the outlook for Negro education was still brighter. This better opportunity was due to the high character of the colonists, to the mutual aid resulting from the proximity of the communities, and to the cooeperation of the Canadians. The previous experience of most of these adventurers as sojourners in the free States developed in them such noble traits that they did not have to be induced to ameliorate their condition. They had already come under educative influences which prepared them for a larger task in Canada. Fifteen thousand of sixty thousand Negroes in Canada in 1860 were free born.[51] Many of those, who had always been free, fled to Canada[52] when the Fugitive Slave Law of 1850 made it possible for even a dark-complexioned Caucasian to be reduced to a state of bondage. Fortunately, too, these people settled in the same section. The colored settlements at Dawn, Colchester, Elgin, Dresden, Windsor, Sandwich, Queens, Bush, Wilberforce, Hamilton, St. Catherines, Chatham, Riley, Anderton, Maiden, Gonfield, were all in Southern Ontario. In the course of time the growth of these groups produced a population sufficiently dense to facilitate cooeperation in matters pertaining to social betterment. The uplift of the refugees was made less difficult also by the self-denying white persons who were their first teachers and missionaries. While the hardships incident to this pioneer effort all but baffled the ardent apostle to the lowly, he found among the Canadian whites so much more sympathy than among the northerners that his work was more agreeable and more successful than it would have been in the free States. Ignoring the request that the refugees be turned from Canada as undesirables, the white people of that country protected and assisted them.[53] Canadians later underwent some change in their attitude toward their newcomers, but these British-Americans never exhibited such militant opposition to the Negroes as sometimes developed in the Northern States.[54]

The educational privileges which the refugees hoped to enjoy in Canada, however, were not easily exercised. Under the Canadian law they could send their children to the common schools, or use their proportionate share of the school funds in providing other educational facilities.[55] But conditions there did not at first redound to the education of the colored children.[56] Some were too destitute to avail themselves of these opportunities; others, unaccustomed to this equality of fortune, were timid about having their children mingle with those of the whites, and not a few clad their youths so poorly that they became too unhealthy to attend regularly[57]. Besides, race prejudice was not long in making itself the most disturbing factor. In 1852 Benjamin Drew found the minds of the people of Sandwich much exercised over the question of admitting Negroes into the public schools. The same feeling was then almost as strong in Chatham, Hamilton, and London[58]. Consequently, "partly owing to this prejudice, and partly to their own preference, the colored people, acting under the provision of the law that allowed them to have separate schools, set up their own schools in Sandwich and in many other parts of Ontario"[59]. There were separate schools at Colchester, Amherstburg, Sandwich, Dawn, and Buxton[60]. It was doubtless because of the rude behavior of white pupils toward the children of the blacks that their private schools flourished at London, Windsor, and other places[61]. The Negroes, themselves, however, did not object to the coeducation of the races. Where there were a few white children in colored settlements they were admitted to schools maintained especially for pupils of African descent.[62] In Toronto no distinction in educational privileges was made, but in later years there flourished an evening school for adults of color.[63]

The most helpful schools, however, were not those maintained by the state. Travelers in Canada found the colored mission schools with a larger attendance and doing better work than those maintained at public expense.[64] The rise of the mission schools was due to the effort to "furnish the conditions under which whatever appreciation of education there was native in a community of Negroes, or whatever taste for it could be awakened there," might be "free to assert itself unhindered by real or imagined opposition."[65] There were no such schools in 1830, but by 1838 philanthropists had established the first mission among the Canadian refugees.[66] The English Colonial Church and School Society organized schools at London, Amherstburg, and Colchester. Certain religious organizations of the United States sent ten or more teachers to these settlements.[67] In 1839 these workers were conducting four schools while Rev. Hiram Wilson, their inspector, probably had several other institutions under his supervision.[68] In 1844 Levi Coffin found a large school at Isaac Rice's mission at Fort Maiden or Amherstburg.[69] Rice had toiled among these people six years, receiving very little financial aid, and suffering unusual hardships.[70] Mr. E. Child, a graduate of Oneida Institute, was later added to the corps of mission teachers.[71] In 1852 Mrs. Laura S. Haviland was secured to teach the

The Education of the Negro

school of the colony of "Refugees' Home," where the colored people had built a structure "for school and meeting purposes."[72] On Sundays the schoolhouses and churches were crowded by eager seekers, many of whom lived miles away. Among these earnest students a traveler saw an aged couple more than eighty years old.[73] These elementary schools broke the way for a higher institution at Dawn, known as the Manual Labor Institute.

With these immigrants, however, this was not a mere passive participation in the work of their amelioration. From the very beginning the colored people partly supported their schools. Without the cooeperation of the refugees the large private schools at London, Chatham, and Windsor could not have succeeded. The school at Chatham was conducted by Alfred Whipper,[74] a colored man, that at Windsor by Mary E. Bibb, the wife of Henry Bibb,[75] the founder of the Refugees' Home Settlement, and that at Sandwich by Mary Ann Shadd, of Delaware.[76] Moreover, the majority of these colonists showed increasing interest in this work of social uplift.[77] Foregoing their economic opportunities many of the refugees congregated in towns of educational facilities. A large number of them left their first abodes to settle near Dresden and Dawn because of the advantages offered by the Manual Labor Institute. Besides, the Negroes organized "True Bands" which effected among other things the improvement of schools and the increase of their attendance [78].

The good results of these schools were apparent. In the same degree that the denial to slaves of mental development tended to brutalize them the teaching of science and religion elevated the fugitives in Canada. In fact, the Negroes of these settlements soon had ideals differing widely from those of their brethren less favorably circumstanced. They believed in the establishment of homes, respected the sanctity of marriage, and exhibited in their daily life a moral sense of the highest order. Travelers found the majority of them neat, orderly, and intelligent[79]. Availing themselves of their opportunities, they quickly qualified as workers among their fellows. An observer reported in 1855 that a few were engaged in shop keeping or were employed as clerks, while a still smaller number devoted themselves to teaching and preaching.[80] Before 1860 the culture of these settlements was attracting the colored graduates of northern institutions which had begun to give men of African blood an opportunity to study in their professional schools.

[1: Siebert, The Underground Railroad, p. 32.]
[2: Ibid., pp. 32 and 37.]
[3: Siebert, The Underground Railroad, p. 249.]
[4: Langston, From the Virginia Plantation to the National Capitol, p. 35.]
[5: Davidson and Stuve, A Complete History of Illinois, pp. 321-322; and Washburne, Sketch of Edward Cole, Second Governor of Illinois, pp. 44 and 53.]
[6: History of Brown County, pp. 313 et seq.; and Lane, Fifty Years and over of Akron and Summit County, Ohio, pp. 579-580.]
[7: Howe, Ohio Historical Collections, p. 356.]
[8: Ibid., p. 356.]
[9: Manuscript in the hands of Dr. J.E. Moreland.]
[10: The African Repository, vol. xxii., pp. 322-323.]
[11: Howe, Ohio Historical Collections, p. 465.]
[12: Ibid., p. 466.]
[13: Simmons, Men of Mark, p. 723.]

Educating Negroes Transplanted to Free Soil

[14: Russell, The Free Negro in Virginia, Johns Hopkins University Studies, Series xxxi., No. 3, p. 492; and Acts of the General Assembly of Virginia, 1848, p. 117.]

[15: Simmons, Men of Mark, p. 352.]

[16: Wright, "Negro Rural Communities" (Southern Workman, vol. xxxvii., p. 158).]

[17: Special Report of the U.S. Com. of Ed., p. 373; and Non-Slaveholder, vol. ii., p. 113.]

[18: Wright, "Negro Rural Communities" (Southern Workman, vol. xxxvii., p. 158); and Bassett, Slavery in North Carolina, p. 68.]

[19: A Brief Statement of the Rise and Progress of the Testimony, etc.]

[20: Wright, "Rural Negro Communities in Indiana" (Southern Workman, vol. xxxvii., pp. 162-166); and Bassett, Slavery in North Carolina, pp. 67 and 68.]

[21: Coffin, Reminiscences, p. 106.]

[22: Birney, James G. Birney and His Times, p. 139.]

[23: Jones, Religious Instruction of the Negroes, p. 115.]

[24: See statistics on pages 237-240.]

[25: STATISTICS OF THE FREE COLORED POPULATION OF THE UNITED STATES IN 1850

	Population	ATTENDING SCHOOL			ADULTS UNABLE TO READ		
		Males	Females	Total	Males	Females	Total
Alabama	2,265	33	35	68	108	127	235
Arkansas	608	6	5	11	61	55	116
California	962	1	0	1	88	29	117
Connecticut	7,693	689	575	1,264	292	273	567
Delaware	18,073	92	95	187	2,724	2,921	5,645
Florida	932	29	37	66	116	154	270
Georgia	2,931	1	0	1	208	259	467
Illinois	5,436	162	161	323	605	624	1,229
Indiana	11,262	484	443	927	1,024	1,146	2,170
Iowa	333	12	5	17	15	18	33
Kentucky	10,011	128	160	288	1,431	1,588	3,029
Louisiana	17,462	629	590	1,219	1,038	2,351	3,389
Maine	1,356	144	137	281	77	58	135
Maryland	74,723	886	730	1,616	9,422	11,640	21,062
Massachusetts	9,064	726	713	1,439	375	431	806
Michigan	2,583	106	101	207	201	168	369
Mississippi	930	0	0	0	75	48	123
Missouri	2,618	23	17	40	271	226	497
New Hampshire	520	41	32	73	26	26	52
New Jersey	23,810	1,243	1,083	2,326	2,167	2,250	4,417
New York	49,069	2,840	2,607	5,447	3,387	4,042	7,429
North Carolina	27,463	113	104	217	3,099	3,758	6,857
Ohio	25,279	1,321	1,210	2,531	2,366	2,624	4,990
Pennsylvania	53,626	3,385	3,114	6,499	4,115	5,229	**9,344

[** was 6,344 in error.**]

The Education of the Negro

	Population	ATTENDING SCHOOL			ADULTS UNABLE TO READ		
		Males	Females	Total	Males	Females	Total
Rhode Island	3,670	304	247	551	130	137	267
South Carolina	8,960	54	26	80	421	459	880
Tennessee	6,422	40	30	70	506	591	1,097
Texas	397	11	9	20	34	24	58
Vermont	718	58	32	90	32	19	51
Virginia	54,333	37	27	64	5,141	6,374	11,515
Wisconsin	635	32	35	67	55	37	92
District of Col.	10,059	232	235	467	1,106	2,108	3,214
Minnesota	30	0	2	2	0	0	0
New Mexico	207	0	0	0	0	0	0
Oregon	24	2	0	2	3	2	5
Utah	22	0	0	0	1	0	1
Total	434,495	13,864	12,597	26,461	40,722	49,800	90,522

See Sixth Census of the United States, 1850.]

[26: See statistics on pages 237-240.]
[27: STATISTICS OF THE FREE COLORED POPULATION OF THE UNITED STATES IN 1860

	Population	ATTENDING SCHOOL			ADULTS UNABLE TO READ		
		Males	Females	Total	Males	Females	Total
Alabama	2,690	48	65	114	192	263	455
Arkansas	144	3	2	5	10	13	23
California	4,086	69	84	153	497	207	704
Connecticut	8,627	737	641	1,378	181	164	345
Delaware	19,829	122	128	250	3,056	3,452	6,508
Florida	932	3	6	9	48	72	120
Georgia	3,500	3	4	7	255	318	573
Illinois	7,628	264	347	611	632	695	1,327
Indiana	11,428	570	552	1,122	869	904	1,773
Iowa	1,069	77	61	138	92	77	169
Kansas	625	8	6	14	25	38	63
Kentucky	10,684	102	107	209	1,113	1,350	2,463
Louisiana	18,647	153	122	275	485	717	1,202
Maine	1,327	148	144	292	25	21	46
Maryland	83,942	687	668	1,355	9,904	11,795	21,699
Massachusetts	9,602	800	815	1,615	291	368	659
Michigan	6,797	555	550	1,105	558	486	1,044
Minnesota	259	8	10	18	6	6	12
Mississippi	773	0	2	2	50	60	110

Educating Negroes Transplanted to Free Soil

	Population	ATTENDING SCHOOL			ADULTS UNABLE TO READ		
		Males	Females	Total	Males	Females	Total
Missouri	3,572	76	79	155	371	514	885
New Hampshire	494	49	31	80	15	19	34
New Jersey	25,318	1,413	1,328	2,741	1,720	2,085	3,805
New York	49,005	2,955	2,739	5,694	2,653	3,260	5,913
North Carolina	30,463	75	58	133	3,067	3,782	6,849
Ohio	36,673	2,857	2,814	5,671	2,995	3,191	6,186
Oregon	128	0	0	2	7	5	12
Pennsylvania	56,949	3,882	3,691	7,573	3,893	5,466	9,359
Rhode Island	3,952	276	256	532	119	141	260
South Carolina	9,914	158	207	365	633	783	1,416
Tennessee	7,300	28	24	52	743	952	1,695
Texas	355	4	7	11	25	37	62
Vermont	709	65	50	115	27	20	47
Virginia	58,042	21	20	41	5,489	6,008	12,397
Wisconsin	1,171	62	50	112	53	45	98
TERRITORIES							
Colorado	46						
No returns Dakota	0	0	0	0	0	0	0
District Columbia	11,131	315	363	678	1,131	2,224	3,375
Nebraska	67	1	1	2	6	7	13
Nevada	45	0	0	0	6	1	7
New Mexico	85	0	0	0	12	15	27
Utah	30	0	0	0	0	0	0
Washington	30	0	0	0	1	0	1
Total	488,070	16,594	16,035	32,629	41,275	50,461	91,736

See Seventh Census of the United States, vol. 1.]
[28: Howe, The Refugee from Slavery, p. 77.]
[29: Russell, The Free Negro in Virginia (Johns Hopkins University Studies, series xxxi., No. 3, p. 107).]
[30: Evans, A History of Scioto County, Ohio, p. 613.]
[31: Siebert, The Underground Railroad, p. 249.]
[32: Ibid., p. 249.]
[33: Ibid., p. 250.]
[34: Wright, "Negro Rural Communities in Indiana," Southern Workman, vol. xxxvii., p. 165; Boone, The History of Education in Indiana, p. 237; and Simmons, Men of Mark, pp. 590 and 948.]
[35: Simmons, Men of Mark, p. 948; and Hickok, The Negro in Ohio, p. 85.]
[36: Howe, Historical Collections of Ohio, p. 355.]
[37: Hickok, The Negro in Ohio, p. 89.]
[38: Wickersham, Education in Pennsylvania, p. 248.]
[39: Life of Martin R. Delaney, p. 33.]
[40: Special Report of the U.S. Com. of Ed., 1871, p. 214.]

[41: Hickok, The Negro in Ohio, p. 88.]
[42: Ibid., p. 83.]
[43: Delany, The Condition of the Colored People, etc., 132.]
[44: This statement is based on the accounts of various western freedmen.]
[45: Simmons, Men of Mark, p. 113.]
[46: Simmons, Men of Mark, p. 829.]
[47: Ibid., p. 948.]
[48: Ibid., p. 590.]
[49: Ibid., p. 1023.]
[50: Wright, "Negro Rural Communities in Indiana," Southern Workman, vol. xxxvii., p. 169.]
[51: Siebert, The Underground Railroad, p. 222.]
[52: Ibid., pp. 247-250.]
[53: Siebert, The Underground Railroad, pp. 201 and 233.]
[54: Ibid., 233.]
[55: Howe, The Refugees from Slavery, p. 77.]
[56: Drew said: "The prejudice against the African race is here [Canada] strongly marked. It had not been customary to levy school taxes on the colored people. Some three or four years since a trustee assessed a school tax on some of the wealthy citizens of that class. They sent their children at once into the public school. As these sat down the white children near them deserted the benches: and in a day or two the white children were wholly withdrawn, leaving the schoolhouse to the teacher and his colored pupils. The matter was at last 'compromised': a notice 'Select School' was put on the schoolhouse: the white children were selected in and the black were selected out." See Drew's. A North-side View of Slavery, etc., p. 341.]
[57: Mitchell, The Underground Railroad, pp. 140, 164, and 165.]
[58: Drew, A North-side View of Slavery, pp. 118, 147, 235, and 342.]
[59: Ibid., p. 341.]
[60: Siebert, The Underground Railroad, p. 229.]
[61: Ibid., p. 229.]
[62: First Annual Report of the Anti-slavery Society of Canada, 1852, Appendix, p. 22.]
[63: Ibid., p. 15.]
[64: Drew, A North-side View of Slavery, pp. 118, 147, 235, 341, and 342.]
[65: Siebert, The Underground Railroad, p. 229.]
[66: Father Henson's Story of His Own Life, p. 209.]
[67: First Annual Report of the Anti-slavery Society of Canada, 1852, p. 22.]
[68: Siebert, The Underground Railroad, p. 199.]
[69: "While at this place we made our headquarters at Isaac J. Rice's missionary buildings, where he had a large school for colored children. He had labored here among the colored people, mostly fugitives, for six years. He was a devoted, self-denying worker, had received very little pecuniary help, and had suffered many privations. He was well situated in Ohio as pastor of a Presbyterian Church, and had fine prospects before him, but believed that the Lord called him to this field of missionary labor among the fugitive slaves, who came here by hundreds and by thousands, poor, destitute, ignorant, suffering from all the evil influences of slavery. We entered into deep sympathy with him and his labors, realizing the great need there was here for just such an institution as he had established. He had sheltered at his missionary home many hundred of

fugitives till other homes for them could be found. This was the great landing point, the principal terminus of the Underground Railroad of the West." See Coffin's Reminiscences, p. 251.]

[70: Ibid., pp. 249-251.]

[71: Siebert, The Underground Railroad, p. 202.]

[72: Haviland, A Woman's Work, pp. 192, 196, 201.]

[73: Haviland, A Woman's Work, pp. 192, 193.]

[74: Drew, A North-side View of Slavery, p. 236.]

[75: Ibid., p. 322.]

[76: Delany, The Condition of the Colored People, etc., 131.]

[77: Howe, The Refugees from Slavery, pp. 70, 71, 108, and 110.]

[78: According to Drew a True Band was composed of colored persons of both sexes, associated for their own improvement. "Its objects," says he, "are manifold: mainly these:--the members are to take a general interest in each other's welfare; to pursue such plans and objects as may be for their mutual advantage; to improve all schools, and to induce their race to send their children into the schools; to break down all prejudice; to bring all churches as far as possible into one body, and not let minor differences divide them; to prevent litigation by referring all disputes among themselves to a committee; to stop the begging system entirely (that is, going to the United States and thereby representing that the fugitives are starving and suffering, raising large sums of money, of which the fugitives never receive the benefit,--misrepresenting the character of the fugitives for industry and underrating the advance of the country, which supplies abundant work for all at fair wages); to raise such funds among themselves as may be necessary for the poor, the sick, and the destitute fugitive newly arrived; and prepare themselves ultimately to bear their due weight of political power." See Drew, A North-side View of Slavery, p. 236.]

[79: According to the report of the Freedmen's Inquiry Commission published by S.G. Howe, an unusually large proportion of the colored population believed in education. He says: "Those from the free States had very little schooling in youth; those from the slave States, none at all. Considering these things it is rather remarkable that so many can now read and write. Moreover, they show their esteem for instruction by their desire to obtain it for their children. They all wish to have their children go to school, and they send them all the time that they can be spared. "Canada West has adopted a good system of public instruction, which is well administered. The common schools, though inferior to those of several of the States of the United States, are good. Colored children are admitted to them in most places; and where a separate school is open for them, it is as well provided by the government with teachers and apparatus as the other schools are. Notwithstanding the growing prejudice against blacks, the authorities evidently mean to deal justly by them in regard to instruction; and even those who advocate separate schools, promise that they shall be equal to white schools. "The colored children in the mixed schools do not differ in their general appearance and behavior from their white comrades. They are usually clean and decently clad. They look quite as the whites; and are perhaps a little more mirthful and roguish. The association is manifestly beneficial to the colored children." See Howe, The Refugees, etc., p. 77.]

[80: Siebert, The Underground Railroad, p. 226.]

Chapter 11

Higher Education

The development of the schools and churches established for these transplanted freedmen made more necessary than ever a higher education to develop in them the power to work out their own salvation. It was again the day of thorough training for the Negroes. Their opportunities for better instruction were offered mainly by the colonizationists and abolitionists.[1] Although these workers had radically different views as to the manner of elevating the colored people, they contributed much to their mental development. The more liberal colonizationists endeavored to furnish free persons of color the facilities for higher education with the hope that their enlightenment would make them so discontented with this country that they would emigrate to Liberia. Most southern colonizationists accepted this plan but felt that those permanently attached to this country should be kept in ignorance; for if they were enlightened, they would either be freed or exterminated. During the period of reaction, when the elevation of the race was discouraged in the North and prohibited in most parts of the South, the colonizationists continued to secure to Negroes, desiring to expatriate themselves, opportunities for education which never would have been given those expecting to remain in the United States.[2]

The policy of promoters of African colonization, however, did not immediately become unprogressive. Their plan of education differed from previous efforts in that the objects of their philanthropy were to be given every opportunity for mental growth. The colonizationists had learned from experience in educating Negroes that it was necessary to begin with the youth.[3] These workers observed, too, that the exigencies of the time demanded more advanced and better endowed institutions to prepare colored men to instruct others in science and religion, and to fit them for "civil offices in Liberia and Hayti."[4] To execute this scheme the leaders of the colonization movement endeavored to educate Negroes in "mechanic arts, agriculture, science, and Biblical literature."[5] Exceptionally bright youths were to be given special training as catechists, teachers, preachers, and physicians.[6] A southern planter offered a plantation for the establishment of a suitable institution of learning,[7] a few masters sent their slaves to eastern schools to be educated, and men organized "education societies" in various parts to carry out this work at shorter range. In 1817 colonizationists opened at Pasippany, New Jersey, a school to give a four-year course to "African youth" who showed "talent, discretion, and piety" and were able to read and write.[8] Twelve years later another effort was made to establish a school of this kind at Newark in that State,[9] while other promoters of that faith were endeavoring to establish a similar institution at Hartford, Connecticut,[10] all hoping to make use of the Kosciuszko fund.[11]

The schemes failed, however, on account of the unyielding opposition of the free Negroes and abolitionists. They could see no philanthropy in educating persons to prepare for doom in a deadly climate. The convention of the free people of color assembled in Philadelphia in 1830, denounced the colonization movement as an evil, and urged their fellows not to support it. Pointing out the impracticability of such schemes, the convention encouraged the race to take steps toward its elevation in this country.[12] Should the colored people be properly educated, the prejudice against them would not continue such as to necessitate their expatriation. The delegates hoped to establish a Manual Labor College at New Haven that Negroes might there acquire that "classical knowledge which promotes genius and causes man to soar up to those high intellectual enjoyments and acquirements which place him in a situation to shed upon a country and people that scientific grandeur which is imperishable by time, and drowns in oblivion's cup their moral degradation."[13]

Influential abolitionists were also attacking this policy of the colonizationists. William Jay, however, delivered against them such diatribes and so wisely exposed their follies that the advocates of colonization learned to consider him as the arch enemy of their cause.[14] Jay advocated the education of the Negroes for living where they were. He could not see how a Christian could prohibit or condition the education of any individual. To do such a thing was tantamount to preventing him from having a direct revelation of God. How these "educators" could argue that on account of the hopelessness of the endeavors to civilize the blacks they should be removed to a foreign country, and at the same time undertake to provide for them there the same facilities for higher education that white men enjoyed, seemed to Jay to be facetiously inconsistent.[15] If the Africans could be elevated in their native land and not in America, it was due to the Caucasians' sinful condition, for which the colored people should not be required to suffer the penalty of expatriation.[16] The desirable thing to do was to influence churches and schools to admit students of color on terms of equality with all other races.

Encountering this opposition, the institutions projected by the colonization society existed in name only. Exactly how and why the organization failed to make good with its educational policy is well brought out by the wailing cry of one of its promoters. He asserted that "every endeavor to divert the attention of the community or even a portion of the means which the present so imperatively calls for, from the colonization society to measures calculated to bind the colored population to this country and seeking to raise them to a level with the whites, whether by founding colleges or in any other way, tends directly in the proportion that it succeeds, to counteract and thwart the whole plan of colonization."[17] The colonizationists, therefore, desisted from their attempt to provide higher education for any considerable number of the belated race. Seeing that they could not count on the support of the free persons of color, they feared that those thus educated would be induced by the abolitionists to remain in the United States. This would put the colonizationists in the position of increasing the intelligent element of the colored population, which was then regarded as a menace to slavery. Consequently these timorous "educators" did practically nothing during the reactionary period to carry out their plan of establishing colleges.

Thereafter the colonizationists found it advisable to restrict their efforts to individual cases. Not much was said about what they were doing, but now and then appeared notices of Negroes who had been privately prepared in the South or publicly in the North for professional work in Liberia. Dr. William Taylor and Dr. Fleet were thus educated in medicine in the District of Columbia.[18]

The Education of the Negro

In the same way John V. DeGrasse, of New York, and Thomas J. White,[19] of Brooklyn, were allowed to complete the Medical Course at Bowdoin in 1849. Garrison Draper, who had acquired his literary education at Dartmouth, studied law in Baltimore under friends of the colonization cause, and with a view to going to Liberia passed the examination of the Maryland Bar in 1857.[20] In 1858 the Berkshire Medical School graduated two colored doctors, who were gratuitously educated by the American Colonization Society. The graduating class thinned out, however, and one of the professors resigned because of their attendance.[21]

Not all colonizationists, however, had submitted to this policy of mere individual preparation of those emigrating to Liberia. Certain of their organizations still believed that it was only through educating the free people of color sufficiently to see their humiliation that a large number of them could be induced to leave this country. As long as they were unable to enjoy the finer things of life, they could not be expected to appreciate the value and use of liberty. It was argued that instead of remaining in this country to wage war on its institutions, the highly enlightened Negroes would be glad to go to a foreign land.[22] By this argument some colonizationists were induced to do more for the general education of the free blacks than they had considered it wise to do during the time of the bold attempts at servile insurrection.[23] In fact, many of the colored schools of the free States were supported by ardent colonizationists.

The later plan of most colonizationists, however, was to educate the emigrating Negroes after they settled in Liberia. Handsome sums were given for the establishment of schools and colleges in which professorships were endowed for men educated at the expense of churches and colonization societies.[24] The first institution of consequence in this field was the Alexander High School. To this school many of the prominent men of Liberia owed the beginning of their liberal education. The English High School at Monrovia, the Baptist Boarding School at Bexley, and the Protestant Episcopal High School at Cape Palmas also offered courses in higher branches.[25] Still better opportunities were given by the College of West Africa and Liberia College. The former was founded in 1839 as the head of a system of schools established by the Methodist Episcopal Church in every county of the Republic.[26] Liberia College was at the request of its founders, the directors of the American Colonization Society, incorporated by the legislature of the country in 1851. As it took some time to secure adequate funds, the main building was not completed, and students were not admitted before 1862.

Though the majority of the colored students scoffed at the idea of preparing for work in Liberia their education for service in the United States was not encouraged. No Negro had graduated from a college before 1828, when John B. Russworm, a classmate of Hon. John P. Hale, received his degree from Bowdoin.[27] During the thirties and forties, colored persons, however well prepared, were generally debarred from colleges despite the protests of prominent men. We have no record that as many as fifteen Negroes were admitted to higher institutions in this country before 1840. It was only after much debate that Union College agreed to accept a colored student on condition that he should swear that he had no Negro blood in his veins.[28]

Having had such a little to encourage them to expect a general admission into northern institutions, free blacks and abolitionists concluded that separate colleges for colored people were necessary. The institution demanded for them was thought to have an advantage over the aristocratic college in that labor would be combined with study, making the stay at school pleasant and enabling the poorest youth to secure an education.[29] It was the kind of higher institution which had already been established in several States to meet the needs of the illiterate whites. Such higher training for the Negroes was considered necessary, also, because their intermediate schools were after the reaction in a languishing state. The children of color were able to advance but little on account of having nothing to stimulate them. The desired college was, therefore, boomed as an institution to give the common schools vigor, "to kindle the flame of emulation," "to open to beginners discerning the mysteries of arithmetic other mysteries beyond," and above all to serve them as Yale or Harvard did as the capstone of the educational system of the other race.[30]

In the course of time these workers succeeded in various communities. The movement for the higher education of the Negroes of the District of Columbia centered largely around the academy established by Miss Myrtilla Miner, a worthy young woman of New York. After various discouragements in seeking a special preparation for life's work, she finally concluded that she should devote her time to the moral and intellectual improvement of Negroes.[31] She entered upon her career in Washington in 1851 assisted by Miss Anna Inman, a native of New York, and a member of the Society of Friends. After teaching the girls French one year Miss Inman returned to her home in Southfield, Rhode Island. [32] Finding it difficult to get a permanent location, Miss Miner had to move from place to place among colored people who were generally persecuted and threatened with conflagration for having a white woman working among them. Driven to the extremity of building a schoolhouse for her purpose, she purchased a lot with money raised largely by Quakers of New York, Philadelphia, and New England, and by Harriet Beecher Stowe.[33] Miss Miner had also the support of Mrs. Means, an aunt of the wife of President Franklin Pierce, and of United States Senator W.H. Seward.[34] Effective opposition, however, was not long in developing. Articles appeared in the newspapers protesting against this policy of affording Negroes "a degree of instruction so far above their social and political condition which must continue in this and every other slaveholding community."[35] Girls were insulted, teachers were abused along the streets, and for lack of police surveillance the house was set afire in 1860. It was sighted, however, in time to be saved.[36]

Undisturbed by these efforts to destroy the institution, Miss Miner persisted in carrying out her plan for the higher education of colored girls of the District of Columbia. She worked during the winter, and traveled during the summer to solicit friends and contributions to keep the institution on that higher plane where she planned it should be. She had the building well equipped with all kinds of apparatus, utilized the ample ground for the teaching of horticulture, collected a large library, and secured a number of paintings and engravings with which she enlightened her pupils on the finer arts. In addition to the conventional teaching of seminaries of that day, Miss Miner provided lectures on scientific and literary subjects by the leading men of that time, and trained her students to teach.[37] She hoped some day to make the seminary a first-class teachers' college. During the Civil War, however, it was difficult for her to find funds, and health having failed her in 1858 she died in 1866 without realizing this dream.[38]

The Education of the Negro

Earlier in the nineteenth century the philanthropists of Pennsylvania had planned to establish for Negroes several higher institutions. Chief among these was the Institute for Colored Youth. The founding of an institution of this kind had been made possible by Richard Humphreys, a Quaker, who, on his death in 1832, devised to a Board of Trustees the sum of $10,000 to be used for the education of the descendants of the African race.[39] As the instruction of Negroes was then unpopular, no steps were taken to carry out this plan until 1839. The Quakers then appointed a Board and undertook to execute this provision of Humphreys's will. In conformity with the directions of the donor, the Board of Trustees endeavored to give the colored youth the opportunity to obtain a good education and acquire useful knowledge of trades and commercial occupations. Humphreys desired that "they might be enabled to obtain a comfortable livelihood by their own industry, and fulfill the duties of domestic and social life with reputation and fidelity as good citizens and pious men."[40] Accordingly they purchased a tract of land in Philadelphia County and taught a number of boys the principles of farming, shoemaking, and other useful occupations.

Another stage in the development of this institution was reached in 1842, the year of its incorporation. It then received several small contributions and the handsome sum of $18,000 from another Quaker, Jonathan Zane. As it seemed by 1846 that the attempt to combine the literary with the industrial work had not been successful, it was decided to dispose of the industrial equipment and devote the funds of the institution to the maintenance of an evening school. An effort at the establishment of a day school was made in 1850, but it was not effected before 1852. A building was then erected in Lombard Street and the school known thereafter as the Institute for Colored Youth was opened with Charles L. Reason of New York in charge. Under him the institution was at once a success in preparing advanced pupils of both sexes for the higher vocations of teaching and preaching. The attendance soon necessitated increased accommodations for which Joseph Dawson and other Quakers liberally provided in later years.[41]

This favorable tendency in Pennsylvania led to the establishment of Avery College at Alleghany City. The necessary fund was bequeathed by Rev. Charles Avery, a rich man of that section, who left an estate of about $300,000 to be applied to the education and Christianization of the African race.[42] Some of this fund was devoted to missionary work in Africa, large donations were made to colored institutions of learning, and another portion was appropriated to the establishment of Avery College. This institution was incorporated in 1849. Soon thereafter it advertised for students, expressing willingness to make every provision without regard to religious proclivities. The school had a three-story brick building, up-to-date apparatus for teaching various branches of natural science, a library of all kinds of literature, and an endowment of $25,000 to provide for its maintenance. Rev. Philotas Dean, the only white teacher connected with this institution, was its first principal. He served until 1856 when he was succeeded by his assistant, M.H. Freeman, who in 1863 was succeeded by George B. Vashon. Miss Emma J. Woodson was an assistant in the institution from 1856 to 1867. After the din of the Civil War had ceased the institution took on new life, electing a new corps of teachers, who placed the work on a higher plane. Among these were Rev. H.H. Garnett, president, B.K. Sampson, Harriet C. Johnson, and Clara G. Toop.[43]

Higher Education

It was due also to the successful forces at work in Pennsylvania that the Ashmun Institute, now Lincoln University, was established in that State. The need of higher education having come to the attention of the Presbytery of New Castle, that body decided to establish within its limits an institution for the "scientific, classical, and theological education of the colored youth of the male sex." In 1853 the Synod approved the plans of the founders and provided that the institution should be under the supervision and control of the Presbytery or Synod within whose bounds it might be located. A committee to solicit funds, find a site, and secure a charter for the school was appointed. They selected for the location Hensonville, Chester County, Pennsylvania.[44] The legislature incorporated the institution in 1854 with John M. Dickey, Alfred Hamilton, Robert P. DuBois, James Latta, John B. Spottswood, James Crowell, Samuel J. Dickey, Alfred Hamilton, John M. Kelton, and William Wilson as trustees. Sufficient buildings and equipment having been provided by 1856, the doors of this institution were opened to young colored men seeking preparation for work in this country and Liberia.[45]

An equally successful plan of workers in the West resulted in the founding of the first higher institution to be controlled by Negroes. Having for some years believed that the colored people needed a college for the preparation of teachers and preachers, the Cincinnati Conference of the Methodist Episcopal Church in session in 1855 appointed Rev. John F. Wright as general agent to execute this design. Addressing themselves immediately to this task Rev. Mr. Wright and his associates solicited from philanthropic persons by 1856 the amount of $13,000. The agents then made the purchase payment on the beautiful site of Tawawa Springs, long known as the healthy summer resort near Xenia, Ohio.[46] That same year the institution was incorporated as Wilberforce University. From 1856 to 1862 the school had a fair student body, consisting of the mulatto children of southern slaveholders.[47] When these were kept away, however, by the operations of the Civil War, the institution declined so rapidly that it had to be closed for a season. Thereafter the trustees appealed again to the African Methodist Episcopal Church which in 1856 had declined the invitation to cooeperate with the founders. The colored Methodists had adhered to their decision to operate Union Seminary, a manual labor school, which they had started near Columbus, Ohio.[48] The proposition was accepted, however, in 1862. For the amount of the debt of $10,000 which the institution had incurred while passing through the crisis, Rev. Daniel A. Payne and his associates secured the transfer of the property to the African Methodist Episcopal Church. These new directors hoped to develop a first-class university, offering courses in law, medicine, literature, and theology. The debt being speedily removed the school showed evidences of new vigor, but was checked in its progress by an incendiary, who burned the main building while the teachers and pupils were attending an emancipation celebration at Xenia, April 14, 1865. With the amount of insurance received and donations from friends, the trustees were able to construct a more commodious building which still marks the site of these early labors.[49]

A brighter day for the higher education of the colored people at home, however, had begun to dawn during the forties. The abolitionists were then aggressively demanding consideration for the Negroes. Men "condescended" to reason together about slavery and the treatment of the colored people. The northern people ceased to think that they had nothing to do with these problems. When these questions were openly discussed in the schools of the North, students and teachers gradually became converted to the doctrine of equality in education. This revolution was instituted by President C.B. Storrs, of Western Reserve College, then at Hudson, Ohio. His doctrine in regard to the training of the mind "was that men are able to be made only by putting youth under the responsibilities of men." He, therefore, encouraged the free discussion of all important subjects, among which was the appeal of the Negroes for enlightenment. This policy gave rise to a spirit of inquiry which permeated the whole school. The victory, however, was not easy. After a long struggle the mind of the college was carried by irresistible argument in favor of fair play for colored youth. This institution had two colored students as early as 1834.[50]

Northern institutions of learning were then reaching the third stage in their participation in the solution of the Negro problem. At first they had to be converted even to allow a free discussion of the question; next the students on being convinced that slavery was a sin, sought to elevate the blacks thus degraded; and finally these workers, who had been accustomed to instructing the neighboring colored people, reached the conclusion that they should be admitted to their schools on equal footing with the whites. Geneva College, then at Northfield, Ohio, now at Beaver Falls, Pennsylvania, was being moved in this manner.[51]

Lane Seminary, however, is the best example of a school which passed through the three stages of this revolution. This institution was peculiar in that the idea of establishing it originated with a southerner, a merchant of New Orleans. It was founded largely by funds of southern Presbyterians, was located in Cincinnati about a mile from slave territory, and was attended by students from that section.[52] When the right of free discussion swept the country many of the proslavery students were converted to abolition. To southerners it seemed that the seminary had resolved itself into a society for the elevation of the free blacks. Students established Sabbath-schools, organized Bible classes, and provided lectures for Negroes ambitious to do advanced work. Measures were taken to establish an academy for colored girls, and a teacher was engaged. But these noble efforts put forth so near the border States soon provoked firm opposition from the proslavery element. Some of the students had gone so far in the manifestation of their zeal that the institution was embarrassed by the charge of promoting the social equality of the races.[53] Rather than remain in Cincinnati under restrictions, the reform element of the institution moved to the more congenial Western Reserve where a nucleus of youth and their instructors had assumed the name of Oberlin College. This school did so much for the education of Negroes before the Civil War that it was often spoken of as an institution for the education of the people of color.

Interest in the higher education of the neglected race, however, was not confined to a particular commonwealth. Institutions of other States were directing their attention to this task. Among others were a school in New York City founded by a clergyman to offer Negroes an opportunity to study the classics,[54] New York Central College at McGrawville, Oneida Institute conducted by Beriah Green at Whitesboro, Thetford Academy of Vermont, and Union Literary Institute in the center of the communities of freedmen transplanted to Indiana. Many other of our best institutions were opening their doors to students of African descent. By 1852 colored students had attended the Institute at Easton, Pennsylvania; the Normal School of Albany, New York; Bowdoin College, Brunswick, Maine; Rutland College, Vermont; Jefferson College,

Higher Education

Pennsylvania; Athens College, Athens, Ohio; Franklin College, New Athens, Ohio; and Hanover College near Madison, Indiana. Negroes had taken courses at the Medical School of the University of New York; the Castleton Medical School in Vermont; the Berkshire Medical School, Pittsfield, Massachusetts; the Rush Medical School in Chicago; the Eclectic Medical School of Philadelphia; the Homeopathic College of Cleveland; and the Medical School of Harvard University. Colored preachers had been educated in the Theological Seminary at Gettysburg, Pennsylvania; the Dartmouth Theological School; and the Theological Seminary of Charleston, South Carolina.[55]

Prominent among those who brought about this change in the attitude toward the education of the free blacks was Gerrit Smith, one of the greatest philanthropists of his time. He secured privileges for Negroes in higher institutions by extending aid to such as would open their doors to persons of color. In this way he became a patron of Oneida Institute, giving it from $3,000 to $4,000 in cash and 3,000 acres of land in Vermont. Because of the hospitality of Oberlin to colored students he gave the institution large sums of money and 20,000 acres of land in Virginia valued at $50,000. New York Central College which opened its doors alike to both races obtained from him several donations.[56] This gentleman proceeded on the presumption that it is the duty of the white people to elevate the colored and that the education of large numbers of them is indispensable to the uplift of the degraded classes.[57] He wanted them to have the opportunity for obtaining either a common or classical education; and hoped that they would go out from our institutions well educated for any work to which they might be called in this country or abroad.[58] He himself established a colored school at Peterboro, New York. As this institution offered both industrial and literary courses we shall have occasion to mention it again. Both a cause and result of the increasing interest in the higher education of Negroes was that these unfortunates had made good with what little training they had. Many had by their creative power shown what they could do in business,[59] some had convinced the world of the inventive genius of the man of color,[60] others had begun to rank as successful lawyers,[61] not a few had become distinguished physicians,[62] and scores of intelligent Negro preachers were ministering to the spiritual needs of their people.[63] S.R. Ward, a scholar of some note, was for a few years the pastor of a white church at Courtlandville, New York. Robert Morris had been honored by the appointment as Magistrate by the Governor of Massachusetts, and in New Hampshire another man of African blood had been elected to the legislature.[64]

Thanks to the open doors of liberal schools, the race could boast of a number of efficient educators.[65] There were Martin H. Freeman, John Newton Templeton, Mary E. Miles, Lucy Stratton, Lewis Woodson, John F. Cook, Mary Ann Shadd, W.H. Allen, and B.W. Arnett. Professor C.L. Reason, a veteran teacher of New York City, was then so well educated that in 1844 he was called to the professorship of Belles-Lettres and the French Language in New York Central College. Many intelligent Negroes who followed other occupations had teaching for their avocation. In fact almost every colored person who could read and write was a missionary teacher among his people.

In music, literature, and journalism the Negroes were also doing well. Eliza Greenfield, William Jackson, John G. Anderson, and William Appo made their way in the musical world. Lemuel Haynes, a successful preacher to a white congregation, took up theology about 1815. Paul Cuffee wrote an interesting account of Sierra Leone. Rev. Daniel Coker published a book on slavery in 1810. Seven years later came the publication of the Law and Doctrine of the African Methodist Episcopal Church and the Standard Hymnal written by Richard Allen. In 1836 Rev. George Hogarth published an addition to this volume and in 1841 brought forward the first magazine of the sect. Edward W. Moore, a colored teacher of white children in Tennessee, wrote an arithmetic. C.L. Remond of Massachusetts was then a successful lecturer and controversialist. James M. Whitefield, George Horton, and Frances E.W. Harper were publishing poems. H.H. Garnett and J.C. Pennington, known to fame as preachers, attained success also as pamphleteers. R.B. Lewis, M.R. Delany, William Nell, and Catto embellished Negro history; William Wells Brown wrote his Three Years in Europe; and Frederick Douglass, the orator, gave the world his creditable autobiography. More effective still were the journalistic efforts of the Negro intellect pleading its own cause. [66] Colored newspapers varying from the type of weeklies like The North Star to that of the modern magazine like The Anglo-African were published in most large towns and cities of the North.

[1: The views of the abolitionists at that time were well expressed by Garrison in his address to the people of color in the convention assembled in Philadelphia in 1830. He encouraged them to get as much education as possible for themselves and their offspring, to toil long and hard for it as for a pearl of great price. "An ignorant people," said he, "can never occupy any other than a degraded place in society; they can never be truly free until they are intelligent. It is an old maxim that knowledge is power; and not only is it power but rank, wealth, dignity, and protection. That capital brings highest return to a city, state, or nation (as the case may be) which is invested in schools, academies, and colleges. If I had children, rather than that they should grow up in ignorance, I would feed upon bread and water: I would sell my teeth, or extract the blood from my veins." See Minutes of the Proceedings of the Convention for the Improvement of the Free People of Color, 1830, pages 10, 11.]

[2: Special Report of the U.S. Com. of Ed., 1871, pp. 213-214; and The African Repository, under the captions of "Education in Liberia," and "African Education Societies," passim.]

[3: African Repository, vol. i., p. 277.]

[4: African Repository, vol. ii., p. 223.]

[5: Ibid., vol. xxviii., pp. 271, 347; Child, An Appeal, p. 144.]

[6: African Repository, vol. i., p. 277.]

[7: Report of the Proceedings at the Organization of the African Education Society, p. 9.]

[8: African Repository, vol. i., p. 276, and Griffin, A Plea for Africa, p. 65.]

[9: African Repository, vol. iv., pp. 186, 193, and 375; and vol. vi., pp. 47, 48, 49, and Report of the Proceedings of the African Education Society, p. 7.]

[10: Ibid., pp. 7 and 8 and African Repository, vol. iv., p. 375.]

[11: What would become of this plan depended upon the changing fortunes of the men concerned. Kosciuszko died in 1817; and as Thomas Jefferson refused to take out letters testamentary under this will, Benjamin Lincoln Lear, a trustee of the African Education Society, who intended to apply for the whole fund, was appointed administrator of it. The fund amounted to about $16,000. Later Kosciuszko Armstrong demanded of the administrator $3704 bequeathed to him by T. Kosciuszko in a will alleged to have been executed in Paris in 1806.

Higher Education

The bill was dismissed by the Circuit Court of the District of Columbia, and the decision of the lower Court was confirmed by the United States Supreme Court in 1827 on the grounds that the said will had not been admitted to probate anywhere. To make things still darker just about the time the trustees of the African Education Society were planning to purchase a farm and select teachers and mechanics to instruct the youth, the heirs of General Kosciuszko filed a bill against Mr. Lear in the Supreme Court of the United States on the ground of the invalidity of the will executed by Kosciuszko in 1798. The death of Mr. Lear in 1832 and that of William Wirt, the Attorney-General of the United States, soon thereafter, caused a delay in having the case decided. The author does not know exactly what use was finally made of this fund. See African Repository, vol. it., pp. 163, 233; also 7 Peters, 130, and 8 Peters, 52.]

[12: Williams, History of the Negro Race, p. 67.]
[13: Ibid., p. 68; and Minutes of the Proceedings of the Third Convention for the Improvement of the Free People of Color, pp. 9, 10, and 11.]
[14: Reese, Letters to Honorable William Jay.]
[15: Jay, Inquiry, p. 26; and Letters, p. 21.]
[16: Ibid., p. 22.]
[17: Hodgkin, Inquiry into the Merits of the Am. Col. Soc., p. 31.]
[18: Special Report of the U.S. Com. of Ed., 1871, and African Repository, vol. x., p. 10.]
[19: Niles Register, vol. lxxv., p. 384.]
[20: African Repository, vol. xxxiv., pp. 26 and 27.]
[21: Ibid., p. 30.]
[22: Boone, The History of Education in Indiana, p. 237; and African Repository, vol. xxx., p. 195.]
[23: Ibid., p. 195.]
[24: African Repository, under the caption of "Education in Liberia" in various volumes; and Alexander, A History of Col., pp. 348, 391.]
[25: Ibid., p. 348.]
[26: Monroe, Cyclopaedia of Education, vol. iv., p. 6.]
[27: Dyer, Speech in Congress on the Progress of the Negro, 1914.]
[28: Clarke, The Condition of the Free People of Color, 1859, p. 3, and the Sixth Annual Report of the American Antislavery Society, p. 11.]
[29: Proceedings of the Third Convention of Free People of Color held in Philadelphia in 1836, pp. 7 and 8; Ibid., Fourth Annual Convention, p. 26; Proceedings of the New England Antislavery Society, 1836, p. 40.]
[30: Minutes and Proceedings of the Third Annual Convention of the Free People of Color, 1836; Garrison's Address.]
[31: O'Connor, Myrtilla Miner, pp. 11, 12.]
[32: Special Report of the U.S. Com. of Ed., 1871, p. 207.]
[33: Ibid., 1871, p. 208.]
[34: Ibid., pp. 208, 209, and 210.]
[35: The National Intelligencer.]
[36: Special Report of the U.S. Com. of Ed., 1871, p. 209.]
[37: Special Report of the U.S. Com. of Ed., 1871, p. 210.]
[38: Those who assisted her were Helen Moore, Margaret Clapp, Anna H. Searing, Amanda Weaver, Anna Jones, Matilda Jones, and Lydia Mann, the sister of Horace Mann, who helped Miss Miner considerably in 1856 at the time of her failing health. Emily Holland was her firm supporter when the institution

was passing through the crisis, and stood by her until she breathed her last. See Special Report of the U.S. Com. of Ed., 1871, p. 210.]

[39: Wickersham, History of Education in Pa., p. 249.]
[40: Special Report of the U.S. Com. of Ed., 1871, p. 379.]
[41: Special Report of the United States Com. of Ed., 1871, p. 380.]
[42: African Repository, vol. xxxiv., p. 156.]
[43: Special Report of the U.S. Com. of Ed., 1871, p. 381.]
[44: Baird, A Collection, etc., p. 819.]
[45: Special Report of the United States Com. of Ed., 1871, p. 382.]
[46: The Non-Slaveholder, vol. ii., p. 113.]
[47: Special Report of the U.S. Com. of Ed., 1871, pp. 372-373.]
[48: History of Greene County, Ohio, chapter on Wilberforce; and Special Report of the U.S. Com. of Ed., 1871, p. 373.]
[49: The Non-Slaveholder, vol. ii., p. 113.]
[50: First Annual Report of the American Anti-Slavery Society, p. 42.]
[51: First Annual Report of the American Anti-slavery Society, 1834. p. 43.]
[52: Ibid., p. 43.]
[53: First Annual Report of the American Anti-Slavery Society, p. 43.]
[54: Simmons, Men of Mark, p. 530.]
[55: These facts are taken from M.R. Delany's The Condition, Elevation, Emigration, and Destiny of the Colored People of the United States Practically Considered, published in 1852; the Reports of the Antislavery and Colonization Societies, and The African Repository.]
[56: Special Report of the U.S. Com. of Ed., 1871, p. 367.]
[57: African Repository, vol. x., p. 312.]
[58: Ibid., p. 312.]
[59: Among these were John B. Smith, Coffin Pitts, Robert Douglas, John P. Bell, Augustus Washington, Alexander S. Thomas, Henry Boyd, P.H. Ray, and L.T. Wilcox.]
[60: A North Carolina Negro had discovered a cure for snakebite; Henry Blair, a slave of Maryland, had invented a corn-planter; and Roberts of Philadelphia had made a machine for lifting railway cars from the tracks.]
[61: The most noted of these lawyers were Robert Morris, Malcolm B. Allen, G.B. Vashon, and E.G. Walker.]
[62: The leading Negroes of this class were T. Joiner White, Peter Ray, John DeGrasse, David P. Jones, J. Gould Bias, James Ulett, Martin Delany, and John R. Peck. James McCrummill, Joseph Wilson, Thos. Kennard, and Wm. Nickless were noted colored dentists of Philadelphia.]
[63: The prominent colored preachers of that day were Titus Basfield, B.F. Templeton, W.T. Catto, Benjamin Coker, John B. Vashon, Robert Purvis, David Ruggles, Philip A. Bell, Charles L. Reason, William Wells Brown, Samuel L. Ward, James McCune Smith, Highland Garnett, Daniel A. Payne, James C. Pennington, M. Haines, and John F. Cook.]
[64: Baldwin, Observations, etc., p. 44.]
[65: James B. Russworm, an alumnus of Bowdoin, was the first Negro to receive a degree from a college in this country.]
[66: In 1827 John B. Russworm and Samuel B. Cornish began the publication of The Freedom's Journal, appearing afterward as Rights to All. Ten years later P.A. Bell was publishing The Weekly Advocate. From 1837 to 1842 Bell and Cornish edited The Colored Man's Journal, while Samuel Ruggles sent

from his press The Mirror of Liberty. In 1847, one year after the appearance of Thomas Van Rensselaer's Ram's Horn, Frederick Douglass started The North Star at Rochester, while G. Allen and Highland Garnett were appealing to the country through The National Watchman of Troy, New York. That same year Martin R. Delany brought out The Pittsburg Mystery, and others The Elevator at Albany, New York. At Syracuse appeared The Impartial Citizen established by Samuel R. Ward in 1848, three years after which L.H. Putnam came before the public in New York City with The Colored Man's Journal. Then came The Philadelphia Freeman, The Philadelphia Citizen, The New York Phalanx, The Baltimore Elevator, and The Cincinnati Central Star. Of a higher order was he Anglo-African, a magazine published in New York in 1859 by Thomas Hamilton, who was succeeded in editorship by Robert Hamilton and Highland Garnett. In 1852 there were in existence The Colored American, The Struggler, The Watchman, The Ram's Horn, The Demosthenian Shield, The National Reformer, The Pittsburg Mystery, The Palladium of Liberty, The Disfranchised American, The Colored Citizen, The National Watchman, The Excelsior, The Christian Herald, The Farmer, The Impartial Citizen, The Northern Star of Albany, and The North Star of Rochester.]

Chapter 12

Vocational Training

Having before them striking examples of highly educated colored men who could find no employment in the United States, the free Negroes began to realize that their preparation was not going hand in hand with their opportunities. Industrial education was then emphasized as the proper method of equipping the race for usefulness. The advocacy of such training, however, was in no sense new. The early anti-slavery men regarded it as the prerequisite to emancipation, and the abolitionists urged it as the only safe means of elevating the freedmen. But when the blacks, converted to this doctrine, began to enter the higher pursuits of labor during the forties and fifties, there started a struggle which has been prolonged even into our day. Most northern white men had ceased to oppose the enlightenment of the free people of color but still objected to granting them economic equality. The same investigators that discovered increased facilities of conventional education for Negroes in 1834 reported also that there existed among the white mechanics a formidable prejudice against colored artisans.[1]

In opposing the encroachment of Negroes on their field of labor the northerners took their cue from the white mechanics in the South. At first laborers of both races worked together in the same room and at the same machine.[2] But in the nineteenth century, when more white men in the South were condescending to do skilled labor and trying to develop manufactures, they found themselves handicapped by competition with the slave mechanics. Before 1860 most southern mechanics, machinists, local manufacturers, contractors, and railroad men with the exception of conductors were Negroes.[3] Against this custom of making colored men such an economic factor the white mechanics frequently protested.[4] The riots against Negroes occurring in Cincinnati, Philadelphia, New York, and Washington during the thirties and forties owed their origin mainly to an ill feeling between the white and colored skilled laborers.[5] The white artisans prevailed upon the legislatures of Pennsylvania, Maryland, and Georgia to enact measures hostile to their rivals.[6] In 1845 the State of Georgia made it a misdemeanor for a colored mechanic to make a contract for the repair or the erection of buildings.[7] The people of Georgia, however, were not unanimously in favor of keeping the Negro artisan down. We have already observed that at the request of the Agricultural Convention of that State in 1852 the legislature all but passed a bill providing for the education of slaves to increase their efficiency and attach them to their masters.[8]

It was unfortunate that the free people of color in the North had not taken up vocational training earlier in the century before the laboring classes realized fraternal consciousness. Once pitted against the capitalists during the Administration of Andrew Jackson the working classes learned to think that their interests differed materially from those of the rich, whose privileges had multiplied at the expense of the poor. Efforts toward effecting organizations to secure to labor adequate protection began to be successful during Van Buren's

Administration. At this time some reformers were boldly demanding the recognition of Negroes by all helpful groups. One of the tests of the strength of these protagonists was whether or not they could induce the mechanics of the North to take colored workmen to supply the skilled laborers required by the then rapid economic development of our free States. Would the whites permit the blacks to continue as their competitors after labor had been elevated above drudgery? To do this meant the continuation of the custom of taking youths of African blood as apprentices. This the white mechanics of the North generally refused to do.[9]

The friends of the colored race, however, were not easily discouraged by that "vulgar race prejudice which reigns in the breasts of working classes."[10] Arthur Tappan, Gerrit Smith, and William Lloyd Garrison made the appeal in behalf of the untrained laborers.[11] Although they knew the difficulties encountered by Negroes seeking to learn trades, and could daily observe how unwilling master mechanics were to receive colored boys as apprentices, the abolitionists persisted in saying that by perseverance these youths could succeed in procuring profitable situations.[12] Garrison believed that their failure to find employment at trades was not due so much to racial differences as to their lack of training. Speaking to the free people of color in their convention in Philadelphia in 1831, he could give them no better advice than that "wherever you can, put your children to trades. A good trade is better than a fortune, because when once obtained it cannot be taken away." Discussing the matter further, he said: "Now, there can be no reason why your sons should fail to make as ingenious and industrious mechanics, as any white apprentices; and when they once get trades, they will be able to accumulate money; money begets influence, and influence respectability. Influence, wealth, and character will certainly destroy those prejudices which now separate you from society."[13]

To expect the cooeperation of the white working classes in thus elevating the colored race turned out to be a delusion. They reached the conclusion that in making their headway against capital they had a better chance without Negroes than with them. White mechanics of the North not only refused to accept colored boys as apprentices, but would not even work for employers who persisted in hiring Negroes. Generally refused by the master mechanics of Cincinnati, a colored cabinet-maker finally found an Englishman who was willing to hire him, but the employees of the shop objected, refusing to allow the newcomer even to work in a room by himself.[14] A Negro who could preach in a white church of the North would have had difficulty in securing the contract to build a new edifice for that congregation. A colored man could then more easily get his son into a lawyer's office to learn law than he could "into a blacksmith shop to blow the bellows and wield the sledge hammer."[15]

Left then in a quandary as to what they should do, northern Negroes hoped to use the then popular "manual labor schools" to furnish the facilities for both practical and classical education. These schools as operated for the whites, however, were not primarily trade schools. Those which admitted persons of African descent paid more attention to actual industrial training for the reason that colored students could not then hope to acquire such knowledge as apprentices. This tendency was well shown by the action of the free Negroes through their delegates in the convention assembled in Philadelphia in 1830. Conversant with the policy of so reshaping the educational system of the country as to carry knowledge even to the hovels, these leaders were easily won to the

The Education of the Negro

scheme of reconstructing their schools "on the manual labor system." In this they saw the redemption of the free Negroes of the North. These gentlemen were afraid that the colored people were not paying sufficient attention to the development of the power to use their hands skillfully.[16] One of the first acts of the convention was to inquire as to how fast colored men were becoming attached to mechanical pursuits,[17] and whether or not there was any prospect that a manual labor school for the instruction of the youth would shortly be established. The report of the committee, to which the question was referred, was so encouraging that the convention itself decided to establish an institution of the kind at New Haven, Connecticut. They appealed to their fellows for help, called the attention of philanthropists to this need of the race, and commissioned William Lloyd Garrison to solicit funds in Great Britain.[18] Garrison found hearty supporters among the friends of freedom in that country. Some, who had been induced to contribute to the Colonization Society, found it more advisable to aid the new movement. Charles Stewart of Liverpool wrote Garrison that he could count on his British co-workers to raise $1000 for this purpose.[19] At the same time Americans were equally active. Arthur Tappan subscribed $1000 on the condition that each of nineteen other persons should contribute the same amount.[20]

Before these well-laid plans could mature, however, unexpected opposition developed in New Haven. Indignation meetings were held, protests against this project were filed, and the free people of color were notified that the institution was not desired in Connecticut.[21] It was said that these memorialists feared that a colored college so near to Yale might cause friction between the two student bodies, and that the school might attract an unusually large number of undesirable Negroes. At their meeting the citizens of New Haven resolved "That the founding of colleges for educating colored people is an unwarrantable and dangerous undertaking to the internal concerns of other states and ought to be discouraged, and that the mayor, aldermen, common council, and freemen will resist the movement by every lawful means."[22] In view of such drastic action the promoters had to abandon their plan. No such protests were made by the citizens of New Haven, however, when the colonizationists were planning to establish there a mission school to prepare Negroes to leave the country.

The movement, however, was not then stopped by this outburst of race prejudice in New Haven. Directing attention to another community, the New England Antislavery Society took up this scheme and collected funds to establish a manual labor school. When the officials had on hand about $1000 it was discovered that they could accomplish their aim by subsidizing the Noyes Academy of Canaan, New Hampshire, and making such changes as were necessary to subserve the purposes intended.[23] The plan was not to convert this into a colored school. The promoters hoped to maintain there a model academy for the co-education of the races "on the manual labor system." The treasurer of the Antislavery Society was to turn over certain moneys to this academy to provide for the needs of the colored students, who then numbered fourteen of the fifty-two enrolled. But although it had been reported that the people of the town were in accord with the principal's acceptance of this proposition, there were soon evidences to the contrary. Fearing imaginary evils, these modern Canaanites destroyed the academy, dragging the building to a swamp with a hundred yoke of oxen.[24] The better element of the town registered against this outrage only a slight protest. H.H. Garnett and Alexander Crummell were among the colored students who sought education at this academy.

This work was more successful in the State of New York. There, too, the cause was championed by the abolitionists.[25] After the emancipation of all Negroes in that commonwealth by 1827 the New York Antislavery Society devoted more time to the elevation of the free people of color. The rapid rise of the laboring classes in this swiftly growing city made it evident to their benefactors that they had to be speedily equipped for competition with white mechanics or be doomed to follow menial employments. The only one of that section to offer Negroes anything like the opportunity for industrial training, however, was Gerrit Smith.[26] He was fortunate in having sufficient wealth to carry out the plan. In 1834 he established in Madison County, New York, an institution known as the Peterboro Manual Labor School. The working at trades was provided not altogether to teach the mechanic arts, but to enable the students to support themselves while attending school. As a compensation for instruction, books, room, fuel, light, and board furnished by the founder, the student was expected to labor four hours daily at some agricultural or mechanical employment "important to his education."[27] The faculty estimated the four hours of labor as worth on an average of about 12-1/2 cents for each student.

Efforts were then being made for the establishment of another institution near Philadelphia. These endeavors culminated in the above-mentioned benefaction of Richard Humphreys, by the will of whom $10,000 was devised to establish a school for the purpose of instructing "descendants of the African race in school learning in the various branches of the mechanical arts and trades and agriculture."[28] In 1839 members of the Society of Friends organized an association to establish a school such as Humphreys had planned. The founders believed that "the most successful method of elevating the moral and intellectual character of the descendants of Africa, as well as of improving their social condition, is to extend to them the benefits of a good education, and to instruct them in the knowledge of some useful trade or business, whereby they may be enabled to obtain a comfortable livelihood by their own industry; and through these means to prepare them for fulfilling the various duties of domestic and social life with reputation and fidelity as good citizens and pious men."[29] Directing their attention first to things practical the association purchased in 1839 a piece of land in Bristol township, Philadelphia County, where they offered boys instruction in farming, shoemaking, and other useful trades. Their endeavors, so far as training in the mechanic arts was concerned, proved to be a failure. In 1846, therefore, the management decided to discontinue this literary, agricultural, and manual labor experiment. The trustees then sold the farm and stock, apprenticed the male students to mechanical occupations, and opened an evening school. Thinking mainly of classical education thereafter, the trustees of the fund finally established the Institute for Colored Youth of which we have spoken elsewhere.

Some of the philanthropists who promoted the practical education of the colored people were found in the Negro settlements of the Northwest. Their first successful attempt in that section was the establishment of the Emlen Institute in Mercer County, Ohio. The founding of this institution was due manly to the efforts of Augustus Wattles who was instrumental in getting a number of emigrating freedmen to leave Cincinnati and settle in this county about 1835. [30] Wattles traveled in almost every colored neighborhood of the State and laid before them the benefits of permanent homes and the education for their children. On his first journey he organized, with the assistance of abolitionists, twenty-five schools for colored children. Interested thereafter in providing a head for this system he purchased for himself ninety acres of land in Mercer County to establish a manual labor institution. He sustained a school on it at his own expense, till the 11th of November, 1842. Wattles then visited Philadelphia where he became acquainted with the trustees of the late Samuel Emlen, a Friend of New Jersey. He had left by his will $20,000 "for the support and education in school learning and mechanic arts and agriculture of boys of African and Indian descent whose parents would give such youths to the Institute."[31] The means of the two philanthropists were united. The trustees purchased a farm and appointed Wattles as superintendent of the establishment, calling it Emlen Institute. Located in a section where the Negroes had sufficient interest in education to support a number of elementary schools, this institution once had considerable influence.[32] It was removed to Bucks County, Pennsylvania, in 1858 and then to Warminster in the same county in 1873.

Another school of this type was founded in the Northwest. This was the Union Literary Institute of Spartanburg, Indiana. The institution owes its origin to a group of bold, antislavery men who "in the heat of the abolition excitement"[33] stood firm for the Negro. They soon had opposition from the pro-slavery leaders who impeded the progress of the institution. But thanks to the indefatigable Ebenezer Tucker, its first principal, the "Nigger School" weathered the storm. The Institute, however, was founded to educate both races. Its charter required that no distinction should be made on account of race, color, rank, or religion. Accordingly, although the student body was from the beginning of the school partly white, the board of trustees represented denominations of both races. Accessible statistics do not show that colored persons ever constituted more than one-third of the students.[34] It was one of the most durable of the manual labor schools, having continued after the Civil War, carrying out to some extent the original designs of its founders. As the plan to continue it as a private institution proved later to be impracticable the establishment was changed into a public school.[35]

Scarcely less popular was the British and American Manual Labor Institute of the colored settlements in Upper Canada. This school was projected by Rev. Hiram Wilson and Josiah Henson as early as 1838, but its organization was not undertaken until 1842. The refugees were then called together to decide upon the expenditure of $1500 collected in England by James C. Fuller, a Quaker. They decided to establish at Dawn "a manual labor school, where children could be taught those elements of knowledge which are usually the occupations of a grammar school, and where boys could be taught in addition the practice of some mechanic art, and the girls could be instructed in those domestic arts which are the proper occupation and ornament of their sex."[36] A tract of three hundred acres of land was purchased, a few buildings were constructed, and pupils were soon admitted. The managers endeavored to make the school, "self-supporting by the employment of the students for certain portions of the time on the land."[37] The advantage of schooling of this kind attracted to Dresden and Dawn sufficient refugees to make these prosperous settlements. Rev. Hiram Wilson, the first principal of the institution, began with fourteen "boarding scholars" when there were no more than fifty colored persons in all the vicinity. In 1852 when the population of this community had increased to five hundred there were sixty students attending the school. Indian and white children were also admitted. Among the students there were also adults varying later in number from fifty-six to one hundred and sixteen.[38] This institution became very influential among the Negroes of Canada. Travelers mentioned the Institute in accounting for the prosperity and good morals of the refugees. [39] Unfortunately, however, after the year 1855 when the school reached its zenith, it began to decline on account of bad feeling probably resulting from a divided management.

Studying these facts concerning the manual labor system of education, the student of education sees that it was not generally successful. This may be accounted for in various ways. One might say that colored people were not desired in the higher pursuits of labor and that their preparation for such vocations never received the support of the rank and file of the Negroes of the North. They saw then, as they often do now, the seeming impracticability of preparing themselves for occupations which they apparently had no chance to follow. Moreover, bright freedmen were not at first attracted to mechanical occupations. Ambitious Negroes who triumphed over slavery and made their way to the North for educational advantages hoped to enter the higher walks of life. Only a few of the race had the foresight of the advocates of industrial training. The majority of the enlightened class desired that they be no longer considered as "persons occupying a menial position, but as capable of the highest development of man."[40] Furthermore, bitterly as some white men hated slavery, and deeply as they seemingly sympathized with the oppressed, they were loath to support a policy which they believed was fatal to their economic interests.[41]

The chief reason for the failure of the new educational policy was that the managers of the manual labor schools made the mistakes often committed by promoters of industrial education of our day. At first they proceeded on the presumption that one could obtain a classical education while learning a trade and at the same time earn sufficient to support himself at school. Some of the managers of industrial schools have not yet learned that students cannot produce articles for market. The best we can expect from an industrial school to-day is a good apprentice.

Another handicap was that at that time conditions were seldom sufficiently favorable to enable the employer to derive profit enough from students' work to compensate for the maintenance of the youth at a manual labor school. Besides, such a school could not be far-reaching in its results because it could not be so conducted as to accommodate a large number of students. With a slight change in its aims the manual labor schools might have been more successful in the large urban communities, but the aim of their advocates was to establish them in the country where sufficient land for agricultural training could be had, and where students would not be corrupted by the vices of the city.

It was equally unfortunate that the teachers who were chosen to carry out this educational policy lacked the preparation adequate to their task. They had any amount of spirit, but an evident lack of understanding as to the meaning of this new education. They failed to unite the qualifications for both the industrial and academic instruction. It was the fault that we find to-day in our industrial schools. Those who were responsible for the literary training knew little of and cared still less for the work in mechanic arts, and those who were employed to teach trades seldom had sufficient education to impart what they knew. The students, too, in their efforts to pursue these uncorrelated courses seldom succeeded in making much advance in either. We have no evidence that many Negroes were equipped for higher service in the manual labor schools. Statistics of 1850 and 1860 show that there was an increase in the number of colored mechanics, especially in Philadelphia, Cincinnati, Columbus, the Western Reserve, and Canada.[42] But this was probably due to the decreasing prejudice of the local white mechanics toward the Negro artisans fleeing from the South rather than to formal industrial training.[43]

Schools of this kind tended gradually to abandon the idea of combining labor and learning, leaving such provisions mainly as catalogue fictions. Many of the western colleges were founded as manual labor schools, but the remains of these beginnings are few and insignificant. Oberlin, which was once operated on this basis, still retains the seal of "Learning and Labor," with a college building in the foreground and a field of grain in the distance. A number of our institutions have recitations now in the forenoon that students may devote the afternoon to labor. In some schools Monday instead of Saturday is the open day of the week because this was wash-day for the manual labor colleges. Even after the Civil War some schools had their long vacation in the winter instead of the summer because the latter was the time for manual labor. The people of our day know little about this unsuccessful system.

It is evident, therefore, that the leaders who had up to that time dictated the policy of the social betterment of the colored people had failed to find the key to the situation. This task fell to the lot of Frederick Douglass, who, wiser in his generation than most of his contemporaries, advocated actual vocational training as the greatest leverage for the elevation of the colored people. Douglass was given an opportunity to bring his ideas before the public on the occasion of a visit to Mrs. Harriet Beecher Stowe. She was then preparing to go to England in response to an invitation from her admirers, who were anxious to see this famous author of Uncle Tom's Cabin and to give her a testimonial. Thinking that she would receive large sums of money in England she desired to get Mr. Douglass's views as to how it could be most profitably spent for the advancement of the free people of color. She was especially interested in those who had become free by their own exertions. Mrs. Stowe informed her guest that several had suggested the establishment of an educational institution pure and simple, but that she had not been able to concur with them, thinking that it would be better to open an industrial school. Douglass was opposed both to the establishment of such a college as was suggested, and to that of an ordinary industrial school where pupils should merely "earn the means of obtaining an education in books." He desired what we now call the vocational school, "a series of workshops where colored men could learn some of the handicrafts, learn to work in iron, wood, and leather, while incidentally acquiring a plain English education."[44]

Under Douglass's leadership the movement had a new goal. The learning of trades was no longer to be subsidiary to conventional education. Just the reverse was true. Moreover, it was not to be entrusted to individuals operating on a small scale; it was to be a public effort of larger scope. The aim was to make the education of Negroes so articulate with their needs as to improve their economic condition. Seeing that despite the successful endeavors of many freedmen to acquire higher education that the race was still kept in penury, Douglass believed that by reconstructing their educational policy the friends of the race could teach the colored people to help themselves. Pecuniary embarrassment, he thought, was the cause of all evil to the blacks, "for poverty kept them ignorant and their lack of enlightenment kept them degraded." The deliverance from these evils, he contended, could be effected not by such a fancied or artificial elevation as the mere diffusion of information by institutions beyond the immediate needs of the poor. The awful plight of the Negroes, as he saw it, resulted directly from not having the opportunity to learn trades, and from "narrowing their limits to earn a livelihood." Douglass deplored the fact that even menial employments were rapidly passing away from the colored people. Under the caption of "Learn Trades or Starve," he tried to drive home the truth that if the free people of color did not soon heed his advice, foreigners then immigrating in large numbers would elbow them from all lucrative positions. In his own words, "every day begins with the lesson and ends with the lesson that colored men must find new employments, new modes of usefulness to society, or that they must decay under the pressing wants to which their condition is bringing them."[45]

Douglass believed in higher education and looked forward to that stage in the development of the Negroes when high schools and colleges could contribute to their progress. He knew, however, that it was foolish to think that persons accustomed to the rougher and harder modes of living could in a single leap from their low condition reach that of professional men. The attainment of such positions, he thought, was contingent upon laying a foundation in things material by passing "through the intermediate gradations of agriculture and the mechanic arts."[46] He was sure that the higher institutions then open to the colored people would be adequate to the task of providing for them all the professional men they then needed, and that the facilities for higher education so far as the schools and colleges in the free States were concerned would increase quite in proportion to the future needs of the race.

Douglass deplored the fact that education and emigration had gone together. As soon as a colored man of genius like Russworm, Garnett, Ward, or Crummell appeared, the so-called friends of the race reached the conclusion that he could better serve his race elsewhere. Seeing themselves pitted against odds, such bright men had had to seek more congenial countries. The training of Negroes merely to aid the colonization scheme would have little bearing on the situation at home unless its promoters could transplant the majority of the free people of color. The aim then should be not to transplant the race but to adopt a policy such as he had proposed to elevate it in the United States.[47]

Vocational education, Douglass thought, would disprove the so-called mental inferiority of the Negroes. He believed that the blacks should show by action that they were equal to the whites rather than depend on the defense of friends who based their arguments not on facts but on certain admitted principles. Believing in the mechanical genius of the Negroes he hoped that in the establishment of this institution they would have an opportunity for development. In it he saw a benefit not only to the free colored people of the North, but also to the slaves. The strongest argument used by the slaveholder in defense of his precious institution was the low condition of the free people of color of the North. Remove this excuse by elevating them and you will hasten the liberation of the slaves. The best refutation of the proslavery argument is the "presentation of an industrious, enterprising, thrifty, and intelligent free black population."[48] An element of this kind, he believed, would rise under the fostering care of vocational teachers.

The Education of the Negro

With Douglass this proposition did not descend to the plane of mere suggestion. Audiences which he addressed from time to time were informed as to the necessity of providing for the colored people facilities of practical education.[49] The columns of his paper rendered the cause noble service. He entered upon the advocacy of it with all the zeal of an educational reformer, endeavoring to show how this policy would please all concerned. Anxious fathers whose minds had been exercised by the inquiry as to what to do with their sons would welcome the opportunity to have them taught trades. It would be in line with the "eminently practical philanthropy of the Negroes' trans-Atlantic friends." America would scarcely object to it as an attempt to agitate the mind on slavery or to destroy the Union. "It could not be tortured into a cause for hard words by the American people," but the noble and good of all classes would see in the effort "an excellent motive, a benevolent object, temperately, wisely, and practically manifested."[50] The leading free people of color heeded this message. Appealing to them through their delegates assembled in Rochester in 1853, Douglass secured a warm endorsement of his plan in eloquent speeches and resolutions passed by the convention.

This great enterprise, like all others, was soon to encounter opposition. Mrs. Stowe was attacked as soliciting money abroad for her own private use. So bitter were these proslavery diatribes that Henry Ward Beecher and Frederick Douglass had some difficulty in convincing the world that her maligners had no grounds for this vicious accusation. Furthermore, on taking up the matter with Mrs. Stowe after her return to the United States, Douglass was disappointed to learn that she had abandoned her plan to found a vocational institution. He was never able to see any force in the reasons for the change of policy; but believed that Mrs. Stowe acted conscientiously, although her action was decidedly embarrassing to him both at home and abroad.[51]

[1: Minutes of the Fourth Annual Convention for the Improvement of the Free People of Color, p. 26.]
[2: Buckingham, Slave States of America, vol. ii., p. 112.]
[3: Du Bois and Dill, The Negro American Artisan, p. 36.]
[4: Du Bois and Dill, The Negro American Artisan, pp. 31, 32, 33.]
[5: Du Bois and Dill, The Negro American Artisan, p. 34, and Special Report of the U.S. Com. of Ed., 1871, p. 365.]
[6: Du Bois and Dill, The Negro American Artisan, pp. 31, 32.]
[7: Du Bois and Dill, The Negro American Artisan, p. 32.]
[8: Special Report of the U.S. Com. of Ed., 1871, p. 339.]
[9: Minutes of the Third Annual Convention of the Free People of Color, p. 18.]
[10: Minutes of the Fourth Annual Convention for the Improvement of the Free People of Color, p. 26.]
[11: This statement is based on articles appearing in The Liberator from time to time.]
[12: Minutes of the Second Annual Convention for the Improvement of the Free People of Color, 1831, p. 10.]
[13: Minutes of the Second Annual Convention for the Improvement of the Free People of Color, 1831, p. II.]
[14: The Liberator, June 13, 1835.]
[15: Douglass, Narrative of the Life of Frederick Douglass, p. 248.]

Vocational Training

[16: Minutes of the Fourth Annual Convention for the Improvement of the Free People of Color, p. 26; and The Liberator, October 22, 1831; and The Abolitionist, November, 1833 (p. 191).]

[17: Minutes of the Fourth Annual Convention for the Improvement of the Free People of Color, p. 27.]

[18: Minutes of the Third Annual Convention for the Improvement of the Free People of Color, p. 34.]

[19: The Abolitionist (November 1833), p. 191.]

[20: The Liberator, October 22, 1831.]

[21: Monroe, Cyclopaedia of Education, vol. iv., p. 406.]

[22: Ibid., vol. iv., p. 406; and The Liberator, July 9, 1831.]

[23: The Liberator, July 4, 1835.]

[24: Minutes and Proceedings of the Third Annual Convention for the Improvement of the Free People of Color, p. 34; and Monroe, Cyclopaedia of Education, vol. iv., p. 406.]

[25: Minutes and Proceedings of the Third Annual Convention for the Improvement of the Free People of Color, p. 25.]

[26: African Repository, vol. x., p. 312.]

[27: Ibid., vol. x., p. 312.]

[28: Special Report of the U.S. Com. of Ed., 1871, p. 379.]

[29: Ibid., 1871, p. 379.]

[30: Howe, Ohio Historical Collections, p. 355.]

[31: Howe, Ohio Historical Collections, p. 356.]

[32: Wickersham, History of Education in Pa., p. 254.]

[33: Boone, The History of Education in Indiana, p. 77.]

[34: According to the Report of the United States Commissioner of Education in 1893 the colored students then constituted about one-third of those then registered at this institution. See p. 1944 of this report.]

[35: Records of the United States Bureau of Education.]

[36: Henson, Life of Josiah Henson, pp. 73, 74.]

[37: Henson, Life of Josiah Henson, p. 115.]

[38: Ibid., p. 117.]

[39: Drew, A North-Side View of Slavery, p. 309; and Coffin, Reminiscences, pp. 249, 250.]

[40: Minutes and Proceedings of the Third Annual Convention, etc., p. 25.]

[41: The Fifth Report of the American Antislavery Society, p. 115; Douglass, The Life and Times of, p. 248.]

[42: Clarke, Present Condition of the Free People of Color of the United States, 1859, pp. 9, 10, 11, 13, and 29.]

[43: Ibid., pp. 9, 10, and 23.]

[44: Douglass, The Life and Times of, p. 248.]

[45: Douglass, The Life and Times of, p. 248.]

[46: Ibid., p. 249.]

[47: Douglass, The Life and Times, p. 250.]

[48: Douglass, The Life and Times of, p. 251.]

[49: African Repository, vol. xxix., p. 136.]

[50: Douglass, Life and Times of, p. 252.]

[51: Ibid., p. 252.]

Chapter 13

Education at Public Expense

The persistent struggle of the colored people to have their children educated at public expense shows how resolved they were to be enlightened. In the beginning Negroes had no aspiration to secure such assistance. Because the free public schools were first regarded as a system to educate the poor, the friends of the free blacks turned them away from these institutions lest men might reproach them with becoming a public charge. Moreover, philanthropists deemed it wise to provide separate schools for Negroes to bring them into contact with sympathetic persons, who knew their peculiar needs. In the course of time, however, when the stigma of charity was removed as a result of the development of the free schools at public expense, Negroes concluded that it was not dishonorable to share the benefits of institutions which they were taxed to support.[1] Unable then to cope with systems thus maintained for the education of the white youth, the directors of colored schools requested that something be appropriated for the education of Negroes. Complying with these petitions boards of education provided for colored schools which were to be partly or wholly supported at public expense. But it was not long before the abolitionists saw that they had made a mistake in carrying out this policy. The amount appropriated to the support of the special schools was generally inadequate to supply them with the necessary equipment and competent teachers, and in most communities the white people had begun to regard the co-education of the races as undesirable. Confronted then with this caste prejudice, one of the hardest struggles of the Negroes and their sympathizers was that for democratic education.

The friends of the colored people in Pennsylvania were among the first to direct the attention of the State to the duty of enlightening the blacks as well as the whites. In 1802, 1804, and 1809, respectively, the State passed, in the interest of the poor, acts which although interpreted to exclude Negroes from the benefits therein provided, were construed, nevertheless, by friends of the race as authorizing their education at public expense. Convinced of the truth of this contention, officials in different parts of the State began to yield in the next decade. At Columbia, Pennsylvania, the names of such colored children as were entitled to the benefits of the law for the education of the poor were taken in 1818 to enable them to attend the free public schools. Following the same policy, the Abolition Society of Philadelphia, seeing that the city had established public schools for white children in 1818, applied two years later for the share of the fund to which the children of African descent were entitled by law. The request was granted. The Comptroller opened in Lombard Street in 1822 a school for children of color, maintained at the expense of the State. This furnished a precedent for other such schools which were established in 1833, and 1841.[2] Harrisburg had a colored school early in the century, but upon the establishment of the Lancastrian school in that city in the thirties, the colored as well as the white children were required to attend it or pay for their education themselves.[3]

In 1834 the legislature of Pennsylvania established a system of public schools, but the claims of the Negroes to public education were neither guaranteed nor denied.[4] The school law of 1854, however, seems to imply that the benefits of the system had always been understood to extend to colored children.[5] This measure provided that the comptrollers and directors of the several school districts of the State could establish within their respective districts separate schools for Negro and mulatto children wherever they could be so located as to accommodate twenty or more pupils. Another provision was that wherever such schools should "be established and kept open four months in the year" the directors and comptrollers should not be compelled to admit colored pupils to any other schools of that district. The law was interpreted to mean that wherever such accommodations were not provided the children of Negroes could attend the other schools. Such was the case in the rural districts where a few colored children often found it pleasant and profitable to attend school with their white friends.[6] The children of Robert B. Purvis, however, were turned away from the public schools of Philadelphia on the ground that special educational facilities for them had been provided.[7] It was not until 1881 that Pennsylvania finally swept away all the distinctions of caste from her public school system.

As the colored population of New Jersey was never large, there was not sufficient concentration of such persons in that State to give rise to the problems which at times confronted the benevolent people of Pennsylvania. Great as had been the reaction, the Negroes of New Jersey never entirely lost the privilege of attending school with white students. The New Jersey Constitution of 1844 provided that the funds for the support of the public schools should be applied for the equal benefit of all the people of that State.[8] Considered then entitled to the benefits of this fund, colored pupils were early admitted into the public schools without any social distinction.[9] This does not mean that there were no colored schools in that commonwealth. Negroes in a few settlements like that of Springtown had their own schools.[10] Separate schools were declared illegal by an act of the General Assembly in 1881.

Certain communities of New York provided separate schools for colored pupils rather than admit them to those open to white children. On recommendation of the superintendent of schools in 1823 the State adopted the policy of organizing schools exclusively for colored people.[11] In places where they already existed, the State could aid the establishment as did the New York Common Council in 1824, when it appropriated a portion of its fund to the support of the African Free Schools.[12] In 1841 the New York legislature authorized any district, with the approbation of the school commissioners, to establish a separate school for the colored children in their locality. The superintendent's report for 1847 shows that schools for Negroes had been established in fifteen counties in the State, reporting an enrollment of 5000 pupils. For the maintenance of these schools the sum of $17,000 had been annually expended. Colored pupils were enumerated by the trustees in their annual reports, drew public money for the district in which they resided, and were equally entitled with white children to the benefit of the school fund. In the rural districts colored children were generally admitted to the common schools. Wherever race prejudice, however, was sufficiently violent to exclude them from the village school, the trustees were empowered to use the Negroes' share of the public money to provide for their education elsewhere. At the same time indigent Negroes were to be exempted from the payment of the "rate bill" which fell as a charge upon the other citizens of the district.[13]

Some trouble had arisen from making special appropriations for incorporated villages. Such appropriations, the superintendent had observed, excited prejudice and parsimony; for the trustees of some villages had learned to expend only the special appropriations for the education of the colored pupils, and to use the public money in establishing and maintaining schools for the white children. He believed that it was wrong to argue that Negroes were any more a burden to incorporated villages than to cities or rural districts, and that they were, therefore, entitled to every allowance of money to educate them.[14]

In New York City much had already been done to enlighten the Negroes through the schools of the Manumission Society. But as the increasing population of color necessitated additional facilities, the Manumission Society obtained from the fund of the Public School Society partial support of its system. The next step was to unite the African Free Schools with those of the Public School Society to reduce the number of organizations participating in the support of Negro education. Despite the argument of some that the two systems should be kept separate, the property and schools of the Manumission Society were transferred to the New York Public School Society in 1834.[15] Thereafter the schools did not do as well as they had done before. The administrative part of the work almost ceased, the schools lost in efficiency, and the former attendance of 1400 startlingly dropped. An investigation made in 1835 showed that many Negroes, intimidated by frequent race riots incident to the reactionary movement, had left the city, while others kept their children at home for safety. It seemed, too, that they looked upon the new system as an innovation, did not like the action of the Public School Society in reducing their schools of advanced grade to that of the primary, and bore it grievously that so many of the old teachers in whom they had confidence, had been dropped. To bring order out of chaos the investigating committee advised the assimilation of the separate schools to the white. Thereupon the society undertook to remake the colored schools, organizing them into a system which offered instruction in primary, intermediate, and grammar departments. The task of reconstruction, however, was not completed until 1853, when the property of the colored schools was transferred to the Board of Education of New York.[16]

The second transfer marked an epoch in the development of Negro education in New York. The Board of Education proceeded immediately to perfect the system begun at the time of the first change. The new directors reclassified the lower grades, opened other grammar schools, and established a normal school according to the recommendation of the investigating committee of 1835. Supervision being more rigid thereafter, the schools made some progress, but failed to accomplish what was expected of them. They were carelessly intrusted for supervision to the care of ward officers, some of whom partly neglected this duty, while others gave the work no attention whatever. It was unfortunate, too, that some of these schools were situated in parts of the city where the people were not interested in the uplift of the despised race, and in a few cases in wards which were almost proslavery. Better results followed after the colored schools were brought under the direct supervision of the Board of Education.

Before the close of the Civil War the sentiment of the people of the State of New York had changed sufficiently to permit colored children to attend the regular public schools in several communities. This, however, was not general. It was, therefore, provided in the revised code of that State in 1864 that the board of education of any city or incorporated village might establish separate schools for children and youth of African descent provided such schools be supported in the same manner as those maintained for white children. The last vestige of caste in the public schools of New York was not exterminated until 1900, in the administration of Theodore Roosevelt as Governor of New York. The legislature then passed an act providing that no one should be denied admittance to any public school on account of race, color, or previous condition of servitude.[17]

In Rhode Island, where the black population was proportionately larger than in some other New England States, special schools for persons of color continued. These efforts met with success at Newport. In the year 1828 a separate school for colored children was established at Providence and placed in charge of a teacher receiving a salary of $400 per annum.[18] A decade later another such school was opened on Pond Street in the same city. About this time the school law of Rhode Island was modified so as to make it a little more favorable to the people of color. The State temporarily adopted a rule by which the school fund was thereafter not distributed, as formerly, according to the number of inhabitants below the age of sixteen. It was to be apportioned, thereafter, according to the number of white persons under the age of ten years, "together with five-fourteenths of the said [colored] population between the ages of ten and twenty-four years." This law remained in force between the years 1832 and 1845. Under the new system these schools seemingly made progress. In 1841 they were no longer giving the mere essentials of reading and writing, but combined the instruction of both the grammar and the primary grades.[19]

Thereafter Rhode Island had to pass through the intense antislavery struggle which had for its ultimate aim both the freedom of the Negro and the democratization of the public schools. Petitions were sent to the legislature, and appeals were made to representatives asking for a repeal of those laws which permitted the segregation of the colored children in the public schools. But intense as this agitation became, and urgently as it was put before the public, it failed to gain sufficient momentum to break down the barriers prior to 1866 when the legislature of Rhode Island passed an act abolishing separate schools for Negroes.[20]

Prior to the reactionary movement the schools of Connecticut were, like most others in New England at that time, open alike to black and white. It seems, too, that colored children were well received and instructed as thoroughly as their white friends. But in 1830, whether on account of the increasing race prejudice or the desire to do for themselves, the colored people of Hartford presented to the School Society of that city a petition that a separate school for persons of color be established with a part of the public school fund which might be apportioned to them according to their number. Finding this request reasonable, the School Society decided to take the necessary steps to comply with it. As such an agreement would have no standing at law the matter was recommended to the legislature of the State, which authorized the establishment in that commonwealth of several separate schools for persons of color.[21] This arrangement, however, soon proved unsatisfactory. Because of the small number of Negroes in Connecticut towns, they found their pro rata inadequate to the maintenance of separate schools. No buildings were provided for them, such schools as they had were not properly supervised, the teachers were poorly paid, and with the exception of a little help from a few philanthropists, the white citizens failed to aid the cause. In 1846, therefore, the pastor of the colored Congregational Church sent to the School Society of Hartford a memorial calling attention to the fact that for lack of means the colored schools had been unable to secure suitable quarters and competent teachers. Consequently the education of their children had been exceedingly irregular, deficient, and onerous. The School Society had done nothing for these institutions but to turn over to them every year their small share of the public fund. These gentlemen then decided to raise by taxation an amount adequate to the support of two better equipped schools and proceeded at once to provide for its collection and expenditure.[22]

The results gave general satisfaction for a while. But as it was a time when much was being done to develop the public schools of New England, the colored people of Hartford could not remain contented. They saw the white pupils housed in comfortable buildings and attending properly graded classes, while their own children continued to be crowded into small insanitary rooms and taught as unclassified students. The Negroes, therefore, petitioned for a more suitable building and a better organization of their schools. As this request came at the time when the abolitionists were working hard to exterminate caste from the schools of New England, the School Committee called a meeting of the memorialists to decide whether they desired to send their children to the white or separate schools.[23] They decided in favor of the latter, provided that the colored people should have a building adequate to their needs and instruction of the best kind.[24] Complying with this decision the School Society erected the much-needed building in 1852. To provide for the maintenance of the separate schools the property of the citizens was taxed at such a rate as to secure to the colored pupils of the city benefits similar to those enjoyed by the white pupils.[25]

Ardent antislavery men believed that this segregation in the schools was undemocratic. They asserted that the colored people would never have made such a request had the teachers of the public schools taken the proper interest in them. The Negroes, too, had long since been convinced that the white people would not maintain separate schools with the same equipment which they gave their own. This arrangement, however, continued until 1868. The legislature then passed an act declaring that the schools of the State should be open to all persons alike between the ages of four and sixteen, and that no person should be denied instruction in any public school in his school district on account of race or color.[26]

In the State of Massachusetts the contest was most ardent. Boston opened its first primary school for colored children in 1820. In other towns like Salem and Nantucket, New Bedford and Lowell, where the colored population was also considerable, the same policy was carried out.[27] Some years later, however, both the Negroes and their friends saw the error of their early advocacy of the establishment of special schools to escape the stigma of receiving charity. After the change in the attitude toward the public free schools and the further development of caste in American education, there arose in Massachusetts a struggle between leaders determined to restrict the Negroes' privileges to the use of poorly equipped separate schools and those contending for equality in education.

Basing their action on the equality of men before the law, the advocates of democratic education held meetings from which went frequent and urgent petitions to school committees until Negroes were accepted in the public schools in all towns in Massachusetts except Boston.[28] Children of African blood were successfully admitted to the New Bedford schools on equality with the white youth in 1838.[29] In 1846 the school committee of that town reported that the colored pupils were regular in their attendance, and as successful in their work as the whites. There were then ninety in all in that system; four in the high school, forty in grammar schools, and the remainder in the primary department, all being scattered in such a way as to have one to four in twenty-one to twenty-eight schools. At Lowell the children of a colored family were not only among the best in the schools but the greatest favorites in the system.[30]

The consolidation of the colored school of Salem with the others of that city led to no disturbance. Speaking of the democracy of these schools in 1846 Mr. Richard Fletcher said: "The principle of perfect equality is the vital principle of the system. Here all classes of the community mingle together. The rich and the poor meet on terms of equality and are prepared by the same instruction to discharge the duties of life. It is the principle of equality cherished in the free schools on which our government and free institutions rest. Destroy this principle in the schools and the people would soon cease to be free." At Nantucket, however, some trouble was experienced because of the admission of pupils of color in 1843. Certain patrons criticized the action adversely and withdrew fourteen of their children from the South Grammar School. The system, however, prospered thereafter rather than declined.[31] Many had no trouble in making the change.[32]

These victories having been won in other towns of the State by 1846, it soon became evident that Boston would have to yield. Not only were abolitionists pointing to the ease with which this gain had been made in other towns, but were directing attention to the fact that in these smaller communities Negroes were both learning the fundamentals and advancing through the lower grades into the high school. Boston, which had a larger black population than all other towns in Massachusetts combined, had never seen a colored pupil prepared for a secondary institution in one of its public schools. It was, therefore, evident to fair-minded persons that in cities of separate systems Negroes would derive practically no benefit from the school tax which they paid.

This agitation for the abolition of caste in the public schools assumed its most violent form in Boston during the forties. The abolitionists then organized a more strenuous opposition to the caste system. Why Sarah Redmond and the other children of a family paying tax to support the schools of Boston should be turned away from a public school simply because they were persons of color was a problem too difficult for a fair-minded man.[33] The war of words came, however, when in response to a petition of Edmund Jackson, H.J. Bowditch, and other citizens for the admission of colored people to the public schools in 1844, the majority of the school committee refused the request. Following the opinion of Chandler, their solicitor, they based their action of making distinction in the public schools on the natural distinction of the races, which "no legislature, no social customs, can efface," and which "renders a promiscuous intermingling in the public schools disadvantageous both to them and to the whites."[34] Questioned as to any positive law providing for such discrimination, Chandler gave his opinion that the School Committee of Boston, under the authority perhaps of the City Council, had a legal right to establish and maintain special primary schools for the blacks. He believed, too, that in the exercise of their lawful discretionary power they could exclude white pupils from certain schools and colored pupils from certain other schools when, in their judgment, the best interests of all would thereby be promoted.[35]

Encouraged by the fact that colored children were indiscriminately admitted to the schools of Salem, Nantucket, New Bedford, and Lowell, in fact, of every city in Massachusetts but Boston, the friends of the colored people fearlessly attacked the false legal theories of Solicitor Chandler. The minority of the School Committee argued that schools are the common property of all, and that each and all are legally entitled without "let or hindrance" to the equal benefits of all advantages they might confer.[36] Any action, therefore, which tended to restrict to any individual or class the advantages and benefits designed for all, was an illegal use of authority, and an arbitrary act used for pernicious purposes.[37] Their republican system, the minority believed, conferred civil equality and legal rights upon every citizen, knew neither privileged nor degraded classes, made no distinctions, and created no differences between rich and poor, learned and ignorant, or white and black, but extended to all alike its protection and benefits.[38] The minority considered it a merit of the school system that it produced the fusion of all classes, promoted the feeling of brotherhood, and the habits of equality. The power of the School Committee, therefore, was limited and constrained by the general spirit of the civil policy and by the letter and spirit of the laws which regulated the system.[39] It was further maintained that to debar the colored youth from these advantages, even if they were assured the same external results, would be a sore injustice and would serve as the surest means of perpetuating a prejudice which should be deprecated and discountenanced by all intelligent and Christian men.[40]

To the sophistry of Chandler, Wendell Phillips also made a logical reply. He asserted that as members of a legal body, the School Committee should have eyes only for such distinctions among their fellow-citizens as the law recognized and pointed out. Phillips believed that they had precedents for the difference of age and sex, for regulation of health, etc., but that when they opened their eyes to the varied complexion, to difference of race, to diversity of creed, to distinctions of caste, they would seek in vain through the laws and institutions of Massachusetts for any recognition of their prejudice. He deplored the fact that they had attempted to foist into the legal arrangements of the land a principle utterly repugnant to the State constitution, and that what the sovereignty of the constitution dared not attempt a school committee accomplished. To Phillips it seemed crassly inconsistent to say that races permitted to intermarry should be debarred by Mr. Chandler's "sapient committee" from educational contact.[41]

This agitation continued until 1855 when the opposition had grown too strong to be longer resisted. The legislature of Massachusetts then enacted a law providing that in determining the qualifications of a scholar to be admitted to any public school no distinction should be made on account of the race, color, or religious opinion of the applicant. It was further provided that a child excluded from school for any of these reasons might bring suit for damages against the offending town.[42]

In other towns of New England, where the black population was considerable, separate schools were established. There was one even in Portland, Maine.[43] Efforts in this direction were made in Vermont and New Hampshire, but because of the scarcity of the colored people these States did not have to resort to such segregation. The Constitution of Vermont was interpreted as extending

Education at Public Expense

to Negroes the benefits of the Bill of Rights, making all men free and equal. Persons of color, therefore, were regarded as men entitled to all the privileges of freemen, among which was that of education at the expense of the State.[44] The framers of the Constitution of New Hampshire were equally liberal in securing this right to the dark race.[45] But when the principal of an academy at Canaan admitted some Negroes to his private institution, a mob, as we have observed above, broke up the institution by moving the building to a swamp, while the officials of the town offered no resistance. Such a spirit as this accounts for the rise of separate schools in places where the free blacks had the right to attend any institution of learning supported by the State.

The problem of educating the Negroes at public expense was perplexing also to the minds of the people of the West. The question became more and more important in Ohio as the black population in that commonwealth increased. The law of 1825 provided that moneys raised from taxation of half a mill on the dollar should be appropriated to the support of common schools in the respective counties and that these schools should be "open to the youth of every class and grade without distinction."[46] Some interpreted this law to include Negroes. To overcome the objection to the partiality shown by school officials the State passed another law in 1829. It excluded colored people from the benefits of the new system, and returned them the amount accruing from the school tax on their property.[47] Thereafter benevolent societies and private associations maintained colored schools in Cincinnati, Columbus, Cleveland, and the southern counties of Ohio.[48] But no help came from the cities and the State before 1849 when the legislature passed a law authorizing the establishment of schools for children of color at public expense.[49]

The Negroes of Cincinnati soon discovered that they had not won a great victory. They proceeded at once to elect trustees, organized a system, and employed teachers, relying on the money allotted them by the law on the basis of a per capita division of the school fund received by the Board of Education of Cincinnati. So great was the prejudice that the school officials refused to turn over the required funds on the grounds that the colored trustees were not electors, and therefore could not be office holders qualified to receive and disburse public funds.[50] Under the leadership of John I. Gaines the trustees called indignation meetings, and raised sufficient money to employ Flamen Ball, an attorney, to secure a writ of mandamus. The case was contested by the city officials even in the Supreme Court of the State which decided against the officious whites.[51]

Unfortunately it turned out that this decision did not mean very much to the Negroes. There were not many of them in certain settlements and the per capita division of the fund did not secure to them sufficient means to support schools. Even if the funds had been adequate to pay teachers, they had no schoolhouses. Lawyers of that day contended that the Act of 1849 had nothing to do with the construction of buildings. After a short period of accomplishing practically nothing material, the law was amended so as to transfer the control of such colored schools to the managers of the white system.[52] This was taken as a reflection on the standing of the blacks of the city and tended to make them refuse to cooeperate with the white board. On account of the failure of this body to act effectively prior to 1856, the people of color were again given power to elect their own trustees.[53]

The Education of the Negro

During the contest for the control of the colored schools certain Negroes of Cincinnati were endeavoring to make good their claim that their children had a right to attend any school maintained by the city. Acting upon this contention a colored patron sent his son to a public school, which on account of his presence became the center of unusual excitement.[54] Miss Isabella Newhall, the teacher to whom he went, immediately complained to the Board of Education, requesting that he be expelled on account of his race. After "due deliberation" the Board of Education decided by a vote of fifteen to ten that he would have to withdraw from that school. Thereupon two members of that body, residing in the district of the timorous teacher, resigned.[55]

Thereafter some progress in the development of separate schools in Cincinnati was noted. By 1855 the Board of Education of that city had established four public schools for the instruction of Negro youths. The colored pupils were showing their appreciation by regular attendance, manly deportment, and rapid progress in the acquisition of knowledge. Speaking of these Negroes in 1855, John P. Foote said that they shared with the white citizens that respect for education, and the diffusion of knowledge, which has ever been one of their "characteristics," and that they had, therefore, been more generally intelligent than free persons of color not only in other States but in all other parts of the world.[56] It was in appreciation of the worth of this class of progressive Negroes that in 1858 Nicholas Longworth built a comfortable school-house for them in Cincinnati, leasing it with the privilege of purchasing it in fourteen years.[57] They met these requirements within the stipulated time, and in 1859 secured through other agencies the construction of another building in the western portion of the city.[58]

The agitation for the admission of colored children to the public schools was not confined to Cincinnati alone, but came up throughout the section north of the Ohio River.[59] Where the black population was large enough to form a social center of its own, Negroes and their friends could more easily provide for the education of colored children. In settlements, however, in which just a few of them were found, some liberal-minded man usually asked the question why persons taxed to support a system of free schools should not share its benefits. To strengthen their position these benevolent men referred to the rapid progress of the belated people, many of whom within less than a generation from their emergence from slavery had become intelligent, virtuous, and respectable persons, and in not a few cases had accumulated considerable wealth.[60] Those who insisted that children of African blood should be debarred from the regular public schools had for their defense the so-called inequality of the races. Some went so far as to concede the claims made for the progressive blacks, and even to praise those of their respective communities. [61] But great as their progress had been, the advocates of the restriction of their educational privileges considered it wrong to claim for them equality with the Caucasian race. They believed that society would suffer from an intermingling of the children of the two races.

In Indiana the problem of educating Negroes was more difficult. R.G. Boone says that, "nominally for the first few years of the educational experience of the State, black and white children had equal privileges in the few schools that existed."[62] But this could not continue long. Abolitionists were moving the country, and freedmen soon found enemies as well as friends in the Ohio valley. Indiana, which was in 1824 so very "solicitous for a system of education which would guard against caste distinction," provided in 1837 that the white inhabitants alone of each congressional township should constitute the local school corporation.[63] In 1841 a petition was sent to the legislature requesting that a reasonable share of the school fund be appropriated to the education of Negroes, but the committee to which it was referred reported that legislation on that subject was inexpedient.[64] With the exception of prohibiting the immigration of such persons into that State not much account of them was taken until 1853. Then the legislature amended the law authorizing the establishment of schools in townships so as to provide that in all enumerations the children of color should not be taken, that the property of the blacks and mulattoes should not be taxed for school purposes, and that their children should not derive any benefit from the common schools of that State.[65] This provision had really been incorporated into the former law, but was omitted by oversight on the part of the engrossing clerk.[66]

A resolution of the House instructing the educational committee to report a bill for the establishment of schools for the education of the colored children of the State was overwhelmingly defeated in 1853. Explaining their position the opponents said that it was held "to be better for the weaker party that no privilege be extended to them," as the tendency to such "might be to induce the vain belief that the prejudice of the dominant race could ever be so mollified as to break down the rugged barriers that must forever exist between their social relations." The friends of the blacks believed that by elevating them the sense of their degradation would be keener, and so the greater would be their anxiety to seek another country, where with the spirit of men they "might breathe fresh air of social as well as political liberty."[67] This argument, however, availed little. Before the Civil War the Negroes of Indiana received help in acquiring knowledge from no source but private and mission schools.

In Illinois the situation was better than in Indiana, but far from encouraging. The constitution of 1847 restricted the benefits of the school law to white children, stipulating the word white throughout the act so as to make clear the intention of the legislators.[68] It seemed to some that, in excluding the colored children from the public schools, the law contemplated the establishment of separate schools in that it provided that the amount of school taxes collected from Negroes should be returned. Exactly what should be done with such money, however, was not stated in the act. But even if that were the object in view, the provision was of little help to the people of color for the reason that the clause providing for the return of school taxes was seldom executed. In the few cases in which it was carried out the fund thus raised was not adequate to the support of a special school, and generally there were not sufficient colored children in a community to justify such an outlay. In districts having control of their local affairs, however, the children of Negroes were often given a chance to attend school.

As this scant consideration given Negroes of Illinois left one-half of the six thousand of their children out of the pale of education, earnest appeals were made that the restrictive word white be stricken from the school law. The friends of the colored people sought to show how inconsistent this system was with the spirit of the constitution of the State, which, interpreted as they saw it, guaranteed all persons equality.[69] They held meetings from which came renewed petitions to their representatives, entreating them to repeal or amend the old school law. It was not so much a question as to whether or not there

The Education of the Negro

should be separate schools as it was whether or not the people of color should be educated. The dispersed condition of their children made it impossible for the State to provide for them in special schools the same educational facilities as those furnished the youth of Caucasian blood. Chicago tried the experiment in 1864, but failing to get the desired result, incorporated the colored children into the white schools the following year.[70] The State Legislature had sufficient moral courage to do away with these caste distinctions in 1874.[71]

In other States of the West and the North where few colored people were found, the solution of the problem was easier. After 1848 Negroes were legal voters in the school meetings of Michigan. Colored children were enumerated with others to determine the basis for the apportionment of the school funds, and were allowed to attend the public schools. Wisconsin granted Negroes equal school privileges.[72] After the adoption of a free constitution in 1857, Iowa "determined no man's rights by the color of his skin." Wherever the word white had served to restrict the privileges of persons of color it was stricken out to make it possible for them not only to bear arms and to vote but to attend public schools.[73]

[1: The Negroes of Baltimore were just prior to the Civil War paying $500 in taxes annually to support public schools which their children could not attend.]
[2: Special Report of the U.S. Com. of Ed., 1871, p. 379.]
[3: Ibid., p. 379.]
[4: Purdon's Digest of the Laws of Pa., p. 291, sections 1-23.]
[5: Stroud and Brightly, Purdon's Digest, p. 1064, section 23.]
[6: Wickersham, History of Education in Pa., p. 253.]
[7: Wigham, The Antislavery Cause in America, p. 103.]
[8: Thorpe, Federal and State Constitutions, vol. v., p. 2604.]
[9: Southern Workman, vol. xxxvii., p. 390.]
[10: Special Report of the U.S. Com. of Ed., 1871, p. 400.]
[11: Randall, Hist. of Common School System of New York, p. 24.]
[12: Ibid., p. 48.]
[13: Randall, Hist. of Common School System of New York, p. 248.]
[14: Randall, Hist. of Common School System of New York, p. 249.]
[15: Special Report of the U.S. Com. of Ed., 1871, p. 366.]
[16: Special Report of the U.S. Com. of Ed., 1871, p. 366.]
[17: Laws of New York, 1900, ch. 492.]
[18: Stockwell, Hist. of Education in R.I., p. 169.]
[19: Stockwell, Hist. of Education in R.I., p. 51.]
[20: Public Laws of the State of Rhode Island, 1865-66, p. 49.]
[21: Special Report of the U.S. Com. of Ed., 1871, p. 334.]
[22: Special Report of the U.S. Com. of Ed., 1871, p. 334.]
[23: Minority Report, etc., p. 21.]
[24: Ibid., p. 22.]
[25: Special Report of the U.S. Com. of Ed., 1871, p. 334.]
[26: Public Acts of the General Assembly of Conn., 1868, p. 296.]
[27: Minority Report, etc., p. 35.]
[28: Ibid., p. 20, and Niles Register, vol. lxvi., p. 320.]
[29: Minority Report, etc., p. 23.]
[30: Minority Report, etc., p. 25.]
[31: Ibid., p. 6.]

[32: Ibid., p. 23.]
[33: Wigham, The Antislavery Cause in America, p. 103.]
[34: Minority Report, etc., p. 31.]
[35: Ibid., p. 30.]
[36: Ibid., p. 3.]
[37 Minority Report, etc. pp. 4 and 5.]
[38: Ibid., pp. 3 et. seq.]
[39: Ibid., p. 4.]
[40: Ibid., p. 5.]
[41: Minority Report, etc., p. 27.]
[42: Acts and Resolves of the General Court of Mass., 1855, ch. 256.]
[43: Adams, Anti-slavery, etc., p. 142.]
[44: Thorpe, Federal and State Constitutions, vol. vi., p. 3762.]
[45: Ibid., vol. iv., p. 2471.]
[46: Laws of Ohio, vol. xxiii., pp. 37 et seq.]
[47: Hickok, The Negro in Ohio, p. 85.]
[48: Simmons, Men of Mark, p. 374.]
[49: Laws of Ohio, vol. liii., pp. 117-118.]
[50: Special Report of the U.S. Com. of Ed., 1871, pp. 371, 372.]
[51: Ibid., 1871, p. 372.]
[52: Laws of the State of Ohio, vol. liii., p. 118.]
[53: Ibid., p. 118.]
[54: New York Tribune, Feb. 19, 1855.]
[55: New York Tribune, Feb. 19, 1855; and Carlier, L'Esclavage, etc., p. 339.]
[56: Foote, The Schools of Cincinnati, p. 92.]
[57: Special Report of the U.S. Com. of Ed., 1871, p. 372.]
[58: Ibid., p. 372.]
[59: Hickok, The Negro in Ohio, ch. iii.; and Boone, History of Education in Indiana, p. 237.]
[60: Foote, The Schools of Cincinnati, p. 93.]
[61: Ibid., p. 92.]
[62: Boone, History of Ed. in Indiana, p. 237.]
[63: Laws of a General Nature of the State of Indiana, 1837, p. 15.]
[64: Boone, History of Education in Indiana, p. 237.]
[65: Laws of a General Nature of the State of Indiana, 1855, p. 161.]
[66: Boone, History of Education in Indiana, p. 237.]
[67: Boone, History of Education in Indiana, p. 237.]
[68: The Constitution of Illinois, in the Journal of the Constitution of the State of Illinois, 1847, p. 344.]
[69: Thorpe, Federal and State Constitutions, Const. of Illinois.]
[70: Special Report of U.S. Com. of Ed., 1871, p. 343.]
[71: Starr and Curtis, Annotated Statutes of Illinois, ch. 105, p. 2261.]
[72: Special Report of the U.S. Com. of Ed., 1871, p. 400.]
[73: Journal of the Constitutional Convention of the State of Iowa, 1857, p. 3 of the Constitution.]

Appendix

The following resolutions on the subject treated in this part (the instruction of Negroes) are from the works of Dr. Cotton Mather.--Bishop William Meade.

1st. I would always remember, that my servants are in some sense my children, and by taking care that they want nothing which may be good for them, I would make them as my children; and so far as the methods of instituting piety into the mind which I use with my children, may be properly and prudently used with my servants, they shall be partakers in them--Nor will I leave them ignorant of anything, wherein I may instruct them to be useful to their generation.

2d. I will see that my servants be furnished with bibles and be able and careful to read the lively oracles. I will put bibles and other good and proper books into their hands; will allow them time to read and assure myself that they do not misspend this time--If I can discern any wicked books in their hands, I will take away those pestilential instruments of wickedness.

3d. I will have my servants present at the religious exercises of my family; and will drop, either in the exhortations, in the prayers or daily sacrifices of the family such pages as may have a tendency to quicken a sense of religion in them.

4th. The article of catechising, as far as the age or state of the servants will permit it to be done with decency, shall extend to them also,--And they shall be concerned in the conferences in which I may be engaged with my family, in the repetition of the public sermons. If any of them when they come to me shall not have learned the catechism, I will take care that they do it, and will give them a reward when they have accomplished it.

5th. I will be very inquisitive and solicitous about the company chosen by my servants; and with all possible earnestness will rescue them from the snares of evil company, and forbid their being the companions of fools.

6th. Such of my servants as may be capable of the task, I will employ to teach lessons of piety to my children, and will recompense them for so doing. But I would, by a particular artifice, contrive them to be such lessons, as may be for their own edification too.

7th. I will sometimes call my servants alone; talk to them about the state of their souls; tell them to close with their only servant, charge them to do well and "lay hold on eternal life," and show them very particularly how they may render all they do for me a service to the glorious Lord; how they may do all from a principle of obedience to him, and become entitled to the "reward of the heavenly inheritance."

To those resolutions did I add the following pages as an appendix:

Age is nearly sufficient, with some masters to obliterate every letter and action in the history of a meritorious life, and old services are generally buried under the ruins of an old carcase. It is a barbarous inhumanity in men towards their servants, to account their small failings as crimes, without allowing their past services to have been virtues; gracious God, keep thy servants from such base ingratitude!

But then O servants, if you would obtain "the reward of inheritance," each of you should set yourself to enquire "how shall I approve myself such a servant, that the Lord may bless the house of my master, the more for my being in it?" Certainly there are many ways by which servants may become blessings. Let your studies with your continual prayers for the welfare of the family to which you belong: and the example of your sober carriage render you such. If you will but remember four words and attempt all that is comprised in them, Obedience, Honesty, Industry, and Piety, you will be the blessings and Josephs of the families in which you live. Let these four words be distinctly and frequently recollected; and cheerfully perform all your business from this consideration-- that it is obedience to heaven, and from thence will leave a recompense. It was the observation even of a pagan, "That a master may receive a benefit from a servant"; and "what is done with the affection of a friend, ceases to be the act of a mere servant." Even the maid-servants of a house may render a great service to it, by instructing the infants and instilling into their minds the lessons of goodness.--In the Appendix of Rev. Thomas Bacon's Sermons Addressed to Masters and Servants.

EDIT DU ROI

Concernant les Esclaves Negres des Colonies, qui seront amenes, ou envoyes en France. Donne a Paris au mois d'Octobre 1716.

I. Nous avons connu la necessite qu'il y a d'y soutenir l'execution de l'edit du mars 1685, qui en maintenant la discipline de l'Eglise Catholique, Apostolique et Romaine, pourvoit a ce qui concerne l'etat et la qualite des Esclaves Negres, qu'on entretient dans lesdites colonies pour la culture des terres; et comme nous avons ete informes que plusieurs habitans de nos Isles de l'Amerique desirent envoyer en France quelques-uns de leur Esclaves pour les confirmer dans les Instructions et dans les Exercices de notre Religion, et pour leur faire apprendre en meme tems quelque Art et Metier dont les colonies recevroient beaucoup d'utilite par le retour de ces Esclaves; mais que les habitans craignaient que les Esclaves ne pretendent etre libres en arrivant en France, ce qui pourroit causer auxdits habitans une perte considerable, et les detourner d'un objet aussi pieux et aussi utile.

II. Si quelques-uns des habitans de nos colonies, ou officiers employes sur l'Etat desdites colonies, veulent amener en France avec eux des Esclaves Negres, de l'un & de l'autre sexe, en qualite de domestique ou autrement pour les fortifier davantage dans notre Religion, tant par les instructions qu'ils recevront, que par l'exemple de nos autre sujets, et pour leur faire apprendre en meme tems quelque Art et Metier, dont les colonies puissent retirer de l'utilite, par le retour de ces Esclaves, lesdits proprietaires seront tenus d'en obtenir la permission des Gouverneurs Generaux, ou Commandans dans chaque Isle, laquelle permission contiendra le nom du proprietaire, celui des Esclaves, leur age & leur signalement.--Code Noir ou Recueil d'edits, declarations, et arrets concernant des Esclaves Negres Discipline el le commerce des Esclaves Negres des isles francaises de l'Amerique (in Recueil de reglemens, edits, declarations, et arrets concernant le commerce, l'administration de la justice et la police des colonies francaises de l'Amerique et les Engages avec le Code Noir et l'addition audit Code) (Jefferson's copy). A Paris chez les Libraires Associes, 1745.

A PROPOSITION FOR ENCOURAGING THE CHRISTIAN EDUCATION OF INDIAN, NEGRO, AND MULATTO CHILDREN AT LAMBETH, VIRGINIA, 1724

"It being a duty of Christianity very much neglected by masters and mistresses of this country (America) to endeavor the good instruction and education of their heathen slaves in the Christian faith,--the said duty being likewise earnestly recommended by his Majesty's instructions,--for the facilitating thereof among the young slaves that are born among us; it is, therefore, humbly proposed that every Indian, Negro, or mulatto child that shall be baptized and afterward brought to church and publicly catechized by the minister in church, and shall, before the fourteenth year of his or her age, give a distinct account of the Creed, the Lord's Prayer and Ten Commandments, and whose master or mistress shall receive a certificate from the minister that he or she hath so done, such Indian, Negro or mulatto child shall be exempted from paying all levies till the age of eighteen years."--Bishop William Meade's Old Churches, Ministers, and Families of Virginia, vol. i., p. 265.

PASTORAL LETTER OF BISHOP GIBSON OF LONDON

To the Masters and Mistresses of Families in the English Plantations abroad; exhorting them to encourage and promote the instruction of their Negroes in the Christian Faith. (About 1727.)

The care of the Plantations abroad being committed to the Bishop of London as to Religious Affairs; I have thought it my duty to make particular Inquiries into the State of Religion in those Parts, and to learn among other Things, what numbers of slaves are employed within the several Governments, and what Means are used for their Instruction in the Christian Faith: I find the Numbers are prodigiously great; and am not a little troubled to observe how small a Progress has been made in a Christian country, towards the delivering those poor Creatures from the Pagan Darkness and Superstition in which they were bred, and the making them Partakers in the Light of the Gospel, and the Blessings and Benefits belonging to it. And what is yet more to be lamented, I find there has not only been very little Progress made in the work but that all Attempts toward it have been by too many industriously discouraged and hindered; partly by magnifying the Difficulties of the Work beyond what they really are; and partly by mistaken Suggestions of the Change which Baptism would make in the Condition of the Negroes, to the Loss and Disadvantage of their Masters.

As to the Difficulties; it may be pleaded, That the Negroes are grown Persons when they come over, and that having been accustomed to the Pagan Rites and Idolatries of their own Country, they are prejudiced against all other Religions, and more particularly against the Christian, as forbidding all that Licentiousness which is usually practiced among the Heathens.... But a farther Difficulty is that they are utter Strangers to our Language, and we to theirs; and the Gift of

Appendix

Tongues being now ceased, there is no Means left of instructing them in the Doctrines of the Christian Religion. And this, I own is a real Difficulty, as long as it continues, and as far as it reaches. But, if I am rightly informed, many of the Negroes, who are grown Persons when they come over, do of themselves obtain so much of our Language, as enables them to understand, and to be understood, in Things which concern the ordinary Business of Life, and they who can go so far of their own Accord, might doubtless be carried much farther, if proper Methods and Endeavors were used to bring them to a competent Knowledge of our Language, with a pious view to instructing them in the Doctrines of our Religion. At least, some of them, who are more capable and more serious than the rest, might be easily instructed both in our Language and Religion, and then be made use of to convey Instruction to the rest in their own Language. And this, one would hope, may be done with great Ease, wherever there is a hearty and sincere Zeal of the Work.

But what Difficulties there may be in instructing those who are grown-up before they are brought over; there are not the like Difficulties in the Case of their Children, who are born and bred in our Plantations, who have never been accustomed to Pagan Rites and Superstitions, and who may easily be trained up, like all other Children, to any Language whatsoever, and particularly to our own; if the making them good Christians be sincerely the Desire and Intention of those, who have Property in them, and Government over them.--Dalcho's An Historical Account of the Protestant Episcopal Church in South Carolina, pp. 104-106.

ANOTHER PASTORAL LETTER OF BISHOP GIBSON OF LONDON

To the Missionaries in the English Plantations (about 1727).

DEAR BROTHER,

Having understood by many Letters from the Plantations, and by the Accounts of Persons who have come from thence, that very little progress hath hitherto been made in the conversion of the Negroes to the Christian Faith; I have thought it proper for me to lay before Masters and Mistresses the Obligations they are under, and to promote and encourage that pious and necessary Work....

As to those Ministers who have Negroes of their own; I cannot but esteem it their indispensable Duty to use their best Endeavors to instruct them in the Christian Religion, in order to their being baptised; both because such Negroes are their proper and immediate Care, and because it is in vain to hope that other Masters and Mistresses will exert themselves in this Work, if they see it wholly neglected, or but coldly pursued, in the Families of the Clergy ...

I would also hope that the Schoolmasters in the several Parishes, part of whose Business it is to instruct Youth in the Principles of Christianity, might contribute somewhat towards the carrying on of this Work; by being ready to bestow upon it some of their Leisure Time, and especially on the Lord's Day, when both they and the Negroes are most at liberty and the Clergy are taken up with the public Duties of their Function.--Dalcho's An Historical Account of the Protestant Episcopal Account of the Protestant Episcopal Church in South Carolina, pages 112-114.

The Education of the Negro

AN EXTRACT FROM A SERMON PREACHED BY BISHOP SECKER OF LONDON IN 1741

"The next Object of the Society's Concern, were the poor Negroes. These unhappy Wretches learn in their Native Country, the grossest Idolatry, and the most savage Dispositions: and then are sold to the best Purchaser: sometimes by their Enemies, who would else put them to Death; sometimes by the nearest Friends, who are either unable or unwilling to maintain them. Their Condition in our Colonies, though it cannot well be worse than it would have been at Home, is yet nearly as hard as possible: their Servitude most laborious, their Punishments most severe. And thus many thousands of them spend their whole Days, one Generation after another, undergoing with reluctant Minds continual Toil in this World, and comforted with no Hopes of Reward in a better. For it is not to be expected that Masters, too commonly negligent of Christianity themselves, will take much Pains to teach it their slaves; whom even the better Part of them are in a great Measure habituated to consider, as they do their Cattle, merely with a view to the Profit arising from them. Not a few, therefore, have openly opposed their Instruction, from an Imagination now indeed proved and acknowledged to be groundless, that Baptism would entitle them to Freedom. Others by obliging them to work on Sundays to provide themselves Necessaries, leave them neither Time to learn Religion, nor any Prospect of being able to subsist, if once the Duty of resting on that Day become Part of their Belief. And some, it may be feared, have been averse to their becoming Christians because after that, no Pretence will remain for not treating them like Men. When these Obstacles are added to the fondness they have for their old Heathenish Rites, and the strong Prejudices they must have against Teachers from among those, whom they serve so unwillingly; it cannot be wondered, if the Progress made in their Conversion prove slow. After some Experience of this kind, Catechists were appointed in two Places, by Way of Trial for Their Instruction alone: whose Success, where it was least, hath been considerable; and so great in the Plantation belonging to the Society that out of two hundred and thirty, at least seventy are now Believers in Christ. And there is lately an Improvement to this Scheme begun to be executed, by qualifying and employing young Negroes, prudently chosen, to teach their Countrymen: from which in the Opinion of the best Judges, we may reasonably promise ourselves, that this miserable People, the Generality of whom have hitherto sat in Darkness, will see great Light."--Seeker's A Sermon Preached before the Incorporated Society for the Propagation of the Gospel in Foreign Parts, 1741.

EXTRACTS FROM THE SERMONS OF REV. THOMAS BACON ADDRESSED TO MASTERS AND SERVANTS ABOUT 1750

"Next to our children and brethren by blood, our servants, and especially our slaves, are certainly in the nearest relation to us. They are an immediate and necessary part of our households, by whose labors and assistance we are enabled to enjoy the gifts of Providence in ease and plenty; and surely we owe them a return of what is just and equal for the drudgery and hardships they go through in our service....

"It is objected, They are such stubborn creatures, there is no dealing with them.

Appendix

"Answer. Supposing this to be true of most of them (which I believe will scarcely be insisted on:) may it not fairly be asked, whence doth this stubbornness proceed?--Is it from nature?--That cannot be:--for I think it is generally acknowledged that new Negroes, or those born in and imported from the coast of Guinea, prove the best and most tractable servants. Is it then from education?--for one or the other it must proceed from.--But pray who had the care of bringing up those that were born here?--Was it not ourselves?--And might not an early care, of instilling good principles into them when young, have prevented much of that stubbornness and untractableness you complain of in country-born negroes?--These, you cry out, are wickeder than the others:--and, pray, where did they learn that wickedness?--Was it not among ourselves?--for those who come immediately from their own country, you say, have more simplicity and honesty. A sad reproach to a Christian people indeed! that such poor ignorant heathens shall bring better morals and dispositions from home with them, that they can learn or actually do contract amongst us!

* * * * *

"It is objected,--they are so ignorant and unteachable, they cannot be brought to any knowledge in these matters.

"Answer. This objection seems to have little or no truth in it, with respect to the bulk of them.--Their ignorance, indeed, about matters of religion, is not to be disputed;--they are sunk in it to a sad and lamentable degree, which has been shown to be chiefly owing to the negligence of their owners.--But that they are so stupid and unteachable, as that they cannot be brought to any competent knowledge in these matters, is false, and contrary to fact and experience. In regard to their work, they learn it, and grow dexterous enough in a short time. Many of them have learned trades and manufactures, which they perform well, and with sufficient ingenuity:--whence it is plain they are not unteachable; do not want natural parts and capacities.--Most masters and mistresses will complain of their art and cunning in contriving to deceive them.--Is it reasonable to deny then they can learn what is good, when it is owned at the same time they can be so artful in what is bad?--Their ignorance, therefore, if born in the country, must absolutely be the fault of their owners:--and such as are brought here from Africa may, surely, be taught something of advantage to their own future state, as well as to work for their masters' present gain.--The difference plainly consists in this;--that a good deal of pains is taken to shew them how to labour, and they are punished if they neglect it.--This sort of instruction their owners take care to give them every day, and look well to it that it be duly followed.--But no such pains are taken in the other case.--They are generally left to themselves, whether they will serve God, or worship Devils--whether they become christians, or remain heathens as long as they live: as if either their souls were not worth the saving, or as if we were under no obligation of giving them any instruction:--which is the true reason why so many of them who are grown up, and lived many years among us, are as entirely ignorant of the principles of religion, as if they had never come into a christian country:--at least, as to any good or practical purposes.

* * * * *

The Education of the Negro

"I have dwelt the longer upon this head, because it is of the utmost importance, and seems to be but little considered among us.--For there is too much reason to fear, that the many vices and immoralities so common among white people;--the lewdness, drunkenness, quarrelling, abusiveness, swearing, lying, pride, backbiting, overreaching, idleness, and sabbath-breaking, everywhere to be seen among us, are a great encouragement to our Negroes to do the like, and help strongly to confirm them in the habits of wickedness and impiety.

"We ought not only to avoid giving them bad examples, and abstain from all appearance of evil, but also strive to set a daily good example before their eyes, that seeing us lead the way in our own person, they may more readily be persuaded to follow us in the wholesome paths of religion and virtue.

* * * * *

"We ought to make this reading and studying the holy scriptures, and the reading and explaining them to our children and slaves, and the catechizing or instructing them in the principles of the Christian religion, a stated duty.

* * * * *

"We ought in a particular manner to take care of the children, and instil early principles of piety and religion into their minds.

"If the grown up slaves, from confirmed habits of vice, are hard to be reclaimed, the children surely are in our power, and may be trained up in the way they should go, with rational hopes that when they are old, they will not depart from it.--We ought, therefore, to take charge of their education principally upon ourselves, and not leave them entirely to the care of their wicked parents.--If the present generation be bad, we may hope by this means that the succeeding ones will be much better. One child well instructed, will take care when grown up to instruct his children; and they again will teach their posterity good things.--And I am fully of opinion, that the common notion of wickedness running in the blood, is not so general in fact as to be admitted for an axiom. And that the vices we see descending from parents to their children are chiefly owing to the malignant influence of bad example and conversation.--And though some persons may be, and undoubtedly are, born with stronger passions and appetites, or with a greater propensity to some particular gratifications or pursuits than others, yet we do not want convincing instances how effectually they may be restrained, or at least corrected and turned to proper and laudable ends, by the force of an early care, and a suitable education.

"To you of the female sex, (whom I have had occasion more than once to take notice of with honor in this congregation) I would address a few words on this head.--You, who by your stations are more confined at home, and have the care of the younger sort more particularly under your management, may do a great deal of good in this way.--I know not when I have been more affected, or my heart touched with stronger and more pleasing emotions, than at the sight and conversation of a little negro boy, not above seven years old, who read to me in the new testament, and perfectly repeated his catechism throughout, and all from the instruction of his careful, pious mistress, now I hope with God, enjoying the blessed fruits of her labours while on earth.--This example I would recommend to your serious imitation, and to enforce it shall only remark, that a shining part of the character of Solomon's excellent daughter is, that she looketh well to the ways of her household."--Rev. Thomas Bacon's Sermons Addressed to Masters and Servants, pp. 4, 48, 49, 51, 64, 65, 69, 70, 73, 74.

PORTIONS OF BENJAMIN FAWCETT's ADDRESS TO THE CHRISTIAN NEGROES IN VIRGINIA ABOUT 1755

"Rejoice and be exceeding glad, that you are delivered either from the Frauds of Mohamet, or Pagan Darkness, and Worship of Daemons; and are not now taught to place your Dependence upon those other dead Men, whom the Papists impiously worship, to the Neglect and Dishonor of Jesus Christ, the one only Mediator between God and Men. Christ, tho' he was dead, is alive again, and liveth forever-more. It is Christ, who is able also to save them to the uttermost, that come unto God by him, seeing he ever liveth to make intercession for them. Bless God, with all your Heart, that the Holy Scriptures are put into your Hands, which are able to make you wise unto Salvation, thro' Faith which is in Christ Jesus. Read and study the Bible for yourselves; and consider how Papists do all they can to hide it from their Followers, for Fear such divine Light should discover the gross Darkness of their false Doctrines and Worship. Be particularly thankful to the Ministers of Christ around you, who are faithfully labouring to teach you the Truth as it is in Jesus....

"Contrary to these evident Truths and precious Comforts of the Word of God, you may perhaps be tempted very unjustly to renounce your Fidelity and Obedience to your Old Masters, in Hope of finding new ones, with whom you may live more happily. At one time or other it will probably be suggested to you, that the French will make better Masters than the English. But I beseech you to consider, that your Happiness as Men and Christians exceedingly depends upon your doing all in your Power to support the British Government, and that kind of Christianity which is called the Protestant Religion; and likewise in opposing, with all your Might, the Power of the French, the Delusions of Popish Priests, and all the Rage and Malice of such Indians, as are in the French Interest. If the Power of France was to prevail in the Country where you now live, you have Nothing to expect but the most terrible Increase of your Sufferings. Your Slavery would then, not merely extend to Body, but also to the Soul; not merely run thro' your Days of Labour, but even thro' your Lord's Days. Your Bibles would then become like a sealed Book, and your Consciences would be fettered with worse than Iron-Chains. Therefore be patient, be submissive and obedient, be faithful and true, even when some of your Masters are most unkind. This is the only way for you to have Consciences void of Offense towards God and Man. This will really be taking the most effectual Measures, to secure for yourselves a Share in the invaluable Blessings and Privileges of the glorious Gospel of the Blessed God, which you have already received thro' the Channel of the British Government, and which no other Government upon the Face of the Earth is so calculated to support and preserve.

"The Lord Jesus Christ is now saying to you, as he did to Peter, when thou art converted strengthen thy Brethren....

"Therefore let me entreat you to look upon your Country-men around you, and pity them, not so much for their being Fellow-Captives with you in a strange Land; as for this, that they are not yet, like you, delivered from the Power of Darkness....

The Education of the Negro

"Invite them to learn to read, and direct them where they may apply for Assistance, especially to those faithful Ministers, who have been your Instructors and Fathers in Christ...."--Fawcett's Address to the Negroes in Virginia, etc., pp. 8, 17, 18, 24, 25.

EXTRACT FROM THE APPENDIX OF BENJAMIN FAWCETT'S "ADDRESS TO THE CHRISTIAN NEGROES IN VIRGINIA"

"The first Account, I ever met with, of any considerable Number of Negroes embracing the Gospel, is in a letter written by Mr. Davies, Minister at Hanover in Virginia, to Mr. Bellamy of Bethlehem in New England, dated June 28, 1751. It appears that the Letter was designed for Publication; and I suppose, was accordingly printed at Boston in New England. It is to be seen in vol. ii., pages 330-338, of the Historical Collections relating to remarkable Periods of the Success of the Gospel, and eminent Instruments employed in promoting it; Compiled by Mr. John Gillies, one of the Ministers of Glasgow: Printed by Foulis in 1754. Mr. Davies fills the greatest part of his Letter, with an Account of the declining State of Religion in Virginia, and the remarkable Means used by Providence to revive it, for a few Years before his Settlement there, which was in 1747; not in the character of a Missionary, but that of a dissenting Minister, invited by a particular People, and fixed with them. Such, he observes, was the scattered State of his Congregation, that he soon found it necessary to license seven Meeting-Houses, the nearest of which are twelve or fifteen Miles distant from each other, and the extremes about Forty; yet some of his People live twenty, thirty, and a few forty Miles from the nearest Meeting-House. He computes his Communicants at about three Hundred. He then says, 'There is also a Number of Negroes. Some times I see a Hundred and more among my Hearers. I have baptized about Forty of them within the last three Years, upon such a Profession of Faith as I then judged credible. Some of them, I fear, have apostatized; but others, I trust, will persevere to the End. I have had as satisfying Evidences of the sincere Piety of several of them, as ever I had from any Person in my Life; and their artless Simplicity, their passionate Aspirations after Christ, their incessant Endeavors to know and do the Will of God, have charmed me. But, alas! while my Charge is so extensive, I cannot take sufficient Pains with them for their Instruction, which often oppresses my Heart....'"

At the Close of the above Letter, in the Historical Collections (vol. ii., page 338), there is added the following Marginal Note.--"May 22, 1754. Mr. G. Tennent and Mr. Davies being at Edinburgh, as Agents for the Trustees of the College of New Jersey, Mr. Davies informs,--that when he left Virginia in August last, there was a hopeful Appearance of a greater Spread of a religious Concern amongst the Negroes;--And a few weeks before he left Home, he baptized in one Day fifteen Negroes, after they had been catechized for some Months, and given credible Evidences of their sincerely embracing the Gospel."

After these Gentlemen had finished the Business of their late Mission in this part of the World, Mr. Davies gave the following Particulars to his Correspondent in London, in a letter which he wrote in the Spring of the previous Year, six Weeks after his safe return to his Family and Friends.--"The Inhabitants of Virginia are computed to be about 300,000 Men, the one-half of which Number are supposed to be Negroes. The Number of those who attend my Ministry at particular Times is uncertain, but generally about three Hundred who give a

Appendix

stated Attendance. And never have I been so much struck with the Appearance of an Assembly, as when I have glanced my Eye to that Part of the Meeting-House, where they usually sit; adorned, for so it had appeared to me, with so many black Countenances, eagerly attentive to every Word they hear, and frequently bathed in Tears. A considerable Number of them, about a Hundred, have been baptized, after the proper Time for Instruction, and having given credible Evidences, not only of their Acquaintance with the important Doctrines of the Christian Religion, but also a deep Sense of them upon their Minds, attested by a Life of the strictest Piety and Holiness. As they are not sufficiently polished to dissemble with a good Grace, they express the sentiments of their Souls so much in the Language of simple Nature, and with such genuine Indications of Sincerity, that it is impossible to suspect their Professions, especially when attended with a truly Christian Life and exemplary Conduct.--My worthy Friend, Mr. Tod, Minister of the next Congregation, has near the same Number under his Instructions, who, he tells me, discover the same serious Turn of Mind. In short, Sir, there are Multitudes of them in different Places, who are willing, and eagerly desirous to be instructed, and embrace every Opportunity of acquainting themselves with the Doctrines of the Gospel; and tho' they have generally very little Help to learn to read, yet, to my agreeable Surprise, many of them, by the Dint of Application in their Leisure-Hours, have made such a Progress, that they can intelligibly read a plain Author, and especially their Bibles; and Pity it is that many of them should be without them. Before I had the Pleasure of being admitted a Member of your Society [Mr. Davies here means the Society for promoting religious Knowledge among the Poor, which was first begun in London in August, 1750] the Negroes were wont frequently to come to me, with such moving Accounts of their Necessities in this Respect, that I could not help supplying them with Books to the utmost of my small Ability; and when I distributed those among them, which my Friends with you sent over, I had Reason to think that I never did an Action in all my Life, that met with so much Gratitude from the Receivers. I have already distributed all the Books I brought over, which were proper for them. Yet still, on Saturday Evenings, the only Time they can spare [they are allowed some short Time, viz., Saturday afternoon, and Sunday, says Dr. Douglass in his Summary. See the Monthly Review for October, 1755, page 274] my House is crowded with Numbers of them, whose very Countenances still carry the air of importunate Petitioners for the same Favors with those who came before them. But, alas! my Stock is exhausted, and I must send them away grieved and disappointed.--Permit me, Sir, to be an Advocate with you, and, by your Means, with your generous Friends in their Behalf. The Books I principally want for them are, Watts' Psalms and Hymns, and Bibles. The two first they cannot be supplied with any other Way than by a Collection, as they are not among the Books which your Society give away. I am the rather importunate for a good Number of these, and I cannot but observe, that the Negroes, above all the Human Species that I ever knew, have an Ear for Musick, and a kind of extatic Delight in Psalmody; and there are no Books they learn so soon, or take so much Pleasure in as those used in that heavenly Part of divine Worship. Some Gentlemen in London were pleased to make me a private Present of these Books for their Use, and from the Reception they met with, and their Eagerness for more, I can easily foresee, how acceptable and useful a larger Number would be among them. Indeed, Nothing would be a greater Inducement to their Industry to learn to read, than the Hope of such a Present; which they would consider, both as a Help, and a Reward for their Diligence"....--Fawcett's Address to the Christian Negroes in Virginia, etc., pp. 33. 34. 35. 36, 37. 38.

EXTRACT FROM JONATHAN BOUCHER'S "A VIEW OF THE CAUSES AND CONSEQUENCES OF THE AMERICAN REVOLUTION"(1763)

"If ever these colonies, now filled with slaves, be improved to their utmost capacity, an essential part of the improvement must be the abolition of slavery. Such a change would be hardly more to the advantage of the slaves than it would be to their owners....

"I do you no more than justice in bearing witness, that in no part of the world were slaves better treated than, in general, they are in the colonies.... In one essential point, I fear, we are all deficient; they are nowhere sufficiently instructed. I am far from recommending it to you, at once to set them free; because to do so would be an heavy loss to you, and probably no gain to them; but I do entreat you to make them some amends for the drudgery of their bodies by cultivating their minds. By such means only can we hope to fulfil the ends, which we may be permitted to believe, Providence had in view in suffering them to be brought among us. You may unfetter them from the chains of ignorance; you may emancipate them from the bondage of sin, the worst slavery to which they can be subjected; and by thus setting at liberty those that are bruised, though they still continue to be your slaves, they shall be delivered from the bondage of corruption into the glorious liberty of the Children of God."--Jonathan Boucher's A View of the Causes and Consequences, etc., pp. 41, 42, 43.

BOUCHER ON AMERICAN EDUCATION IN 1773

"You pay far too little regard to parental education....
"What is still less credible is that at least two-thirds of the little education we receive is derived from instructors who are either indented servants or transported felons. Not a ship arrives either with redemptioners or convicts, in which schoolmasters are not as regularly advertised for sale as weavers, tailors, or any other trade; with little other difference, that I can hear of, excepting perhaps that the former do not usually fetch so good a price as the latter....

"I own, however, that I dislike slavery and among other reasons because as it is here conducted it has pernicious effects on the social state, by being unfavorable to education. It certainly is no necessary circumstance, essential to the condition of a slave, that he be uneducated; yet this is the general and almost universal lot of the slaves. Such extreme, deliberate, and systematic inattention to all mental improvement, in so large portion of our species, gives far too much countenance and encouragement to those abject persons who are contented to be rude and ignorant."--Jonathan Boucher's A View of the Causes and Consequences of the American Revolution, pp. 183, 188, 189.

A PORTION OF AN ESSAY OF BISHOP PORTEUS TOWARD A PLAN FOR THE MORE EFFECTUAL CIVILIZATION AND CONVERSION OF THE NEGRO SLAVES ON THE TRENT ESTATE IN BARBADOES BELONGING TO THE SOCIETY FOR THE PROPAGATION OF THE GOSPEL IN FOREIGN PARTS. (WRITTEN IN 1784)

Appendix

"We are expressly commanded to preach the gospel to every creature; and therefore every human creature must necessarily be capable of receiving it. It may be true, perhaps, that the generality of the Negro slaves are extremely dull of apprehension, and slow of understanding; but it may be doubted whether they are more so than some of the lowest classes of our own people; at least they are certainly not inferior in capacity to the Greenlanders, many of whom have made very sincere Christians. Several travellers of good credit speak in very favorable terms, both of the understandings and dispositions of the native Africans on the coast of Guinea; and it is a well-known fact, that many even of the Negro slaves in our islands, although laboring under disadvantages and discouragements, that might well depress and stupefy even the best understandings, yet give sufficient proofs of the great quickness of parts and facility in learning. They have, in particular, a natural turn to the mechanical arts, in which several of them show much ingenuity, and arrive at no small degree of perfection. Some have discovered marks of genius for music, poetry, and other liberal accomplishments; and there are not wanting instances among them of a strength of understanding, and a generosity, dignity, and heroism of mind, which would have done honour to the most cultivated European. It is not, therefore, to any natural or unconquerable disability in the subject we had to work upon, that the little success of our efforts is to be ascribed. This would indeed be an insuperable obstacle, and must put an effectual stop to all future attempts of the same nature; but as this is far from being the case, we must look for other causes of our disappointment; which may perhaps appear to be, though of a serious, yet less formidable nature, and such as it is in the power of human industry and perseverance, with the blessing of Providence, to remove. The principal of them, it is conceived, are these which here follow:

1. "Although several of our ministers and catechists in the college of Barbadoes have been men of great worth and piety, and good intentions, yet in general they do not appear (if we may judge from their letters to the Board) to have possessed that peculiar sort of talents and qualifications, that facility and address in conveying religious truths, that unconquerable activity, patience, and perseverance, which the instruction of dull and uncultivated minds requires, and which we sometimes see so eminently and successfully displayed in the missionaries of other churches.

"And indeed the task of instructing and converting near three hundred Negro slaves, and of educating their children in the principles of morality and religion, is too laborious for any one person to execute well; especially when the stipend is too small to animate his industry, and excite his zeal.

2. "There seems also to have been a want of other modes of instruction, and of other books and tracts for that purpose, besides those made use of hitherto by our catechists. And there is reason moreover to believe, that the time allotted to the instruction of the Negroes has not been sufficient.

3. "Another impediment to the progress of our slaves in Christian knowledge has been their too frequent intercourse with the Negroes of the neighboring plantations, and the accession of fresh slaves to our own, either hired from other estates, or imported from Africa. These are so many constant temptations in their way to revert to their former heathenish principles and savage manners, to

which they have always a strong natural propensity; and when this propensity is continually inflamed by the solicitations of their unconverted brethren, or the arrival of new companions from the coast of Guinea, it frequently becomes very difficult to be resisted, and counteracts, in a great degree, all the influence and exhortations of their religious teachers.

4. "Although this society has been always most honourably distinguished by the gentleness with which the negroes belonging to its trust estates have been generally treated, yet even these (by the confession of our missionaries) are in too abject, and depressed, and uncivilized a state to be proper subjects for the reception of the divine truths of revelation. They stand in need of some further marks of the society's regard and tenderness for them, to conciliate their affections, to invigorate their minds, to encourage their hopes, and to rouse them out of that state of languor and indolence and insensibility, which renders them indifferent and careless both about this world and the next.

5. "A still further obstacle to the effectual conversion of the Negroes has been the almost unrestrained licentiousness of their manner, the habits of vice and dissoluteness in which they are permitted to live, and the sad examples they too frequently see in their managers and overseers. It can never be expected that people given up to such practices as these, can be much disposed to receive a pure and undefiled religion: or that, if after their conversion they are allowed, as they generally are, to retain their former habits, their christianity can be anything more than a mere name.

"These probably the society will, on inquiry, find to have been the principal causes of the little success they have hitherto had in their pious endeavors to render their own slaves real christians. And it is with a view principally to the removal of these obstacles that the following regulations are, with all due deference to better judgments, submitted to their consideration.

"The first and most essential step towards a real and effectual conversion of our Negroes would be the appointment of a missionary (in addition to the present catechist) properly qualified for that important and difficult undertaking. He should be a clergyman sought out for in this country, of approved ability, piety, humanity, industry, and a fervent, yet prudent zeal for the interests of religion, and the salvation of those committed to his care; and should have a stipend not less than 200 f. sterling a year if he has an apartment and is maintained in the College, or 300 f. a year if he is not.

"This clergyman might be called (for a reason to be hereafter assigned) 'The Guardian of the Negroes'; and his province should be to superintend the moral and spiritual concern of the slaves, to take upon himself the religious instruction of the adult Negroes, and to take particular care that all the Negro children are taught to read by the catechist and the two assistant women (now employed by the society) and also that they are diligently instructed by the catechist in the principles of the Christian religion, till they are fifteen years of age, when they shall be instructed by himself with the adult Negroes.

"This instruction of the Negro children from their earliest years is one of the most important and essential parts of the whole plan; for it is to the education of the young Negroes that we are principally to look for the success of our spiritual labours. These may be easily taught to understand and to speak the English language with fluency; these may be brought up from their earliest

Appendix

youth in habits of virtue, and restrained from all licentious indulgences: these may have the principles and the precepts of religion impressed so early upon their tender minds as to sink deep, and to take firm root, and bring forth the fruits of a truly Christian life. To this great object, therefore, must our chief attention be directed; and as almost everything must depend on the ability, the integrity, the assiduity, the perseverance of the person to whom we commit so important a charge, it is impossible for us to be too careful and too circumspect in our choice of a CATECHIST. He must consider it his province, not merely to teach the Negroes the use of letters, but the elements of Christianity; not only to improve their understandings, but to form their hearts. For this purpose they must be put into his hands the moment they are capable of articulating their words, and their instruction must be pursued with unrelenting diligence. So long as they continue too young to work, they may be kept constantly in the school; as they grow fit to labour, their attendance on the CATECHIST must gradually lessen, till at length they take their full share of work with the grown Negroes.

"A school of this nature was formerly established by the society of Charlestown in South Carolina, about the year 1745, under the direction of Mr. Garden, the Bishop of London's commissary in that province. This school flourished greatly, and seemed to answer their utmost wishes. There were at one time sixty scholars in it, and twenty young Negroes were annually sent out from it well instructed in the English language, and the Christian faith. Mr. Garden, in his letters to the society, speaks in the highest terms of the progress made by his scholars, and says, that the Negroes themselves were highly pleased with their own acquirements. But it is supposed that on a parochial establishment being made in Charlestown by government, this excellent institution was dropt; for after the year 1751, no further mention is made of it in the minutes of the society. From what little we know of it, however, we may justly conceive the most pleasing hopes from a similar foundation at Barbadoes."--The Works of Bishop Porteus, vi., pp., 171-179.

EXTRACT FROM "THE ACTS OF DR. BRAY'S VISITATION HELD AT ANNAPOLIS IN MARYLAND, MAY 23, 24, 25, ANNO 1700"

Words of Dr. Bray
"I think, my REVEREND BRETHREN, that we are now gone through such measures as may be necessary to be considered for the more universal as well as successful Catechising, and Instruction of Youth. And I heartily thank you for your so ready Concurrence in every thing that I have offered to you: And which, I hope, will appear no less in the Execution, than it has been to the Proposals.

"And that proper Books may not be wanting for the several Classes of Catechumens, there is care taken for the several sorts, which may be all had in this Town. And it may be necessary to acquaint you, that for the poor Children and Servants, they shall be given Gratis."--Hawks's Ecclesiastical History of the United States, vol. ii., pp. 503-504.

The Education of the Negro

EXTRACTS FROM THE MINUTES OF THE MEETINGS OF THE SOCIETY OF FRIENDS....

FROM THE MINUTES OF THE YEARLY MEETING OF THE FRIENDS OF PENNSYLVANIA AND NEW JERSEY, 1774

"And having grounds to conclude that there are some brethren who have these poor captives under their care, and are desirous to be wisely directed in the restoring them to liberty: Friends who may be appointed by quarterly and monthly meetings on the service now proposed, are earnestly desired to give their weighty and solid attention for the assistance of such who are thus honestly and religiously concerned for their own relief, and the essential benefit of the negro. And in such families where there are young ones, or others of suitable age, that they excite the masters, or those who have them, to give them sufficient instruction and learning, in order to qualify them for the enjoyment of liberty intended, and that they may be instructed by themselves, or placed out to such masters and mistresses who will be careful of their religious education, to serve for such time, and no longer, as is prescribed by law and custom, for white people."--A Brief Statement of the Rise and Progress of the Testimony of the Religious Society of Friends against Slavery and the Slave Trade. Published by direction of the Yearly Meeting, held in Philadelphia, in the Fourth Month, 1843, p. 38.

FROM THE MINUTES OF THE YEARLY MEETING OF THE FRIENDS OF PHILADELPHIA AND NEW JERSEY, 1779

"A tender Christian sympathy appears to be awakened in the minds of many who are not in religious profession with us, who have seriously considered the oppressions and disadvantages under which those people have long laboured; and whether a pious care extended to their offspring is not justly due from us to them, is a consideration worthy of our serious and deep attention; or if this obligation did not weightily lay upon us, can benevolent minds be directed to any object more worthy of their liberality and encouragement, than that of laving a foundation in the rising generation for their becoming good and useful men? remembering what was formerly enjoined, 'If thy brethren be waxen poor, and fallen in decay with thee, then thou shalt relieve him; yea, though he be a stranger, or a sojourner; that he may live with thee.'"--Ibid., p. 38.

FROM THE MINUTES OF THE QUARTERLY MEETING OF THE FRIENDS OF CHESTER

"The consideration of the temporal and spiritual welfare of the Africans, and the necessary instruction of their offspring now being resumed, and after some time spent thereon, it is closely recommended to our several monthly meetings to pay due attention to the advice of the Yearly Meeting on this subject, and proceed as strength may be afforded, in looking after them in their several habitations by a religious visit; giving them such counsel as their situation may require."--Ibid., p. 39.

Appendix

FROM THE MINUTES OF THE HADDONFIELD QUARTERLY MEETING

"In Haddonfield Quarterly Meeting, a committee was kept steadily under appointment for several years to assist in manumissions, and in the education of the negro children. Religious meetings were frequently held for the people of color; and Haddonfield Monthly Meeting raised on one occasion 131 pounds, for the education of negro children.

"In Salem Monthly Meeting, frequent meetings of worship for the people of color were held by direction of the monthly meeting; funds were raised for the education of their children, and committees appointed in the different meetings to provide books, place the children at school, to visit the schools, and inspect their conduct and improvement.

"Meetings for Divine worship were regularly held for people of color, at least once in three months, under the direction of the monthly meetings of Friends in Philadelphia; and schools were also established at which their children were gratuitously instructed in useful learning. One of these, originally instituted by Anthony Benezet, is now in operation in the city of Philadelphia, and has been continued under the care of one of the monthly meetings of Friends of that city, and supported by funds derived from voluntary contributions of the members, and from legacies and bequests, yielding an income of about $1000 per annum. The average number of pupils is about sixty-eight of both sexes."--Ibid., pp. 40-41.

FROM THE MINUTES OF THE RHODE ISLAND QUARTERLY MEETING OF THE FRIENDS, 1769

A committee reported "that having met, and entered into a solemn consideration of the subject, they were of the mind that a useful alteration might be made in the query referred to; yet apprehending some further Christian endeavors in labouring with such who continue in possession of slaves should be first promoted, by which means the eyes of Friends may be more clearly opened to behold the iniquity of the practice of detaining our fellow creatures in bondage, and a disposition to set such free who are arrived to mature age; and when the labour is performed and report made to the meeting, the meeting may be better capable of determining what further step to take in this affair, which hath given so much concern to faithful Friends, and that in the meantime it should be enforced upon Friends that have them in possession, to treat them with tenderness; impress God's fear on their minds; promote their attending places of religious worship; and give such as are young, so much learning, that they may be capable of reading.

"Are Friends clear of importing, buying, or any ways disposing of negroes or slaves; and do they use those well who are under their care, and not in circumstances, through nonage or incapacity, to be set at liberty? And do they give those that are young such an education as becomes Christians; and are the others encouraged in a religious and virtuous life? Are all set at liberty that are of age, capacity, and ability suitable for freedom?"--Ibid., pp. 45,46.

The Education of the Negro

FROM THE MINUTES OF THE YEARLY MEETING OF THE FRIENDS OF VIRGINIA IN 1757 AND 1773

"Are Friends clear of importing or buying negroes to trade on; and do they use those well which they are possessed of by inheritance or otherwise, endeavoring to train them in the principles of the Christian religion?"

The meeting of 1773 recommended to Friends, "seriously to consider the circumstances of these poor people, and the obligation we are under to discharge our religious duties to them, which being disinterestedly pursued, will lead the professor to Truth, to advise and assist them on all occasions, particularly in promoting their instruction in the principles of the Christian religion, and the pious education of their children; also to advise them in their worldly concerns, as occasions offer; and it advised that Friends of judgment and experience may be nominated for this necessary service, it being the solid sense of this meeting, that we, of the present generation, are under strong obligations to express our love and concern for the offspring of those people, who, by their labours, have greatly contributed toward the cultivation of these colonies, under the afflictive disadvantage of enduring a hard bondage; and many amongst us are enjoying the benefit of their toil."--Ibid., pp. 51, 52, and 54.

EXTRACT FROM THE MINUTES OF THE METHODIST CONFERENCE, 1785

"Q. What directions shall we give for the promotion of the spiritual welfare of the colored people?

"A. We conjure all our ministers and preachers, by the love of God and the salvation of souls, and do require them, by all the authority that is invested in us, to leave nothing undone for the spiritual benefit and salvation of them, within their respective circuits or districts; and for this purpose to embrace every opportunity of inquiring into the state of their souls, and to unite in society those who appear to have a real desire of fleeing from the wrath to come, to meet such a class, and to exercise the whole Methodist Discipline among them."

"Q. What can be done in order to instruct poor children, white and black to read?

"A. Let us labor, as the heart of one man, to establish Sunday schools, in or near the place of public worship. Let persons be appointed by the bishop, elders, deacons, or preachers, to teach gratis all that will attend or have the capacity to learn, from six o'clock in the morning till ten, and from two o'clock in the afternoon till six, where it does not interfere with public worship. The council shall compile a proper school book to teach them learning and piety."--Rev. Charles Elliott's History of the Great Secession front the Methodist Episcopal Church, etc., p. 35.

A PORTION OF AN ACT OF THE GENERAL ASSEMBLY OF THE PRESBYTERIAN CHURCH IN 1800.

The Assembly recommended:

Appendix

"2. The instruction of Negroes, the poor and those who are destitute of the means of grace in various parts of this extensive country; whoever contemplates the situation of this numerous class of persons in the United States, their gross ignorance of the plainest principles of religion, their immorality and profaneness, their vices and dissoluteness of manners, must be filled with anxiety for their present welfare, and above all for their future and eternal happiness.

"3. The purchasing and disposing of Bibles and also of books and short essays on the great principles of religion and morality, calculated to impress the minds of those to whom they are given with a sense of their duty both to God and man, and consequently of such a nature as to arrest the attention, interest the curiosity and touch the feelings of those to whom they are given."--Act and Proceedings of the General Assembly of the Presbyterian Church in the U.S.A. in the Year 1800, Philadelphia.

AN ACT OF THE GENERAL ASSEMBLY OF THE PRESBYTERIAN CHURCH IN 1801

"The Assembly resumed the consideration of the communication from the Trustees of the General Assembly and having gone through the same, thereupon resolved,

"5. That there be made a purchase of so many cheap and pious books as a due regard to the other objects of the Assembly's funds will admit, with a view of distributing them not only among the frontiers of these States, but also among the poorer classes of people, and the blacks, or wherever it is thought useful; which books shall be given away, or lent, at the discretion of the distributor; and that there be received from Mr. Robert Aitken, toward the discharge of his debt, books to such amount as shall appear proper to the Trustees of the Assembly, who are hereby requested to take proper measures for the distribution of same."--Act and Proceedings of the General Assembly of the Presbyterian Church in the U.S.A.

PLAN FOR IMPROVING THE CONDITION OF THE FREE BLACKS

The business relative to free blacks shall be transacted by a committee of twenty-four persons, annually elected by ballot at a meeting of this Society, in the month called April, and in order to perform the different services with expedition, regularity and energy this committee shall resolve itself into the following sub-committees, viz.:

I. A Committee of Inspection, who shall superintend the morals, general conduct, and ordinary situation of the free negroes, and afford them advice and instruction, protection from wrongs, and other friendly offices.

II. A Committee of Guardians, who shall place out children and young people with suitable persons, that they may (during a moderate time of apprenticeship or servitude) learn some trade or other business of subsistence. The committee may effect this partly by a persuasive influence on parents and the persons concerned, and partly by cooeperating with the laws, which are or may be enacted for this and similar purposes. In forming contracts of these occasions, the committee shall secure to the Society as far as may be practicable the right of guardianship over the person so bound.

III. A Committee of Education, who shall superintend the school instruction of the children and youth of the free blacks. They may either influence them to attend regularly the schools already established in this city, or form others with this view; they shall, in either case, provide, that the pupils may receive such learning as is necessary for their future situation in life, and especially a deep impression of the most important and generally acknowledged moral and religious principles. They shall also procure and preserve a regular record of the marriages, births, and manumissions of all free blacks.

IV. The Committee of Employ, who shall endeavor to procure constant employment for those free negroes who are able to work; as the want of this would occasion poverty, idleness, and many vicious habits. This committee will by sedulous inquiry be enabled to find common labor for a great number; they will also provide that such as indicate proper talents may learn various trades, which may be done by prevailing upon them to bind themselves for such a term of years as shall compensate their masters for the expense and trouble of instruction and maintenance. The committee may attempt the institution of some simple and useful manufactures which will require but little skill, and also may assist, in commencing business, such as appear to be qualified for it.

Whenever the Committee of Inspection shall find persons of any particular description requiring attention, they shall immediately direct them to the committee of whose care they are the proper objects.

In matters of a mixed nature, the committee shall confer, and, if necessary, act in concert. Affairs of great importance shall be referred to the whole committee.

The expense incurred by the prosecution of this plan, shall be defrayed by a fund, to be formed by donations or subscriptions for these particular purposes, and to be kept separate from the other funds of the Society.

The Committee shall make a report on their proceedings, and of the state of their stock, to the Society, at their quarterly meetings, in the months called April and October.--Smyth's Writings of Benjamin Franklin, vol. x, p. 127.

EXTRACT FROM THE "ADDRESS OF THE AMERICAN CONVENTION OF DELEGATES FROM THE ABOLITION SOCIETIES, 1795"

"We cannot forbear expressing to you our earnest desire, that you will continue, without ceasing, to endeavor, by every method in your power which can promise any success, to procure, either an absolute repeal of all the laws in your state, which countenance slavery, or such an amelioration of them as will gradually produce an entire abolition. Yet, even should that great end be happily attained, it cannot put a period to the necessity of further labor. The education of the emancipated, the noblest and most arduous task which we have to perform, will require all our wisdom and virtue, and the constant exercise of the greatest skill and discretion. When we have broken his chains, and restored the African to the enjoyment of his rights, the great work of justice and benevolence is not accomplished--The new born citizen must receive that instruction, and those powerful impressions of moral and religious truths, which will render him capable and desirous of fulfilling the various duties he owes to himself and to his country. By educating some in the higher branches of science, and all the useful parts of learning, and in the precepts of religion and morality, we shall not only do away with the reproach and calumny so unjustly lavished upon us, but confound the enemies of truth, by evincing that the unhappy sons of Africa, in spite of the degrading influence of slavery, are in no wise inferior to the more fortunate inhabitants of Europe and America.

"As a means of effectuating, in some degree, a design so virtuous and laudable, we recommend to you to appoint a committee, annually, or for any other more convenient period, to execute such plans, for the improvement of the condition and moral character of the free blacks in your state, as you may think best adapted to your particular situation."--Minutes of the Proceedings of the Second Convention of Delegates, 1795.

A PORTION OF THE "ADDRESS OF THE AMERICAN CONVENTION OF DELEGATES TO THE FREE AFRICANS AND OTHER FREE PEOPLE OF COLOR, 1796"

"In the first place, We earnestly recommend to you, a regular attention to the duty of public worship; by which means you will evince gratitude to your CREATOR, and, at the same time, promote knowledge, union, friendship, and proper conduct among yourselves.

"Secondly, we advise such of you, as have not been taught reading, writing, and the first principles of arithmetic, to acquire them as early as possible. Carefully attend to the instruction of your children in the same simple and useful branches of education. Cause them, likewise, early and frequently to read the holy Scriptures. They contain, among other great discoveries, the precious record of the original equality of mankind, and of the obligations of universal justice and benevolence, which are derived from the relation of the human race to each other in a COMMON FATHER.

"Thirdly, Teach your children useful trades, or to labor with their hands in cultivating the earth. These employments are favorable to health and virtue. In the choice of masters, who are to instruct them in the above branches of business, prefer those who will work with them; by this means they will acquire habits of industry, and be better preserved from vice, than if they worked alone, or under the eye of persons less interested in their welfare. In forming contracts for yourselves or children, with masters, it may be useful to consult such persons as are capable of giving you the best advice, who are known to be your friends, in order to prevent advantages being taken of your ignorance of the laws and customs of your country."--Minutes of the Proceedings of the Third Convention of Delegates, 1796. American Convention of Abolition Societies, Minutes, 1795-1804

A PORTION OF THE ADDRESS TO THE FREE PEOPLE OF COLOR BY THE AMERICAN CONVENTION FOR PROMOTING THE ABOLITION OF SLAVERY, 1819

"The great work of emancipation is not to be accomplished in a day;--it must be the result of time, of long and continued exertions: it is for you to show by an orderly and worthy deportment that you are deserving of the rank which you have attained. Endeavor as much as possible to use economy in your expenses, so that you may be enabled to save from your earnings, something for the education of your children, and for your support in time of sickness and in old age: and let all those who by attending to this admonition, have acquired the means, send their children to school as soon as they are old enough, where their morals will be the object of attention, as well as their improvement in school learning; and when they arrive at a suitable age, let it be your especial care to have them instructed in some mechanical art suited to their capacities, or in agricultural pursuits; by which they may afterwards be enabled to support themselves and a family. Encourage also, those among you who are qualified as teachers of schools, and when you are of ability to pay, never send your children to free schools; this may be considered as robbing the poor, of the opportunities which were intended for them alone."

THE WILL OF KOSCIUSZKO

I, Thaddeus Kosciuszko, being just on my departure from America, do hereby declare and direct, that, should I make no other testamentary disposition of my property in the United States, I hereby authorize my friend, Thomas Jefferson, to employ the whole thereof in purchasing Negroes from his own or any others, and giving them liberty in my name, in giving them an education in trade or otherwise, and in having them instructed for their new condition in the duties of morality, which may make them good neighbors, good fathers or mothers, husbands or wives in their duties as citizens, teaching them to be defenders of their liberty and country, and of the good order of society, and in whatsoever may make them happy and useful. And I make the said Thomas Jefferson my executor of this.

(Signed) T. KOSCIUSZKO. May 5, 1798. [See African Repository, vol. xi., p. 294.]

FROM WASHINGTON'S WILL

"Upon the decease of my wife, it is my will and desire that all the slaves whom I now hold in my own right shall receive their freedom.... And whereas among those who will receive freedom according to this devise, there may be some who, from old age or bodily infirmities, and others who on account of their infancy will be unable to support themselves, it is my will and desire that all who come under the first and second description, shall be comfortably clothed and fed by my heirs while they live; and that such of the latter description as have no parents living, or if living are unable or unwilling to provide for them, shall be bound by the court until they shall arrive at the age of twenty-five years; and in cases where no record can be produced, whereby their ages can be ascertained, the judgement of court upon its own view of the subject shall be adequate and final. The negroes thus bound are (by their masters or mistresses) to be taught to read and write, and to be brought up to some useful occupation, agreeable to the laws of the Commonwealth of Virginia, providing for the support of orphan and other poor children."--Benson J. Lossing's Life of George Washington, vol. iii., p. 537.

Appendix

THIS INTERESTING DIALOGUE WAS WRITTEN BY AN AMERICAN ABOUT 1800

The following dialogue took place between Mr. Jackson the master of a family, and the slave of one of his neighbors who lived adjoining the town, on this occasion. Mr. Jackson was walking through the common and came to a field of this person's farm. He there saw the slave leaning against the fence with a book in his hand, which he seemed to be very intent upon; after a little time he closed the book, and clasping it in both his hands, looked upwards as if engaged in mental prayer; after this, he put the book in his bosom, and walked along the fence near where Mr. Jackson was standing. Surprised at seeing a person of his color engaged with a book, and still more by the animation and delight that he observed in his countenance; he determines to enquire about it, and calls to him as he passes.

Mr. J. So I see you have been reading, my lad?

Slave. Yes, sir.

Mr. J. Well, I have a great curiosity to see what you were reading so earnestly; will you show me the book?

Slave. To be sure, sir. (And he presented it to him very respectfully.)

Mr. J. The Bible!--Pray when did you get this book? And who taught you to read it?

Slave. I thank God, sir, for the book. I do not know the good gentleman who gave it to me, but I am sure God sent it to me. I was learning to read in town at nights, and one morning a gentleman met me in the road as I had my spelling book open in my hand: he asked me if I could read, I told him a little, and he gave me this book and told me to make haste and learn to read it, and to ask God to help me, and that it would make me as happy as any body in the world.

Mr. J. Well did you do so?

Slave. I thought about it for some time, and I wondered that any body should give me a book or care about me; and I wondered what that could be which could make a poor slave like me so happy; and so I thought more and more of it, and I said I would try and do as the gentleman bid me, and blessed be God! he told me nothing but the truth.

Mr. J. Who is your master?

Slave. Mr. Wilkins, sir, who lives in that house.

Mr. J. I know him; he is a very good man; but what does he say to your leaving his work to read your book in the field?

Slave. I was not leaving his work, sir. This book does not teach me to neglect my master's work. I could not be happy if I did that.--I have done my breakfast, sir, and am waiting till the horses are done eating.

Mr. J. Well, what does that book teach you?

Slave. Oh, sir! every thing that I want to know--all I am to do, this book tells me, and so plain. It shew me first that I was a wretched, ruined sinner, and what would become of me if I died in that state, and then when I was day and night in dread of God's calling me to account for my wickedness, and did not know which way to look for my deliverance, reading over and over again those dreadful words, "depart from me ye cursed into everlasting fire," then it revealed to me how Jesus Christ had consented to come and suffer punishment for us in our stead, and bought pardon for us by his blood, and how by believing on him and serving him, I might become a child of God, so that I need be no more terrified by the thoughts of God's anger but sure of his forgiveness and love....

(Here Mr. J. pursued his walk; but soon reflecting on what he had heard, he resolved to walk by Mr. Wilkins's house and enquire into this affair from him. This he did, and finding him the following conversation took place between them.)

Mr. J. Sir, I have been talking with a man of yours in that field, who was engaged, while his horses were eating, in reading a book; which I asked him to shew me and found it was the Bible; thereupon I asked him some questions and his answers, and the account he gave of himself, have surprised me greatly.

Mr. W. I presume it was Will--and though I do not know what he may have told you, yet I will undertake to say that he has told you nothing but the truth. I am always safe in believing him, and do not believe he would tell me an untruth for any thing that could be offered him....

Mr. J. Well, sir, you have seen I trust in your family, good fruits from the beginning.

Mr. W. Yes indeed, sir, and that man was most instrumental in reconciling and encouraging all my people in the change. From that time I have regarded him as more a friend and assistant, than a slave. He has taught the younger ones to read, and by his kindness and example, has been a great benefit to all. I have told them that I would do what I could to instruct and improve them; and that if I found any so vicious, that they would not receive it and strive to amend, I would not keep them; that I hoped to have a religious, praying family, and that none would be obstinately bent on their own ruin. And from time to time, I endeavored to convince them that I was aiming at their own good. I cannot tell you all the happiness of the change, that God has been pleased to make among us, all by these means. And I have been benefited both temporally and spiritually by it; for my work is better done, and my people are more faithful, contented, and obedient than before; and I have the comfort of thinking that when my Lord and master shall call me to account for those committed to my charge, I shall not be ashamed to present them.--Bishop William Meade's "Tracts and Dialogues," etc., in the Appendix of Thomas Bacon's Sermons Addressed to Masters and Servants.

A TRUE ACCOUNT OF A PIOUS NEGRO

(Written about 1800)

Some years ago an English gentleman had occasion to be in North America, where, among other adventures, the following circumstances occurred to him which are related in his own words.

"Every day's observation convinces me that the children of God, viz. those who believe in him, and on such terms are accepted by him through Jesus Christ, are made so by his own especial grace and power inclining them to what is good, and, assisting them when they endeavor to be and continue so.

"In one of my excursions, while I was in the province of New York, I was walking by myself over a considerable plantation, amused with its husbandry, and comparing it with that of my own country, till I came within a little distance of a middle aged negro, who was tilling the ground. I felt a strong inclination to converse with him. After asking him some little questions about his work, which he answered very sensibly, I wished him to tell me, whether his state of slavery was not disagreeable to him, and whether he would not gladly exchange it for his liberty?"

"Massah," said he, looking seriously upon me, "I have wife and children; my massah takes care of them, and I have no care to provide anything; I have a good massah, who teach me to read; and I read good book, that makes me happy." "I am glad," replied I, "to hear you say so; and pray what is the good book you read?" "The Bible, massah, God's own good book." "Do you understand, friend, as well as read this book? for many can read the words well, who cannot get hold of the true and good sense." "O massah," says he, "I read the book much before I understand; but at last I found things in the book which made me very uneasy." "Aye," said I, "and what things were they?" "Why massah, I found that I was a sinner, massah, a very great sinner, I feared that God would destroy me, because I was wicked, and done nothing as I should do. God was holy, and I was very vile and naughty; so I could have nothing from him but fire and brimstone in hell, if I continued in this state." In short, he fully convinced me that he was thoroughly sensible of his errors, and he told me what scriptures came to his mind, which he had read, that both probed him to the bottom of his sinful heart, and were made the means of light and comfort to his soul. I then inquired of him, what ministry or means he made use of and found that his master was a Quaker, a plain sort of man who had taught his slaves to read, and had thus afforded him some means of obtaining religious knowledge, though he had not ever conversed with this negro upon the state of his soul. I asked him likewise, how he got comfort under all his trials? "O massah," said he, "it was God gave me comfort by his word. He bade me come unto him, and he would give me rest, for I was very weary and heavy laden." And here he went through a line of the most striking texts in the Bible, showing me, by his artless comment upon them as he went along, what great things God had done in the course of some years for his soul....--Bishop William Meade's "Tracts, Dialogues," etc., in the Appendix of Thomas Bacon's Sermons Addressed to Masters and Servants.

LETTER TO ABBE GREGOIRE, OF PARIS, 1809

I have received the favor of your letter of August 19th, and with it the volume you were so kind as to send me on the Literature of Negroes. Be assured that no person living wishes more sincerely than I do to see a complete refutation of the doubts I have myself entertained and expressed on the grade of understanding allotted to them by nature and to find that in this respect they are on par with ourselves. My doubts were the result of personal observation in the limited sphere of my own state, where the opportunities for the development of their genius were not favorable, and those of exercising it still less so. I expressed them therefore with great hesitation; but whatever be their degree of talent it is no measure of their rights. Because Sir Isaac Newton was superior to others in understanding, he was not therefore lord of the person and property of others. On this subject they are gaining daily in the opinions of nations, and hopeful advances are making towards their re-establishment on an equal footing with the other colors of the human family. I pray you therefore to accept my thanks for the many instances you have enabled me to observe of respectable intelligence in that race of men, which cannot fail to have effect in hastening the day of their relief; and to be sure of the sentiments of the high and just esteem and consideration which I tender to yourself with all sincerity.--Writings of Thomas Jefferson, Memorial Edition, 1904, vol. xii., p. 252.

PORTION OF JEFFERSON'S LETTER TO M.A. JULIEN, JULY 23, 1818

Referring to Kosciuszko, Jefferson said:
"On his departure from the United States in 1798 he left in my hands an instrument appropriating after his death all the property he had in our public funds, the price of his military services here, to the education and emancipation of as many of the children of bondage in this country as this should be adequate to. I am now too old to undertake a business de si longue haleine; but I am taking measures to place it in such hands as will ensure a faithful discharge of the philanthropic intentions of the donor. I learn with pleasure your continued efforts for the instruction of the future generations of men, and, believing it the only means of effectuating their rights, I wish them all possible success, and to yourself the eternal gratitude of those who will feel their benefits, and beg leave to add the assurance of my high esteem and respect."--Writings of Thomas Jefferson, Memorial Edition. 1904, vol. xv., pp. 173-174.

FROM MADISON'S LETTER TO MISS FRANCES WRIGHT, SEPTEMBER 1, 1825

"Supposing these conditions to be duly provided for, particularly the removal of the emancipated blacks, the remaining questions relate to the aptitude and adequacy of the process by which the slaves are at the same time to earn funds, entire or supplemental, required for their emancipation and removal; and to be sufficiently educated for a life of freedom and of social order....
"With respect to the proper course of education, no serious difficulties present themselves. As they are to continue in a state of bondage during the preparatory period, and to be within the jurisdiction of States recognizing ample authority over them, a competent discipline cannot be impracticable. The degree in which this discipline will enforce the needed labour, and in which a voluntary industry will supply the defect of compulsory labour, are vital points, on which it may not be safe to be very positive without some light from actual experiment.
"Considering the probable composition of the labourers, and the known fact that, where the labour is compulsory, the greater the number of labourers brought together (unless, indeed, where co-operation of many hands is rendered essential by a particular kind of work or of machinery) the less are the proportional profits, it may be doubted whether the surplus from that source merely, beyond the support of the establishment, would sufficiently accumulate in five, or even more years, for the objects in view. And candor obliges me to say that I am not satisfied either that the prospect of emancipation at a future day will sufficiently overcome the natural and habitual repugnance to labour, or that there is such an advantage of united over individual labour as is taken for granted.
"In cases where portions of time have been allotted to slaves, as among the Spaniards, with a view to their working out their freedom, it is believed that but few have availed themselves of the opportunity by a voluntary industry; and such a result could be less relied on in a case where each individual would feel

that the fruits of his exertions would be shared by others, whether equally or unequally making them, and that the exertions of others would equally avail him, notwithstanding a deficiency in his own. Skilful arrangements might palliate this tendency, but it would be difficult to counteract it effectually.

"The examples of the Moravians, the Harmonites, and the Shakers, in which the united labours of many for a common object have been successful, have, no doubt, an imposing character. But it must be recollected that in all these establishments there is a religious impulse in the members, and a religious authority in the head, for which there will be no substitutes of equivalent efficacy in the emancipating establishment. The code of rules by which Mr. Rapp manages his conscientious and devoted flock, and enriches a common treasury, must be little applicable to the dissimilar assemblage in question. His experience may afford valuable aid in its general organization, and in the distribution of details of the work to be performed. But an efficient administration must, as is judiciously proposed, be in hands practically acquainted with the propensities and habits of the members of the new community."

FROM FREDERICK DOUGLASS'S PAPER, 1853: "LEARN TRADES OR STARVE"

These are the obvious alternatives sternly presented to the free colored people of the United States. It is idle, yea even ruinous, to disguise the matter for a single hour longer; every day begins and ends with the impressive lesson that free negroes must learn trades, or die.

The old avocations, by which colored men obtained a livelihood, are rapidly, unceasingly and inevitably passing into other hands; every hour sees the black man elbowed out of employment by some newly arrived emigrant, whose hunger and whose color are thought to give him a better title to the place; and so we believe it will continue to be until the last prop is levelled beneath us.

As a black man, we say if we cannot stand up, let us fall down. We desire to be a man among men while we do live; and when we cannot, we wish to die. It is evident, painfully evident to every reflecting mind, that the means of living, for colored men, are becoming more and more precarious and limited. Employments and callings formerly monopolized by us, are so no longer.

White men are becoming house-servants, cooks and stewards on vessels-- at hotels.--They are becoming porters, stevedores, wood-sawers, hod-carriers, brick-makers, white-washers and barbers, so that the blacks can scarcely find the means of subsistence--a few years ago, a white barber would have been a curiosity--now their poles stand on every street. Formerly blacks were almost the exclusive coachmen in wealthy families: this is so no longer; white men are now employed, and for aught we see, they fill their servile station with an obsequiousness as profound as that of the blacks. The readiness and ease with which they adapt themselves to these conditions ought not to be lost sight of by the colored people. The meaning is very important, and we should learn it. We are taught our insecurity by it. Without the means of living, life is a curse, and leaves us at the mercy of the oppressor to become his debased slaves. Now, colored men, what do you mean to do, for you must do something? The American Colonization Society tells you to go to Liberia. Mr. Bibb tells you to go to Canada. Others tell you to go to school. We tell you to go to work; and to work you must go or die. Men are not valued in this country, or in any country, for what they are; they are valued for what they can do. It is in vain that we talk of being men, if we do not the work of men. We must become valuable to society in other departments of industry than those servile ones from which we are rapidly being excluded. We must show that we can do as well as be; and to this end we must learn trades. When we can build as well as live in houses; when we can make as well as wear shoes; when we can produce as well as consume wheat, corn and rye--then we shall become valuable to society. Society is a hard-hearted affair.--With it the helpless may expect no higher dignity than that of paupers. The individual must lay society under obligation to him, or society will honor him only as a stranger and sojourner. How shall this be done? In this manner; use every means, strain every nerve to master some important mechanical art. At present, the facilities for doing so are few--institutions of learning are more readily opened to you than the work-shop; but the Lord helps them who will help themselves, and we have no doubt that new facilities will be presented as we press forward.

If the alternative were presented to us of learning a trade or of getting an education, we would learn the trade, for the reason, that with the trade we could get the education while with the education we could not get the trade. What we, as a people, most need, is the means for our own elevation.--An educated colored man, in the United States, unless he has within him the heart of a hero, and is willing to engage in a lifelong battle for his rights, as a man, finds few inducements to remain in this country. He is isolated in the land of his birth--debarred by his color from congenial association with whites; he is equally cast out by the ignorance of the blacks. The remedy for this must comprehend the elevation of the masses; and this can only be done by putting the mechanic arts within the reach of colored men.

We have now stated pretty strongly the case of our colored countrymen; perhaps some will say, too strongly, but we know whereof we affirm.

In view of this state of things, we appeal to the abolitionists. What Boss anti-slavery mechanic will take a black boy into his wheelwright's shop, his blacksmith's shop, his joiner's shop, his cabinet shop? Here is something practical; where are the whites and where are the blacks that will respond to it? Where are the antislavery milliners and seamstresses that will take colored girls and teach them trades, by which they can obtain an honorable living? The fact that we have made good cooks, good waiters, good barbers, and white-washers, induces the belief that we may excel in higher branches of industry. One thing is certain; we must find new methods of obtaining a livelihood, for the old ones are failing us very fast.

We, therefore, call upon the intelligent and thinking ones amongst us, to urge upon the colored people within their reach, in all seriousness, the duty and the necessity of giving their children useful and lucrative trades, by which they may commence the battle of life with weapons, commensurate with the exigencies of conflict.--African Repository, vol. xxix., pp. 136, 137.

EDUCATION OF COLORED PEOPLE

(Written by a highly respectable gentleman of the South in 1854)
Several years ago I saw in the Repository, copied from the Colonization Herald, a proposal to establish a college for the education of young colored men in this country. Since that time I have neither seen nor heard anything

Appendix

more of it, and I should be glad to hear whether the proposed plan was ever carried into execution.

Four years ago I conversed with one of the officers of the Colonization Society on the subject of educating in this country colored persons intending to emigrate to Liberia, and expressed my firm conviction of the paramount importance of high moral and mental training as a fit preparation for such emigrants.

To my great regret the gentleman stated that under existing circumstances the project, all important as he confessed it to be, was almost impracticable; so strong being the influence of the enemies of colonization that they would dissuade any colored persons so educated from leaving the United States.

I know that he was thoroughly acquainted with the subject in all its bearings, and therefore felt that he must have good reasons for what he said; still I hoped the case was not so bad as he thought, and, at any rate, I looked forward with strong hope to the time when the colored race would, as a body, open their eyes to the miserable, unnatural position they occupy in America; when they would see who were their true friends, those who offered them real and complete freedom, social and political, in a land where there is no white race to keep them in subjection, where they govern themselves by their own laws; or those pretended friends who would keep the African where he can never be aught but a serf and bondsman of a despised caste, and who, by every act of their pretended philanthropy, make the colored man's condition worse.

Most happily, since that time, the colored race has been aroused to a degree never before known, and the conviction has become general among them that they must go to Liberia if they would be free and happy.

Under these circumstances the better the education of the colored man the more keenly will he feel his present situation and the more clearly he will see the necessity of emigration.

Assuming such to be the feelings of the colored race, I think the immense importance of a collegiate institution for the education of their young must be felt and acknowledged by every friend of the race. Some time since the legislature of Liberia passed an act to incorporate a college in Liberia, but I fear the project has failed, as I have heard nothing more of it since. Supposing however the funds raised for such an institution, where are the professors to come from? They must be educated in this country; and how can that be done without establishing an institution specially for young colored men?

There is not a college in the United States where a young man of color could gain admission, or where, supposing him admitted, he could escape insult and indignity. Into our Theological Seminaries a few are admitted, and are, perhaps, treated well; but what difficulty they find in obtaining a proper preparatory education. The cause of religion then, no less than that of secular education, calls for such a measure.

I think a strong and earnest appeal ought to be made to every friend of colonization throughout the United States to support the scheme with heart, hand and purse. Surely there are enough friends of the cause to subscribe at least a moderate sum for such a noble object; and in a cause like this, wealthy colored persons ought to, and doubtless will, subscribe according to their means. In addition to the general appeal through the Repository, let each individual friend of colonization use all his influence with his personal friends and acquaintances, especially with such as are wealthy. I know from my own experience how much can be done by personal application, even in cases where success appears nearly hopeless.--I will pledge myself to use my humble endeavors to the utmost with my personal acquaintances. A large sum would not be absolutely necessary to found the college; and it would certainly be better to commence in the humblest way than to give up the scheme altogether.

Buildings for instance might be purchased in many places for a very moderate sum that would answer every purpose, or they might be built in the cheapest manner; in short, everything might be commenced on the most economical scale and afterwards enlarged as funds increased.

Those who are themselves engaged in teaching, such as the faculties of colleges, etc., would, of course, be most competent to prepare a plan for the proposed institution, and the ablest of them should be consulted; meantime almost anyone interested in the cause may offer some useful hint. In that spirit, I would myself offer a few brief suggestions, in case this appeal should be favorably received.

Probably few men of my time of life have studied the character and condition of the African race more attentively than I have, with what success I cannot presume to say, but the opinion of any one devoting so much of his time to the subject ought to be of some value.

My opinion of their capacity has been much raised during my attempts at instructing them, but at the same time, I am convinced that they require a totally different mode of training from whites, and that any attempt to educate the two races together must prove a failure. I now close these desultory remarks with the hope that some one more competent than myself will take up the cause and urge it until some definite plan is formed.--African Repository, vol. xxx., pp. 194, 195, 196.

FROM A MEMORIAL TO THE LEGISLATURE OF NORTH CAROLINA, CIRCULATED AMONG THE CITIZENS OF THAT STATE IN 1855, TO SECURE THE MODIFICATION OF CERTAIN LAWS REGULATING SLAVES AND FREE PERSONS OF COLOR.

ELEVATION OF THE COLORED RACE

The Memorial is thus introduced:
"Your memorialists are well aware of the delicate nature of the subject to which the attention of the Legislature is called, and of the necessity of proceeding with deliberation and caution. They propose some radical changes in the law of slavery, demanded by our common christianity, by public morality, and by the common weal of the whole South. At the same time they have no wish or purpose inconsistent with the best interests of the slaveholder, and suggest no reform which may impair the efficiency of slave labor. On the contrary, they believe that the much desired modifications of our slave code will redound to the welfare of all classes, and to the honor and character of the State throughout the civilized world."

The attention of the Legislature was then asked to the following propositions: "1. That it behooves us as christian people to establish the institution of matrimony among our slaves, with all its legal obligations and guarantees as to its duration between the parties. 2. That under no circumstances should masters be permitted to disregard these natural and sacred ties of relationship among their slaves, or between slaves belonging to different masters. 3. That the

Appendix

parental relation to be acknowledged by law; and that the separation of parents from their young children, say of twelve years and under, be strictly forbidden, under heavy pains and penalties. 4. That the laws which prohibit the instruction of slaves and free colored persons, by teaching them to read the Bible and other good books, be repealed."--African Repository, vol. xxxi., pp. 117, 118.

A LAWYER FOR LIBERIA

On the sailing of almost every expedition we have had occasion to chronicle the departure of missionaries, teachers, or a physician, but not until the present time, that of a lawyer. The souls and bodies of the emigrants have been well cared for; now, it is no doubt supposed, they require assistance in guarding their money, civil rights, etc. Most professional emissaries have been educated at public expense, either by Missionary or the Colonization Societies, but the first lawyer goes out independent of any associated aid. Mr. Garrison Draper, a colored man of high respectability, and long a resident of Old Town, early determined on educating his only son for Africa. He kept him at some good public school in Pennsylvania till fitted for college, then sent him to Dartmouth where he remained four years and graduated, maintaining always a very respectable standing, socially, and in his class. After much consultation with friends, he determined upon the study of law. Mr. Charles Gilman, a retired member of the Baltimore Bar, very kindly consented to give young Draper professional instruction, and for two years he remained under his tuition. Not having any opportunities for acquiring a knowledge of the routine of professional practice, the rules, habits, and courtesy of the Bar, in Baltimore, Mr. Draper spent some few months in the office of a distinguished lawyer in Boston. On returning to the city to embark for Liberia, he underwent an examination by Judge Lee of the Superior Court, and obtained from him a certificate of his fitness to practice the profession of law, a copy of which we append hereto.

We consider the settlement of Mr. Draper in the Republic as an event of no little importance. It seemed necessary that there should be one regularly educated lawyer in a community of several thousand people, in a Republic of freemen. True, there are many very intelligent, well informed men now in the practice of law in Liberia, but they have not been educated to the profession, and we believe, no one makes that his exclusive business. We doubt not that they will welcome Mr. Draper as one of their fraternity. To our Liberia friends we commend him as a well-educated, intelligent man, of good habits and principles; one in whom they may place the fullest confidence, and we bespeak for him, at their hands, kind considerations and patronage.

STATE OF MARYLAND,
CITY OF BALTIMORE,
October 29, 1857.

Upon the application of Charles Gilman, Esq., of the Baltimore Bar, I have examined Edward G. Draper, a young man of color, who has been reading law under the direction of Mr. Gilman, with the view of pursuing its practice in Liberia, Africa. And I have found him most intelligent and well informed in his answers to the questions propounded by me, and qualified in all respects to be admitted to the Bar in Maryland, if he was a free white citizen of this State.

Mr. Gilman, in whom I have the highest confidence, has also testified to his good moral character.

This certificate is therefore furnished to him by me, with a view to promote his establishment and success in Liberia at the Bar there.

Z. COLLINS LEE,
Judge of Superior Court, Balt., Md.
African Repository, vol. xxxiv., pp. 26 and 27.

Bibliography

There is no helpful bibliography on the early education of the American Negro. A few books treating the recent problems of education in this country give facts about the enlightenment of the colored people before their general emancipation, but the investigator has to depend on promiscuous sources for adequate information of this kind. With the exception of a survey of the Legal Status of the Colored Population in Respect to Schools and Education in the Different States, published in the Report of the United States Commissioner of Education in 1871, there has been no attempt at a general treatment of this phase of our history. This treatise, however, is too brief to inculcate an appreciation of the extensive efforts to enlighten the ante-bellum Negro.

Considered as a local problem this question has received more attention. A few writers have undertaken to sketch the movement to educate the colored people of certain communities before the Civil War. Their objective point, however, has been rather to treat of later periods. The books mentioned below give some information with respect to the period treated in this monograph.

BOOKS ON EDUCATION

Andrews, C.C. The history of the New York African Free Schools from their Establishment in 1787 to the Present Time. (New York, 1830.) Embraces a period of more than forty years, also a brief account of the successful labors of the New York Manumission Society, with an appendix containing specimens of original composition, both in prose and verse, by several of the pupils; pieces spoken at public examinations; an interesting dialogue between Doctor Samuel L. Mitchell, of New York, and a little boy of ten years old, and lines illustrative of the Lancastrian system of instruction. Andrews was a white man who was for a long time the head of this colored school system.

Boese, Thomas. Public Education in the City of New York, Its History, Condition, and Statistics, an Official Report of the Board of Education. (New York, 1869.) While serving as clerk of the Board of Education Boese had an opportunity to learn much about the New York African Free Schools.

Boone, R.G. A History of Education in Indiana. (New York, 1892.) Contains a brief account of the work of the Abolitionists in behalf of the education of the Negroes of that commonwealth.

BUTLER, N.M. Education in the United States. A series of monographs. (New York, 1910.)

The Education of the Negro

FOOTE, J.P. The Schools of Cincinnati and Its Vicinity. (Cincinnati, 1855.) A few pages of this book are devoted to the establishment and the development of colored schools in that city.

GOODWIN, M.B. "History of Schools for the Colored Population in the District of Columbia." (Published in the Report of the United States Commissioner of Education in 1871.) This is the most thorough research hitherto made in this field. The same system has been briefly treated by W.S. Montgomery in his Historical Sketch of Education for the Colored Race in the District of Columbia, 1807-1907. (Washington, D.C., 1907.) A less detailed account of the same is found in James Storum's "The Colored Public Schools of Washington,--Their Origin, Growth, and Present Condition." (A.M.E. Church Review, vol. v., p. 279.)

JONES, C.C. The Religious Instruction of the Negroes in the United States. (Savannah, 1842.) In trying to depict the spiritual condition of the colored people the writer tells also what he thought about their intellectual status.

MERIWETHER, C. History of Higher Education in South Carolina, with a Sketch of the Free School System. (Washington, 1889.) The author accounts for the early education of the colored people in that commonwealth but gives no details.

MILLER, KELLY. "The Education of the Negro." Constitutes Chapter XVI. of the Report of the United States Commissioner of Education for the year 1901. Contains a brief sketch of the early education of the Negro race in this country.

ORR, GUSTAVUS. The Need of Education in the South. (Atlanta, 1880.) An address delivered before the Department of Superintendence of the National Educational Association in 1879. Mr. Orr referred to the first efforts to educate the Negroes of the South.

PLUMER, W.S. Thoughts on the Religious Instruction of Negroes. Reference is made here to the early work of the Moravians among the colored people.

RANDALL, SAMUEL SIDWELL. The Common School System of the State of New York. (New York, 1851.) Comprises the several laws relating to common schools, together with full expositions, instructions, and forms, to which is prefixed an historical sketch of the system. Prepared in pursuance of an act of the legislature, under the direction of the Honorable Christopher Morgan, Superintendent of Common Schools.

STOCKWELL, THOMAS B. A History of Public Education in Rhode Island from 1636 to 1876. (Providence, 1876.) Compiled by authority of the Board of Education of Providence. Takes into account the various measures enacted to educate the Negroes of that commonwealth.

WICKERSHAM, J.P. A History of Education in Pennsylvania, Private and Public, Elementary and Higher, from the Time the Swedes Settled on the

Bibliography

Delaware to the Present Day. (Lancaster, Pa., 1886.) Considerable space is given to the education of the Negroes.

WRIGHT, R.R., SR. A Brief Historical Sketch of Negro Education in Georgia. (Savannah, 1894.) The movement during the early period in that State is here disposed of in a few pages.
A Brief Sketch of the Schools for the Black People and their Descendants, Established by the Society of Friends, etc. (Philadelphia, 1824.)

BOOKS OF TRAVEL BY FOREIGNERS

ABDY, E.S. Journal of a Residence and Tour in the United States from April, 1833, to October, 1834. Three volumes. (London, 1835.) Abdy was a fellow of Jesus College, Cambridge.

ALLIOT, PAUL. Reflexions historiques et politigues sur la Louisiane. (Cleveland, 1911.) Good for economic conditions. Valuable for information concerning New Orleans about the beginning of the nineteenth century.

ARFWEDSON, C.D. The United States and Canada in 1833 and 1834. Two volumes. (London, 1834.) Somewhat helpful.

BREMER, FREDERIKA. The Homes of the New World; Impressions of America. Translated by M. Howitt. Two volumes. (London, 1853.) The teaching of Negroes in the South is mentioned in several places.

BRISSOT DE WARVILLE, J.P. New Travels in the United States of America: including the Commerce of America with Europe, particularly with Great Britain and France. Two volumes. (London, 1794.) Gives general impressions, few details.

BUCKINGHAM, J.S. America, Historical, Statistical, and Descriptive. Two volumes. (New York, 1841.)
---- Eastern and Western States of America. Three volumes. (London and Paris, 1842.) Contains useful information.

BULLOCK, W. Sketch of a Journey through the Western States of North America from New Orleans by the Mississippi, Ohio, City of Cincinnati, and Falls of Niagara to New York. (London, 1827.) The author makes mention of the condition of the Negroes.

COKE, THOMAS. Extracts from the Journals of the Rev. Dr. Coke's Three Visits to America. (London, 1790.) Contains general information.
---- A Journal of the Reverend Doctor Coke's Fourth Tour on the Continent of America. (London, 1792.) Brings out the interest of this churchman in the elevation of the Negroes.

CUMING, F. Sketches of a Tour to the Western Country through the States of Kentucky and Ohio; a Voyage down the Ohio and Mississippi Rivers and a Trip through the Mississippi Territory and Part of West Florida, Commenced at Philadelphia in the Winter of 1807 and Concluded in 1809. (Pittsburg, 1810.) Gives a few facts.

FAUX, W. Venerable Days in America. (London, 1823.) A "journal of a tour in the United States principally undertaken to ascertain by positive evidence, the condition and probable prospects of British emigrants, including accounts of Mr. Kirkbeck's settlement in Illinois and intended to show men and things as they are in America." The Negroes are casually mentioned.

HUMBOLDT, FRIEDRICH HEINRICH ALEXANDER, FREIHERR VON. The Travels and Researches of Friedrich Heinrich Alexander von Humboldt. (London, 1833.) The author gives a "condensed narrative of his journeys in the equinoctial regions in America and in Asiatic Russia." The work contains also analyses of his important investigations. He throws a little light on the condition of the mixed breeds of the Western Hemisphere.

KEMBLE, FRANCES ANNE. Journal of a Residence on a Plantation in 1838-1839. (New York, 1863.) This diary is quoted extensively as one of the best sources for Southern conditions before the Civil War.

LAMBERT, JOHN. Travels through Canada and the United States, in the Years 1806, 1807, and 1808. Two volumes. (London, 1813.) To this journal are added notices and anecdotes of some of the leading characters in the United States. This traveler saw the Negroes.

PONS, FRANCOIS RAYMOND DE. Travels in Parts of South America, during the Years 1801, 1802, 1803, and 1804. (London, 1806.) Contains a description of Caracas; an account of the laws, commerce, and natural productions of that country; and a view of the customs and manners of the Spaniards and native Indians. Negroes are mentioned.

PRIEST, WILLIAM. Travels in the United States Commencing in the Year 1793 and ending in the Year 1797. (London, 1802.) Priest made two voyages across the Atlantic to appear at the theaters of Baltimore, Boston, and Philadelphia. He had something to say about the condition of the Negroes.

ROCHEFOUCAULD-LIANCOURT, DUC DE. Travels through the United States of America, the Country of the Iroquois, and Upper Canada in the Years 1795, 1796, and 1797. (London, 1799.) The author discusses the attitude of the people toward the uplift of the Negroes.

SCHOEPF, JOHANN DAVID. Reise durch der Mittlern und Sudlichen Vereinigten Nordamerikanischen Staaten nach Ost-Florida und den Bahama Inseln unternommen in den Jahren 1783 und 1784. (Cincinnati, 1812.) A translation of this work was published by Alfred J. Morrison at Philadelphia in 1911. Gives general impressions.

SMYTH, J.F.D. A Tour in the United States. (London, 1848.) This writer incidentally mentions the people of color.

Bibliography

SUTCLIFF, ROBERT. Travels in Some Parts of North America in the Years 1804, 1805, and 1806. (Philadelphia, 1812.) While traveling in slave territory Sutcliff studied the mental condition of the colored people.

BOOKS OF TRAVEL BY AMERICANS

BROWN, DAVID. The Planter, or Thirteen Years in the South. (Philadelphia, 1853.) Here we get a Northern white man's view of the heathenism of the Negroes.

BURKE, EMILY. Reminiscences of Georgia. (Oberlin, Ohio, 1850.) Presents the views of a woman who was interested in the uplift of the Negro race.

EVANS, ESTWICK. A Pedestrious Tour of Four Thousand Miles through the Western States and Territories during the Winter and Spring of 1818. (Concord, N.H., 1819.) Among the many topics treated is the author's contention that the Negro is capable of the highest mental development.

OLMSTED, FREDERICK LAW. A Journey in the Seaboard Slave States, with Remarks on their Economy. (New York, 1859.)
---- A Journey in the Back Country. (London, i860.)
---- Journeys and Explorations in the Cotton Kingdom. (London, 1861.)
Olmsted was a New York farmer. He recorded a few important facts about the education of the Negroes immediately before the Civil War.

PARSONS, E.G. Inside View of Slavery, or a Tour among the Planters. (Boston, 1855.) The introduction was written by Harriet Beecher Stowe. It was published to aid the antislavery cause, but in describing the condition of Negroes the author gave some educational statistics.

REDPATH, JAMES. The Roving Editor, or Talks with Slaves in Southern States. (New York 1859.) The slaves are here said to be telling their own story.

SMEDES, MRS. SUSAN (DABNEY). Memorials of a Southern Planter. (Baltimore, 1887.) The benevolence of those masters who had their slaves taught in spite of public opinion and the law, is well brought out in this volume.

TOWER, REVEREND PHILO. Slavery Unmasked. (Rochester, 1856.) Valuable chiefly for the author's arraignment of the so-called religious instruction of the Negroes after the reactionary period.

WOOLMAN, JOHN. Journal of John Woolman, with an Introduction by John G. Whittier. (Boston, 1873.) Woolman traveled so extensively in the colonies that he probably knew more about the mental state of the Negroes than any other Quaker of his time.

LETTERS

JEFFERSON, THOMAS. Letters of Thomas Jefferson to Abbe Gregoire, M.A. Julien, and Benjamin Banneker. In Jefferson's Works, Memorial Edition, xii. and xv. He comments on Negroes' talents.

The Education of the Negro

MADISON, JAMES. Letter to Prances Wright. In Madison's Works, vol. iii., p. 396. The training of Negroes is discussed.

MAY, SAMUEL JOSEPH. The Right of the Colored People to Education. (Brooklyn, 1883.) A collection of public letters addressed to Andrew T. Judson, remonstrating on the unjust procedure relative to Miss Prudence Crandall.

MCDONOGH, JOHN. "A Letter of John McDonogh on African Colonization addressed to the Editor of The New Orleans Commercial Bulletin," McDonogh was interested in the betterment of the colored people and did much to promote their mental development.

SHARPE, H. ED. The Abolition of Negro Apprenticeship. A letter to Lord Brougham. (London, 1838.)
A Southern Spy, or Curiosities of Negro Slavery in the South. Letters from a Southern to a Northern Gentleman. The comment of a passer-by.
A Letter to an American Planter from his Friend in London in 1781. The writer discussed the instruction of Negroes.

BIOGRAPHIES

BIRNEY, CATHERINE H. The Grimke Sisters; Sara and Angelina Grimke, the First American Women Advocates of Abolition and Woman's Rights. (Boston, 1885.) Mentions the part these workers played in the secret education of Negroes in the South.

BIRNEY, WILLIAM. James G. Birney and His Times. (New York, 1890.) A sketch of an advocate of Negro education.

BOWEN, CLARENCE W. Arthur and Lewis Tappan. A paper read at the fiftieth anniversary of the New York Anti-Slavery Society, at the Broadway Tabernacle, New York City, October 2, 1883. An honorable mention of two promoters of the colored manual labor schools.

CHILD, LYDIA MARIA. Isaac T. Hopper: A True Life. (Boston and Cleveland, 1853.)

CONWAY, MONCURE DANIEL. Benjamin Banneker, the Negro Astronomer. (London, 1864.)

(COOPER, JAMES F.) Notions of the Americans Picked up by a Traveling Bachelor. (Philadelphia, 1828.) General.

DREW, BENJAMIN. A North-side View of Slavery. The Refugee: or the Narratives of Fugitive Slaves in Canada. Related by themselves, with an Account of the History and Condition of the Colored Population of Upper Canada. (New York and Boston, 1856.)

GARRISON, FRANCIS AND WENDELL P. William Lloyd Garrison, 1805-1879. The Story of his Life told by his Children. Four volumes. (Boston

Bibliography

and New York, 1894.) Includes a brief account of what he did for the education of the colored people.

HALLOWELL, A.D. James and Lucretia Mott; Life and Letters. (Boston, 1884.) These were ardent abolitionists who advocated the education of the colored people.

JOHNSON, OLIVER. William Lloyd Garrison and his Times. (Boston, 1880. New edition, revised and enlarged, Boston, 1881.)

LOSSING, BENSON J. Life of George Washington, a Biography, Military and Political. Three volumes. (New York, 1860.) Gives the will of George Washington, who provided that at the stipulated time his slaves should be freed and that their children should be taught to read.

MATHER, COTTON. The Life and Death of the Reverend John Elliot who was the First Preacher of the Gospel to the Indians in America. The third edition carefully corrected. (London, 1694.) Sets forth the attitude of John Elliot toward the teaching of slaves.

MOTT, A. Biographical Sketches and Interesting Anecdotes of Persons of Color; with a Selection of Pieces of Poetry. (New York, 1826.) Some of these sketches show how ambitious Negroes learned to read and write in spite of opposition.

SIMMONS, W.J. Men of Mark: Eminent, Progressive, and Rising, with an Introductory Sketch of the Author by Reverend Henry M. Turner. (Cleveland, Ohio, 1891.) Accounts for the adverse circumstances under which many antebellum Negroes acquired knowledge.

SNOWDEN, T.B. The Autobiography of John B. Snowden. (Huntington, W. Va., 1900.)

WIGHTMAN, WILLIAM MAY. Life of William Capers, one of the Bishops of the Methodist Episcopal Church South; including an Autobiography. (Nashville, Tenn., 1858.) Shows what Capers did for the religious instruction of the colored people.

AUTOBIOGRAPHIES

ASBURY, BISHOP FRANCIS. The Journal of the Reverend Francis Asbury, Bishop of the Methodist Episcopal Church, from August 7, 1781, to December 7, 1815. Three volumes. (New York, 1821.)

COFFIN, LEVI. Reminiscences of Levi Coffin, reputed President of the Under Ground Railroad. (Second edition, Cincinnati, 1880.) Mentions the teaching of slaves.

The Education of the Negro

DOUGLASS, FREDERICK. Narrative of the Life of Frederick Douglass, as an American Slave. Written by himself. (Boston, 1845.) Gives several cases of secret Negro schools.

---- The Life and Times of Frederick Douglass from 1817 to 1882. Written by himself. Illustrated. With an Introduction by the Right Honorable John Bright, M.P. Edited by John Loeb, F.R.G.S., of the Christian Age, Editor of Uncle Tom's Story of his Life. (London, 1882.) Contains Douglass's appeal in behalf of vocational training.

FLINT, TIMOTHY. Recollections of the last Ten Years. A series of letters to the Reverend James Flint of Salem, Massachusetts, by T. Flint, Principal of the Seminary of Rapide, Louisiana. (Boston, 1826.) Mentions the teaching of Negroes.

GENERAL HISTORIES

BANCROFT, GEORGE. History of the United States. Ten volumes. (Boston, 1857-1864.)

HART, A.B., Editor. American History told by Contemporaries. Four volumes. (New York, 1898.)

---- The American Nation; A history, etc. Twenty-seven volumes. (New York, 1904-1908.) The volumes which have a bearing on the subject treated in this monograph are Bourne's Spain in America, Edward Channing's Jeffersonian System, F.J. Turner's Rise of the New West, and Hart's Slavery and Abolition.

HERRERA Y TORDESILLAS, ANTONIO DE. Historia General de los hechos de los Castellanos en las islas i tierra firme del mar oceano. Escrito por Antonio herrera coronista mayor de Sr. M. de las Indias y si coronista de Castilla. En Quatro decadas desde el ano de 1492 hasta el de 1554. Decada primera del rey Nuro Senor. (En Madrid en la Imprenta real de Nicolas Rodriguez Franco, ano 1726-1727.)

MCMASTER, JOHN B. History of the United States. Six volumes. (New York, 1900.)

RHODES, J.F. History of the United States from the Compromise of 1850 to the Final Restoration of Home Rule in the South. (New York and London, Macmillan & Company, 1892-1906.)

VON HOLST, HERMAN. The Constitutional and Political History of the United States of America. (Seven volumes. Chicago, 1877.)

STATE HISTORIES

ASHE, S.A. History of North Carolina. (Greensboro, 1908.)

BANCROFT, HUBERT HOWE. History of Arizona and New Mexico, 1530-1888. (San Francisco, 1890.)

Bibliography

BEARSE, AUSTIN. Reminiscences of Fugitive Slave Days in Boston. (Boston, 1880.)

BETTLE, EDWARD. "Notices of Negro Slavery as Connected with Pennsylvania." Read before the Historical Society of
Pennsylvania, 8th Mo., 7th, 1826. Memoirs of Historical Society of Pennsylvania.

BRACKETT, JEFFREY R. The Negro in Maryland. Johns Hopkins University Studies. (Baltimore, 1889.)

COLLINS, LEWIS. Historical Sketches of Kentucky. (Maysville, Ky., and Cincinnati, Ohio, 1847.)

JONES, CHARLES COLCOCK, JR. History of Georgia. (Boston, 1883.)

MCCRADY, EDWARD. The History of South Carolina under the Royal Government, 1719-1776, by Edward McCrady, a Member of the Bar of South Carolina and President of the Historical Society of South Carolina, Author of A History of South Carolina under the Proprietary Government. (New York and London, 1899.)

STEINER, B.C. History of Slavery in Connecticut. (Johns Hopkins University Studies, 1893.)

STUVE, BERNARD, and Alexander Davidson. A Complete History of Illinois from 1673 to 1783. (Springfield, 1874.)

TREMAIN, MARY M.A. Slavery in the District of Columbia. (University of Nebraska Seminary Papers, April, 1892.)
History of Brown County, Ohio. (Chicago, 1883.)
"Slavery in Illinois, 1818-1824." (Massachusetts Historical Society Collections, volume x.)

CHURCH HISTORIES

BANGS, NATHAN. A History of the Methodist Episcopal Church. Four volumes. (New York, 1845.)

BENEDICT, DAVID. A General History of the Baptist Denomination in America and in Other Parts of the World. (Boston, 1813.)
---- Fifty Years among the Baptists. (New York, 1860.)

DALCHO, FREDERICK. An Historical Account of the Protestant Episcopal Church in South Carolina, from the First Settlement of the Province to the War of the Revolution; with notices of the present State of the Church in each Parish: and some Accounts of the early Civil History of Carolina never before published. To which are added: the Laws relating to Religious Worship, the Journal and Rules of the Convention of South Carolina; the Constitution and

Canons of the Protestant Episcopal Church and the Course of Ecclesiastical Studies. (Charleston, 1820.)

DAVIDSON, REV. ROBERT. History of the Presbyterian Church in the State of Kentucky; with a Preliminary Sketch of the Churches in the Valley of Virginia. (New York, Pittsburgh, and Lexington, Kentucky, 1847.)

HAMILTON, JOHN T. A History of the Church Known as the Moravian Church, or the Unitas Fratrum, or the Unity of Brethren during the Eighteenth and Nineteenth Centuries. (Bethlehem, Pa., 1900.)

HAWKS, FRANCIS L. Ecclesiastical History of the United States. (New York, 1836.)

JAMES, CHARLES P. Documentary History of the Struggle for Religious Liberty in Virginia. (Lynchburg, Va., 1900.)

MATLACK, LUCIUS. The History of American Slavery and Methodism from 1780 to 1849: and History of the Wesleyan Methodist Connection of America. In Two Parts with an Appendix. (New York, 1849.)

MCTYEIRE, HOLLAND N. A History of Methodism; comprising a View of the Rise of the Revival of Spiritual Religion in the First Half of the Eighteenth Century, and the Principal Agents by whom it was promoted in Europe and America, with some Account of the Doctrine and Polity of Episcopal Methodism in the United States and the Means and Manner of its Extension down to 1884. (Nashville, Tenn., 1884.) McTyeire was one of the bishops of the Methodist Episcopal Church South.

REICHEL, L.T. The Early History of the Church of the United Brethren (Unitas Fratrum) commonly Called Moravians in North America, from 1734 to 1748. (Nazareth, Pa., 1888.)

RUSH, CHRISTOPHER. A Short Account of the African Methodist Episcopal Church in America. Written by the aid of George Collins. Also a view of the Church Order or Government from Scripture and from some of the best Authors relative to Episcopacy. (New York, 1843.)

SEMPLE, R.B. History of the Rise and Progress of the Baptists in Virginia. (Richmond, 1810.)

SERMONS, ORATIONS, ADDRESSES

BACON, THOMAS. Sermons Addressed to Masters and Servants. Published in 1743. Republished with other tracts by Rev. William Meade. (Winchester, Va., 1805.)

BOUCHER, JONATHAN. "American Education." This address is found in the author's volume entitled A View of the Causes and Consequences of

Bibliography

the American Revolution; in thirteen discourses, preached in North America between the years 1763 and 1775: with an historical preface. (London, 1797.)

BUCHANAN, GEORGE. An Oration upon the Moral and Political Evil of Slavery. Delivered at a Public Meeting of the Maryland Society for Promoting the Abolition of Slavery, and Relief of Free Negroes and others unlawfully held in Bondage. Baltimore, July 4, 1791. (Baltimore, 1793.)

CATTO, WILLIAM T. A Semicentenary Discourse Delivered in the First African Presbyterian Church, Philadelphia, on the 4th Sabbath of May, 1857: with a History of the Church from its first organization; including a brief Notice of Reverend John Gloucester, its First Pastor. Also an appendix containing sketches of all the Colored Churches in Philadelphia. (Philadelphia, 1857.) The author was then pastor of this church.

DANA, JAMES. The African Slave Trade. A Discourse delivered in the City of New Haven, September 9, 1790, before the Connecticut Society for the Promotion of Freedom. (New Haven, 1790.) Dr. Dana was at that time the pastor of the First Congregational Church of New Haven.

FAWCETT, BENJAMIN. A Compassionate Address to the Christian Negroes in Virginia, and other British Colonies in North America. With an appendix containing some account of the rise and progress of Christianity among that poor people. (The second edition, Salop, printed by F. Edwards and F. Cotton.)

GARRISON, WILLIAM LLOYD. An Address Delivered before the Free People of Color in Philadelphia, New York, and other Cities during the Month of June, 1831. (Boston, 1831.)

GRIFFIN, EDWARD DORR. A Plea for Africa. A Sermon preached October 26, 1817, in the First Presbyterian Church in the City of New York before the Synod of New York and New Jersey at the Request of the Board of Directors of the African School established by the Synod. (New York, 1817.) The aim was to arouse interest in this school.

JONES, CHARLES COLCOCK. The Religious Instruction of Negroes. A Sermon delivered before the Association of the Planters in Liberty and McIntosh Counties, Georgia. (Princeton, N.J., 1832.) Jones was then engaged in the work which he was discussing.

MAYO, A.D. "Address on Negro Education." (Springfield Republican, July 9, 1897; and the New England Magazine, October, 1898.)

RUSH, BENJAMIN. An Address to the Inhabitants of the British Settlements in America upon Slave Keeping. The second edition with observations on a pamphlet entitled Slavery not Forbidden by the Scripture or a Defense of the West Indian Planters by a Pennsylvanian. (Philadelphia, 1773.) The Negroes' need of education is pointed out.

The Education of the Negro

SECKER, THOMAS, Archbishop of Canterbury. A Sermon Preached before the Incorporated Society for the Propagation of the Gospel in Foreign Parts; at their Anniversary Meeting in the Parish Church of St. Mary-le-Bow, on Friday, February 20, 1741. (London 1741.) In this discourse Secker set forth his plan of teaching the Negroes to elevate themselves.

SIDNEY, JOSEPH. An Oration Commemorative of the Abolition of the Slave Trade in the United States Delivered before the Wilberforce Philanthropic Association in the City of New York on January 2, 1809. (New York, 1809.) The speaker did not forget the duty of all men to uplift those unfortunates who had already been degraded.

SMITH, THOMAS P. An Address before the Colored Citizens of Boston in Opposition to the Abolition of Colored Schools, 1849. (Boston, 1850.)

WARBURTON, WILLIAM, Bishop of Gloucester. A Sermon Preached before the Incorporated Society for the Propagation of the Gospel in Foreign Parts; at their Anniversary Meeting in the Parish Church of St. Mary-le-Bow on Friday, February 21, 1766. (London, 1766.) The speaker urged his hearers to enlighten the Indians and Negroes.

REPORTS ON THE EDUCATION OF THE COLORED PEOPLE

Report of the Proceedings at the Formation of the African Education Society; instituted at Washington, December 28, 1829. With an Address to the Public by the Board of Managers. (Washington, 1830.)

Report of the Minority of the Committee of the Primary School Board on the Caste Schools of the City of Boston. With some remarks on the City Solicitor's Opinion, by Wendell Phillips. (Boston, 1846.)

Report of a Special Committee of the Grammar School Board of Boston, Massachusetts. Abolition of the Smith Colored School. (Boston, 1849.)

Report of the Primary School Committee, Boston, Massachusetts. Abolition of the Colored Schools. (Boston, 1846.)

Report of the Minority of the Committee upon the Petition of J.T. Hilton and other Colored Citizens of Boston, Praying for the Abolition of the Smith Colored School. (Boston, 1849.)

Opinion of Honorable Richard Fletcher as to whether Colored Children can be Lawfully Excluded from Free Public Schools. (Boston, 1846.)

Special Report of the Commissioner of Education on the Improvement of the Public Schools in the District of Columbia, containing M.B. Goodwin's "History of Schools for the Colored Population in the District of Columbia." (Washington, 1871.)

Thirty-Seventh Annual Report of the New York Public School Society, 1842. (New York, 1842.)

STATISTICS

CLARKE, J.F. Present Condition of the Free Colored People of the United States. (New York and Boston, the American Antislavery Society, 1859.) Published also in the March number of the Christian Examiner.

Bibliography

Condition of the Free People of Color in Ohio. With interesting anecdotes. (Boston, 1839.)

Institute for Colored Youth. (Philadelphia, 1860-1865.) Contains a list of the officers and students.

Report of the Condition of the Colored People of Cincinnati, 1835. (Cincinnati, 1835.)

Report of a Committee of the Pennsylvania Society of Abolition on Present Condition of the Colored People, etc., 1838. (Philadelphia, 1838.)

Statistical Inquiry into the Condition of the People of Color of the City and Districts of Philadelphia. (Philadelphia, 1849.) Statistics of the Colored People of Philadelphia in 1859, compiled by Benj. C. Bacon. (Philadelphia, 1859.)

Statistical Abstract of the United States, 1898. Prepared by the Bureau of Statistics. (Washington, D.C., 1899.)

Statistical View of the Population of the United States, A, 1790-1830. (Published by the Department of State in 1835.)

The Present State and Condition of the Free People of Color of the city of Philadelphia and adjoining districts as exhibited by the Report of a Committee of the Pennsylvania Society for Promoting the Abolition of Slavery. Read First Month (January), 5th, 1838. (Philadelphia, 1838.)

Trades of the Colored People. (Philadelphia, 1838.)

United States Censuses of 1790, 1800, 1810, 1820, 1830, 1840, 1850, and 1860.

VARLE, CHARLES. A Complete View of Baltimore; with a Statistical Sketch of all the Commercial, Mercantile, Manufacturing, Literary, Scientific Institutions and Establishments in the same Vicinity ... derived from personal Observation and Research. (Baltimore, 1833.)

CHURCH REPORTS

A Brief Statement of the Rise and Progress of the Testimony of Friends against Slavery and the Slave Trade. Published by direction of the Yearly Meeting held in Philadelphia in the Fourth Month, 1843. Shows the action taken by various Friends to educate the Negroes.

A Collection of the Acts, Deliverances, and Testimonies of the Supreme Judicatory of the Presbyterian Church, from its Origin in America to the Present Time. By Samuel J. Baird. (Philadelphia, 1856.)

Acts and Proceedings of the General Assembly of the Presbyterian Church in the United States of America in the Year 1800. (Philadelphia, 1800.) The question of instructing the Negroes came up in this meeting.

PASCOE, C.F. Classified Digest of the Records of the Society for the Propagation of the Gospel in Foreign Parts, 1701-1892, with much Supplementary Information. (London, 1893.) A good source for the accounts of the efforts of this organization among Negroes.

"Minutes of the Methodist Conference, 1785." Found in Rev. Charles Elliott's History of the Great Secession from the Methodist Episcopal Church, etc. This conference discussed the education of the colored people.

The Education of the Negro

REPORTS OF THE AMERICAN CONVENTION, 1794-1831

American Convention of Abolition Societies. Minutes of the Proceedings of a Convention of Delegates from the Abolition Societies established in different Parts of the United States, assembled at Philadelphia on the first Day of January, one thousand seven hundred and ninety-four, and continued by Adjournments, until the seventh Day of the same Month, inclusive. (Philadelphia, 1794.)

--Minutes of the Proceedings of the Second Convention of Delegates from the Abolition Societies established in different Parts of the United States, assembled at Philadelphia on the seventh Day of January, one thousand seven hundred and ninety-five, and continued by Adjournments until the fourteenth Day of the same Month, inclusive. (Philadelphia, 1795.)

--Minutes of the Proceedings of the Third Convention of Delegates from the Abolition Societies established in different Parts of the United States, assembled at Philadelphia on the first Day of January, one thousand seven hundred and ninety-six, and continued, by Adjournments, until the seventh Day of the same Month, inclusive. (Philadelphia, 1796.)

--Address to Free Africans and other Free People of Colour in the United States. (1796.)

--Minutes of the Proceedings of the Fourth Convention of Delegates from the Abolition Societies established in different Parts of the United States, assembled at Philadelphia on the third Day of May, one thousand seven hundred and ninety-seven, and continued by Adjournments, until the ninth Day of the same Month, inclusive. (Philadelphia, 1797.)

--Minutes of the Proceedings of the Fifth Convention of Delegates from the Abolition Societies established in different Parts of the United States, assembled at Philadelphia on the first Day of June, one thousand seven hundred and ninety-eight, and continued, by Adjournments, until the sixth Day of the same Month, inclusive. (Philadelphia, 1798.)

American Convention of Abolition Societies. Minutes of the Proceedings of the Sixth Convention of Delegates from the Abolition Societies established in different parts of the United States, assembled at Philadelphia, on the fourth Day of June, one thousand eight hundred, and continued by Adjournments, until the sixth Day of the same Month, inclusive. (Philadelphia, 1800.)

--Minutes of the Proceedings of the Seventh Convention of Delegates from the Abolition Societies established in different parts of the United States, assembled at Philadelphia on the third Day of June, one thousand eight hundred and one, and continued by Adjournments until the sixth Day of the same Month, inclusive. (Philadelphia, 1801.)

--Minutes of the Proceedings of the Eighth Convention of Delegates from the Abolition Societies established in different parts of the United States, assembled at Philadelphia, on the tenth Day of January, one thousand eight hundred and three, and continued by Adjournments until the fourteenth Day of the same Month, inclusive. (Philadelphia, 1803.)

--Minutes of the Proceedings of the Ninth American Convention for promoting the Abolition of Slavery and improving the Condition of the African Race; assembled at Philadelphia on the ninth Day of January, one thousand eight hundred and four, and continued by Adjournments until the thirteenth Day of the same Month, inclusive. (Philadelphia, 1804.)

Bibliography

--Address of the American Convention for promoting the Abolition of Slavery and improving the Condition of the African Race, assembled at Philadelphia, in January, 1804, to the People of the United States. (Philadelphia, 1804.)

--Minutes of the Proceedings of the Tenth American Convention for promoting the Abolition of Slavery and improving the Condition of the African Race; assembled at Philadelphia on the fourteenth Day of January, one thousand eight hundred and five, and continued by Adjournments until the seventeenth Day of the same Month, inclusive. (Philadelphia, 1805.)

--Minutes of the Proceedings of the Eleventh American Convention for promoting the Abolition of Slavery and improving the Condition of the African Race; assembled at Philadelphia, on the thirteenth Day of January, one thousand eight hundred and six, and continued by Adjournments until the fifteenth Day of the same Month, inclusive. (Philadelphia, 1806.)

--Minutes of the Proceedings of a Special Meeting of the Fifteenth American Convention for promoting the Abolition of Slavery and improving the Condition of the African Race; assembled at Philadelphia on the tenth Day of December, 1818, and continued by Adjournments until the fifteenth Day of the same Month, inclusive. (Philadelphia, 1818.)

--Constitution of the American Convention for promoting the Abolition of Slavery, and improving the Condition of the African Race. Adopted on the eleventh Day of December, 1818, to take effect on the fifth Day of October, 1819. (Philadelphia, 1819.)

--Minutes of the Eighteenth Session of the American Convention for promoting the Abolition of Slavery, and improving the Condition of the African Race. Convened at Philadelphia, on the seventh Day of October, 1823. (Philadelphia, 1823.)

--To the Clergy and Pastors throughout the United States. (Dated Philadelphia, September 18, 1826.)

--Minutes of the Adjourned Session of the Twentieth Biennial American Convention for promoting the Abolition of Slavery. Held at Baltimore, November 28. (Philadelphia, 1828.)

REPORTS OF ANTI-SLAVERY SOCIETIES

The Annual Report of the American and Foreign Anti-Slavery Societies, presented at New York, May 6, 1847, with the Addresses and Resolutions. (New York, 1847.)

The Annual Report of the American and Foreign Anti-Slavery Societies, with the Addresses and Resolutions. (New York, 1851.)

The First Annual Report of the American Anti-Slavery Society, with the Speeches Delivered at the Anniversary Meeting held in Chatham Street Chapel in the City of New York, on the sixth Day of May by Adjournment on the eighth, in the Rev. Dr. Lansing's Church, and the Minutes of the Society for Business. (New York, 1834.)

The Second Annual Report of the American Anti-Slavery Society, held in the City of New York, on the twelfth of May, 1835, and the Minutes and Proceedings of the Society for Business. (New York, 1835.)

The Third Annual Report of the American Anti-Slavery Society, with the Speeches delivered at the Anniversary Meeting held in the City of New York on

May the tenth, 1836, and Minutes of the Meetings of the Society for Business. (New York, 1836.)

The Fourth Annual Report of the American Anti-Slavery Society, with the Speeches delivered at the Anniversary Meeting held in the City of New York on the ninth of May, 1837. (New York, 1837.)

The Fifth Annual Report of the American Anti-Slavery Society, with the Speeches delivered at the Anniversary Meeting and the Minutes and Proceedings of the Society for Business. (New York, 1838.)

The Sixth Annual Report of the American Anti-Slavery Society, with the Speeches delivered at the Anniversary Meeting held in the City of New York, on the seventh Day of May, 1839, and the Minutes of the Meetings of the Society for Business, held on the evenings of the three following days. (New York, 1839.)

The Annual Report of the American Anti-Slavery Society by the Executive Committee for the year ending May 1, 1859. (New York, 1860.)

The Third Annual Report of the Managers of the New England Anti-Slavery Society presented June 2, 1835. (Boston, 1835.)

Annual Reports of the Massachusetts (or New England) Anti-Slavery Society, 1831-end.

Reports of the National Anti-Slavery Convention, 1833-end.

REPORTS OF COLONIZATION SOCIETIES

Reports of the American Colonization Society, 1818-1832.

Report of the New York Colonization Society, October 1, 1823. (New York, 1823.)

The Seventh Annual Report of the Colonization Society of the City of New York. (New York, 1839.)

Proceedings of the New York State Colonization Society, 1831. (Albany, 1831.)

The Eighteenth Annual Report of the Colonization Society of the State of New York. (New York, 1850.)

REPORTS OF CONVENTIONS OF FREE NEGROES

Minutes and Proceedings of the First Annual Convention of the People of Color. Held by Adjournment in the City of Philadelphia, from the sixth to the eleventh of June, inclusive, 1831.
(Philadelphia, 1831.)

Minutes and Proceedings of the Second Annual Convention for the Improvement of the Free People of Color in these United States. Held by Adjournments in the City of Philadelphia, from the 4th to the 13th of June, inclusive, 1832,(Philadelphia, 1832.)

Minutes and Proceedings of the Third Annual Convention for the Improvement of the Free People of Color in these United States. Held by Adjournments in the city of Philadelphia, in 1833. (New York, 1833.) These proceedings were published also in the New York Commercial Advertiser, April 27, 1833.

Minutes and Proceedings of the Fourth Annual Convention for the Improvement of the Free People of Color in the United States. held by

Bibliography

Adjournments in the Asbury Church, New York, from the 2d to the 12th of June, 1834. (New York, 1834.)

Proceedings of the Convention of the Colored Freedmen of Ohio at Cincinnati, January 14, 1852. (Cincinnati, Ohio, 1852.)

MISCELLANEOUS BOOKS AND PAMPHLETS

ADAMS, ALICE DANA. The Neglected Period of Anti-Slavery in America. Radcliffe College Monographs No. 14. (Boston and London, 1908.) Contains some valuable facts about the education of the Negroes during the first three decades of the nineteenth century.

ADAMS, JOHN. The Works of John Adams, Second President of the United States; with a Life of the Author, Notes, and Illustrations by his Grandson, Charles Francis Adams. Ten volumes. Volume x., shows the attitude of James Otis toward the Negroes.

ADAMS, NEHEMIAH. A South-Side View of Slavery; or Three Months at the South in 1854. (Boston, 1854.) The position of the South on the education of the colored people is well set forth.

AGRICOLA (pseudonym). An Impartial View of the Real State of the Black Population in the United States. (Philadelphia, 1824.)

ALBERT, O.V. The House of Bondage; or Charlotte Brooks and other Slaves Original and Life-like as they appeared in their Plantation and City Slave Life; together with pen Pictures of the peculiar Institution, with Sights and Insights into their new Relations as Freedmen, Freemen, and Citizens, with an Introduction by Reverend Bishop Willard Mallalieu. (New York and Cincinnati, 1890.)

ALEXANDER, A. A History of Colonization on the Western Continent of Africa. (Philadelphia, 1846.) Treats of education in "An Account of the Endeavors used by the Society for the Propagation of the Gospel in Foreign Parts, to instruct Negroes in the City of New York, together with two of Bishop Gibson's Letters on that subject, being an Extract from Dr. Humphrey's Historical Account of the Incorporated Society for the Propagation of the Gospel in Foreign Parts from its Foundation in the Year 1728." (London, 1730.)

An Address to the People of North Carolina on the Evils of Slavery, by the Friends of Liberty and Equality, 1830. (Greensborough, 1830.)

An Address to the Presbyterians of Kentucky proposing a Plan for the Instruction and Emancipation of their Slaves by a Committee of the Synod of Kentucky. (Newburyport, 1836.)

ANDERSON, MATTHEW. Presbylerianism--Its Relation to the Negro. (Philadelphia, 1897.)

ANDREWS, E.E. Slavery and the Domestic Slave Trade in the United States. In a series of letters addressed to the Executive Committee of the American Union for the Relief and Improvement of the Colored Race. (Boston, 1836.)

The Education of the Negro

BALDWIN, EBENEZER. Observations on the Physical and Moral Qualities of our Colored Population with Remarks on the Subject of Emancipation and Colonization. (New Haven, 1834.)

BASSETT, J.S. Slavery and Servitude in the Colony of North Carolina. (Johns Hopkins University Studies in Historical and Political Science. Fourteenth Series, iv.-v. Baltimore, 1896.)
---- Slavery in the State of North Carolina. (Johns Hopkins University Studies in Historical and Political Science. Series XVII., Nos. 7-8. Baltimore, 1899.)
---- Anti-Slavery Leaders of North Carolina. (Johns Hopkins University Studies in Historical and Political Science. Series XVI., No. 6. Baltimore, 1898.)

BAXTER, RICHARD. Practical Works. Twenty-three volumes. (London, 1830.)

BENEZET, ANTHONY. A Caution to Great Britain and Her Colonies in a Short Representation of the calamitous state of the enslaved Negro in the British Dominions. (Philadelphia, 1784.)
---- The Case of our Fellow-Creatures, the Oppressed Africans, respectfully recommended to the serious Consideration of the Legislature of Great Britain, by the People called Quakers. (London, 1783.)
---- Observations on the enslaving, importing, and purchasing of Negroes; with some advice thereon, extracted from the Epistle of the Yearly-Meeting of the People called Quakers, held at London in the Year 1748. (Germantown, 1760.)
---- The Potent Enemies of America laid open: being some Account of the baneful Effects attending the Use of distilled spirituous Liquors, and the Slavery of the Negroes. (Philadelphia.)
---- A Short Account of that Part of Africa, inhabited by the Negroes. With respect to the Fertility of the Country; the good Disposition of many of the Natives, and the Manner by which the Slave Trade is carried on. (Philadelphia, 1792.)
---- Short Observations on Slavery, Introductory to Some Extracts from the Writings of the Abbe Raynal, on the Important Subject.
---- Some Historical Account of Guinea, its Situation, Produce, and the General Disposition of its Inhabitants. With an Inquiry into the Rise and Progress of the Slave Trade, its Nature and Lamentable Effects. (London, 1788.)

BIRNEY, JAMES G. The American Churches, the Bulwarks of American Slavery, by an American. (Newburyport, 1842.)

BIRNEY, WILLIAM. James G. Birney and his Times. The Genesis of the Republican Party, with Some Account of the Abolition Movements in the South before 1828. (New York, 1890.)

BOURNE, WILLIAM O. History of the Public School Society of the City of New York, with Portraits of the Presidents of the Society. (New York, 1870.)

BRACKETT, JEFFERY R. The Negro in Maryland. A Study of the Institution of Slavery. (Baltimore, Johns Hopkins University, 1889).

Bibliography

BRANAGAN, THOMAS. A Preliminary Essay on the Oppression of the Exiled Sons of Africa, Consisting of Animadversions on the Impolicy and Barbarity of the Deleterious Commerce and Subsequent Slavery of the Human Species. (Philadelphia: Printed for the Author by John W. Scott, 1804.)

BRANAGAN, T. Serious Remonstrances Addressed to the Citizens of the Northern States and their Representatives, being an Appeal to their Natural Feelings and Common Sense; Consisting of Speculations and Animadversions, on the Recent Revival of the Slave Trade in the American Republic. (Philadelphia, 1805.)

BROWN, W.W. My Southern Home. (Boston, 1882.)

CHILD, LYDIA MARIA. An Appeal in Favor of that Class of Americans Called Africans. (Boston: Allen & Ticknor, 1833, and New York: J.S. Taylor, 1836.)

CHANNING, WILLIAM E. Slavery. (Boston: J. Munroe & Co., 1835.)
---- Remarks on the Slavery Question. (Boston: J. Munroe & Co., 1839.)

COBB, T.R.R. An Historical Sketch of Slavery. (Philadelphia: T. & J.W. Johnson, 1858.)
---- An Inquiry into the Law of Negro Slavery in the United States of America. To which is Prefixed an Historical Sketch of Slavery by Thomas R.R. Cobb of Georgia. (Philadelphia and Savannah, 1858.)

COFFIN, JOSHUA. An Account of Some of the Principal Slave Insurrections and Others which have Occurred or been attempted in the United States and Elsewhere during the Last Two Centuries. With Various Remarks. Collected from Various Sources. (New York, 1860.)

CONWAY, MONCURE DANIEL. Testimonies Concerning Slavery. (London: Chapman & Hall, 1865.) The author was a native of Virginia.

CULP, D.W. Twentieth Century Negro Literature, or a Cyclopedia of Thought, Vital Topics Relating to the American Negro by One Hundred of America's Greatest Negroes. (Toronto, Naperville, Ill., and Atlanta, Ga., 1902.)

DE BOW, J.D.B. Industrial Resources of the Southern and Western States. (New Orleans, 1852-1853.)

DELANY, M.R. The Condition of the Colored People in United States. (Boston, 1852.)

DRESSER, AMOS. The Narrative of Amos Dresser with Stone's Letters from Natchez--an Obituary Notice of the Writer and Two Letters from Tallahassee Relating to the Treatment of Slaves. (New York, 1836.)

DREWERY, WILLIAM SIDNEY. Slave Insurrections in Virginia, 1830-1865. (Washington, 1900.)

DUBOIS, W.E.B. The Philadelphia Negro. (Philadelphia, 1896.)

---- The Suppression of the African Slave Trade to the United States of America, 1638-1870. Harvard Historical Studies, Vol. i. (New York, London, and Bombay, 1896.)

---- Atlanta University Publications, The Negro Common School. (Atlanta, 1901.)

---- The College-Bred Negro. (Atlanta, 1900.)

---- The Negro Church. (Atlanta, 1903.)

---- and Dill, A.G. The College-Bred Negro American. (Atlanta, 1910.)

---- The Common School and the Negro American. (Atlanta, 1911.)

---- The Negro American Artisan. (Atlanta, 1912.)

ELLIOTT, REV. CHARLES. History of the Great Secession from the Methodist Episcopal Church, etc.
Exposition of the Object and Plan of the American Union for the Relief and Improvement of the Colored Race. (Boston, 1835.)

FEE, JOHN G. Anti-Slavery Manual. (Maysville, 1848.)

FISH, C.R. Guide to the Materials for American History in Roman and Other Italian Archives. (Washington, D.C., Carnegie Institution, 1911.)

FRANKLIN, BENJAMIN. The Writings of Benjamin Franklin Collected and Edited with a Life and Introduction by Albert Henry Smyth. (New York, 1905-1907.)

FROST, W.G. "Appalachian America." In vol. i. of The Americana (New York, 1912.)

GARNETT, H.H. The Past and Present Condition and the Destiny of the Colored Race. (Troy, 1848.)

GOODLOE, D.R. The Southern Platform. (Boston, 1858.)

GREGOIRE, BISHOP. De la Litterature des Negres. (Paris, 1808.) Translated and published by D.B. Warden at Brooklyn, in 1810.

HARRISON, SAMUEL ALEXANDER. Wenlock Christison, and the Early Friends in Talbot County, Maryland. A Paper read before the Maryland Historical Society, March 9, 1874. (Baltimore, 1878.)

HENSON, JOSIAH. The Life of Josiah Henson. (Boston, 1849.)

HICKOK, CHARLES THOMAS. The Negro in Ohio, 1802-1870. (Cleveland, 1896.)

HODGKIN, THOMAS A. Inquiry into the Merits of the American Colonization Society and Reply to the Charges Brought against it, with an Account of the British African Colonization Society. (London, 1833.)

Bibliography

HOLLAND, EDWIN C. Refutation of Calumnies Circulated against the Southern and Western States. (Charleston, 1822.)

HOWE, SAMUEL G. The Refugees from Slavery in Canada West. Report to the Freedmen's Inquiry Committee. (Boston, 1864.)

INGLE, EDWARD. The Negro in the District of Columbia. (Johns Hopkins Studies in Historical and Political Sciences, vol. xi., Baltimore, 1893.)

JAY, JOHN. The Correspondence and Public Papers of John Jay, First Chief Justice of the United States and President of the Continental Congress, Member of the Commission to Negotiate the Treaty of Independence, Envoy to Great Britain, Governor of New York, etc., 1782-1793. (New York and London, 1891.) Edited by Henry P. Johnson, Professor of History in the College of the City of New York.

JAY, WILLIAM. An Inquiry into the Character and Tendencies of the American Colonization and American Anti-Slavery Societies. Second edition. (New York, 1835.)

JEFFERSON, THOMAS. The Writings of Thomas Jefferson. Memorial Edition. Autobiography, Notes on Virginia, Parliamentary Manual, Official Papers, Messages and Addresses, and Other Writings Official and Private, etc. (Washington, 1903.)
Johns Hopkins University Studies in Historical and Political Science. H.B. Adams, Editor. (Baltimore, Johns Hopkins Press.)

JONES, C.C. A Catechism of Scripture, Doctrine, and Practice. (Philadelphia, 1852.)

KIRK, EDWARD E. Educated Labor, etc. (New York, 1868.)

LANGSTON, JOHN M. From the Virginia Plantation to the National Capital; or, The First and Only Negro Representative in Congress from the Old Dominion. (Hartford, 1894.)
L'Esclavage dans les Etats Confederes par un missionaire. Deuxieme edition. (Paris, 1865.)

LOCKE, M.S. Anti-Slavery in America, from the Introduction of African Slaves to the Prohibition of the Slave Trade, 1619-1808. Radcliffe College Monographs, No. 11. (Boston, 1901.)

LONG, J.D. Pictures of Slavery in Church and State, Including Personal Reminiscences, Biographical Sketches, Anecdotes, etc., with Appendix Containing the Views of John Wesley and Richard Watson on Slavery. (Philadelphia, 1857.)

LOWERY, WOODBURY. The Spanish Settlements within the Present Limits of the United States. Florida, 1562-1574. (New York and London, 1905.)

The Education of the Negro

MADISON, JAMES. Letters and Other Writings of James Madison Published by Order of Congress. Four volumes. (Philadelphia, 1865.)

MALLARY, R.O. Maybank: Some Memoirs of a Southern Christian Household; Family Life of C.C. Jones.

MAY, S.J. Some Recollections of our Anti-Slavery Conflict.

MCLEOD, ALEXANDER. Negro Slavery Unjustifiable. A Discourse by the Late Alexander McLeod, 1802, with an Appendix. (New York, 1863.)

MEADE, BISHOP WILLIAM. Old Churches, Ministers, and Families, of Virginia. (Philadelphia, 1897.)

MONROE, JAMES. The Writings of James Monroe, Including a Collection of his Public and Private Papers and Correspondence now for the First Time Printed, Edited by S.M. Hamilton. (Boston, 1900.)

MOORE, GEORGE H. Notes on the History of Slavery in Massachusetts by George H. Moore, Librarian of the New York Historical Society and Corresponding Member of the Massachusetts Historical Society. (New York, 1866.)

MORGAN, THOMAS J. The Negro in America. (Philadelphia, 1898.)

NEEDLES, EDWARD. Ten Years' Progress, or a Comparison of the State and Condition of the Colored People in the City and County of Philadelphia from 1837 to 1847. (Philadelphia, 1849.)

OTHELLO (PSEUDONYM). "Essays on Negro Slavery." Published in The American Museum in 1788. Othello was a free Negro.

OVINGTON, M.W. Half-a-Man. (New York, 1911.) Treats of the Negro in the State of New York. A few pages are devoted to the education of the colored people.

PARRISH, JOHN. Remarks on the Slavery of the Black People; Addressed to the Citizens of the United States, Particularly to those who are in Legislative or Executive Stations in the General or State Governments; and also to Such Individuals as Hold them in Bondage. (Philadelphia, 1806.)

PLUMER, W.S. Thoughts on the Religious Instruction of the Negroes of this Country. (Savannah, 1848.)

Plymouth Colony, New. Records of the Colony of New Plymouth in New England. Printed by Order of the Legislature of the Commonwealth of Massachusetts. Edited by Nathaniel B. Shurtleff, Member of the Massachusetts Historical Society, and Fellow of the Antiquarians of London. (Boston, 1855.)

PORTEUS, BISHOP BEILBY. The Works of the Rev. Beilby Porteus, D.D., Late Bishop of London, with his Life by the Rev. Robert Hodgson, A.M., F.R.S.,

Bibliography

Rector of St. George's, Hanover Square, and One of the Chaplains in ordinary to His Majesty. A new edition in six volumes. (London, 1816.)

POWER, REV. JOHN H. Review of the Lectures of William A. Smith, D.D., on the Philosophy and Practice of Slavery as Exhibited in the Institution of Domestic Slavery in the United States, with the Duties of Masters to Slaves in a Series of Letters addressed to the Author. (Cincinnati, 1859.)
Quaker Pamphlet.

RICE, DAVID. Slavery Inconsistent with Justice and Good Policy: Proved by a Speech Delivered in the Convention Held at Danville, Kentucky. (Philadelphia, 1792, and London, 1793.)

SCOBER, J. Negro Apprenticeship in the Colonies. (London, 1837.)

SECKER, THOMAS. The Works of the Right Reverend Thomas Seeker, Archbishop of Canterbury with a Review of his Life and Character by B. Porteus. (New edition in six volumes, London, 1811.)

SIEBERT, WILBUR H. The Underground Railroad from Slavery to Freedom, by W.H. Siebert, Associate Professor of History in the Ohio State University, with an Introduction by A.B. Hart. (New York, 1898.)

SMITH, WILLIAM A. Lectures on the Philosophy and Practice of Slavery as Exhibited in the Institution of Domestic Slavery in the United States, with the Duties of Masters to Slaves. (Nashville, Tenn., 1856.) Doctor Smith was the President and Professor of Moral and Intellectual Philosophy of Randolph-Macon College.
Slavery and the Internal Slave Trade in the United States of America, being Inquiries to Questions Transmitted by the Committee of the British and Foreign Anti-Slavery Society for the Abolition of Slavery and the Slave Trade throughout the World. Presented to the General Anti-Slavery Convention Held in London, June, 1840, by the Executive Committee of the American Anti-Slavery Society. (London, 1841.)
The Enormity of the Slave Trade and the Duty of Seeking the Moral and Spiritual Elevation of the Colored Race. (New York.) This work includes speeches of Wilberforce and other documents.
The Jesuit Relations and Allied Documents, Travels, and Explorations of the Jesuit Missionaries in New France, 1610-1791. The Original French, Latin, and Italian Texts with English Translations and Notes; Illustrated by Portraits, Maps, and Facsimiles. Edited by Reuben Gold Thwaites, Secretary of the State Historical Society of Wisconsin. (Cleveland, 1896.)
The South Vindicated from the Treason and Fanaticism of the Northern Abolitionists. (Philadelphia, 1836.)

THOMPSON, GEORGE. Speech at the Meeting for the Extinction of Negro Apprenticeship. (London, 1838.)
---- The Free Church Alliance with Manstealers. Send Back the Money. Great Anti-Slavery Meeting in the City Hall, Glasgow, Containing the Speeches Delivered by Messrs. Wright, Douglass, and Buffum, from America, and by

George Thompson of London, with a Summary Account of a Series of Meetings Held in Edinburgh by the Abovenamed Gentlemen. (Glasgow, 1846.)

TORREY, JESSE, JR. A Portraiture of Domestic Slavery in the United States, with Reflections on the Practicability of Restoring the Moral Rights of the Slave, without Impairing the Legal Privileges of the Possessor, and a Project of a Colonial Asylum for Free Persons of Color, Including Memoirs of Facts on the Interior Traffic in Slaves, and on Kidnapping, Illustrated with Engravings by Jesse Torrey, Jr., Physician, Author of a Series of Essays on Morals and the Diffusion of Knowledge. (Philadelphia, 1817.)
---- American Infernal Slave Trade; with Reflections on the Project for forming a Colony of Blacks in Africa. (London, 1822.)

TOWER, PHILO. Slavery Unmasked: Being a Truthful Narrative of Three Years' Residence and Journeying in Eleven Southern States; to which is Added "The Invasion of Kansas," Including the Last Chapter of her Wrongs. (Rochester, 1856.)

TURNER, E.R. The Negro in Pennsylvania. (Washington, 1911.)
Tyrannical Libertymen: a Discourse upon Negro Slavery in the United States; Composed at---- in New Hampshire; on the Late Federal Thanksgiving Day. (Hanover, N.H., 1795.)

VAN EVRIE, JOHN H. Negroes and Negro Slavery, by J.H. Van Evrie, M.D. Introductory Chapter: Causes of Popular Delusion on the Subject. (Washington, 1853.)
---- White Supremacy and Negro Subordination; or, Negroes a Subordinate Race, and So-called Slavery its Normal Condition. With an Appendix Showing the Past and Present Condition of the Countries South of us. (New York, 1868.)

WALKER, DAVID. Walker's Appeal in Four Articles, together with a Preamble, to the Colored Citizens of the World, but in Particular and very Expressly to those of the United States of America. Written in Boston, State of Massachusetts, September 28, 1820. Second edition. (Boston, 1830.) Walker was a Negro who hoped to arouse his race to self-assertion.

WASHINGTON, B.T. The Story of the Negro. Two volumes (New York, 1909.)

WASHINGTON, GEORGE. The Writings of George Washington, being his Correspondence, Addresses, Messages, and other Papers, Official and Private, Selected and Published from the Original Manuscripts with the Life of the Author, Notes and Illustrations, by Jared Sparks. (Boston, 1835.)

WEEKS, STEPHEN B. Southern Quakers and Slavery. A Study in Institutional History. (Baltimore, The Johns Hopkins Press, 1896.)
---- The Anti-Slavery Sentiment in the South; with Unpublished Letters from John Stuart Mill and Mrs. Stowe. (Southern History Association Publications. Volume ii., No. 2, Washington, D. C, April, 1898.)

Bibliography

WESLEY, JOHN. Thoughts upon Slavery. In the Potent Enemies of America Laid Open.... London, printed: Reprinted in Philadelphia with Notes, and Sold by Joseph Cruikshank. 1774.

WIGHAM, ELIZA. The Anti-Slavery Cause in America and its Martyrs. (London, 1863.)

WILLIAMS, GEORGE W. History of the Negro Race in the United States from 1619-1880. Negroes as Slaves, as Soldiers, and as Citizens: together with a Preliminary Consideration of the Unity of the Human Family, an Historical Sketch of Africa and an Account of the Negro Governments of Sierra Leone and Liberia. (New York, 1883.)

WOOLMAN, JOHN. The Works of John Woolman. In two parts. Part I: a Journal of the Life, Gospel-Labors, and Christian Experiences of that Faithful Minister of Christ, John Woolman, Late of Mount Holly, in the Province of New Jersey. (London, 1775.)
---- Same. Part Second. Containing his Last Epistle and other Writings. (London, 1775.)
---- Some Considerations on the Keeping of Negroes. Recommended to the Professors of Christianity of every Denomination. (Philadelphia, 1754.)
---- Considerations on Keeping Negroes; Recommended to the Professors of Christianity of every Denomination. Part Second. (Philadelphia, 1762.)

WRIGHT, R.R., JR. The Negro in Pennsylvania. (Philadelphia, 1912.)

MAGAZINES

The Abolitionist, or Record of the New England Anti-Slavery Society. Edited by a committee. Appeared in January, 1833.
The African Methodist Episcopal Church Review. Valuable for the following articles:
"The Colored Public Schools of Washington," by James Storum, vol. v., p. 279.
"The Negro as an Inventor," by R.R. Wright, vol. ii., p. 397. "Negro Poets," vol. iv., p. 236.
"The Negro in Journalism," vols. vi., 309, and xx., 137.
The African Repository. Published by the American Colonization Society from 1826 to 1832. A very good source for the development of Negro education both in this country and Liberia. Some of its most valuable articles are: "Learn Trades or Starve," by Frederick Douglass, vol. xxix., pp. 136 and 137. Taken from Frederick Douglass's Paper.
"Education of the Colored People," by a highly respectable gentleman of the South, vol. xxx., pp. 194, 195, and 196.
"Elevation of the Colored Race," a memorial circulated in North Carolina, vol. xxxi., pp. 117 and 118.
"A Lawyer for Liberia," a sketch of Garrison Draper, vol. xxxiv., pp. 26 and 27.
Numerous articles on the religious instruction of the Negroes occur throughout the foregoing volumes. Information about the actual literary training of the colored people is given as news items.

The Education of the Negro

The American Museum, or Repository of Ancient and Modern Fugitive Pieces, etc., Prose and Poetical. Vols. i.-iv. (First and second editions, Philadelphia, 1788. Third edition, Philadelphia, 1790.) Contains some interesting essays on the intellectual status of the Negroes, etc., contributed by "Othello," a free Negro.

The Colonizationist and Journal of Freedom. The author has been able to find only the volume which contains the numbers for the year 1834.

The Crisis. A record of the darker races published by the National Association for the Advancement of Colored People.

The Maryland Journal of Colonization. Published as the official organ of the Maryland Colonization Society. Among its important articles are: "The Capacities of the Negro Race," vol. iii., p. 367; and "The Educational Facilities of Liberia," vol. vii., p. 223.

The Non-Slaveholder. Two volumes of this publication are now found in the Library of Congress.

The School Journal.

The Southern Workman. Volume xxxvii. contains Dr. R.R. Wright's valuable dissertation on "Negro Rural Communities in Indiana."

NEWSPAPERS

District of Columbia. The Daily National Intelligencer.
Louisiana The New Orleans Commercial Bulletin.
Maryland. The Maryland Journal and Baltimore Advertiser. The Maryland Gazette. Dunlop's Maryland Gazette or The Baltimore Advertiser.
Massachusetts. The Liberator.
New York. The New York Daily Advertiser. The New York Tribune.
North Carolina. The State Gazette of North Carolina. The Newbern Gazette.
Pennsylvania. The Philadelphia Gazette.
South Carolina. The City Gazette and Commercial Daily Advertiser. The State Gazette of South Carolina. The Charleston Courier. The South Carolina Weekly Advertiser. The Carolina Gazette. The Columbian Herald.
Virginia. The Richmond Enquirer. The Norfolk and Portsmouth Herald. The Virginia Herald. (Fredericksburg.) The Norfolk and Portsmouth Chronicle.

LAWS, DIGESTS, CHARTERS, CONSTITUTIONS, AND REPORTS

GENERAL

Code Noir ou Recueil d'edits, declarations et arrets concernant la Discipline et le commerce des esclaves Negres des isles francaises de l'Amerique (in Recueils de reglemens, edits, declarations et arrets, concernant le commerce, l'administration de la justice et la police des colonies francaises de l'Amerique, et les engages avec le Code Noir, et l'addition audit code). (Paris, 1745.)

GOODELL, WILLIAM. The American Slave Code in Theory and Practice: Its Distinctive Features Shown by its Statutes, Judicial Decisions, and Illustrative Facts. (New York, 1853.)

PETERS, RICHARD. Condensed Reports of Cases Argued and Adjudged in the Supreme Court of the United States. Six volumes. (Philadelphia, 1830-1834.)

Bibliography

THORPE, F.N. Federal and State Constitution, Colonial Charters, and Other Organic Laws of the States, Territories, and Colonies now or heretofore Forming the United States of America. Compiled and Edited under an Act of Congress, June 30, 1906. (Washington, 1909.)

STATE

Alabama. Acts of the General Assembly Passed by the State of Alabama. CLAY, C.C. Digest of the Laws of the State of Alabama to 1843. (Tuscaloosa, 1843.)

Connecticut. Public Acts Passed by the General Assembly of Connecticut.

Delaware. Laws of the State of Delaware Passed by the General Assembly.

District of Columbia. BURCH, SAMUEL. A Digest of the Laws of the Corporation of the City of Washington, with an Appendix of the Laws of the United States Relating to the District of Columbia. (Washington, 1823.)

Florida. Acts of the Legislative Council of the Territory of Florida. Acts and Resolutions of the General Assembly of the State of Florida.

Georgia. Laws of the State of Georgia. COBB, HOWELL. A Digest of the Statutes of Georgia in General Use to 1846. (New York, 1846.) DAWSON, WILLIAM. A Compilation of the Laws of the State of Georgia to 1831. (Milledgeville, 1831.) PRINCE, O.H. A Digest of the Laws of the State of Georgia to 1837. (Athens, 1837.)

Illinois. Laws of the State of Illinois Passed by the General Assembly. STARR, M., and RUSSELL H. CURTIS. Annotated Statutes of Illinois in Force, January 1, 1885.

Indiana. Laws of a General Nature Passed by the State of Indiana.

Kentucky. Acts of the General Assembly of the Commonwealth of Kentucky.

Louisiana. Acts Passed by the Legislature of the State of Louisiana. BULLARD, HENRY A., and THOMAS CURRY. A New Digest of the Statute Laws of the State of Louisiana to 1842. (New Orleans, 1842.)

Maryland. Laws Made and Passed by the General Assembly of the State of Maryland.

Massachusetts. Acts and Resolves Passed by the General Court of Massachusetts. QUINCY, JOSIAH, JR. Reports of Cases, Superior Court of Judicature of the Province of Massachusetts Bay, 1761-1772. (Boston, 1865.)

Mississippi. Laws of the State of Mississippi Passed at the Regular Sessions of the Legislature. POINDEXTER, GEORGE. Revised Code of the Laws of Mississippi. (Natchez, 1824.) HUTCHINSON, A. Code of Mississippi. (Jackson, 1848.)

Missouri. Acts of the General Assembly of the State of Missouri.

New Jersey. Acts of the General Assembly of the State of New Jersey.

New York. Laws of the State of New York.

Ohio. Acts of a General Nature Passed by the General Assembly of the State of Ohio. Acts of a Local Nature Passed by the General Assembly of the State of Ohio.

Pennsylvania. Laws of the General Assembly of the State of Pennsylvania. BRIGHTLY, FRANK F. A Digest of the Laws of Pennsylvania. STROUD, G.M. Purdon's Digest of the Laws of Pennsylvania from 1700 to 1851. (Philadelphia, 1852.)

Rhode Island. Acts and Resolves Passed by the General Assembly of the State of Rhode Island and Providence Plantations.

South Carolina. Acts and Resolutions of the General Assembly of the State of South Carolina. BREVARD, JOSEPH. An Alphabetical Digest of the Public Statute Laws of South Carolina from 1692 to 1813. Three volumes. (Charleston, 1814.)

Tennessee. Acts of the General Assembly of the State of Tennessee.

Virginia. Acts of the General Assembly of Virginia. HENING, W.W. Statutes at Large: A Collection of all the Laws of Virginia from the First Session of the Legislature in the Year 1816. (Richmond, 1819 to 1823.) Published pursuant to an act of the General Assembly of Virginia, passed on the 5th of February, 1808. The work was extended by S. Shepherd who published three additional volumes in 1836. Chief source of historical material for the history of Virginia. TATE, Joseph. A Digest of the Laws of Virginia. (Richmond, 1841.)

The Mis-education of the Negro

by
Carter G. Woodson

Contents

Introduction
Forward
Preface

1. The Seat of the Trouble 225
2. How We Missed the Mark 228
3. How We Drifted Away from the Truth 231
4. Education Under Outside Control 235
5. The Failure to Learn to Make a Living 240
6. The Educated Negro Leaves the Masses 245
7. Dissension and Weakness 249
8. Professional Education Discouraged 254
9. Political Education Neglected 258
10. The Loss of Vision 263
11. The Need for Service Rather than Leadership 269
12. Hirelings in the Place of Public Servants 273
13. Understand the Negro 278
14. The New Program 283
15. Vocational Guidance 288
16. The New Type of Professional Man Required 294
17. Higher Strivings in the Service of the Country 297
18. The Study of the Negro 301

Appendix
Notes

Introduction

Considerable time has passed since the first printing of this volume, but it is significant that it has meaning and direct implications for today's consideration. While it does not relate exclusively to Black History it does emphasize its instruction, research and writing. In substance Carter Woodson has produced a definitive and constructive critique of the educational system, with special reference to its blighting effects on the Negro; and the term he used, Mis-education, was the most apt and descriptive word available. It is still, in 1969, equally as relevant and expressive. Now, however, it is loudly articulated by many voices of Whites as well as Blacks, who likewise challenge the system.

The most imperative and crucial element in Woodson's concept of mis-education hinged on the education system's failure to present authentic Negro History in schools and the bitter knowledge that there was a scarcity of literature available for such a purpose, because most history books gave little or no space to the black man's presence in America. Some of them contained casual references to Negroes but these generally depicted them in menial, subordinate roles, more or less sub-human. Such books stressed their good fortune at having been exposed, through slavery, to the higher (white man's) civilization. There were included derogatory statements relating to the primitive, heathenish quality of the African background, but nothing denoting skills, abilities, contributions or potential in the image of the Blacks, in Africa or America. Woodson considered this state of affairs deplorable, an American tragedy, dooming the Negro to a brain-washed acceptance of the inferior role assigned to him by the dominant race, and absorbed by him through his schooling.

Moreover, the neglect of Afro-American History and distortion of the facts concerning Negroes in most history books, deprived the black child and his whole race of a heritage, and relegated him to nothingness and nobodyness. This was Woodson's conviction as he stated it in this book and as he lived by it. In his Annual Report of the Association for the Study of Negro Life and History for the year ending June 30, 1933, the publication period of Mis-Education, he stated:

Regarding the Negro race as a factor in world culture rather than as an element in a sequestered sphere, the Director (Woodson) has recently made two trips to Europe to extend the study of the notice taken of Negroes by European authors and artists, and to engage a larger number of Europeans and Africans in the study of the past of the Negro [1]

Thus it is evident that the stress which Dr. Woodson places on historical research, writing, and teaching in this volume was not theoretical jargon. It represented rather, a firm belief; also a judgement of the available type of education that was so strongly oriented as to warrant his complete and selfless dedication to its betterment. This devotion became a crusade which, in the above instance, carried him to Europe in an effort to open new avenues for recreating and writing of the black man's past. This was in line with his basic charges against the omission by most historians of such an important part of history.

Mis-Education criticizes the system, and explains the vicious circle that results from mis-educated individuals graduating, then proceeding to teach and mis-educate others. But the book is by no means a study in negation. The author goes to great lengths in tracing the historical foundations of the problem, its development, and its influence on interpersonal relations and historical scholarship. Numerous other scholars now follow its example.

The youths of the race were Woodson's particular concern because he recognized that it was with, the boys and girls that Mis-education began, later crystallizing into deep-seated insecurities, intra-racial cleavages, and inter-racial antagonisms. All of these factors have been discussed over and over in the immediate past, by historians, sociologists, psychiatrists, and laymen, but Dr. Woodson, and a pitifully small number of others, had pointed the way a full generation earlier.

More so than most of his contemporaries did Woodson contribute because he gave up a prestigious educational career, including a school principalship in Washington, D.C., the position of Dean at both Howard University and West Virginia State College. He decided instead to devote his finances and energies to an association which would help to overcome the inadequacies of the system which promoted mis-education. This was not by any means his first book but the views expressed herein form a sort of core or center, to and from which his texts and other writings protrude and revert.

All of this scholar's researches and writings were designed to provide educational sustenance, to fill the void which existed by reason of neglect of Black Studies. As has been already observed, however, he was no mere theorist, he was an activist and a pragmatist. He knew that writing alone would be inadequate for the enormity of the need. Consequently he, with four others, founded The Association for the Study of Negro Life and History, established the Journal of Negro History, and concentrated mightily on the educational aspect of his program, trying to counteract the poison of mis-education. In regard to these efforts he reported:

The calls on the Research Department for assistance to teachers and students have multiplied so as to make this phase of the work a heavy burden on a small staff. Instructors now taking up the study of the Negro require help in working out courses in this new field; and their students are urged to make frequent use of the Department by correspondence or a visit to the home of the Association.[2]

That statement is just as relevant in today's situation as it was when Woodson made it! As a matter of fact it might be copied and used by the present Director of the Association and it would be true except that the demand for services has increased a thousand-fold. The study of the Black man is still new in this generation, but such advances as have been made are in large part due to the vision, insight, writings, and publishing of pioneers like Carter Woodson. Indeed his analyses and conclusions regarding the entire educational system and its unrelatedness to future needs of the students stand firm, on solid ground. They were extendable to the 1960's, and student attitudes and actions make it quite clear that the reasoning and recommendations of Mis-Education constitute a convenient point of departure for the current reformation of educational institutions.

Introduction

If Woodson had been content with merely writing his own articles and books his contribution would have been monumental, because his production was tremendous and his methodology was scientific. He, however, conceived of this historical vacuum in terms of such magnitude that no one historian could possibly do enough research and writing to seek the facts, organize and present them, and correct the false and distorted information which had been passed off for true history for many generations. Consequently he sought, encouraged, and published the works of other scholars who shared his convictions and his sense of urgency in the premises.

As one noteworthy example, Lawrence D. Reddick has an analytical article of forty pages in the Journal of Negro History entitled "Racial Attitudes in American History Textbooks of the South."[3] In line with Woodson's complaints this author pointed out that the average pupil received a picture of slavery which generally managed to justify it, to explain the climate and economic conditions which fastened it to the South, and to minimize the hardships for blacks by emphasizing their good nature and song-singing. The textbook authors stressed the fact that there had been no practical way to free southern slaves, and blamed the northern abolitionists for the hardening of southern attitudes.

There was virtually nothing in the textbooks he explored that referred to the role and development of the Negro in national life after Reconstruction. His activities in the wars and national defense were completely ignored, and illustrations for all periods were almost non-existent. Thus this article, accepted, edited, and published by Woodson, in all respects bore out his grievance against Mis-education, and it went to the very heart of his thesis.

In the same issue of the Journal of Negro History another article reinforced his views from a different investigative angle. Thomas L. Dabney made a survey of Negro and white colleges to determine the ones which offered courses in Negro History and/or Literature, or Race Relations; the Negro public schools which offered Negro History and/or Negro Literature; and the enrollment figures for both colleges and pre-college students. He also explained the purposes and progress of Negro History Week, as well as the home study courses offered by the Association for the Study of Negro Life and History, and its clubs in their states.[4]

Another respected educator, Dr. Horace Mann Bond, was strongly aware of the substantive character of Dr. Woodson's charges of Mis-Education, particularly with regard to the curriculum under which the southern Negro child studied. In that connection he wrote, "The activities of the Association for the Study of Negro Life and History may ... be said to represent a Negro nationalism which is a reaction against the 'white' nationalism of the American people."[5]

Then, referring to the curriculum builders who took "for granted that white supremacy had to be maintained," Bond declared:

> The load of what appears to the present writer, and Dr. Woodson, as propaganda, was not so considered by the former writers of southern textbooks, nor is it today.[6]

Thus it is apparent that Dr. Bond was either influenced by or was in agreement with the mis-education ideas which constituted so vital a part of Dr. Woodson's entire theory of the unfavorable effect of the American educational system on black children.

The Mis-Education of the Negro

Many of the investigations were concentrated on the Southland and that is understandable. The hulk of the Negro population then lived below the Mason-Dixon line where no blacks were admitted to the white schools or colleges, and the dual system of education was obviously and definitely designed to perpetuate the Negro-inferiority image of the slavery period. Dr. Woodson also condemned the North for discrimination. As one who had studied at northern universities, The University of Chicago, and Harvard University, where he received the Ph.D degree, his experiences and observations enabled him to make valid judgments about that section.

One of his intellectual contemporaries, another Harvard-trained scholar, W. E. B. DuBois, was especially outspoken on northern education for Negroes, believing with Woodson, that it propagandized and indoctrinated youth, draining them of self-confidence, self-respect, and self-knowledge.

In 1935 DuBois wrote:

... race prejudice in the United States today is such that most Negroes cannot receive proper education in white institutions ... many public school systems in the North where Negroes are admitted and tolerated but they are not educated; they are crucified ... certain Northern universities where Negro students ... cannot get fair recognition, either in classroom or on the campus, in dining hall or student activities, or in human common courtesy ... at Harvard, Yale, and Columbia, Negroes are admitted but not welcomed; while in other institutions like Princeton they cannot even enroll.[7]

In further development of his thesis that Blacks needed special education, Dr. DuBois made a point-blank statement with respect to a constructive means of overcoming the mis-education to which they were subjected:

Negroes must know the history of the Negro race in America, and this they will seldom get in white institutions. Their children ought to study textbooks like Brawley's "Short History," the first edition of Woodson's "Negro in Our History," and Cromwell, Turner, and Dykes' "Readings from Negro Authors." Negroes who celebrate the birthdays of Washington and Lincoln, and relatively unimportant "founders" of various Negro colleges, ought not to forget the 5th of March,—that first national holiday of this country, which commemorates the martyrdom of Crispus Attucks. They ought to celebrate Negro Health Week and Negro History Week. They ought to study intelligently and from their own point of view, the slave trade, slavery, emancipation, Reconstruction and present economic development.[8]

Dr. DuBois proceeded then to explain in careful detail that he was making no special plea for segregated schools, or mixed schools, but for education. To use his language:

... a separate Negro school where children are treated like human beings, trained by teachers of their own race, who know what it means to be black in the year of salvation 1935, is infinitely better than making our boys and girls doormats to be spit and trampled upon and lied to by ignorant social climbers, whose sole claim to superiority is ability to kick "niggers" when they are down.[9]

The foregoing observations relate directly to the problems of mis-education, well understood and posed by Woodson; and the same problems are at long

Introduction

last being faced and attacked by the very universities identified by DuBois and many others. These institutions, formerly known only as "white" colleges, are now heeding the black demands, and are soliciting black students, even at the expense of the "quota systems," once so firmly entrenched. The "cry in the wilderness" of Woodson in Mis-Education, and his few like-minded cohorts, has become a resounding chorus, and the reverberations will in time shake the mis from Mis-education.

The scholars under discussion all shared a common goal, namely, to provide for Negro youth access to historical information and education which would be true and thus nullify or diminish the false and belittling propaganda type of history which had been handed to them by whites. This, it was felt, would build up the black child's self and race knowledge as well as his self-respect. In a larger sense they expected that their publications would at least partly fill the unjustifiable void in American History and its antecedents, reveal the existing distortions of actual facts, and constitute a service to the entire field of historical and social science writing and understanding.

Ultimately, thought Woodson and those who had similar beliefs, the program would be a responsible factor in regenerating race relations in all areas and not only in education. Without detracting from any other efforts (and there were others) it is reasonably certain that those writers who tried so zealously to right the wrongs of mis-education exerted a positive influence in that direction. As a result the democratic practices of this society are beginning to reach for its ideology, thus narrowing the long-existing cultural lag.

It is, in fact, quite clear that Woodson regarded this book as historical only in its most inclusive sense—history as interrelated with social customs, literature, economic and political matters and all else that affects society. This is a sensible and legitimate approach, as such historians as Spengler and Toynbee have demonstrated by popularizing broad areas and issues. Woodson was familiar with the tendency to include the intangible factors that influence the course of history—psychological elements and traditional sensitivities, based of course on valid historical methodology. He fitted Mis-Education into that framework.

Necessarily he thought in terms of other aspects of society which influenced education and which were, in turn influenced by it, because all of his writings show that he was convinced of the interrelations of all types of social phenomena. Furthermore, when he published Mis-Education, the nation was in the throes of a paralyzing economic depression, and President Franklin D. Roosevelt was on the verge of his vigorous and innovative administration. The "separate but equal" myth then afforded respectable legal sanction for an unequal, caste-like society, in education and all areas of national life. Permissive resignation had settled over much of the Negro population, and a majority rationalized that the caricature of education that they received was at least "better than it used to be."

The debilitating depression had thrust the problems of the Negro, as the lowest socioeconomic class, into the forefront of those in dire need. As an educator of stature who was already engaged in his intensive writing and publishing program, the role of the disadvantageous educational system in keeping the black people on the lowest level, became abundantly clear to Woodson. Hence his attempts to analyze the problem and to define and castigate the type of education that confined Negroes in a vice-like grip of inferiority was designed not only to inform other historians and educators of their own derelictions, but to arouse the black people from their apathy. Mis-Education did not immediately have the impact that he hoped, but in the long run it merges now with the researches of the awakened historians and other educators; the demands of several minority groups, which have discovered each other; the insistence of students on racial equality and relevant curricula; and the clamor of the downtrodden masses for appropriate treatment as fellow human beings.

Dr. Woodson, in adopting a comprehensive, overall view of the problem of education in this book, was strongly prophetic, and showed a rare intellectual kinship with those who would move to the forefront in the next generation. His statement (p. 114), "The warring area, then, is in the cities," is highly pertinent to current circumstances, as are also the points in context which he connected with it. Another idea that he expressed with clarity (p. 117) in the sentences which follow, will be recognized at once for its present relevance:

The race will free itself from exploiters just as soon as it decides to do so. No one else can accomplish this task for the race. It must plan and do for itself.

Another matter connected with Mis-education should be noted. The inferior character of black education was made inevitable by virtue of the poor financing of the segregated school systems. Although most Northern states had some racially-mixed schools, education in the sixteen southern, former slave states, plus Oklahoma and the District of Columbia, forming a bloc, provided the pattern, the atmosphere, and the reflection of Negro problems and general attitudes of whites about black education in the United States.

This southern bloc maintained a completely segregated system, and though there were differences in one category or another in spending money for education among its jurisdictions they had one common denominator—there were great differentials between moneys allocated for white education and black education. In 1930 the average expenditure per school-age child was $45.00 per white pupil and $14.95 per Negro pupil. Average southern investment in public school property per school-child amounted to $120.09 for whites and $29.62 for Negroes. Figures for 1928-1929 disclose that the average southern white teacher's pupil load was 31 for a school term of 164 days, while the average black teacher instructed about 44 pupils for 144 days. The average white teacher's salary was $1020, while the average black teacher earned $524.[10]

These figures were frustratingly well known to Dr. Woodson. As a participator in the field of education, an observer, a scholar and a reformer, he had long studied the disparities in the dual system. Before 1930 he had become thoroughly alarmed because the differentials between white and black education were increasing rather than diminishing, and that knowledge undoubtedly motivated some of the pessimism which creeps through in this volume.

Early in his Preface to Mis-Education the author takes a positive stand for tax money to be allocated in such manner that "every individual in the social order" should be given the opportunity to do his best. He rejected the objective notion of "progress" taken from statistical data, and injected a qualitative criteria which would judge the effectiveness of education by whether it was instrumental in making an individual "do and think for himself." With respect to Negro education in particular, it would require much study of the race and the role of its members in society. The dual system did not afford the opportunity for such study. As Woodson evaluated then, the inequity of the two societies within the nation, black and white, with its financial and propagandistic suppression of blacks through education and otherwise, was efficiently responsible for the social ills that he so deplored. He was really aiming a direct blow at the rationale

Introduction

which the South used to justify the dual school system; and his position was vindicated by the United States Supreme Court in the 1950's, and subsequently by public opinion. When he suggested equal educational opportunities regardless of financial status or race he was more or less anticipating the "social citizen" concept of the incoming administration, although President Roosevelt did not implement his concept to its logical conclusion.

When Woodson likewise made observations to the effect that information alone was not education, he was not stating a unique or isolated theory. Other educators agreed, but many who professed to adhere to the notion did so in a merely abstract fashion. The author of this book very carefully elaborated and illustrated the thesis. He sought for meaningful, qualitative training, yet most educational institutions held fast to their rigid, inflexible programs, under which much of the required subject-matter might prove useful as intellectual discipline, but not to the life interests of the hapless, captive students. It was Woodson's idea that this system was most devastating to the black children whose schools were inferior, and whose future life interests were farthest removed from the traditional curricula. In recent years, and frequently by reason of student pressures, colleges have been reappraising and restructuring their programs, not necessarily because of Woodson's long-ago reasoning but surely in line with it.

The Preface to Mis-Education also contains a statement that the educational systems of both Europe and the United States were antiquated and failed to hit the mark for either race. A bold and daring assertion in 1933, to be sure, but Woodson had successfully pursued education in both Europe and America. It is evident now that his judgement was projected far beyond its utterance, as witness the student movements which are presently accelerating, and assuming differing and ever more demanding forms. In further attestation note also the trend toward "vocational" education; and the frenzied effort to incorporate Black Studies at all educational levels.

Indeed long before this present climactic phase, there had been a rising racial consciousness and a new stridency to the demands by American Negroes. By the start of World War II the sacred cow of segregation was being reexamined more vigorously than ever before. Such scholars as Frazier, Myrdal, Silberman and others were writing sociologically with candor and verve on racial problems, while Woodson continued his even and uninterrupted interpretation of these problems, plus writing historical books, papers, and engaging in other journalistic endeavors. Cynicism and disillusionment among blacks had spread and become crystallized into a determination to make equality real. The indictments against discrimination were even more virile than Woodson's had been in Mis-Education some years earlier, and they covered more thoroughly the entire spectrum of race relations, but there was a direct line of descent from the educational castigation of 1933 to the more vigorous racial agitation and writings of the next decade.

Carter G. Woodson did not propose, in Mis-Education, such drastic action as the mass protest movement of A. Phillip Randolph in 1941, but then he did not have the type of support which later materialized; nor had there been in 1933 the mass militancy to which World War II gave birth. His was a modest demand, as really were the goals of Randolph's movement when judged by the scope of later demands and achievements. But if one seeks to comprehend the present culmination period in race relations, he must turn back to those earlier efforts and acknowledge the ideas and the work which "seeded the ground" as it were, and made possible a climate of opinion within which concerted action for equality could germinate and grow to fruition. This intellectual climate was possible because the research, writings, and publications of a dedicated scholar like Woodson had provided the historical information, the impetus, and the inspiration for black people to acquire a worthwhile self and race image, to make a start toward overcoming the inferiority complex which had for so long been an emotional prison. Looking back in such manner is a major purpose of history, and in that context the reissuing of this book is both appropriate and necessary.

It will be of great interest for readers to note the similarity in Woodson, the critic, as he looks at education in his day and the day in which we live. Black youth seems to be asking for what Woodson wanted as he expressed it in these pages. His philosophy was not only sound for him but it is sound for them, as they make the same demands of administrators for Black Studies, Black Curricula and Black personnel. It is for this reason that we publish this volume. It had a message for Yesterday and it has a message which Black and white should know for Today.

Charles H. Wesley and Thelma D. Perry

Forward

THE thoughts brought together in this volume have been expressed in recent addresses and articles written by the author. From time to time persons deeply interested in the point of view therein presented have requested that these comments on education be made available in book form. To supply this demand this volume is given to the public.

In the preparation of the volume the author has not followed in detail the productions upon which most of the book is based. The aim is to set forth only the thought developed in passing from the one to the other. The language in some cases, then, is entirely new; and the work is not a collection of essays. In this way repetition has been avoided except to emphasize the thesis which the author sustains.

Carter Godwin Woodson Washington, D. C.
January, 1933.

Preface

HEREIN are recorded not opinions but the reflections of one who for forty years has participated in the education of the black, brown, yellow and white races in both hemispheres and in tropical and temperate regions. Such experience, too, has been with students in all grades from the kindergarten to the university. The author, moreover, has traveled around the world to observe not only modern school systems in various countries but to study the special systems set up by private agencies and governments to educate the natives in their colonies and dependencies. Some of these observations, too, have been checked against more recent studies on a later tour.

Discussing herein the mistakes made in the education of the Negro, the writer frankly admits that he has committed some of these errors himself. In several chapters, moreover, he specifically points out wherein he himself has strayed from the path of wisdom. This book, then, is not intended as a broadside against any particular person or class, but it is given as a corrective for methods which have not produced satisfactory results.

The author does not support the once popular view that in matters of education Negroes are rightfully subjected to the will of others on the presumption that these poor people are not large taxpayers and must be content with charitable contributions to their uplift. The author takes the position that the consumer pays the tax, and as such every individual of the social order should be given unlimited opportunity make the most of himself. Such opportunity, too, should not be determined from without by forces set to direct the proscribed element in a way to redound solely to the good of others but should be determined by the make-up of the Negro himself and by what his environment requires of him.

This new program of uplift, the author contends, should not be decided upon by the trial and error method in the application of devices used in dealing with others in a different situation and at another epoch. Only by careful study of the Negro himself and the life which he is forced to lead can we arrive at the proper procedure in this crisis. The mere imparting of information is not education. Above all things, the effort must result in making a man think and do for himself just as the Jews have done in spite of universal persecution.

In thus estimating the results obtained from the so-called education of the Negro the author does not go to the census figures to show the progress of the race. It may be of no importance to the race to be able to boast today of many times as many "educated" members as it had in 1865. If they are of the wrong kind the increase in numbers will be a disadvantage rather than an advantage. The only question which concerns us here is whether these "educated" persons are actually equipped to face the ordeal before them or unconsciously contribute to their own undoing by perpetuating the regime of the oppressor.

Herein, however, lies no argument for the oft-heard contention that education for the white man should mean one thing and for the Negro a different thing. The element of race does not enter here. It is merely a matter of exercising common sense in approaching people through their environment in order to deal with conditions as they are rather than as you would like to see them or imagine that they are. There may be a difference in method of attack, but the principle remains the same.

"Highly educated" Negroes denounce persons who advocate for the Negro a sort of education different in some respects from that now given the white man. Negroes who have been so long inconvenienced and denied opportunities for development are naturally afraid of anything that sounds like discrimination. They are anxious to have everything the white man has even if it is harmful. The possibility of originality in the Negro, therefore, is discounted one hundred per cent to maintain a nominal equality. If the whites decide to take up Mormonism the Negroes must follow their lead. If the whites neglect such a study, then the Negroes must do likewise.

The author, however, does not have such an attitude. He considers the educational system as it has developed both in Europe and America an antiquated process which does not hit the mark even in the case of the needs of the white man himself. If the white man wants to hold on to it, let him do so; but the Negro, so far as he is able, should develop and carry out a program of his own.

The so-called modern education, with all its defects, however, does others so much more good than it does the Negro, because it has been worked out in conformity to the needs of those who have enslaved and oppressed weaker peoples. For example, the philosophy and ethics resulting from our educational system have justified slavery, peonage, segregation, and lynching. The oppressor has the right to exploit, to handicap, and to kill the oppressed. Negroes daily educated in the tenets of such a religion of the strong have accepted the status of the weak as divinely ordained, and during the last three generations of their nominal freedom they have done practically nothing to change it. Their pouting and resolutions indulged in by a few of the race have been of little avail.

No systematic effort toward change has been possible, for, taught the same economics, history, philosophy, literature and religion which have established the present code of morals, the Negro's mind has been brought under the control of his oppressor. The problem of holding the Negro down, therefore, is easily solved. When you control a man's thinking you do not have to worry about his actions. You do not have to tell him not to stand here or go yonder. He will find his "proper place" and will stay in it. You do not need to send him to the back door. He will go without being told. In fact, if there is no back door, he will cut one for his special benefit. His education makes it necessary.

The same educational process which inspires and stimulates the oppressor with the thought that he is everything and has accomplished everything worth while, depresses and crushes at the same time the spark of genius in the Negro by making him feel that his race does not amount to much and never will measure up to the standards of other peoples. The Negro thus educated is a hopeless liability of the race.

The difficulty is that the "educated Negro" is compelled to live and move among his own people whom he has been taught to despise. As a rule, therefore, the "educated Negro" prefers to buy his food from a white grocer because he has been taught that the Negro is not clean. It does not matter how often a Negro washes his hands, then, he cannot clean them, and it does not matter how often a white man uses his hands he cannot soil them. The educated Negro, moreover, is disinclined to take part in Negro business, because he has been taught in economics that Negroes cannot operate in this particular sphere. The "educated Negro" gets less and less pleasure out of the Negro church, not on account of its primitiveness and increasing corruption, but because of his preference for the seats of "righteousness" controlled by his oppressor. This has been his education, and nothing else can be expected of him.

If the "educated Negro" could go off and be white he might be happy, but only a mulatto now and then can do this. The large majority of this class, then, must go through life denouncing white people because they are trying to run away from the blacks and decrying the blacks because they are not white.

Chapter 1

The Seat of the Trouble

THE "educated Negroes" have the attitude of contempt toward their own people because in their own as well as in their mixed schools Negroes are taught to admire the Hebrew, the Greek, the Latin and the Teuton and to despise the African. Of the hundreds of Negro high schools recently examined by an expert in the United States Bureau of Education only eighteen offer a course taking up the history of the Negro, and in most of the Negro colleges and universities where the Negro is thought of, the race is studied only as a problem or dismissed as of little consequence. For example, an officer of a Negro university, thinking that an additional course on the Negro should be given there, called upon a Negro Doctor of Philosophy of the faculty to offer such work. He promptly informed the officer that he knew nothing about the Negro. He did not go to school to waste his time that way. He went to be educated in a system which dismisses the Negro as a nonentity.

At a Negro summer school two years ago, a white instructor gave a course on the Negro, using for his text a work which teaches that whites are superior to the blacks. When asked by one of the students why he used such a textbook the instructor replied that he wanted them to get that point of view. Even schools for Negroes, then, are places where they must be convinced of their inferiority.

The thought of the inferiority of the Negro is drilled into him in almost every class he enters and in almost every book he studies. If he happens to leave school after he masters the fundamentals, before he finishes high school or reaches college, he will naturally escape some of this bias and may recover in time to be of service to his people.

Practically all of the successful Negroes in this country are of the uneducated type or of that of Negroes who have had no formal education at all. The large majority of the Negroes who have put on the finishing touches of our best colleges are all but worthless in the development of their people. If after leaving school they have the opportunity to give out to Negroes what traducers of the race would like to have it learn such persons may thereby earn a living at teaching or preaching what they have been taught but they never become a constructive force in the development of the race. The so-called school, then, becomes a questionable factor in the life of this despised people.

As another has well said, to handicap a student by teaching him that his black face is a curse and that his struggle to change his condition is hopeless is the worst sort of lynching. It kills one's aspirations and dooms him to vagabondage and crime. It is strange, then, that the friends of truth and the promoters of freedom have not risen up against the present propaganda in the schools and crushed it. This crusade is much more important than the anti-lynching movement, because there would be no lynching if it did not start in the schoolroom. Why not exploit, enslave, or exterminate a class that everybody is taught to regard as inferior?

The Mis-Education of the Negro

To be more explicit we may go to the seat of the trouble. Our most widely known scholars have been trained in universities outside of the South. Northern and Western institutions, however, have had no time to deal with matters which concern the Negro especially. They must direct their attention to the problems of the majority of their constituents, and too often they have stimulated their prejudices by referring to the Negro as unworthy of consideration. Most of what these universities have offered as language, mathematics, and science may have served a good purpose, but much of what they have taught as economics, history, literature, religion and philosophy is propaganda and cant that involved a waste of time and misdirected the Negroes thus trained.

And even in the certitude of science or mathematics it has been unfortunate that the approach to the Negro has been borrowed from a "foreign" method. For example, the teaching of arithmetic in the fifth grade in a backward county in Mississippi should mean one thing in the Negro school and a decidedly different thing in the white school. The Negro children, as a rule, come from the homes of tenants and peons who have to migrate annually from plantation to plantation, looking for light which they have never seen. The children from the homes of white planters and merchants live permanently in the midst of calculations, family budgets, and the like, which enable them sometimes to learn more by contact than the Negro can acquire in school. Instead of teaching such Negro children less arithmetic, they should be taught much more of it than the white children, for the latter attend a graded school consolidated by free transportation when the Negroes go to one-room rented hovels to be taught without equipment and by incompetent teachers educated scarcely beyond the eighth grade.

In schools of theology Negroes are taught the interpretation of the Bible worked out by those who have justified segregation and winked at the economic debasement of the Negro sometimes almost to the point of starvation. Deriving their sense of right from this teaching, graduates of such schools can have no message to grip the people whom they have been ill trained to serve. Most of such mis-educated ministers, therefore, preach to benches while illiterate Negro preachers do the best they can in supplying the spiritual needs of the masses.

In the schools of business administration Negroes are trained exclusively in the psychology and economics of Wall Street and are, therefore, made to despise the opportunities to run ice wagons, push banana carts, and sell peanuts among their own people. Foreigners, who have not studied economics but have studied Negroes, take up this business and grow rich.

In schools of journalism Negroes are being taught how to edit such metropolitan dailies as the Chicago Tribune and the New York Times, which would hardly hire a Negro as a janitor; and when these graduates come to the Negro weeklies for employment they are not prepared to function in such establishments, which, to be successful, must be built upon accurate knowledge of the psychology and philosophy of the Negro.

When a Negro has finished his education in our schools, then, he has been equipped to begin the life of an Americanized or Europeanized white man, but before he steps from the threshold of his alma mater he is told by his teachers that he must go back to his own people from whom he has been estranged by a vision of ideals which in his disillusionment he will realize that he cannot attain. He goes forth to play his part in life, but he must be both social and bisocial at the same time. While he is a part of the body politic, he is in addition to this a member of a particular race to which he must restrict himself in all matters social. While serving his country he must serve within a special group. While being a good American, he must above all things be a "good Negro"; and to perform this definite function he must learn to stay in a "Negro's place."

For the arduous task of serving a race thus handicapped, however, the Negro graduate has had little or no training at all. The people whom he has been ordered to serve have been belittled by his teachers to the extent that he can hardly find delight in undertaking what his education has led him to think is impossible. Considering his race as blank in achievement, then, he sets out to stimulate their imitation of others The performance is kept up a while; but, like any other effort at meaningless imitation, it results in failure.

Facing this undesirable result, the highly educated Negro often grows sour. He becomes too pessimistic to be a constructive force and usually develops into a chronic fault-finder or a complainant at the bar of public opinion. Often when he sees that the fault lies at the door of the white oppressor whom he is afraid to attack, he turns upon the pioneering Negro who is at work doing the best he can to extricate himself from an uncomfortable predicament.

In this effort to imitate, however, these "educated people" are sincere. They hope to make the Negro conform quickly to the standard of the whites and thus remove the pretext for the barriers between the races. They do not realize, however, that even if the Negroes do successfully imitate the whites, nothing new has thereby been accomplished. You simply have a larger number of persons doing what others have been doing. The unusual gifts of the race have not thereby been developed, and an unwilling world, therefore, continues to wonder what the Negro is good for.

These "educated" people, however, decry any such thing as race consciousness; and in some respects they are right. They do not like to hear such expressions as "Negro literature," "Negro poetry," "African art," or "thinking black"; and, roughly speaking, we must concede that such things do not exist. These things did not figure in the courses which they pursued in school, and why should they? "Aren't we all Americans? Then, whatever is American is as much the heritage of the Negro as of any other group in this country."

The "highly educated" contend, moreover, that when the Negro emphasizes these things he invites racial discrimination by recognizing such differentness of the races. The thought that the Negro is one thing and the white man another is the stock-in-trade argument of the Caucasian to justify segregation. Why, then, should the Negro blame the white man for doing what he himself does?

These "highly educated" Negroes, however, fail to see that it is not the Negro who takes this position. The white man forces him to it, and to extricate himself therefrom the Negro leader must so deal with the situation as to develop in the segregated group the power with which they can elevate themselves. The differentness of races, moreover, is no evidence of superiority or of inferiority. This merely indicates that each race has certain gifts which the others do not possess. It is by the development of these gifts that every race must justify its right to exist.

Chapter 2

How We Missed the Mark

How we have arrived at the present state of affairs can be understood only by studying the forces effective in the development of Negro education since it was systematically undertaken immediately after Emancipation. To point out merely the defects as they appear today will be of little benefit to the present and future generations. These things must be viewed in their historic setting. The conditions of today have been determined by what has taken place in the past, and in a careful study of this history we may see more clearly the great theatre of events in which the Negro has played a part. We may understand better what his rôle has been and how well he has functioned in it.

The idea of educating the Negroes after the Civil War was largely a prompting of philanthropy. Their white neighbors failed to assume this responsibility. These black people had been liberated as a result of a sectional conflict out of which their former owners had emerged as victims. From this class, then, the freedmen could not expect much sympathy or cooperation in the effort to prepare themselves to figure as citizens of a modern republic.

From functionaries of the United States Government itself and from those who participated in the conquest of the secessionists early came the plan of teaching these freedmen the simple duties of life as worked out by the Freedmen's Bureau and philanthropic agencies. When systematized this effort became a program for the organization of churches and schools and the direction of them along lines which had been considered most conducive to the progress of people otherwise circumstanced. Here and there some variation was made in this program in view of the fact that the status of the freedmen in no way paralleled that of their friends and teachers, but such thought was not general. When the Negroes in some way would learn to perform the duties which other elements of the population had prepared themselves to discharge they would be duly qualified, it was believed, to function as citizens of the country.

Inasmuch as most Negroes lived in the agricultural South, moreover, and only a few of them at first acquired small farms there was little in their life which any one of thought could not have easily understood. The poverty which afflicted them for a generation after Emancipation held them down to the lowest order of society, nominally free but economically enslaved. The participation of the freedmen in government for a few years during the period known as the Reconstruction had little bearing on their situation except that they did join with the uneducated poor whites in bringing about certain much-desired social reforms, especially in giving the South its first plan of democratic education in providing for a school system at public expense.

Neither this inadequately supported school system nor the struggling higher institutions of a classical order established about the same time, however, connected the Negroes very closely with life as it was. These institutions were concerned rather with life as they hoped to make it. When the Negro found himself deprived of influence in politics, therefore, and at the same time unprepared to participate in the higher functions in the industrial development which this country began to undergo, it soon became evident to him that he was losing ground in the basic things of life. He was spending his time studying about the things which had been or might be, but he was learning little to help him to do better the tasks at hand. Since the Negroes believed that the causes of this untoward condition lay without the race, migration was attempted, and emigration to Africa was again urged. At this psychological moment came the wave of industrial education which swept the country by storm. The educational authorities in the cities and States throughout the Black Belt began to change the course of study to make the training of the Negro conform to this policy.

The missionary teachers from the North in defense of their idea of more liberal training, however, fearlessly attacked this new educational policy; and the Negroes participating in the same dispute arrayed themselves respectively on one side or the other. For a generation thereafter the quarrel as to whether the Negro should be given a classical or a practical education was the dominant topic in Negro schools and churches throughout the United States. Labor was the most important thing of life, it was argued; practical education counted in reaching that end; and the Negro worker must be taught to solve this problem of efficiency before directing attention to other things.

Others more narrow-minded than the advocates of industrial education, seized upon the idea, feeling that, although the Negro must have some semblance of education, it would be a fine stroke to be able to make a distinction between the training given the Negro and that provided for the whites. Inasmuch as the industrial educational idea rapidly gained ground, too, many Negroes for political purposes began to espouse it; and schools and colleges hoping thereby to obtain money worked out accordingly makeshift provisions for such instruction, although they could not satisfactorily offer it. A few real industrial schools actually equipped themselves for this work and turned out a number of graduates with such preparation.

Unfortunately, however, the affair developed into a sort of battle of words, for in spite of all they said and did the majority of the Negroes, those who did make some effort to obtain an education, did not actually receive either the industrial or the classical education. Negroes attended industrial schools, took such training as was prescribed, and received their diplomas; but few of them developed adequate efficiency to be able to do what they were supposedly trained to do. The schools in which they were educated could not provide for all the experience with machinery which white apprentices trained in factories had. Such industrial education as these Negroes received, then, was merely to master a technique already discarded in progressive centres; and even in less complicated operations of industry these schools had no such facilities as to parallel the numerous processes of factories conducted on the plan of the division of labor. Except what value such training might have in the development of the mind by making practical applications of mathematics and science, then, it was a failure.

The majority of Negro graduates of industrial schools, therefore, have gone into other avenues, and too often into those for which they have had no preparation whatever. Some few who actually prepared for the industrial sphere by self-improvement likewise sought other occupations for the reason that Negroes were generally barred from higher pursuits by trades unions; and, being unable to develop captains of industry to increase the demand for persons in these lines, the Negroes have not opened up many such opportunities for themselves.

During these years, too, the schools for the classical education for Negroes have not done any better. They have proceeded on the basis that every ambitious person needs a liberal education when as a matter of fact this does not necessarily follow. The Negro trained in the advanced phases of literature, philosophy, and politics has been unable to develop far in using his knowledge because of having to function in the lower spheres of the social order. Advanced knowledge of science, mathematics and languages, moreover, has not been much more useful except for mental discipline because of the dearth of opportunity to apply such knowledge among people who were largely common laborers in towns or peons on the plantations. The extent to which such higher education has been successful in leading the Negro to think, which above all is the chief purpose of education, has merely made him more of a malcontent when he can sense the drift of things and appreciate the impossibility of success in visioning conditions as they really are.

It is very clear, therefore, that we do not have in the life of the Negro today a large number of persons who have been benefited by either of the systems about which we have quarreled so long. The number of Negro mechanics and artisans have comparatively declined during the last two generations. The Negroes do not proportionately represent as many skilled laborers as they did before the Civil War. If the practical education which the Negroes received helped to improve the situation so that it is today no worse than what it is, certainly it did not solve the problem as was expected of it.

On the other hand, in spite of much classical education of the Negroes we do not find in the race a large supply of thinkers and philosophers. One excuse is that scholarship among Negroes has been vitiated by the necessity for all of them to combat segregation and fight to retain standing ground in the struggle of the races. Comparatively few American Negroes have produced creditable literature, and still fewer have made any large contribution to philosophy or science. They have not risen to the heights of black men farther removed from the influences of slavery and segregation. For this reason we do not find among American Negroes a Pushkin, a Gomez, a Geoffrey, a Captein or a Dumas. Even men like Roland Hayes and Henry O. Tanner have risen to the higher levels by getting out of this country to relieve themselves of our stifling traditions and to recover from their education.

Chapter 3
How We Drifted Away From the Truth

How, then, did the education of the Negro take such a trend? The people who maintained schools for the education of certain Negroes before the Civil War were certainly sincere; and so were the missionary workers who went South to enlighten the freedmen after the results of that conflict had given the Negroes a new status. These earnest workers, however, had more enthusiasm than knowledge. They did not understand the task before them. This undertaking, too, was more of an effort toward social uplift than actual education. Their aim was to transform the Negroes, not to develop them. The freedmen who were to be enlightened were given little thought, for the best friends of the race, ill-taught themselves, followed the traditional curricula of the times which did not take the Negro into consideration except to condemn or pity him.

In geography the races were described in conformity with the program of the usual propaganda to engender in whites a race hate of the Negro, and in the Negroes contempt for themselves. A poet of distinction was selected to illustrate the physical features of the white race, a bedecked chief of a tribe those of the red a proud warrior the brown, a prince the yellow, and a savage with a ring in his nose the black The Negro, of course, stood at the foot of the social ladder.

The description of the various parts of the world was worked out according to the same Plan. The parts inhabited by the Caucasian were treated in detail. Less attention was given to the yellow people, still less to the red, very little to the brown, and practically none to the black race. Those people who are far removed from the physical characteristics of the Caucasians or who do not materially assist them in the domination or exploitation of others were not mentioned except to be belittled or decried.

From the teaching of science the Negro was likewise eliminated. The beginnings of science in various parts of the Orient were mentioned, but the Africans' early advancement in this field was omitted. Students were not told that ancient Africans of the interior knew sufficient science to concoct poisons for arrowheads, to mix durable colors for paintings, to extract metals from nature and refine them for development in the industrial arts. Very little was said about the chemistry in the method of Egyptian embalming which was the product of the mixed breeds of Northern Africa, now known in the modern world as "colored people."

In the study of language in school pupils were made to scoff at the Negro dialect as some peculiar possession of the Negro which they should despise rather than directed to study the background of this language as a broken-down African tongue—in short to understand their own linguistic history, which is certainly more important for them than the study of French Phonetics or Historical Spanish Grammar. To the African language as such no attention was given except in case of the preparation of traders, missionaries and public functionaries to exploit the natives. This number of persons thus trained, of course, constituted a small fraction hardly deserving attention.

From literature the African was excluded altogether. He was not supposed to have expressed any thought worth knowing. The philosophy in the African proverbs and in the rich folklore of that continent was ignored to give preference to that developed on the distant shores of the Mediterranean. Most missionary teachers of the freedmen, like most men of our time, had never read the interesting books of travel in Africa, and had never heard of the Tarikh Es-Soudan.

In the teaching of fine arts these instructors usually started with Greece by showing how that art was influenced from without, but they omitted the African influence which scientists now regard as significant and dominant in early Hellas. They failed to teach the student the Mediterranean Melting Pot with the Negroes from Africa bringing their wares, their ideas and their blood therein to influence the history of Greece, Carthage, and Rome. Making desire father to the thought, our teachers either ignored these influences or endeavored to belittle them by working out theories to the contrary.

The bias did not stop at this point, for it invaded the teaching of the professions. Negro law students were told that they belonged to the most criminal element in the country; and an effort was made to justify the procedure in the seats of injustice where law was interpreted as being one thing for the white man and a different thing for the Negro. In constitutional law the spinelessness of the United States Supreme Court in permitting the judicial nullification of the Fourteenth and Fifteenth Amendments was and still is boldly upheld in our few law schools.

In medical schools Negroes were likewise convinced of their inferiority in being reminded of their rôle as germ carriers. The prevalence of syphilis and tuberculosis among Negroes was especially emphasized without showing that these maladies are more deadly among the Negroes for the reason that they are Caucasian diseases; and since these plagues are new to Negroes, these sufferers have not had time to develop against them the immunity which time has permitted in the Caucasian. Other diseases to which Negroes easily fall prey were mentioned to point out the race as an undesirable element when this condition was due to the Negroes' economic and social status. Little emphasis was placed upon the immunity of the Negro from diseases like yellow fever and influenza which are so disastrous to whites. Yet, the whites were not considered inferior because of this differential resistance to these plagues.

In history, of course, the Negro had no place in this curriculum. He was pictured as a human being of the lower order, unable to subject passion to reason, and therefore useful only when made the hewer of wood and the drawer of water for others. No thought was given to the history of Africa except so far as it had been a field of exploitation for the Caucasian. You might study the history as it was offered in our system from the elementary school throughout the university, and you would never hear Africa mentioned except in the negative. You would never thereby learn that Africans first domesticated the sheep, goat, and cow, developed the idea of trial by jury, produced the first stringed instruments, and gave the world its greatest boon in the discovery of iron. You would never know that prior to the Mohammedan invasion about 1000 A.D. these natives in the heart of Africa had developed powerful kingdoms which were later organized as the Songhay Empire on the order of that of the Romans and boasting of similar grandeur.

How We Drifted Away from the Truth

Unlike other people, then, the Negro, according to this point of view, was an exception to the natural plan of things, and he had no such mission as that of an outstanding contribution to culture. The status of the Negro, then, was justly fixed as that of an inferior. Teachers of Negroes in their first schools after Emancipation did not proclaim any such doctrine, but the content of their curricula justified these inferences.

An observer from outside of the situation naturally inquires why the Negroes, many of whom serve their race as teachers, have not changed this program. These teachers, however, are powerless. Negroes have no control over their education and have little voice in their other affairs pertaining thereto. In a few cases Negroes have been chosen as members of public boards of education, and some have been appointed members of private boards, but these Negroes are always such a small minority that they do not figure in the final working out of the educational program. The education of the Negroes, then, the most important thing in the uplift of the Negroes, is almost entirely in the hands of those who have enslaved them and now segregate them.

With "mis-educated Negroes" in control themselves, however, it is doubtful that the system would be very much different from what it is or that it would rapidly undergo change. The Negroes thus placed in charge would be the products of the same system and would show no more conception of the task at hand than do the whites who have educated them and shaped their minds as they would have them function. Negro educators of today may have more sympathy and interest in the race than the whites now exploiting Negro institutions as educators, but the former have no more vision than their competitors. Taught from books of the same bias, trained by Caucasians of the same prejudices or by Negroes of enslaved minds, one generation of Negro teachers after another have served for no higher purpose than to do what they are told to do. In other words, a Negro teacher instructing Negro children is in many respects a white teacher thus engaged, for the program in each case is about the same.

There can be no reasonable objection to the Negro's doing what the white man tells him to do, if the white man tells him to do what is right; but right is purely relative. The present system under the control of the whites trains the Negro to be white and at the same time convinces him of the impropriety or the impossibility of his becoming white. It compels the Negro to become a good Negro for the performance of which his education is ill-suited. For the white man's exploitation of the Negro through economic restriction and segregation the present system is sound and will doubtless continue until this gives place to the saner policy of actual interracial cooperation—not the present farce of racial manipulation in which the Negro is a figurehead. History does not furnish a case of the elevation of a people by ignoring the thought and aspiration of the people thus served.

This is slightly dangerous ground here, however, for the Negro's mind has been all but perfectly enslaved in that he has been trained to think what is desired of him. The "highly educated" Negroes do not like to hear anything uttered against this procedure because they make their living in this way, and they feel that they must defend the system. Few mis-educated Negroes ever act otherwise; and, if they so express themselves, they are easily crushed by the large majority to the contrary so that the procession may move on without interruption.

The result, then, is that the Negroes thus mis-educated are of no service to themselves and none to the white man. The white man does not need the

The Mis-Education of the Negro

Negroes' professional, commercial or industrial assistance; and as a result of the multiplication of mechanical appliances he no longer needs them in drudgery or menial service. The "highly educated" Negroes, moreover, do not need the Negro professional or commercial classes because Negroes have been taught that whites can serve them more efficiently in these spheres. Reduced, then, to teaching and preaching, the Negroes will have no outlet but to go down a blind alley, if the sort of education which they are now receiving is to enable them to find the way out of their present difficulties.

Chapter 4
Education Under Outside Control

"IN the new program of educating the Negro what would become of the white teachers of the race?" some one recently inquired. This is a simple question requiring only a brief answer. The remaining few Christian workers who went South not so long after the Civil War and established schools and churches to lay the foundation on which we should now be building more wisely than we do, we would honor as a martyred throng. Anathema be upon him who would utter a word derogatory to the record of these heroes and heroines! We would pay high tribute also to unselfish Southerners like Hay-good, Curry, Ruffner, Northern, and Vance, and to white men of our time, who believe that the only way to elevate people is to help them to help themselves.

The unfortunate successors of the Northern missionary teachers of Negroes, however, have thoroughly demonstrated that they have no useful function in the life of the Negro. They have not the spirit of their predecessors and do not measure up to the requirements of educators desired in accredited colleges. If Negro institutions are to be as efficient as those for the whites in the South the same high standard for the educators to direct them should be maintained. Negro schools cannot go forward with such a load of inefficiency and especially when the white presidents of these institutions are often less scholarly than Negroes who have to serve under them.

By law and custom the white presidents and teachers of Negro schools are prevented from participating freely in the life of the Negro. They occupy, therefore, a most uncomfortable dual position. When the author once taught in a school with a mixed faculty the white women connected with the institution would bow to him in patronizing fashion when on the campus, but elsewhere they did not see him. A white president of one Negro school never entertains a Negro in his home, preferring to shift such guests to the students' dining-room. Another white president of a Negro college maintains on the campus a guest cottage which Negroes can enter only as servants. Still another such functionary does not allow students to enter his home through the front door. Negroes trained under such conditions without protest become downright cowards, and in life will continue as slaves in spite of their nominal emancipation.

"What different method of approach or what sort of appeal would one make to the Negro child that cannot be made just as well by a white teacher?" some one asked not long ago. To be frank we must concede that there is no particular body of facts that Negro teachers can impart to children of their own race that may not be just as easily presented by persons of another race if they have the same attitude as Negro teachers; but in most cases tradition, race hate, segregation, and terrorism make such a thing impossible. The only thing to do in this case, then, is to deal with the situation as it is.

Yet we should not take the position that a qualified white person should not teach in a Negro school. For certain work which temporarily some whites may be able to do better than the Negroes there can be no objection to such service, but if the Negro is to be forced to live in the ghetto he can more easily develop out of it under his own leadership than under that which is super-imposed. The Negro will never be able to show all of his originality as long as his efforts are directed from without by those who socially proscribe him. Such "friends" will unconsciously keep him in the ghetto.

Herein, however, the emphasis is not upon the necessity for separate systems but upon the need for common sense schools and teachers who understand and continue in sympathy with those whom they instruct. Those who take the position to the contrary have the idea that education is merely a process of imparting information. One who can give out these things or devise an easy plan for so doing, then, is an educator. In a sense this is true, but it accounts for most of the troubles of the Negro. Real education means to inspire people to live more abundantly, to learn to begin with life as they find it and make it better, but the instruction so far given Negroes in colleges and universities has worked to the contrary. In most cases such graduates have merely increased the number of malcontents who offer no program for changing the undesirable conditions about which they complain. One should rely upon protest only when it is supported by a constructive program.

Unfortunately Negroes who think as the author does and dare express themselves are branded as opponents of interracial cooperation. As a matter of fact, however, such Negroes are the real workers in carrying out a program of interracial effort. Cooperation implies equality of the participants in the particular task at hand. On the contrary, however, the usual way now is for the whites to work out their plans behind closed doors, have them approved by a few Negroes serving nominally on a board, and then employ a white or mixed staff to carry out their program. This is not interracial cooperation. It is merely the ancient idea of calling upon the "inferior" to carry out the orders of the "superior." To express it in post-classic language, as did Jessie O. Thomas, "The Negroes do the `coing' and the whites the `operating.'"

This unsound attitude of the "friends" of the Negro is due to the persistence of the mediaeval idea of controlling underprivileged classes. Behind closed doors these "friends" say you need to be careful in advancing Negroes to commanding positions unless it can be determined beforehand that they will do what they are told to do. You can never tell when some Negroes will break out and embarrass their "friends." After being advanced to positions of influence some of them have been known to run amuck and advocate social equality or demand for their race the privileges of democracy when they should restrict themselves to education and religious development.

It is often said, too, that the time is not ripe for Negroes to take over the administration of their institutions, for they do not have the contacts for raising money; but what becomes of this argument when we remember what Booker T. Washington did for Tuskegee and observe what R. R. Moton and John Hope are doing today? As the first Negro president of Howard University Mordecai W. Johnson has raised more money for that institution among philanthropists than all of its former presidents combined. Furthermore, if, after three generations the Negro colleges have not produced men qualified to administer their affairs, such an admission is an eloquent argument that they have failed ingloriously and should be immediately closed.

Education Under Outside Control

Recently some one asked me how I connect my criticism of the higher education of the Negroes with new developments in this sphere and especially with the four universities in the South which are to be made possible by the millions obtained from governments, boards, and philanthropists. I believe that the establishment of these four centres of learning at Washington, Atlanta, Nashville, and New Orleans can be so carried out as to mark an epoch in the development of the Negro race. On the other hand, there is just as much possibility for a colossal failure of the whole scheme. If these institutions are to be the replica of universities like Harvard, Yale, Columbia and Chicago, if the men who are to administer them and teach in them are to be the products of roll-top desk theorists who have never touched the life of the Negro, the money thus invested will be just as profitably spent if it is used to buy peanuts to throw at the animals in a circus.

Some of the thought behind the new educational movement is to provide in the South for educating the Negroes who are now crowding Northern universities, especially the medical schools, many of which will not admit Negroes because of the racial friction in hospital practice. In the rush merely to make special provisions for these "undesirable students," however, the institutions which are to train them may be established on false ideas and make the same blunders of the smaller institutions which have preceded them. It will hardly help a poisoned patient to give him a large dose of poison.

In higher institutions for Negroes, organized along lines required for people differently circumstanced, some few may profit by being further grounded in the fundamentals, others may become more adept in the exploitation of their people, and a smaller number may cross the divide and join the whites in useful service; but the large majority of the products of such institutions will increase rather than diminish the load which the masses have had to carry ever since their emancipation. Such ill-prepared workers will have no foundation upon which to build. The education of any people should begin with the people themselves, but Negroes thus trained have been dreaming about the ancients of Europe and about those who have tried to imitate them.

In a course at Harvard, for example, students were required to find out whether Pericles was justly charged with trying to supplant the worship of Jupiter with that of Juno. Since that time Negroes thus engaged have learned that they would have been much better prepared for work among the Negroes in the Black Belt if they had spent that time learning why John Jasper of "sun-do-move" fame joined with Joshua in contending that the planet stood still "in the middle of the line while he fought the battle the second time."

Talking the other day with one of the men now giving the millions to build the four Negro universities in the South, however, I find that he is of the opinion that accredited institutions can be established in mushroom fashion with theorists out of touch with the people. In other words, you can go almost anywhere and build a three million dollar plant, place in charge a white man to do what you want accomplished, and in a short while he can secure or have trained to order the men necessary to make a university. "We want here," he will say, "a man who has his Master's degree in English. Send me another who has his Doctor's degree in sociology, and I can use one more in physics."

Now, experience has shown that men of this type may "fill in," but a university cannot be established with such raw recruits. The author once had some experience in trying to man a college in this fashion, and the result was a story that would make an interesting headline for the newspapers. When Dr. William Bainey Harper was establishing the University of Chicago he called to the headship of the various departments only men who had distinguished themselves in the creative world. Some had advanced degrees, and some had not. Several of them had never done any formal graduate work at all. All of them, however, were men whose thought was moving the world. It may be argued that the Negroes have no such men and must have them trained, but such a thing cannot be forced as we are now doing it. It would be much better to stimulate the development of the more progressive teachers of old than experiment with novices produced by the degradation of higher education.

The degradation of the doctorate especially dawned upon the author the other day more clearly than ever when a friend of his rushed into his office saying, "I have been trying to see you for several days. I have just failed to get a job for which I had been working, and I am told that I cannot expect a promotion until I get my 'darkter's 'gree.'" That is what he called it. He could not even pronounce the words, but he is determined to have his "darkter's 'gree" to get the job in sight.

This shameful status of higher education is due in a large measure to low standards of institutions with a tendency toward the diplomamill procedure. To get a job or to hold one you go in and stay until they "grind" you out a "darkter's 'gree." And you do not have to worry any further. The assumption is that almost any school will be glad to have you thereafter, and you will receive a large salary.

Investigation has shown, however, that men who have the doctorate not only lose touch with the common people, but they do not do as much creative work as those of less formal education. After having this honor conferred upon them, these so-called scholars often rest on their oars. Few persons have thought of the seriousness of such inertia among men who are put in the lead of things because of meeting statutory requirements of frontier universities which are not on the frontier.

The General Education Board and the Julius Rosenwald Fund have a policy which may be a partial solution of the undeveloped Negro college instructor's problem. These foundations are giving Negro teachers scholarships to improve themselves for work in the sphere in which they are now laboring in the South. These boards, as a rule, do not send one to school to work for the Doctor's degree. If they find a man of experience and good judgment, showing possibilities for growth, they will provide for him to study a year or more to refresh his mind with whatever there is new in his field. Experience has shown that teachers thus helped have later done much better work than Doctors of Philosophy made to order.

The Northern universities, moreover, cannot do graduate work for Negroes along certain lines when they are concentrating on the educational needs of people otherwise circumstanced. The graduate school for Negroes studying chemistry is with George W. Carver at Tuskegee. At least a hundred youths should wait daily upon the words of this scientist to be able to pass on to the generations unborn his great knowledge of agricultural chemistry. Negroes desiring to specialize in agriculture should do it with workers like T. M. Campbell and B. F. Hubert among the Negro farmers of the South.

In education itself the situation is the same. Neither Columbia nor Chicago can give an advanced course in Negro rural education, for their work in education is based primarily upon what they know of the educational needs of the whites.

Such work for Negroes must be done under the direction of the trail blazers who are building school houses and reconstructing the educational program of those in the backwoods. Leaders of this type can supply the foundation upon which a university of realistic education may be established.

We offer no argument here against earning advanced degrees, but these should come as honors conferred for training crowned with scholastic distinction, not to enable a man to increase his salary or find a better paying position. The schools which are now directing attention exclusively to these external marks of learning will not contribute much to the uplift of the Negro.

In Cleveland not long ago the author found at the Western Reserve University something unusually encouraging. A native of Mississippi, a white man trained in a Northern university and now serving as a professor in one, has under him in sociology a Negro student from Georgia. For his dissertation this Negro is collecting the sayings of his people in everyday life—their morning greetings, their remarks about the weather, their comments on things which happen around them, their reactions to things which strike them as unusual, and their efforts to interpret life as the panorama passes before them. This white Mississippian and black Georgian are on the right way to understand the Negro and, if they do not fall out about social equality, they will serve the Negro much better than those who are trying to find out whether Henry VIII lusted more after Anne Boleyn than after Catherine of Aragon or whether Elizabeth was justly styled as more untruthful than Philip II of Spain.

Chapter 5
The Failure to Learn To Make a Living

THE greatest indictment of such education as Negroes have received, however, is that they have thereby learned little as to making a living, the first essential in civilization. Rural Negroes have always known something about agriculture, and in a country where land is abundant they have been able to make some sort of living on the soil even though they have not always employed scientific methods of farming. In industry where the competition is keener, however, what the Negro has learned in school has had little bearing on the situation, as pointed out above. In business the rôle of education as a factor in the uplift of the Negro has been still less significant. The Negroes of today are unable to employ one another, and the whites are inclined to call on Negroes only when workers of their own race have been taken care of. For the solution of this problem the "mis-educated" Negro has offered no remedy whatever.

What Negroes are now being taught does not bring their minds into harmony with life as they must face it. When a Negro student works his way through college by polishing shoes he does not think of making a special study of the science underlying the production and distribution of leather and its products that he may some day figure in this sphere. The Negro boy sent to college by a mechanic seldom dreams of learning mechanical engineering to build upon the foundation his father has laid, that in years to come he may figure as a contractor or a consulting engineer. The Negro girl who goes to college hardly wants to return to her mother if she is a washerwoman, but this girl should come back with sufficient knowledge of physics and chemistry and business administration to use her mother's work as a nucleus for a modern steam laundry. A white professor of a university recently resigned his position to become rich by running a laundry for Negroes in a Southern city. A Negro college instructor would have considered such a suggestion an insult. The so-called education of Negro college graduates leads them to throw away opportunities which they have and to go in quest of those which they do not find.

In the case of the white youth in this country, they can choose their courses more at random and still succeed because of numerous opportunities offered by their people, but even they show so much more wisdom than do Negroes. For example, a year or two after the author left Harvard he found out West a schoolmate who was studying wool. "How did you happen to go into this sort of thing?" the author inquired. His people, the former replied, had had some experience in wool, and in college he prepared for this work. On the contrary, the author studied Aristotle, Plato, Marsiglio of Padua, and Pascasius Rathbertus when he was in college. His friend who studied wool, however, is now independently rich and has sufficient leisure to enjoy the cultural side of life which his knowledge of the science underlying his business developed, but the author has to make his living by begging for a struggling cause.

The Failure to Learn to Make a Living

An observer recently saw at the market near his office a striking example of this inefficiency of our system. He often goes over there at noon to buy a bit of fruit and to talk with a young woman who successfully conducts a fruit stand there in cooperation with her mother. Some years ago he tried to teach her in high school; but her memory was poor, and she could not understand what he was trying to do. She stayed a few weeks, smiling at the others who toiled, and finally left to assist her mother in business. She learned from her mother, however, how to make a living and be happy. This observer was reminded of this young woman soon thereafter when there came to visit him a friend who succeeded in mastering everything taught in high school at that time and later distinguished himself in college. This highly educated man brought with him a complaint against life. Having had extreme difficulty in finding an opportunity to do what he is trained to do, he has thought several times of committing suicide. A friend encouraged this despondent man to go ahead and do it. The sooner the better. The food and air which he is now consuming may then go to keep alive some one who is in touch with life and able to grapple with its problems. This man has been educated away from the fruit stand.

This friend had been trying to convince this misfit of the unusual opportunities for the Negroes in business, but he reprimanded his adviser for urging him to take up such a task when most Negroes thus engaged have been failures.

"If we invest our money in some enterprise of our own," said he, "those in charge will misuse or misappropriate it. I have learned from my study of economics that we had just as well keep on throwing it away."

Upon investigation, however, it was discovered that this complainant and most others like him have never invested anything in any of the Negro enterprises, although they have tried to make a living by exploiting them. But they feel a bit guilty on this account, and when they have some apparent ground for fault-finding they try to satisfy their conscience which all but condemns them for their suicidal course of getting all they can out of the race while giving nothing back to it.

Gossiping and scandal-mongering Negroes, of course, come to their assistance. Mis-educated by the oppressors of the race, such Negroes expect the Negro business man to fail anyway. They seize, then, upon unfavorable reports, exaggerate the situation, and circulate falsehoods throughout the world to their own undoing. You read such headlines as GREATEST NEGRO BUSINESS FAILS, NEGRO BANK ROBBED BY ITS OFFICERS, and THE TWILIGHT OF NEGRO BUSINESS. The mis-educated Negroes, then, stand by saying:

"I told you so. Negroes cannot run business. My professors pointed that out to me years ago when I studied economics in college; and I never intend to put any of my money in any Negro enterprise."

Yet, investigation shows that in proportion to the amount of capital invested Negro enterprises manifest about as much strength as businesses of others similarly situated. Negro business men have made mistakes, and they are still making them; but the weak link in the chain is that they are not properly supported and do not always grow strong enough to pass through a crisis. The Negro business man, then, has not failed so much as he has failed to get support of Negroes who should be mentally developed sufficiently to see the wisdom of supporting such enterprises. Now the "highly educated" Negroes who have studied economics at Harvard, Yale, Columbia, and Chicago, will say that the Negro cannot succeed in business because their professors who have never had a moment's experience in this sphere have written accordingly. The whites, they say, have the control of the natural resources and so monopolize the production of raw materials as to eliminate the competition of the Negro. Apparently this is true. All things being equal from the point of view of the oppressor, he sees that the Negro cannot meet the test.

The impatient, "highly educated" Negroes, therefore, say that since under the present system of capitalism the Negro has no chance to toil upward in the economic sphere, the only hope for bettering his condition in this respect is through socialism, the overthrow of the present economic régime, and the inauguration of popular control of resources and agencies which are now being operated for personal gain. This thought is gaining ground among Negroes in this country, and it is rapidly sweeping them into the ranks of what are commonly known as "Communists."

There can be no objection to this radical change, if it brings with it some unselfish genius to do the task better than it is now being done under the present régime of competition. Russia so far has failed to do well this particular thing under a proletarian dictatorship in an agricultural country. But whether this millennium comes or not, the capitalistic system is so strongly intrenched at present that the radicals must struggle many years to overthrow it; and if the Negro has to wait until that time to try to improve his condition he will be starved out so soon that he will not he here to tell the story. The Negro, therefore, like all other oppressed people, must learn to do the so-called "impossible."

The "uneducated" Negro business man, however, is actually at work doing the very thing which the "mis-educated" Negro has been taught to believe cannot be done. This much-handicapped Negro business man could do better if he had some assistance, but our schools are turning out men who do as much to impede the progress of the Negro in business as they do to help him. The trouble is that they do not think for themselves. If the "highly educated" Negro would forget most of the untried theories taught him in school, if he could see through the propaganda which has been instilled into his mind under the pretext of education, if he would fall in love with his own people and begin to sacrifice for their uplift—if the "highly educated" Negro would do these things, he could solve some of the problems now confronting the race.

During recent years we have heard much of education in business administration departments in Negro colleges; but if they be judged by the products turned out by these departments they are not worth a "continental." The teachers in this field are not prepared to do the work, and the trustees of our institutions are spending their time with trifles instead of addressing themselves to the study of a situation which threatens the Negro with economic extermination.

Recently the author saw the need for a change of attitude when a young woman came almost directly to his office after her graduation from a business school to seek employment. After hearing her story he finally told her that he would give her a trial at fifteen dollars a week.

"Fifteen dollars a week!" she cried, "I cannot live on that, sir."

"I do not see why you cannot," he replied. "You have lived for some time already, and you say that you have never had permanent employment, and you have none at all now."

"But a woman has to dress and to pay board," said she; "and how can she do it on such a pittance?" The amount offered was small, but it was a great deal more than she is worth at present. In fact, during the first six or nine months

The Failure to Learn to Make a Living

of her connection with some enterprise it will be of more service to her than she will be to the firm. Coming out of school without experience, she will be a drag on a business until she learns to discharge some definite function in it. Instead of requiring the firm to pay her she should pay it for training her. Negro business today, then, finds the "mis-educated employees" its heaviest burden. Thousands of graduates of white business schools spend years in establishments in undergoing apprenticeship without pay and rejoice to have the opportunity thus to learn how to do things.

The schools in which Negroes are now being trained, however, do not give our young people this point of view. They may occasionally learn the elements of stenography and accounting, but they do not learn how to apply what they have studied. The training which they undergo gives a false conception of life when they believe that the business world owes them a position of leadership. They have the idea of business training that we used to have of teaching when it was thought that we could teach anything we had studied.

Graduates of our business schools lack the courage to throw themselves upon their resources and work for a commission. The large majority of them want to be sure of receiving a certain amount at the end of the week or month. They do not seem to realize that the great strides in business have been made by paying men according to what they do. Persons with such false impressions of life are not good representatives of schools of business administration.

Not long ago a firm of Washington, D. C., appealed to the graduates of several of our colleges and offered them an inviting proposition on the commission basis, but only five of the hundreds appealed to responded and only two of the five gave satisfaction. Another would have succeeded, but he was not honest in handling money because he had learned to purloin the treasury of the athletic organization while in college. All of the others, however, were anxious to serve somewhere in an office for a small wage a week.

Recently one of the large insurance companies selected for special training in this line fifteen college graduates of our accredited institutions and financed their special training in insurance. Only one of the number, however, rendered efficient service in this field. They all abandoned the effort after a few days' trial and accepted work in hotels and with the Pullman Company, or they went into teaching or something else with a fixed stipend until they could enter upon the practice of professions. The thought of the immediate reward, shortsightedness, and the lack of vision and courage to struggle and win the fight made them failures to begin with. They are unwilling to throw aside their coats and collars and do the groundwork of Negro business and thus make opportunities for themselves instead of begging others for a chance.

The educated Negro from the point of view of commerce and industry, then, shows no mental power to understand the situation which he finds. He has apparently read his race out of that sphere, and with the exception of what the illiterate Negroes can do blindly the field is left wide open for foreign exploitation. Foreigners see this opportunity as soon as they reach our shores and begin to manufacture and sell to Negroes especially such things as caps, neckties, and housedresses which may be produced at a small cost and under ordinary circumstances. The main problem with the Negro in this field, however, is salesmanship; that is where he is weak.

It is unfortunate, too, that the educated Negro does not understand or is unwilling to start small enterprises which make the larger ones possible. If he cannot proceed according to the methods of the gigantic corporations about which he reads in books, he does not know how to take hold of things and organize the communities of the poor along lines of small businesses. Such training is necessary, for the large majority of Negroes conducting enterprises have not learned business methods and do not understand the possibilities of the field in which they operate. Most of them in the beginning had had no experience, and started out with such knowledge as they could acquire by observing some one's business from the outside. One of them, for example, had waited on a white business club in passing the members a box of cigars or bringing a pitcher of water. When they began to discuss business, however, he had to leave the room. About the only time he could see them in action was when they were at play, indulging in extravagances which the Negro learned to take up before he could afford them.

Negro businesses thus handicapped, therefore, have not developed stability and the capacity for growth. Practically all worth while Negro businesses which were flourishing in 1900 are not existing today. How did this happen? Well, Negro business men have too much to do. They have not time to read the business literature and study the market upon which they depend, and they may not be sufficiently trained to do these things. They are usually operating in the dark or by the hit-or-miss method. They cannot secure intelligent guidance because the schools are not turning out men properly trained to take up Negro business as it is to develop and make it what it ought to be rather than find fault with it. Too often when the founder dies, then, the business dies with him; or it goes to pieces soon after he passes away, for nobody has come into sufficiently close contact with him to learn the secret of his success in spite of his handicaps.

The business among Negroes, too, continues individualistic in spite of advice to the contrary. The founder does not take kindly to the cooperative plan, and such business education as we now give the youth does not make their suggestions to this effect convincing. If the founder happens to be unusually successful, too, the business may outgrow his knowledge, and becoming too unwieldy in his hands, may go to pieces by errors of judgment; or because of mismanagement it may go into the hands of whites who are usually called in at the last hour to do what they call refinancing but what really means the actual taking over of the business from the Negroes. The Negroes, then, finally withdraw their patronage because they realize that it is no longer an enterprise of the race, and the chapter is closed.

All of the failures of the Negro business, however, are not due to troubles from without. Often the Negro business man lacks common sense. The Negro in business, for example, too easily becomes a social "lion." He sometimes plunges into the leadership in local matters. He becomes popular in restricted circles, and men of less magnetism grow jealous of his inroads. He learns how richer men of other races waste money. He builds a finer home than anybody else in the community, and in his social program he does not provide for much contact with the very people upon whom he must depend for patronage. He has the finest car, the most expensive dress, the best summer home, and so far outdistances his competitors in society that they often set to work in child-like fashion to bring him down to their level.

Chapter 6
The Educated Negro Leaves the Masses

ONE of the most striking evidences of the failure of higher education among Negroes is their estrangement from the masses, the very people upon whom they must eventually count for carrying out a program of progress. Of this the Negro churches supply the most striking illustration. The large majority of Negro communicants still belong to these churches, but the more education the Negroes undergo the less comfort they seem to find in these evangelical groups. These churches do not measure up to the standard set by the university preachers of the Northern centres of learning. Most Negroes returning as finished products from such institutions, then, are forever lost to the popular Negro churches. The unchurched of this class do not become members of such congregations, and those who have thus connected themselves remain chiefly for political or personal reasons and tend to become communicants in name only.

The Negro church, however, although not a shadow of what it ought to be, is the great asset of the race. It is a part of the capital that the race must invest to make its future. The Negro church, has taken the lead in education in the schools of the race, it has supplied a forum for the thought of the "highly educated" Negro, it has originated a large portion of the business controlled by Negroes, and in many cases it has made it possible for Negro professional men to exist. It is unfortunate, then, that these classes do not do more to develop the institution. In thus neglecting it they are throwing away what they have, to obtain something which they think they need. In many respects, then, the Negro church during recent generations has become corrupt. It could be improved, but those Negroes who can help the institution have deserted it to exploiters, grafters, and libertines. The "highly educated" Negroes have turned away from the people in the churches, and the gap between the masses and the "talented tenth" is rapidly widening.

Of this many examples may be cited. When the author recently attended in Washington, D. C., one of the popular Negro churches with a membership of several thousands he saw a striking case in evidence. While sitting there he thought of what a power this group could become under the honest leadership of intelligent men and women. Social uplift, business, public welfare—all have their possibilities there if a score or more of our "highly educated" Negroes would work with these people at that center. Looking carefully throughout the audience for such persons, however, he recognized only two college graduates, Kelly Miller and himself; but the former had come to receive from the church a donation to the Community Chest, and the author had come according to appointment to make an appeal in behalf of Miss Nannie H. Burroughs' school. Neither one had manifested any interest in that particular church. This is the way most of them receive attention from our "talented tenth."

Some "highly educated" Negroes say that they have not lost their interest in religion, that they have gone into churches with a more intellectual atmosphere in keeping with their new thoughts and aspirations. And then there is a sort of contagious fever which takes away from the churches of their youth others of less formal education. Talking with a friend from Alabama, the other day, the author found out that after her father had died and she had moved to Washington she forsook the Baptist church in which he had been a prominent worker and joined a ritualistic church which is more fashionable.

Such a change of faith is all right in a sense, for no sensible person today would dare to make an argument in favor of any particular religion. Religion is but religion, if the people live up to the faith they profess. What is said here with respect to the popular churches of Negroes, which happen to be chiefly Methodist and Baptist, would hold also if they were mainly Catholic and Episcopal, provided the large majority of Negroes belonged to those churches. The point here is that the ritualistic churches into which these Negroes have gone do not touch the masses, and they show no promising future for racial development. Such institutions are controlled by those who offer the Negroes only limited opportunity and then sometimes on the condition that they be segregated in the court of the gentiles outside of the temple of Jehovah.

How an "educated Negro" can thus leave the church of his people and accept such jimcrowism has always been a puzzle. He cannot be a thinking man. It may be a sort of slave psychology which causes this preference for the leadership of the oppressor. The excuse sometimes given for seeking such religious leadership is that the Negro evangelical churches are "fogy," but a thinking man would rather be behind the times and have his self-respect than compromise his manhood by accepting segregation. They say that in some of the Negro churches bishoprics are actually bought, but it is better for the Negro to belong to a church where one can secure a bishopric by purchase than be a member of one which would deny the promotion on account of color.

With respect to developing the masses, then, the Negro race has lost ground in recent years. In 1880 when the Negroes had begun to make themselves felt in teaching, the attitude of the leaders was different from what it is today. At that time men went off to school to prepare themselves for the uplift of a downtrodden people. In our time too many Negroes go to school to memorize certain facts to pass examinations for jobs. After they obtain these positions they pay little attention to humanity. This attitude of the "educated Negro" toward the masses results partly from the general trend of all persons toward selfishness, but it works more disastrously among the Negroes than among the whites because the lower classes of the latter have had so much more opportunity.

For some time the author has been making a special study of the Negroes in the City of Washington to compare their condition of today with that of the past. Now although the "highly educated" Negroes of the District of Columbia have multiplied and apparently are in better circumstances than ever, the masses show almost as much backwardness as they did in 1880. Sometimes you find as many as two or three store-front churches in a single block where Negroes indulge in heathen-like practices which could hardly be equaled in the jungle. The Negroes in Africa have not descended to such depths. Although born and brought up in the Black Belt of the South the author never saw there such idolatrous tendencies as he has seen under the dome of the Capitol.

Such conditions show that the undeveloped Negro has been abandoned by those who should help him. The educated white man, said an observer recently, differs from the "educated Negro" who so readily forsakes the belated element

The Educated Negro Leaves the Masses

of his race. When a white man sees persons of his own race tending downward to a level of disgrace he does not rest until he works out some plan to lift such unfortunates to higher ground; but the Negro forgets the delinquents of his race and goes his way to feather his own nest, as he has done in leaving the masses in the popular churches.

This is sad indeed, for the Negro church is the only institution the race controls. With the exception of the feeble efforts of a few all but starved-out institutions, the education of the Negroes is controlled by the other element; and save the dramatization of practical education by Booker T. Washington, Negroes have not influenced the system at all in America. In business, the lack of capital, credit, and experience has prevented large undertakings to accumulate the wealth necessary for the ease and comfort essential to higher culture.

In the church, however, the Negro has had sufficient freedom to develop this institution in his own way; but he has failed to do so. His religion is merely a loan from the whites who have enslaved and segregated the Negroes; and the organization, though largely an independent Negro institution, is dominated by the thought of the oppressors of the race. The "educated" Negro minister is so trained as to drift away from the masses and the illiterate preachers into whose hands the people inevitably fall are unable to develop a doctrine and procedure of their own. The dominant thought is to make use of the dogma of the whites as means to an end. Whether the system is what it should be or not it serves the purpose.

In chameleon-like fashion the Negro has taken up almost everything religious which has come along instead of thinking for himself. The English split off from the Catholics because Henry VIII had difficulty in getting sanction from the Church to satisfy his lust for amorous women, and Negroes went with this ilk, singing "God save the King." Others later said the thing necessary is baptism by immersion; and the Negroes joined them as Baptists. Another circle of promoters next said we must have a new method of doing things and we shall call ourselves Methodists; and the Negroes, then, embraced that faith. The Methodists and Baptists split up further on account of the custom of holding slaves; and the Negroes arrayed themselves on the respective sides. The religious agitators divided still more on questions beyond human power to understand; and the Negroes started out in similar fashion to imitate them.

For example, thirty of the two hundred and thirteen religious bodies reported in 1926 were exclusively Negro, while thirty which were primarily white denominations had one or more Negro churches among their number. In other words, Negroes have gone into practically all sects established by the whites; and, in addition to these, they have established thirty of their own to give the system further complication and subdivision. The situation in these churches is aggravated, too, by having too many ministers and about five times as many supervisory officials as a church embracing all Negro communicants would actually need. All of the Negro Methodists in the world, if united, would not need more than twelve bishops, and these would have time to direct the affairs of both Methodists and Baptists in a united church. There is no need for three or four bishops, each teaching the same faith and practice while duplicating the work of the other in the same area merely because a long time ago somebody following the ignorant oppressors of the race in these churches committed the sin of dissension and strife. For all of this unnecessary expense impoverished Negroes have to pay.

The "theology" of "foreigners," too, is the important factor in this disunion of churches and the burden which they impose on an unenlightened people. Theologians have been the "bane of bliss and source of woe." While bringing the joy of conquest to their own camp they have confused the world with disputes which have divided the church and stimulated division and subdivision to the extent that it no longer functions as a Christian agency for the uplift of all men.

To begin with, theology is of pagan origin. Albert Magnus and Thomas Aquinas worked out the first system of it by applying to religious discussion the logic of Aristotle, a pagan philosopher, who believed neither in the creation of the world nor the immortality of the soul. At best it was degenerate learning, based upon the theory that knowledge is gained by the mind working upon itself rather than upon matter or through sense perception. The world was, therefore, confused with the discussion of absurdities as it is today by those of prominent churchmen. By their peculiar "reasoning," too, theologians have sanctioned most of the ills of the ages. They justified the Inquisition, serfdom, and slavery. Theologians of our time defend segregation and the annihilation of one race by the other. They have drifted away from righteousness into an effort to make wrong seem to be right.

While we must hold the Negroes responsible for following these ignorant theorists, we should not charge to their account the origination of this nonsense with which they have confused thoughtless people. As said above, the Negro has been so busy doing what he is told to do that he has not stopped long enough to think about the meaning of these things. He has borrowed the ideas of his traducers instead of delving into things and working out some thought of his own. Some Negro leaders of these religious factions know better, but they hold their following by keeping the people divided, in emphasizing nonessentials the insignificance of which the average man may not appreciate. The "highly educated" Negroes who know better than to follow these unprincipled men have abandoned these popular churches.

While serving as the avenue of the oppressor's propaganda, the Negro church, although doing some good, has prevented the union of diverse elements and has kept the race too weak to overcome foes who have purposely taught Negroes how to quarrel and fight about trifles until their enemies can overcome them. This is the keynote to the control of the so-called inferior races by the self-styled superior. The one thinks and plans while the other in excited fashion seizes upon and destroys his brother with whom he should cooperate.

Chapter 7

Dissension and Weakness

IN recent years the churches in enlightened centres have devoted less attention to dissension than formerly, but in the rural districts and small cities they have not changed much; and neither in urban communities nor in the country has any one succeeded in bringing these churches together to work for their general welfare. The militant sects are still fighting one another, and in addition to this the members of these sects are contending among themselves. The spirit of Christ cannot dwell in such an atmosphere.

Recent experiences show that these dissensions are about as rank as ever. For example, a rural community, in which an observer spent three weeks a year ago, has no church at all, although eight or ten families live there. No church can thrive among them because, with one or two exceptions, each family represents a different denomination, and the sectarian bias is so pronounced that one will not accept the procedure of the other. Each one loves his fellow man if he thinks as he does; but if his fellow man does not, he hates and shuns him.

In another rural community where the same observer recently spent two weeks he found a small and poorly attended Methodist church. Worshiping there one Sunday morning, he counted only four persons who lived in the community. Others might have come, for there was no other church for them in that place; but this particular church was not of their faith, and their number was too small to justify the establishment of one to their liking. The support given the unfortunate pastor there is so meager that he can hardly afford to come to them once a month, and consequently these peasants are practically without spiritual leadership. People who are so directed as to develop such an attitude are handicapped for life.

Some one recently inquired as to why the religious schools do not teach the people how to tolerate differences of opinion and to cooperate for the common good. This, however, is the thing which these institutions have refused to do. Religious schools have been established, but they are considered necessary to supply workers for denominational outposts and to keep alive the sectarian bias by which the Baptists hope to outstrip the Methodists or the latter the former. No teacher in one of these schools has advanced a single thought which has become a working principle in Christendom, and not one of these centres is worthy of the name of a school of theology. If one would bring together all of the teachers in such schools and carefully sift them he would not find in the whole group a sufficient number qualified to conduct one accredited school of religion. The large majority of them are engaged in imparting to the youth worn-out theories of the ignorant oppressor.

This lack of qualified teachers in Negro schools of theology, however, is not altogether the fault of the teachers themselves. It is due largely to the system to which they belong. Their schools of "theology" are impoverished by their unnecessary multiplication, and consequently the instructors are either poorly paid or not compensated at all. Many of them have to farm, conduct enterprises, or pastor churches to make a living while trying to teach. Often, then, only the inefficient can be retained under such circumstances. Yet those who see how they have failed because of these things nevertheless object to the unification of the churches as taught by Jesus of Nazareth, whom they have all but ceased to follow because of their sectarian bias obtained from thumb-worn books of misguided Americans and Europeans.

Recently an observer saw a result of this in the sermon of a Negro college graduate, trying to preach to a church of the masses. He referred to all the great men in the history of a certain country to show how religious they were, whether they were or not. When he undertook to establish the Christian character of Napoleon, however, several felt like leaving the place in disgust. The climax of the service was a prayer by another "mis-educated" Negro who devoted most of the time to thanking God for Cicero and Demosthenes. Here, then, was a case of the religion of the pagan handed down by the enslaver and segregationist to the Negro.

Returning from the table where he had placed his offering in a church on a Sunday morning not long thereafter, this observer saw another striking example of this failure to hit the mark. He stopped to inquire of his friend, Jim Minor, as to why he had not responded to the appeal for a collection.

"What!" said Jim, "I ain't givin' that man nothing. That man ain't fed me this morning, and I ain't feedin' him."

This was Jim's reaction to a "scholarly" sermon entitled "The Humiliation of the Incarnation." During the discourse, too, the minister had had much to say about John Knox Orthodox, and another of the communicants bowing at that shrine inquired of the observer later as to who this John Knox Orthodox was and where he lived. The observer could not answer all of the inquiries thus evoked, but he tried to explain the best he could that the speaker had "studied" history and theology.

This was the effect this sermon had on an earnest congregation. The minister had attended a school of theology but had merely memorized words and phrases, which meant little to him and nothing to those who heard his discourse. The school in which he had been trained followed the traditional course for ministers, devoting most of the time to dead languages and dead issues. He had given attention to polytheism, monotheism, and the doctrine of the Trinity. He had studied also the philosophical basis of the Caucasian dogma, the elements of that theology, and the schism by which fanatics made religion a football and multiplied wars only to moisten the soil of Europe with the blood of unoffending men.

This minister had given no attention to the religious background of the Negroes to whom he was trying to preach. He knew nothing of their spiritual endowment and their religious experience as influenced by their traditions and environment in which the religion of the Negro has developed and expressed itself. He did not seem to know anything about their present situation. These honest people, therefore, knew nothing additional when he had finished his discourse. As one communicant pointed out, their wants had not been supplied, and they wondered where they might go to hear a word which had some bearing upon the life which they had to live.

Not long ago when the author was in Virginia he inquired about a man who was once a popular preacher in that state. He is here, they said, but he is not preaching now. He went off to school, and when he came back the people could not understand what he was talking about. Then he began to find fault with the people because they would not come to church. He called them fogy, because they did not appreciate his new style of preaching and the things he talked about. The church went down to nothing, and he finally left it and took up farming.

In a rural community, then, a preacher of this type must fail unless he can organize separately members of the popular Methodist and Baptist churches who go into the ritualistic churches or establish certain "refined" Methodist or Baptist churches catering to the "talented tenth." For lack of adequate numbers, however, such churches often fail to develop sufficient force to do very much for themselves or for anybody else. On Sunday morning, then, their pastors have to talk to the benches. While these truncated churches go higher in their own atmosphere of self-satisfaction the mentally undeveloped are left to sink lower because of the lack of contact with the better trained. If the latter exercised a little more judgment, they would be able to influence these people for good by gradually introducing advanced ideas.

Because our "highly educated" people do not do this, large numbers of Negroes drift into churches led by the "uneducated" ministers who can scarcely read and write. These preachers do not know much of what is found in school books and can hardly make use of a library in working out a sermon; but they understand the people with whom they deal, and they make such use of the human laboratory that sometimes they become experts in solving vexing problems and meeting social needs. They would be much better preachers if they could have attended a school devoted to the development of the mind rather than to cramming it with extraneous matters which have no bearing on the task which lies before them. Unfortunately, however, very few of such schools of religion now exist.

For lack of intelligent guidance, then, the Negro church often fulfills a mission to the contrary of that for which it was established. Because the Negro church is such a free field and it is controlled largely by the Negroes themselves, it seems that practically all the incompetents and undesirables who have been barred from other walks of life by race prejudice and economic difficulties have rushed into the ministry for the exploitation of the people. Honest ministers who are trying to do their duty, then, find their task made difficult by these men who stoop to practically everything conceivable. Almost anybody of the lowest type may get into the Negro ministry. The Methodists claim that they have strict regulations to prevent this, but their net draws in proportionately as many undesirables as one finds among the Baptists.

As an evidence of the depths to which the institution has gone a resident of Cincinnati recently reported a case of its exploitation by a railroad man who lost his job and later all his earnings in a game in a den of vice in that city. To refinance himself he took an old black frock coat and a Bible and went into the heart of Tennessee, where he conducted at various points a series of distracted, protracted meetings which netted him two hundred and ninety-nine converts to the faith and four hundred dollars in cash. He was enabled thereby to return to the game in Cincinnati and he is still in the lead. Other such cases are frequently reported.

The large majority of Negro preachers of today, then, are doing nothing more than to keep up the mediaeval hell-fire scare which the whites have long since abandoned to emphasize the humanitarian trend in religion through systematized education. The young people of the Negro race could be held in the church by some such program, but the Negro's Christianity does not conceive of social uplift as a duty of the church; and consequently Negro children have not been adequately trained in religious matters to be equal to the social demands upon them. Turning their back on medievalism, then, these untrained youth think nothing of taking up moonshining, gambling, and racketeering as occupations; and they find great joy in smoking, drinking, and fornication as diversions. They cannot accept the old ideas, and they do not understand the new.

What the Negro church is, however, has been determined largely by what the white man has taught the race by precept and example. We must remember that the Negroes learned their religion from the early white Methodists and Baptists who evangelized the slaves and the poor whites when they were barred from proselytizing the aristocracy. The American white people themselves taught Negroes to specialize unduly in the "Praise the Lord," "Hallelujah" worship. In the West Indies among the Anglicans and among the Latin people Negroes do not show such emotionalism. They are cold and conservative.

Some of the American whites, moreover, are just as far behind in this respect as are the Negroes who have had less opportunity to learn better. While in Miami, Florida, not long ago the author found in two interracial "Holiness Churches" that the following was a third or fourth white. The whites joined whole-heartedly with the Negroes in their "holy rolling" and some of them seemed to be "rollers not holy."

A few months ago in Huntington, West Virginia, where the author was being entertained by friends, the party was disturbed throughout the evening by the most insane outbursts of white worshippers in a "Church of God" across the street. There they daily indulged in such whooping and screaming in "unknown tongues" that the Negroes have had to report them to the police as a nuisance. The author has made a careful study of the Negro church, but he has never known Negroes to do anything to surpass the performance of those heathen.

The American Negroes' ideas of morality, too, were borrowed from their owners. The Negroes could not be expected to raise a higher standard than their aristocratic governing class that teemed with sin and vice. This corrupt state of things did not easily pass away. The Negroes have never seen any striking examples among the whites to help them in matters of religion. Even during the colonial period the whites claimed that their ministers sent to the colonies by the Anglican Church, the progenitor of the Protestant Episcopal Church in America, were a degenerate class that exploited the people for money to waste it in racing horses and drinking liquor. Some of these ministers were known to have illicit relations with women and, therefore, winked at the sins of the officers of their churches, who sold their own offspring by slave women.

Although the author was born ten years after the Civil War the morals and religion of that régime continued even into his time. Many of the rich or well-to-do white men belonging to the churches in Buckingham County, Virginia, indulged in polygamy. They raised one family by a white woman and another by a colored or poor white woman. Both the owner of the largest slate quarry and the proprietor of the largest factory in that county lived in this fashion. One was an outstanding Episcopalian and the other a distinguished Catholic.

One day the foreman of the factory, a polygamous deacon of the local white Baptist Church, called the workmen together at noon for a short memorial service in honor of Parson Taylor, for almost half a century the pastor of the large white Baptist church in that section. The foreman made some remarks on the life of the distinguished minister, and then all sang "Shall We Meet Beyond the River?" But "to save his life" the author could not restrain himself from wondering all that time whether the foreman's white wife or colored paramour would greet him on the other side, and what a conflict there would be if they happened to get into an old-fashioned hair-pulling. In spite of his libertine connections, however, this foreman believed that he was a Christian, and when he died his eulogist commended his soul to God.

Some years later when the author was serving his six years' apprenticeship in the West Virginia coal mines he found at Nutallburg a very faithful vestryman of the white Episcopal Church at that point. He was one of the most devout from the point of view of his co-workers. Yet, privately, this man boasted of having participated in that most brutal lynching of the four Negroes who thus met their doom at the hands of an angry mob in Clifton Forge, Virginia, in 1892.

It is very clear, then, that if Negroes got their conception of religion from slaveholders, libertines, and murderers, there may be something wrong about it, and it would not hurt to investigate it. It has been said that the Negroes do not connect morals with religion. The historian would like to know what race or nation does such a thing. Certainly the whites with whom the Negroes have come into contact have not done so.

Chapter 8
Professional Education Discouraged

IN the training for professions other than the ministry and teaching the Negro has not had full sway. Any extensive comment on professional education by the Negro, then, must be mainly negative. We have not had sufficient professional schools upon which we can base an estimate of what the Negro educator can do in this sphere. If mistakes have been made in mis-educating the Negro professionally it must be charged not so much to the account of the Negroes themselves as to that of their friends who have performed this task. We are dealing here, then, mainly with information obtained from the study of Negroes who have been professionally trained by whites in their own schools and in mixed institutions.

The largest numbers of Negroes in professions other than the ministry or education are physicians, dentists, pharmacists, lawyers and actors. The numbers in these and other lines have not adequately increased because of the economic status of the Negroes and probably because of a false conception of the rôle of the professional man in the community and its relation to him. The people whom the Negro professional men have volunteered to serve have not always given them sufficient support to develop that standing and solidarity which will make their position professional and influential. Most whites in contact with Negroes, always the teachers of their brethren in black, both by precept and practice, have treated the professions as aristocratic spheres to which Negroes should not aspire. We have had, then, a much smaller number than those who under different circumstances would have dared to cross the line; and those that did so were starved out by the whites who would not treat them as a professional class. This made it impracticable for Negroes to employ them in spheres in which they could not function efficiently. For example, because of a law that a man could not be admitted to the bar in Delaware without practicing a year under some lawyer in the state (and no white lawyer would grant a Negro such an opportunity until a few years ago) it was only recently that a Negro was admitted there.

Negroes, then, learned from their oppressors to say to their children that there were certain spheres into which they should not go because they would have no chance therein for development. In a number of places young men were discouraged and frightened away from certain professions by the poor showing made by those trying to function in them. Few had the courage to face this ordeal; and some professional schools in institutions for Negroes were closed about thirty or forty years ago, partly on this account.

This was especially true of the law schools, closed during the wave of legislation against the Negro, at the very time the largest possible number of Negroes needed to know the law for the protection of their civil and political rights. In other words, the thing which the patient needed most to pass the crisis was taken from him that he might more easily die. This one act among many others is an outstanding monument to the stupidity or malevolence of those in charge of Negro schools, and it serves as a striking demonstration of the mis-education of the race.

Almost any observer remembers distinctly the hard trials of the Negro lawyers. A striking example of their difficulties was supplied by the case of the first to be permanently established in Huntington, West Virginia. The author had entrusted to him the matter of correcting an error in the transfer of some property purchased from one of the most popular white attorneys in the state. For six months this simple transaction was delayed, and the Negro lawyer could not induce the white attorney to act. The author finally went to the office himself to complain of the delay. The white attorney frankly declared that he had not taken up the matter because he did not care to treat with a Negro attorney; but he would deal with the author, who happened to be at that time the teacher of a Negro school, and was, therefore, in his place.

At one time the Negroes in medicine and correlated fields were regarded in the same light They had difficulty in making their own people believe that they could cure a complaint, fill a tooth, or compound a prescription. The whites said that they could not do it; and, of course, if the whites said so, it was true, so far as most Negroes were concerned. In those fields, however, actual demonstrations to the contrary have convinced a sufficient number of both Negroes and whites that such an attitude toward these classes is false, but there are many Negroes who still follow those early teachings, especially the "highly educated" who in school have been given the "scientific" reasons for it. It is a most remarkable process that while in one department of a university a Negro may be studying for a profession, in another department of the same university he is being shown how the Negro professional man cannot succeed. Some of the "highly educated," then, give their practice to those who are often inferior to the Negroes whom they thus pass by. Although there has been an increase in these particular spheres, however, the professions among Negroes, with the exception of teaching and preaching, are still undermanned.

In the same way the Negro was once discouraged and dissuaded from taking up designing, drafting, architecture, engineering and chemistry. The whites, they were told, will not employ you and your people cannot provide such opportunities. The thought of pioneering or of developing the Negro to the extent that he might figure in this sphere did not dawn on those monitors of the Negroes preparing for their life's work. This tradition is still a heavy load in Negro education, and it forces many Negroes out of spheres in which they might function into those for which they may not have any aptitude.

In music, dramatics and correlated arts, too, the Negro has been unfortunately misled. Because the Negro is gifted as a singer and can render more successfully than others the music of his own people, he has been told that he does not need training. Scores of those who have undertaken to function in this sphere without adequate education, then, have developed only to a certain point beyond which they have not had ability to go. We cannot easily estimate how popular Negro musicians and their music might have become had they been taught to the contrary.

Of these, several instances may be cited. A distinguished man, talking recently as a member of a large Episcopal church, which maintains a Negro mission, mentioned his objection to the budget of fifteen hundred dollars a year for music for these segregated communicants. Inasmuch as the Negroes were naturally gifted in music he did not believe that any expensive training or direction was required. The small number of Negro colleges and universities which undertake the training of the Negro in music is further evidence of the belief that the Negro is all but perfect in this field and should direct his attention to the traditional curricula.

The same misunderstanding with respect to the Negro in dramatics is also evident. We have long had the belief that the Negro is a natural actor who does not require any stimulus for further development. In this assertion is the idea that because the Negro is good at dancing, joking, minstrelsy and the like he is "in his place" when "cutting a shine" and does not need to be trained to function in the higher sphere of dramatics. Thus misled, large numbers of Negroes ambitious for the stage have not bloomed forth into great possibilities. Too many of them have finally ended with rôles in questionable cafés, cabarets, and night clubs of America and Europe; and instead of increasing the prestige of the Negro they have brought the race into disgrace.

We scarcely realize what a poor showing we make in dramatics in spite of our natural aptitude in this sphere. Only about a half dozen Negro actors have achieved greatness, but we have more actors and showmen than any other professionals except teachers and ministers. Where are these thousands of men and women in the histrionic sphere? What do we hear of them? What have they achieved? Their record shows that only a few measure up to the standard of the modern stage. Most of these would-be artists have no preparation for the tasks undertaken.

A careful study of the Negro in dramatics shows that only those who have actually taken the time to train themselves as they should be have finally endured. Their salvation has been to realize that adequate training is the surest way to attain artistic maturity. And those few who have thus understood the situation clearly demonstrate our ineptitude in the failure to educate the Negroes along the lines in which they could have admirably succeeded. Some of our schools have for some time undertaken this work as imitators of institutions dealing with persons otherwise circumstanced. Desirable results, therefore, have not followed, and the Negro on the stage is still mainly the product of the trial and error method.

Several other reasons may be given for the failure of a larger number of Negro actors to reach a higher level. In the first place, they have been recognized by the white man only in parely plantation comedy and minstrelsy, and because of the large number entering the field it has failed to offer a bright future for many of such aspirants. Repeatedly told by the white man that he could not function as an actor in a different sphere, the American Negro has all but ceased to attempt anything else. The successful career of Ira Aldridge in Shakespeare was forgotten until recently recalled by the dramatic success of Paul Robeson in Othello. The large majority of Negroes have settled down, then, to contentment as ordinary clowns and comedians. They have not had the courage or they have not learned how to break over the unnatural barriers and occupy higher ground.

The Negro author is no exception to the traditional rule. He writes, but the white man is supposed to know more about everything than the Negro. So who wants a book written by a Negro about one? As a rule, not even a Negro himself, for if he is really "educated," he must show that he has the appreciation for the best in literature. The Negro author, then, can neither find a publisher

Professional Education Discouraged

nor a reader; and his story remains untold. The Negro editors and reporters were once treated the same way, but thanks to the uneducated printers who founded most of our newspapers which have succeeded, these men of vision have made it possible for the "educated" Negroes to make a living in this sphere in proportion as they recover from their education and learn to deal with the Negro as he is and where he is.

Chapter 9

Political Education Neglected

SOME time ago when Congressman Oscar De Priest was distributing by thousands copies of the Constitution of the United States certain wiseacres were disposed to make fun of it. What purpose would such an act serve? These critics, however, probably did not know that thousands and thousands of Negro children in this country are not permitted to use school books in which are printed the Declaration of Independence or the Constitution of the United States. Thomas Jefferson and James Madison are mentioned in their history as figures in politics rather than as expounders of liberty and freedom. These youths are not permitted to learn that Jefferson believed that government should derive its power from the consent of the governed.

Not long ago a measure was introduced in a certain State Legislature to have the Constitution of the United States thus printed in school histories, but when the bill was about to pass it was killed by some one who made the point that it would never do to have Negroes study the Constitution of the United States. If the Negroes were granted the opportunity to peruse this document, they might learn to contend for the rights therein guaranteed; and no Negro teacher who gives attention to such matters of the government is tolerated in those backward districts. The teaching of government or the lack of such instruction, then, must be made to conform to the policy of "keeping the Negro in his place."

In like manner, the teaching of history in the Negro area has had its political significance. Starting out after the Civil War, the opponents of freedom and social justice decided to work out a program which would enslave the Negroes' mind inasmuch as the freedom of body had to be conceded. It was well understood that if by the teaching of history the white man could be further assured of his superiority and the Negro could be made to feel that he had always been a failure and that the subjection of his will to some other race is necessary the freedman, then, would still be a slave. If you can control a man's thinking you do not have to worry about his action. "When you determine what a man shall think you do not have to concern yourself about what he will do. If you make a man feel that he is inferior, you do not have to compel him to accept an inferior status, for he will seek it himself. If you make a man think that he is justly an outcast, you do not have to order him to the back door. He will go without being told; and if there is no back door, his very nature will demand one.

This program, so popular immediately after the Civil War, was not new, but after this upheaval, its execution received a new stimulus. Histories written elsewhere for the former slave area were discarded, and new treatments of local and national history in conformity with the recrudescent propaganda were produced to give whites and blacks the biased point of view of the development of the nation and the relations of the races. Special treatments of the Reconstruction period were produced in apparently scientific form by propagandists who went into the first graduate schools of the East to learn modern historiography about half a century ago. Having the stamp of science, the thought of these polemics was accepted in all seats of learning. These rewriters of history fearlessly contended that slavery was a benevolent institution; the masters loved their slaves and treated them humanely; the abolitionists meddled with the institution which the masters eventually would have modified; the Civil War brought about by "fanatics" like William Lloyd Garrison and John Brown was unnecessary; it was a mistake to make the Negro a citizen, for he merely became worse off by incurring the displeasure of the master class that will never tolerate him as an equal; and the Negro must live in this country in a state of recognized inferiority.

Some of these theories may seem foolish, but historians even in the North have been won to this point of view. They ignore the recent works of Miss Elizabeth Donnan, Mrs. H. T. Catterall, and Dr. Frederic Bancroft, who have spent years investigating slavery and slavetrading. These are scientific productions with the stamp of the best scholarship in America, treatises produced from such genuine documents as the court records of the slaveholding section itself, and these authors have rendered the public a valuable service in removing the whitewash which pseudo-historians have been giving to slavery and slaveholders for more than a century.

In the preparation of Negroes, many of whom teach in the South, these biased Northern historians even convert them to such a faith. A few years ago the author happened to listen to a conversation of Negro lawyers in one of our Southern cities, in which they unanimously conceded practically every contention set forth in this program of propaganda. They denounced, therefore, all reconstructionists who advocated equality and justice for all. These Negroes had the biased point of view of the rewriters like Claude Bowers and had never been directed to the real history of that drama as set forth by A. A. Taylor, Francis B. Simkins and Robert H. Woodly of the new Southern school of thought. These Negro critics were especially hard on Negroes of our day who engage in agitation for actual democracy. Negroes themselves in certain parts join with the whites, then, in keeping out of the schools teachers who may be bold enough to teach the truth as it is. They usually say the races here are getting along amicably now, and we do not want these peaceful relations disturbed by the teaching of new political thought.

What they mean to say with respect to the peaceful relation of the races, then, is that the Negroes have been terrorized to the extent that they are afraid even to discuss political matters publicly. There must be no exposition of the principles of government in the schools, and this must not be done in public among Negroes with a view to stimulating political activity. Negroes engaged in other spheres in such communities finally come to the point of accepting silence on these matters as a fixed policy. Knowing that action to the contrary means mob rule which may destroy the peace and property of the community, they constitute themselves a sort of a vigilant committee to direct their fellows accordingly.

A few years ago a rather youthful looking high school principal in one of the large cities was unceremoniously dismissed because he said jocosely to the president of the board of education, in reply to his remark about his youthful bearing, "I am old enough to vote." "Horrors!" said the infuriated official. "Put him out. We brought him here to teach these Negroes how to work, and here he is thinking about voting," A few prominent Negroes of the place muttered a little, but they did nothing effective to correct this injustice.

The Mis-Education of the Negro

In certain parts, therefore, the Negroes under such terrorism have ceased to think of political matters as their sphere. Where such things come into the teaching in more advanced work they are presented as matters of concern to a particular element rather than as functions in which all citizens may participate. The result is that Negroes grow up without knowledge of political matters which should concern all elements. To prevent the Negroes from learning too much about these things the whites in the schools are sometimes neglected also, but the latter have the opportunity to learn by contact, close observation, and actual participation in the affairs of government.

Negroes in certain parts, then, have all but abandoned voting even at points where it might be allowed. In some cases not as many as two thousand Negroes vote in a whole state. By special legislation providing for literacy tests and the payment of taxes their number of voters has been reduced to a negligible quantity, and the few who can thus function do not do so because they are often counted out when they have the deciding vote.

The tests established for the restriction of suffrage were not intended to stimulate political education but to eliminate the Negro vote by subterfuge. Negroes presenting themselves for registration are asked to do the all but impossible thing of expounding parts of the Constitution which have baffled high courts; but whites are asked simple questions which almost any illiterate man can answer. In this way the Negroes, however intelligent, are turned down; and all ignorant whites are permitted to vote. These laws, then, have retarded rather than stimulated the political education of both races. Such knowledge is apparently useless for Negroes and unnecessary for the whites, for the Negroes do not immediately profit by having it and the whites may function as citizens without it.

The effect of such a one-sided system is decidedly bad. One does not realize it until he talks with men and women of these districts, who because of the denial of these privileges have lost interest in political matters. A book agent working in the plantation area of Mississippi tested the knowledge of Negroes of these matters by asking them questions about the local and State government. He discovered that they knew practically nothing in this sphere. It was difficult to find any who knew who was president of the United States. One meets teachers, physicians, and ministers who do not know the ordinary operations of courts, the functions of the counsel, jury or judge, unless such knowledge has come by the bitter experience of having been imposed upon by some tribunal of injustice. Some of the "educated" Negroes do not pay attention to such important matters as "the assessment of property and the collection of taxes, and they do not inform themselves as to how these things are worked out. An influential Negro in the South, then, is one who has nothing to do or say about politics and advises others to follow the same course.

The elimination of the Negro from politics, then, has been most unfortunate. The whites may have profited thereby temporarily, but they showed very little foresight. How the whites can expect to make of the Negroes better citizens by leading them to think that they should have no part in the government of this country is a mystery. To keep a man above vagabondage and crime he needs among other things the stimulus of patriotism, but how can a man be patriotic when the effect of his education is to the contrary?

What little chance the Negro has to learn by participation in politics in most parts of the South is unfortunately restricted now to corruption. The usual

Political Education Neglected

stir about electing delegates to the National Republican Convention from the Southern States and the customary combat the Negroes have with Lily-white corruptionists are about all the political matters which claim their attention in the Lower South. Neither the white nor the black faction, as a rule, makes any effort to restore suffrage to Negroes. The objective is merely the control of delegates and Federal patronage for the financial considerations involved. To do this they resort to numerous contests culminating in closing hotels and bolting doors for secret meetings. Since this is the only activity in which Negroes can participate they have learned to look upon it as honorable. Large numbers of Negroes become excited over the contest and give much publicity to it on the rostrum and in the press as a matter of great importance. The methods of these corruptionists of both races, however, should be condemned as a disgrace to the state and nation.

Instead of doing something to get rid of this ilk, however, we find the "highly educated" Negroes trying to plunge also into the mire. One of the most discouraging aspects in Negro life recently observed was that of a presidential campaign. Prominent Negroes connected with three of our leading institutions of learning temporarily abandoned their work to round up Negro votes for one of the candidates. The objective, of course, was to control the few ordinary jobs which are allotted to Negro politicians for their campaign services. When the successful candidate had been inaugurated, however, he carefully ignored them in the make-up of the personnel of his administration and treated Negroes in general with contempt. When you think of the fact that the Negroes who are being thus used are supposedly the most reputable Negro leaders and our most highly educated men you have to wonder whether the Negro has made any progress since Emancipation. The only consolation one can get out of it is that they may not represent the whole race.

In the North the Negroes have a better chance to acquire knowledge of political matters of the simple kind, but the bosses do not think it is advisable to enlighten them thoroughly. Negroes in parts are employed in campaigns, but they are not supposed to discuss such issues of the day as free trade, tariff for protection, the World Court, and the League of Nations. These Negro workers are supposed to tell their people how one politician seeking office has appointed more Negro messengers or charwomen in the service than the other or how the grandfather of the candidate stood with Lincoln and Grant through their ordeal and thus brought the race into its own. Another important task of these Negroes thus employed is also to abuse the opposing party, showing how hostile it has been to the Negro while the highly favorable party was doing so much for the race.

The course of these bosses has been interesting. At first the white man used the Negro leader by giving him a drink occasionally. The next step was to give him sufficient money to set up drinks in the name of the white candidate. When drinking at the expense of the candidate became too common the politicians fell back on the distribution of funds in small amounts. When this finally proved to be insufficient, however, the politicians had to go a bit further and provide Jim Crow jobs in certain backrooms with the understanding that the functions of the so-called office would be merely nominal and the incumbents would have no close contact with white people. In this stage the Negroes find themselves today.

The Mis-Education of the Negro

The undesirable aspect of the affair is that the Negro in spite of the changes from one method of approach to that of another is never brought into the inner circle of the party with which he is affiliated. He is always kept on the outside and is used as a means to an end. To obtain the meager consideration which he receives the Negro must work clandestinely through the back door. It has been unnecessary for the white man to change this procedure, for until recent years he has generally found it possible to satisfy the majority of Negroes with the few political positions earmarked as "Negro jobs" and to crush those who clamor for more recognition.

It is unfortunate, too, that such a large number of Negroes do not know any better than to stake their whole fortune on politics. History does not show that any race, especially a minority group, has ever solved an important problem by relying altogether on one thing, certainly not by parking its political strength on one side of the fence because of empty promises. There are Negroes who know better, but such thinkers are kept in the background by the traducers of the race to prevent the enlightenment of the masses. The misleading politicians are the only persons through whom the traducers act with respect to the Negro, and there are always a sufficient number of mentally undeveloped voters who will supply them a large following.

Even the few Negroes who are elected to office are often similarly uninformed and show a lack of vision. They have given little attention to the weighty problems of the nation; and in the legislative bodies to which they are elected, they restrict themselves as a rule to matters of special concern to the Negroes themselves, such as lynching, segregation and disfranchisement, which they have well learned by experience. This indicates a step backwards, for the Negroes who sat in Congress and in the State Legislatures during the Reconstruction worked for the enactment of measures of concern to all elements of the population regardless of color. Historians have not yet forgot what those Negro statesmen did in advocating public education, internal improvements, labor arbitration, the tariff, and the merchant marine.

Chapter 10

The Loss of Vision

HISTORY shows, then, that as a result of these unusual forces in the education of the Negro he easily learns to follow the line of least resistance rather than battle against odds for what real history has shown to be the right course. A mind that remains in the present atmosphere never undergoes sufficient development to experience what is commonly known as thinking. No Negro thus submerged in the ghetto, then, will have a clear conception of the present status of the race or sufficient foresight to plan for the future; and he drifts so far toward compromise that he loses moral courage. The education of the Negro, then, becomes a perfect device for control from without. Those who purposely promote it have every reason to rejoice, and Negroes themselves exultingly champion the cause of the oppressor.

A comparison of the record of the spokesmen of the race today with that of those of the eighteenth century shows a moral surrender. During the prolonged struggle between the French and English in America the Negroes held the balance of power at several strategic points and used it accordingly; today the Negro finds himself inconsequential because he can be parked on one side of the fence. The same balance of power was evident also during the American Revolution when Negro soldiers insisted on serving side by side with others; today many Negroes are content as menials in the army. At that time Negroes preached to mixed congregations; today we find Negroes busy separating them. The eighteenth-century Negro resented any such thing as social distinctions; today Negroes are saying that they do not want social equality. Negroes of that epoch said with the ancient poet, "I am a man and deem nothing that relates to man a matter of indifference to me"; today, however, the average Negro says, "Now, I am a colored man, and you white folks must settle that matter among yourselves."

At a still later date the American Negro showed more courage than he does today with all of his so-called enlightenment. When the free Negroes were advised a hundred years ago to go to Africa they replied that they would never separate themselves from the slave population of this country as they were brethren by the "ties of consanguinity, of suffering, and of wrong." Today, however, the Negro in the North turns up his nose at the crude migrant from the South who brings to the North the race problem but along with it more thrift and actual progress than the Northern Negro ever dreamed of.

When, again in 1816, free Negroes like Richard Allen, James Forten, and Robert Purvis, were referred to as a foreign element whose social status might not be secure in this country, instead of permitting the colonizationists to shove them aside as criminals to be deported to a distant shore, they replied in no uncertain terms that this soil in America which gave them birth is their only true home. "Here their fathers fought, bled, and died for this country and here they intended to stay." Today when such things come up you find Negroes appearing upon the scene to see how much pay they can obtain to assist in the proposed undoing of the race.

Further emphasizing this thought of resistance a few years later, Nathaniel Paul, a Baptist preacher of Albany, informed the colonizationists that the free Negroes would not permit their traducers to formulate a program for the race. You may go ahead with your plan to deport this element in order to make slavery secure, he warned; but the free Negroes will never emigrate to Africa. "We shall stay here and fight until the foul monster is crushed. Slavery must go."

"Did I believe it would always continue," said he, "and that man to the end of time would be permitted with impunity to usurp the same undue authority over his fellow, I would disavow any allegiance or obligation I was under to my fellow creatures, or any submission that I owed to the laws of my country! I would deny the superintending power of divine Providence in the affairs of this life; I would ridicule the religion of the Savior of the world, and treat as the worst of men the ministers of the everlasting gospel; I would consider my Bible as a book of false and delusive fables, and commit it to the flames; nay, I would still go farther; I would at once confess myself an atheist, and deny the existence of a holy God."

And these Negroes of a century ago stood their ground and fought the pro-slavery deportationists to a standstill, for with the exception of a few pioneers the emigrants to Liberia were largely slaves manumitted on the condition that they would settle in Africa. These freedmen, then, could have no ideals but those of the slave-holding section from which they were sent. They established, therefore, a slavocracy in Liberia. If Liberia has failed, then, it is no evidence of the failure of the Negro in government. It is merely evidence of the failure of slavery.

The Negroes attacking Jim-Crowism almost a century ago fearlessly questioned the constitutionality of such a provision. Speaking through Charles Lenox Remond of that day, they said, "There is a distinction between social and civil rights. We all claim the privilege of selecting our society and associations, but, in civil rights, one man has not the prerogative to define rights for another. These [race] distinctions react in all their wickedness—to say nothing of their concocted and systematized odiousness and absurdity—upon those who are illiberal and mean enough to practice them."

In our day, however, we find some "highly educated" Negroes approving such Jim-Crowism. For example, not many years ago an outstanding Baptist preacher, dabbling in politics in West Virginia, suggested to the whites that they enact a Jim Crow car law in that State, and we had difficulty in crushing that sentiment. A few years thereafter the author heard one of our bishops say that we should not object to such separation, for we want to be by ourselves. When this distinguished churchman died the traducers of the Negro lauded him to the skies; and thoughtless members of the race, thinking that he deserved it, joined in the loud acclaim.

In this way the large majority of "educated" Negroes in the United States have accepted segregation and have become its fearless champions. Their filled but undeveloped minds do not enable them to understand that, although an opiate furnishes temporary relief, it does not remove the cause of the pain. In this case we have yielded on principle to satisfy the mob, but have not yet found an ultimate solution of the problem at hand. In our so-called democracy we are accustomed to give the majority what they want rather than educate them to

The Loss of Vision

understand what is best for them. We do not show the Negro how to overcome segregation, but we teach him how to accept it as final and just.

Numerous results from this policy may be cited. The white laboring man refuses to work with Negroes because of the false tradition that the Negro is an inferior, and at the same time the Negro for the same reason becomes content with menial service and drudgery. The politician excludes the Negro from the councils of his party and from the government because he has been taught that such is necessary to maintain the supremacy of his race; the Negro, trained in the same school of thought, accepts this as final and contends for such meager consideration as the bosses may begrudgingly grant him. An irate resident in an exclusive district protests against an invasion by Negroes because he has learned that these poverty-stricken people are carriers of disease and agents of crime; the Negroes, believing that such is the truth, remain content in the ghetto. The irrational parent forces the separation of the races in some schools because his child must occupy a seat next to a pupil of "tainted" African blood; the educated Negro accepts this as inevitable and welcomes the makeshift for his people. Children of Negroes are excluded from the playgrounds because of the assertion that they will contaminate those of the whites; the Negroes yielding, settle down to a policy of having their children grow up in neglected fashion in the most undesirable part of the city. The Negro is forced to ride in a Jim Crow car to stamp upon him more easily the badge of his "inferiority"; the "educated Negro" accepts it as settled and abandons the fight against this social proscription.

And thus goes segregation which is the most far-reaching development in the history of the Negro since the enslavement of the race. In fact, it is a sequel of slavery. It has been made possible by our system of mis-educating innocent people who did not know what was happening. It is so subtle that men have participated in promoting it without knowing what they were doing.

There are a few defenders of segregation who are doubtless sincere. Although nominally free they have never been sufficiently enlightened to see the matter other than as slaves. One can cite cases of Negroes who opposed emancipation and denounced the abolitionists. A few who became free reenslaved themselves. A still larger number made no effort to become free because they did not want to disconnect themselves from their masters, and their kind still object to full freedom.

Ever since the Civil War when Negroes were first given a chance to participate in the management of their affairs they have been inconsistent and compromising. They have tried to gain one thing on one day by insisting on equality for all, while at the same time endeavoring to gain another point the next day by segregation. At one moment Negroes fight for the principle of democracy, and at the very next moment they barter it away for some temporary advantage. You cannot have a thing and dispose of it at the same time.

For example, the Negro political leaders of the Reconstruction period clamored for suffrage and the right of holding office, serving in the militia, and sitting on the jury; but few of them wanted white and colored children to attend the same school. When expressing themselves on education most of them took the position of segregationists; and Charles Sumner in his fight for the civil rights of the Negro had to eliminate mixed schools from his program not only because many whites objected but also because the Negroes themselves did not seem to want them. All of these leaders might not have been looking for jobs in those days; but as nominal freemen, who were still slaves, they did not feel comfortable in the presence of their former masters.

These timorous men were very much like some Negroes who were employed near the author's home in Virginia by a Northern farmer, who had moved into the State after the Civil War. When breakfast time came the first morning he called them in to eat at the table with his family. These actual slaves, however, immediately lost their appetite. One finally called the employer aside and settled the matter in another way. He said:

"Now boss, you ain't used to de rules ob dis country. We just can't sit at de table wid wite folks. We been use ter eating a cake er bread out yonder 'tween de plow handles. Les us go out dar."

The system, therefore, has extended from one thing to another until the Negroes today find themselves hedged in by the color bar almost every way they turn; and, set off by themselves, the Negroes cannot learn from the example of others with whom they might come into contact. In the ghetto, too, they are not permitted to construct and carry out a program of their own. These segregating institutions interfere with the development of self-help among Negroes, for often Negroes fail to raise money to establish institutions which they might control, but they readily contribute large sums for institutions which segregate persons of African blood.

Denied participation in the higher things of life, the "educated" Negro himself joins, too, with ill-designing persons to handicap his people by systematized exploitation. Feeling that the case of the Negro is hopeless, the "educated" Negro decides upon the course of personally profiting by whatever he can do in using these people as a means to an end. He grins in their faces while "extracting money" from them, hut his heart shows no fond attachment to their despised cause. With a little larger income than they receive he can make himself somewhat comfortable in the ghetto; and he forgets those who have no way of escape.

Some of this "educated" class join with unprincipled real estate men in keeping Negroes out of desirable parts of the city and confining them to unsanitary sections. Such persons help the profiteer to collect from Negroes thus cornered a larger rental than that exacted from whites for the same property. In similar fashion a Negro minister sometimes goes into a community where the races are moving along amicably together in their churches and rents a shack or an old empty store to start a separate church for "our people," not to supply any practical need but to exploit those who have never learned to think. Professional men, too, walking in their footsteps, impose also upon the poor innocent Negroes who do not know when they are being treated properly and when they are not, but high fees may be obtained from them inasmuch as they cannot always go to others for service.

Settling in a community with mixed schools, the educated Negro often advocates their separation that his daughter may secure a position in the system. The Negro politician is accustomed to corner the Negro vote, by opening a separate office from which he may bargain with the chieftains of the machine for the highest price available. When paid off by some position, which is not very lofty, this office-holder accepts such employment with the understanding that he will be set off by himself as if he were destructive of the rest of mankind.

In the present crisis, however, the "highly educated" Negroes find very little to exploit, and in their untoward condition they have no program of finding a way out. They see numerous instances of Negroes losing their jobs in white establishments. In fact, these things occur daily. Janitors who have been giving satisfaction are abruptly told that they will no longer be needed. Negro waiters in hotels are being informed that their places will go to white workers. Negro truck drivers are ordered to step down and let the needy of the other race go up. We hear so much of this that we wonder what the outcome will be.

In this readjustment, of course, when there are fewer opportunities left for those who cannot or do not have the opportunity to operate machines the Negroes will naturally be turned out of their positions by their employers who think first of their own race. In the ultimate passing of the depression, however, Negroes will not be much better off when some of the whites now displacing them will rise to higher levels. In the economic order of tomorrow there will be little use for the factotum or scullion. Man will not need such personal attention when he can buy a machine to serve him more efficiently. The menial Negroes, the aggregate of parasites whom the "highly educated" Negro has exploited, will not be needed on tomorrow. What, then, will become of "our highly educated" Negroes who have no initiative?

We have appealed to the talented tenth for a remedy, but they have nothing to offer. Their minds have never functioned in this all-important sphere. The "educated" Negro shows no evidence of vision. He should see a new picture. The Negroes are facing the alternative of rising in the sphere of production to supply their proportion of the manufacturers and merchants or of going down to the graves of paupers. The Negro must now do for himself or die out as the world undergoes readjustment. If the whites are to continue for some time in doing drudgery to the exclusion of Negroes, the latter must find another way out. Nothing forces this upon one more dramatically than when he learns that white women in Montgomery, Alabama, are coming to the back door of Negro homes asking for their washing. If the whites have reached this extremity, and they must be taken care of first, what will be left for the Negroes?

At this moment, then, the Negroes must begin to do the very thing which they have been taught that they cannot do. They still have some money, and they have needs to supply. They must begin immediately to pool their earnings and organize industries to participate in supplying social and economic demands. If the Negroes are to remain forever removed from the producing atmosphere, and the present discrimination continues, there will be nothing left for them to do.

There is no reason for lack of confidence because of the recent failure of Negro enterprises, although the "highly educated" Negroes assert the contrary. This lack of confidence is the cause of the failure of these enterprises. If the Negroes had manifested enough confidence in them and had properly supported them, they would have been strong enough to stand the test in the crisis. Negro banks, as a rule, have failed because the people, taught that their own pioneers in business cannot function in this sphere, withdrew their deposits. An individual cannot live after you extract the blood from his veins. The strongest bank in the United States will last only so long as the people will have sufficient confidence in it to keep their money there. In fact, the confidence of the people is worth more than money.

The lack of confidence of the Negro in himself and in his possibilities is what has kept him down. His mis-education has been a perfect success in this respect. Yet it is not necessary for the Negro to have more confidence in his own workers than in others. If the Negro would be as fair to his own as he has been to others, this would be all that is necessary to give him a new lease on life and start the trend upward.

Here we find that the Negro has failed to recover from his slavish habit of berating his own and worshipping others as perfect beings. No progress has been made in this respect because the more "education" the Negro gets the worse off he is. He has just had so much longer to learn to decry and despise himself. The race looking to this educated class for a solution of its problems does not find any remedy; and, on the contrary, sees itself further and further away from those things to which it has aspired. By forgetting the schoolroom for the time being and relying upon an awakening of the masses through adult education we can do much to give the Negro a new point of view with respect to economic enterprise and group cooperation. The average Negro has not been sufficiently mis-educated to become hopeless.

Our minds must become sufficiently developed to use segregation to kill segregation, and thus bring to pass that ancient and yet modern prophecy, "The wrath of man shall praise thee." If the Negro in the ghetto must eternally be fed by the hand that pushes him into the ghetto, he will never become strong enough to get out of the ghetto. This assumption of Negro leadership in the ghetto, then, must not be confined to matters of religion, education, and social uplift; it must deal with such fundamental forces in life as make these things possible. If the Negro area, however, is to continue as a district supported wholly from without, the inept dwellers therein will merit and will receive only the contempt of those who may occasionally catch glimpses of them in their plight.

As Frederick Douglass said in 1852, "It is vain that we talk of being men, if we do not the work of men. We must become valuable to society in other departments of industry than those servile ones from which we are rapidly being excluded. We must show that we can do as well as they. When we can build as well as live in houses; when we can make as well as wear shoes; when we can produce as well as consume wheat, corn and rye—then we shall become valuable to society.

"Society," continued Douglass, "is a hard-hearted affair. With it the helpless may expect no higher dignity than that of paupers. The individual must lay society under obligation to him or society will honor him only as a stranger and sojourner."

Chapter 11
The Need for Service Rather Than Leadership

IN this untoward situation the Negro finds himself at the close of the third generation from Emancipation. He has been educated in the sense that persons directed a certain way are more easily controlled, or as Ovid remarked, "In time the bull is brought to bear the yoke." The Negro in this state continues as a child. He is restricted in his sphere to small things, and with these he becomes satisfied. His ambition, does not rise any higher than to plunge into the competition with his fellows for these trifles. At the same time those who have given the race such false ideals are busy in the higher spheres from which Negroes by their mis-education and racial guidance have been disbarred.

Examples of this failure of the mis-educated Negro to have high ideals may be cited. The author has known numerous cases of Negro lawyers, physicians and business men who, while attending local Sunday schools, churches, and lodges, have fallen out about trifles like a resolution or the chairmanship of a committee, which so embittered them as to make themselves enemies for life and stumbling blocks preventing any such thing as organization or community cooperation.

It is a common on occurrence to see a Negro well situated as a minister or teacher aspiring to a political appointment which temporarily pays little more than what he is receiving and offers no distinction except that of being earmarked as a Jim Crow job set aside for some Negro who has served well the purposes of the bosses as a wardheeler in a campaign. Negroes who have begun promising business enterprises sometimes abandon them temporarily for the same sort of empty honor. In this way they have been known to hamper their business by incurring the displeasure of ambitious politicians who might otherwise patronize them.

Negroes of this point of view have developed in that part of the country where it is thought that the most distinguished persons in the community are those who hold and exploit the local offices or those who are further honored with positions in the state and nation. While this may apply in the case of their oppressors the few positions allotted the Negroes are magnified beyond all reasonable bounds. This comes as a natural result, however, for the "education" of the Negro requires it. The ambitious mis-educated Negro in the struggle for the little things allotted by others prevents any achievement of the people in matters more constructive. Potentially the colored people are strong although they are actually weak.

This much-ado-about-nothing renders impossible cooperation, the most essential thing in the development of a people. The ambitious of this class do more to keep the race in a state of turmoil and to prevent it from serious community effort than all the other elements combined. The one has a job that the other wants; or the one is a leader of a successful faction, and the other is struggling to supplant him. Everything in the community, then, must yield ground to this puerile contest.

In one city of a few thousand Negroes there is no chance for community cooperation because of the antagonism of the Methodist and Baptist preachers in charge of the two largest churches. The one is determined to dictate the appointment of the teaching corps and the social welfare workers; the other is persistently struggling to undo everything accomplished by his opponent. The one is up today, and the other in ascendency tomorrow. Several efforts have been made to start business enterprises there, but none has succeeded because one faction tears down what the other builds up.

In another city the cleavage is along political lines. Preachers are there, but a lawyer and a dentist plunging into politics have dispossessed the clergy of the stage. The leader of one faction is so bitterly opposed to the other that he even warns strangers against going to the home of his adversary. To present a sane proposition to the community through one of these leaders means local warfare rather than an effort to work together for the common good. Consequently, although there are thousands of Negroes living together in one quarter they have no business enterprises of worth. The selfish struggle for personal aggrandizement, which has not yet brought either faction more than an appointment on the police force or a clerkship in one of the city offices, thus blocks the social and economic progress of thousands of unoffending people.

In another state the ambition of the highly educated Negro is restricted to becoming principals of the high schools. The neglected state school has not developed sufficiently to become attractive. The warring area, then, is in the cities. In one of them, where several Negroes own considerable wealth which, if pooled and properly used, would produce all but wonderful results, the petty strife has been most disastrous. Little thought is given to social uplift, and economic effort is crushed by factional wrangling. Before the author had been in one of the towns an hour a stalwart of one faction sounded him on becoming a candidate for the position held by the principal of the high school. A few minutes thereafter another approached him for advice as to how "to get him out."

The high cost of this childishness to the community can be estimated only by taking into consideration the fact that this strife is all but endless. If it were a matter that developed now and then only to be forgotten by people directing their attention thereafter to more important things, it would not do much harm; but this confusion continues for years. Sometimes it grips a community for a whole generation, vitiating the entire life of the people.

In spite of the meager rewards, however, the idea of leadership looms high in the Negro mind. It always develops thus among oppressed people. The oppressor must have some dealing with the despised group, and rather than have contact with individuals he approaches the masses through his own spokesman. The term itself connotes a backward condition. In its strides upward a race shuffles off its leaders because they originate outside of the group. They constitute a load that sinks the oppressed in the mire of trials and tribulations.

Leadership is usually superimposed for the purpose of "directing the course of the ostracized group along sane lines." This was accomplished during the days of slavery by restricting the assembly of Negroes to certain times and places and compelling them to meet in the presence of a stipulated number of the "wisest and discreetest men of the community." These supervisors of the conduct of

The Need for Service Rather Than Leadership

Negroes would prevent them from learning the truth which might make them "unruly" or ambitious to become free.

After the Negroes became free the same end was reached by employing a Negro or some white man to spy upon and report behind closed doors on a plan to enslave the Negroes' minds. In case that actual employment as a spy seemed too bold, the person to be used as such an instrument took up some sort of enterprise which the oppressors of the race warmly supported to give him the desired influence in the community. This "racial racketeer" might be a politician, minister, teacher, director of a community center, or head of a "social uplift agency." As long as he did certain things and expressed the popular opinion on questions he lacked nothing, and those who followed him found their way apparently better paid as the years went by. His leadership, then, was recognized and the ultimate undoing of the Negroes in the community was assured.

Such leadership, too, has continued into our day and it goes from bad to worse. The very service which this racial toady renders hardens him to the extent that he loses his soul. He becomes equal to any task the oppressor may impose upon him, and at the same time he becomes artful enough to press his case convincingly before the thoughtless multitude. What is right is sacrificed because everything that is right is not expedient; and what is expedient soon becomes unnecessary.

Recently a citizen, observing how we have been thus betrayed, suggested that there be called a national meeting to take steps for a program of development of the race from within under "a new leadership." Such a movement can be made to mean something, and then it can degenerate into an assembly of abuse and vituperation followed by the usual whereas-therefore-be-it-resolved effort which has never meant anything in the awakening and the development of an oppressed people.

The Negroes, however, will not advance far if they continue to waste their energy abusing those who misdirect and exploit them. The exploiters of the race are not so much at fault as the race itself. If Negroes persist in permitting themselves to be handled in this fashion they will always find some one at hand to impose upon them. The matter is one which rests largely with the Negroes themselves. The race will free itself from exploiters just as soon as it decides to do so. No one else can accomplish this task for the race. It must plan and do for itself.

Checking up on what they do, Negroes often find themselves giving money and moral support to various persons and institutions which influence the course of the race in the wrong way. They do not often ask themselves whether the support thus given will redound in the long run to the good of the people with whom they are identified. They do not inquire whether the assistance thus given offers temporary relief but eventually results in irreparable loss. So many Negroes often do themselves harm when they actually believe that they are doing good. Under their present teachers they cannot easily learn to do any better, for such training as we undergo does not open our eyes sufficiently for us to see far ahead of us.

If the Negro could abandon the idea of leadership and instead stimulate a larger number of the race to take up definite tasks and sacrifice their time and energy in doing these things efficiently the race might accomplish something. The race needs workers, not leaders. Such workers will solve the problems which race leaders talk about and raise money to enable them to talk more and more about. When you hear a man talking, then, always inquire as to what he is doing or what he has done for humanity. Oratory and resolutions do not avail much. If they did, the Negro race would be in a paradise on earth. It may be well to repeat here the saying that old men talk of what they have done, young men of what they are doing, and fools of what they expect to do. The Negro race has a rather large share of the last mentioned class.

If we can finally succeed in translating the idea of leadership into that of service, we may soon find it possible to lift the Negro to a higher level. Under leadership we have come into the ghetto; by service within the ranks we may work our way out of it. Under leadership we have been constrained to do the biddings of others; by service we may work out a program in the light of our own circumstances. Under leadership we have become poverty-stricken; by service we may teach the masses how to earn a living honestly. Under leadership we have been made to despise our own possibilities and to develop into parasites; by service we may prove sufficient unto the task of self-development and contribute our part to modern culture.

Chapter 12
Hirelings in the Place of Public Servants

IF the highly educated Negroes have not learned better the simple lessons of life one cannot expect the laboring classes to conduct themselves differently. In the large number of cases the employers of Negroes in common labor, in which most of them are now engaged, assert that there is no hope for advancement of Negroes in their employ because Negroes will not work under foremen of their own color. In other words, the average Negro has not yet developed to the point that one is willing to take orders from another of his own race.

While it is true that such an answer is often given as a mere excuse for not placing Negroes in responsible positions when it can be done without any particular trouble, the investigation among Negroes themselves reveals numerous facts to prove that there is more truth than falsehood in this statement. Hundreds of employes of African blood frankly say that they will not work under a Negro. One is afraid that the other may prosper more than he does and be recognized accordingly.

Some of these instances are interesting. A head of one of the Government departments, in which Negro women are employed to do unskilled labor, reports that he placed in charge of the group of these workers an intelligent colored woman who seemed to have all of the necessary qualifications which he had found in other women thus employed. Those working under her, however, refused to obey instructions, kept the place in turmoil and soon destroyed the morale of the whole force. As soon as he placed a white woman in charge, however, order was reestablished on the premises, and everything moved along smoothly.

Another employer conducting a wholesale business placed a Negro foreman in charge of others of his race to function as one of the important departments of the establishment. The Negroes working under him, who had formerly taken orders without question from the white foreman, soon undertook to take liberties with the promoted Negro and to ignore his orders. Knowing that the Negro foreman was well qualified, however, and being personally interested in him, the employer instead of doing what so many others under such circumstances had done, dismissed those who refused to cooperate and supplied the vacancies with others until an efficient working force could thus be obtained. Only a few employers, however, have had such patience and have manifested such interest in the advancement of the Negro. As a rule they merely dispose of Negro foremen with the excuse that one Negro will not take orders from another.

This refusal of Negroes to take orders from one another is due largely to the fact that slaveholders taught their bondmen that they were as good as or better than any others and, therefore, should not be subjected to any member of their race. If they were to be subordinated to some one it should be to the white man of superior culture and social position. This keeps the whole race on a lower level, restricted to the atmosphere of trifles which do not concern their traducers. The greater things of life which can be attained only by wise leadership, then, they have no way to accomplish.

The strong have always used this as a means of dealing with the so-called weaker races of the world. The Caucasian arrays the one against the other so that they may never combine their forces and thus deprive their so-called superiors of control over them, which they could easily do if organized. One white man was thus able to maintain himself on a plantation where there were thirty or forty slaves because the Negroes were mis-educated in such a way as to keep them divided into distinct factions. In petty strife their power would be lost in the process of attrition. Today we find the same thing in Africa where this end is reached by embittering one tribe against another; and it worked the same way in India until recently when it began to break down under the masterful leadership of Mahatma Gandhi.

The Negroes of the United States have followed leadership slavishly but sometimes unfortunately that of those leaders who are selected for them by the traducers of the race. The enemies of the race, for example, will find a Negro willing to do certain things they desire to have accomplished and will finance him and give him sufficient publicity to get before the world, for the few favors which he may dispense among his followers as a result of his influence and economic position will bring to him the adequate number of Negroes for the constituency which he desires.

Negroes, however, sometimes choose their own leaders but unfortunately they are too often of the wrong kind. Negroes do not readily follow persons with constructive programs. Almost any sort of exciting appeal or trivial matter presented to them may receive immediate attention and temporarily at least liberal support. When the bubble collapses, of course, these same followers will begin to decry Negro leadership and call these misrepresentatives of the group rascals and scoundrels. Inasmuch as they have failed to exercise foresight, however, those who have deceived them should not be blamed so much as those who have liberally supported these impostors. Yet the fault here is not inherently in the Negro but in what he has been taught.

The Negroes' point of view, therefore, must be changed before they can construct a program which will bring them out of the wilderness. For example, no good can be expected from one of our teachers who said that she had to give up her class in Sunday school to accept an extra job of waiting on table at that hour because she had bought a twenty-four-hundred-dollar coat and her husband had purchased an expensive car. Such a teacher has no message for the Negro child. Her example would tend to drag the youth downward, and the very thought of having such a person in the schoolroom is most depressing.

We must feel equally discouraged when we see a minister driving up to his church on Sunday morning in a Cadillac. He does not come to feed the multitude spiritually. He comes to fleece the flock. The appeal he makes is usually emotional. While the people are feeling happy the expensive machine is granted, and the prolonged vacation to use it is easily financed. Thus the thoughtless drift backward toward slavery.

When you see a physician drive to one's door in his Pierce Arrow, you cannot get the impression he has come to treat the patient for a complaint. He has come to treat him for a dollar. Such physicians, as a rule, know less and less medicine as the years go by, although they make much money by learning human psychology and using it for personal gain. With leeches of this type feeding upon an all but impoverished people and giving them nothing back there can be no hope for advancement.

No people can go forward when the majority of those who should know better have chosen to go backward, but this is exactly what most of our misleaders do. Not being learned in the history and background of the race, they figure out that there is no hope for the masses; and they decide, then, that the best thing they can do is to exploit these people for all they can and use the accumulations selfishly. Such persons have no vision and therefore perish at their own hands.

It is an injustice to the Negro, however, to mis-educate him and suffer his manners to be corrupted from infancy unto old age and then blame him for making the mistakes which such guidance necessitates. "People who have been restricted and held down naturally condescend to the lower levels of delinquency. When education has been entirely neglected or improperly managed we see the worst passions ruling with uncontrolled and incessant sway. Good sense degenerates into craft, anger wrangles into malignity, restraint which is thought most solitary comes too late, and the most judicial admonitions are urged in vain."

Philosophers have long conceded, however, that every man has two educations: "that which is given to him, and the other that which he gives himself. Of the two kinds the latter is by far the more desirable. Indeed all that is most worthy in man he must work out and conquer for himself. It is that which constitutes our real and best nourishment. What we are merely taught seldom nourishes the mind like that which we teach ourselves."

The same eternal principle applies to a race forced to live apart from others as a separate and distinct group. Inasmuch as the education of the Negro has come from without we can clearly see that he has received only a part of the development which he should have undergone or he has developed negatively. The Negro lacks mental power, which cannot be expected from ill-fed brains.

This naturally brings up a serious question. The people on the outside, who are directing the race from afar, will take this condition of affairs as evidence that the Negro is not prepared for leadership. What they ought to say is that they have not prepared the Negro to assume the responsibility of his own uplift. Instead of doing this, however, they play up this result of their own failure as an argument for imposing upon the Negro race the guidance of others from without.

As to whether or not a white man should be a leader of the Negroes may be dismissed as a silly question. What has the color to do with it? Such a worker may be white, brown, yellow, or red, if he is heart and soul with the people whom he would serve. It just happens, however, that most white men now in control of Negro institutions are not of this required type. Practically all of those with whom I have talked and communicated believe in imposing some sort of disability upon Negroes. Some object to the freedom of intermarriage as a substitute for concubinage, scoff at the idea of the enfranchisement of the Negroes, approve their segregation, and justify the economic exploitation of the race. Now if these are the persons to elevate the Negroes, to what point do they expect to lift them, and what will the Negroes be when they get there?

With this same thought in mind a white director of Negroes recently said to the author:

"I realize that I have no useful function in my present position as a president of a Negro institution. I do not approve of their aspirations to many things. I cannot accept the students in my house as I would white students because it might lead to an interracial romance. Marrying is such a difficult problem at the best that I should not like to see one of my children make a failure in life by marrying a Negro."

"In other words," continued he, "we live in two different worlds. While I am among them I cannot become a part of them. How then can I help them under these circumstances?"

I am acquainted with another white educator at the head of a Negro institution, who will not address a colored girl as Miss, and to avoid the use of a title in speaking to women of the race he addresses them as his kin. One of them was sharp enough to reply to him thus when he accosted her as auntie:

"Oh, I am so glad that I have found my lost relatives at last. My mother often told me that I had some distinguished kin, and just to think that you are my nephew makes me feel glad."

Another such exploiter in charge of a Negro college never wears his hat on the campus. His confidential explanation is that he might have to lift it when he meets a Negro woman. Of course, that would never do. "White supremacy" would be lost in the Negro school.

As we realize more and more that education is not merely imparting information which is expected to produce certain results, we see very clearly the inconsistency of the position of white persons as executives of Negro institutions. These misfits belong to the very group working out the segregation of the Negro, and they come into these institutions mainly to earn a living. They make no particular contribution to the development of education, for they are not scholarly enough to influence educational theory; and they are so far out of sympathy with the Negro that they cannot make any contribution to educational practice. These "foreigners" are not bringing to such institutions large sums of money which the Negroes cannot obtain, for the institutions now directed by Negroes are receiving larger appropriations than those under the management of whites.

Our so-called thinkers, however, seldom see the inevitable results of this unsound policy. Not long ago when the author wrote the textbook entitled NEGRO MAKERS OF HISTORY it was adversely criticised by a Negro who said that the book should have had as an illustration the cut of the white man who established a certain Negro college. The author had to explain that the book was to give an account of what the Negro has done, not of what has been done for him.

The school referred to, moreover, was in no sense a Negro school. It had very few Negro teachers and only one Negro trustee. The policy of the school was determined altogether by others without giving the Negro credit for having a thought on education. In other words, it was merely a school which Negroes were permitted to attend. If they picked up here and there something to help them, well and good; if not, may God help them!

It is all right to have a white man as the head of a Negro college or to have a red man at the head of a yellow one, if in each case the incumbent has taken out his naturalization papers and has identified himself as one of the group which he is trying to serve. It seems that the white educators of this day are unwilling to do this, and for that reason they can never contribute to the actual development of the Negro from within. You cannot serve people by giving them orders as to what to do. The real servant of the people must live among them, think with them, feel for them, and die for them.

Hirelings in the Place of Public Servants

The white worker in Negro institutions, too, can never be successful without manifesting some faith in the people with whom he has cast his lot. His efforts must not be merely an attempt to stimulate their imitation of things in a foreign sphere. He must study his community sufficiently to discover the things which have a trend in the proper direction that he may stimulate such forces and thus help the community to do better the good things which it may be capable of doing and at the same time may be interested in doing. If these people are to be brought the ideas of "foreigners," and must be miraculously transformed into something else before anything can be made of them, such effort will be a fruitless task like most of the so-called education and uplift of the Negroes in America.

The Negro, in spite of his confinement to the ghetto, has some opportunities to develop his special capacities if they are properly studied and understood. The real servant of the people, then, will give more attention to those to be served than to the use that somebody may want to make of them. He will be more concerned with what he can do to increase the ease, comfort, and happiness of the Negro than with how the Negro may be used to contribute to the ease, comfort, and happiness of others.

The servant of the people, unlike the leader, is not on a high horse elevated above the people and trying to carry them to some designated point to which he would like to go for his own advantage. The servant of the people is down among them, living as they live, doing what they do and enjoying what they enjoy. He may be a little better informed than some other members of the group; it may be that he has had some experience that they have not had, but in spite of this advantage he should have more humility than those whom he serves, for we are told that "Whosoever is greatest among you, let him be your servant."

Chapter 13

Understand the Negro

"WE do not offer here any course in Negro history, Negro literature, or race relations," recently said a professor of a Negro college. "We study the Negro along with other people."

"An excellent idea," the interviewer replied. "No one should expect you to do any more than this, but how do you-do it when the Negro is not mentioned in your textbooks except to be condemned? Do you, a teacher in a Negro school, also condemn the race in the same fashion as the writers of your textbooks of history and literature?"

"No," said he, "we bring the Negro in here and there."

"How often does 'here and there' connote?"

"Well, you know," said he, "Negroes have not done much; and what they have accomplished may be briefly covered by referring to the achievements of a few men and women.

"Why do you emphasize the special study of the Negro?" said he further. "Why is it necessary to give the race special attention in the press, on the rostrum, or in the schoolroom? This idea of projecting the Negro into the foreground does the race much harm by singing continually of his woes and problems and thus alienating the public which desires to give its attention to other things."

It is true that many Negroes do not desire to hear anything about their race, and few whites of today will listen to the story of woe. With most of them the race question has been settled. The Negro has been assigned to the lowest drudgery as the sphere in which the masses must toil to make a living; and socially and politically the race has been generally proscribed. Inasmuch as the traducers of the race have "settled" the matter in this fashion, they naturally oppose any effort to change this status.

Many Negro professional men who are making a living attending to the affairs of these laborers and servants in their mentally undeveloped state and many teachers who in conservative fashion are instructing their children to maintain the status quo ante bellum, also oppose any movement to upset this arrangement. They are getting paid for their efforts Why should they try innovations? The gods have so decreed it. Human beings cannot change it. Why be foolish?

A Negro with sufficient thought to construct a program of his own is undesirable, and the educational systems of this country generally refuse to work through such Negroes in promoting their cause. The program for the uplift of the Negroes in this country must be handed over to an executive force like orders from the throne, and they must carry it out without question or get out of line and let the procession go on. Although the Negro is being daily forced more and more by segregation into a world peculiarly his own, his unusually perplexing status is given little or no thought, and he is not considered capable of thinking for himself.

Understand the Negro

The chief difficulty with the education of the Negro is that it has been largely imitation resulting in the enslavement of his mind. Somebody outside of the race has desired to try out on Negroes some experiment which interested him and his coworkers; and Negroes, being objects of charity, have received them cordially and have done what they required. In fact, the keynote in the education of the Negro has been to do what he is told to do. Any Negro who has learned to do this is well prepared to function in the American social order as others would have him.

Looking over the courses of study of the public schools, one finds little to show that the Negro figures in these curricula. In supplementary matter a good deed of some Negro is occasionally referred to, but oftener the race is mentioned only to be held up to ridicule. With the exception of a few places like Atlantic City, Atlanta, Tulsa, St. Louis, Birmingham, Knoxville, and the states of Louisiana and North Carolina no effort is made to study the Negro in the public schools as they do the Latin, the Teuton, or the Mongolian. Several mis-educated Negroes themselves contend that the study of the Negro by children would bring before them the race problem prematurely and, therefore, urge that the study of the race be deferred until they reach advanced work in the college or university. These misguided teachers ignore the fact that the race question is being brought before black and white children daily in their homes, in the streets, through the press and on the rostrum. How, then, can the school ignore the duty of teaching the truth while these other agencies are playing up falsehood?

The experience of college instructors shows that racial attitudes of the youth are not easily changed after they reach adolescence. Although students of this advanced stage are shown the fallacy of race superiority and the folly of social distinctions, they nevertheless continue to do the illogical thing of still looking upon these despised groups as less worthy than themselves and persist in treating them accordingly. Teachers of elementary and secondary schools giving attention to this interracial problem have succeeded in softening and changing the attitude of children whose judgment has not been so hopelessly warped by the general attitude of the communities in which they have been brought up.

In approaching this problem in this fashion to counteract the one-sided education of youth the thinking people of this country have no desire to upset the curricula of the schools or to force the Negro as such into public discussion; but, if the Negro is to be elevated he must be educated in the sense of being developed from what he is, and the public must be so enlightened as to think of the Negro as a man. Furthermore, no one can be thoroughly educated until he learns as much about the Negro as he knows about other people.

Upon examining the recent catalogues of the leading Negro colleges, one finds that invariably they give courses in ancient, mediaeval, and modern Europe, but they do not give such courses in ancient, mediaeval, and modern Africa. Yet Africa, according to recent discoveries, has contributed about as much to the progress of mankind as Europe has, and the early civilization of the Mediterranean world was decidedly influenced by Africa.

Negro colleges offer courses bearing on the European colonists prior to their coming to America, their settlement on these shores, and their development here toward independence. Why are they not equally generous with the Negroes in treating their status in Africa prior to enslavement, their first transplantation to the West Indies, the Latinization of certain Negroes in contradistinction to the development of others under the influence of the Teuton, and the effort of the race toward self-expression?

A further examination of their curricula shows, too, that invariably these Negro colleges offer courses in Greek philosophy and in that of modern European thought, but they direct no attention to the philosophy of the African. Negroes of Africa have and always have had their own ideas about the nature of the universe, time, and space, about appearance and reality, and about freedom and necessity. The effort of the Negro to interpret man's relation to the universe shows just as much intelligence as we find in the philosophy of the Greeks. There were many Africans who were just as wise as Socrates.

Again, one observes in some of these catalogues numerous courses in art but no well defined course in Negro or African art which early influenced that of the Greeks. Thinkers are now saying that the early culture of the Mediterranean was chiefly African. Most of these colleges do not even direct special attention to Negro music in which the Negro has made his outstanding contribution in America. The unreasonable attitude is that because the whites do not have these things in their schools the Negroes must not have them in theirs. The Catholics and Jews, therefore, are wrong in establishing special schools to teach their principles of religion, and the Germans in America are unwise in having their children taught their mother tongue.

Such has been the education of Negroes. They have been taught facts of history, but have never learned to think. Their conception is that you go to school to find out what other people have done, and then you go out in life to imitate them. What they have done can be done by others, they contend; and they are right. They are wrong, however, in failing to realize that what others have done, we may not need to do. If we are to do identically the same thing from generation to generation, we would not make any progress. If we are to duplicate from century to century the same feats, the world will grow tired of such a monotonous performance.

In this particular respect "Negro education" is a failure, and disastrously so, because in its present predicament the race is especially in need of vision and invention to give humanity something new. The world does not want and will never have the heroes and heroines of the past. What this age needs is an enlightened youth not to undertake the tasks like theirs but to imbibe the spirit of these great men and answer the present call of duty with equal nobleness of soul.

Not only do the needs of generations vary, but the individuals themselves are not duplicates the one of the other; and being different in this respect, their only hope to function efficiently in society is to know themselves and the generation which they are to serve. The chief value in studying the records of others is to become better acquainted with oneself and with one's possibilities to live and to do in the present age. As long as Negroes continue to restrict themselves to doing what was necessary a hundred or a thousand years ago, they must naturally expect to be left out of the great scheme of things as they concern men of today.

The most inviting field for discovery and invention, then, is the Negro himself, but he does not realize it. Frederika Bremer, when reflecting upon her visit to America about 1850, gave this country a new thought in saying to Americans, "The romance of your history is the fate of the Negro." In this very thought lies unusual possibilities for the historian, the economist, the artist, and the philosopher. Why should the Negro writer seek a theme abroad when he has the greatest of all at home?

The bondage of the Negro brought captive from Africa is one of the greatest dramas in history, and the writer who merely sees in that ordeal something to approve or condemn fails to understand the evolution of the human race. Negroes now studying dramatics go into our schools to reproduce Shakespeare, but mentally developed members of this race would see the possibilities of a greater drama in the tragedy of the man of color. Negroes graduating from conservatories of music dislike the singing of our folk songs. For some reason such misguided persons think that they can improve on the productions of the foreign drama or render the music of other people better than they can themselves.

A knowledge of real history would lead one to think that slavery was one of the significant developments which, although evil in themselves, may redound sometimes to the advantage of the oppressed rather than to that of the oppressor. Some one has said that the music of Poland was inspired by incidents of a struggle against the despots invading and partitioning their prostrate land. The Greeks never had an art until the country was overrun by hostile Orientals. Some one then began to immortalize in song the sons who went forth to fight for the native land. Another carved in marble the thought evoked by the example of the Greek youth who blocked the mountain pass with his body or who bared his breast to the javelin to defend the liberty of his country. These things we call art.

In our own country the other elements of the population, being secure in their position, have never faced such a crisis; and the Europeans, after whose pattern American life is fashioned, have not recently had such experience. White Americans, then, have produced no art at all, and that of Europe has reached the point of stagnation. Negroes who are imitating whites, then, are engaged in a most unprofitable performance. Why not interpret themselves anew to the world?

If we had a few thinkers we could expect great achievements on tomorrow. Some Negro with unusual insight would write an epic of bondage and freedom which would take its place with those of Homer and Virgil. Some Negro with esthetic appreciation would construct from collected fragments of Negro music a grand opera that would move humanity to repentance. Some Negro of philosophic penetration would find a solace for the modern world in the soul of the Negro, and then men would be men because they are men.

The Negro in his present plight, however, does not see possibilities until it is too late He exercises much "hindsight," and for that reason he loses ground in the hotly contested battles of life. The Negro as a rule waits until a thing happens before he tries to avert it. He is too much like a man whom the author once saw knocked down in a physical combat. Instead of dodging the blow when it was being dealt he arose from his prostration dodging it.

For example, the author has just received a letter from a lady in Pittsburgh complaining that the librarian in one of its schools insists upon reading to the children "a great deal of literature containing such words as 'nigger,' 'Blackie,' 'Little Black Sambo,' etc." This lady, therefore, would like to place in that school some books by Negro authors. This is a commendable effort, but it comes a little late; we hope not too late.

For centuries such literature has been circulated among the children of the modern world; and they have, therefore, come to regard the Negro as inferior.

Now that some of our similarly mis-educated Negroes are seeing how they have been deceived they are awakening to address themselves to a long neglected work. They should have been thinking about this generations ago, for they have a tremendous task before them today in dispelling this error and counteracting the results of such bias in our literature.

There has just come, too, from a friend of humanity in Edinburgh, Scotland, a direful account of the increase in race prejudice in those parts. Sailors who had frequented the stronghold of race prejudice in South Africa undertook recently to prevent Negro men from socializing with Scotch women at a dance; and certain professors of the University of Edinburgh with the same attitude show so much of it in their teaching that this friend entreats us to send them informing books on the Negro. We are doing it.

Here again, however, the effort to uproot error and popularize the truth comes rather late. The Negro since freedom has gone along grinning, whooping, and "cutting capers" while the white man has applied himself to the task of defining the status of the Negro and compelling him to accept it as thus settled forever. While the Negro has been idle, propaganda has gone far ahead of history. Unfortunately, too, Negro "scholars" have assisted in the production of literature which gives this point of view.

Chapter 14

The New Program

IT seems only a reasonable proposition, then, that, if under the present system which produced our leadership in religion, politics, and business we have gone backward toward serfdom or have at least been kept from advancing to real freedom, it is high time to develop another sort of leadership with a different educational system. In the first place, we must bear in mind that the Negro has never been educated. He has merely been informed about other things which he has not been permitted to do. The Negroes have been shoved out of the regular schools through the rear door into the obscurity of the backyard and told to imitate others whom they see from afar, or they have been permitted in some places to come into the public schools to see how others educate themselves. The program for the uplift of the Negro in this country must be based upon a scientific study of the Negro from within to develop in him the power to do for himself what his oppressors will never do to elevate him to the level of others.

Being without actual education, we have very few persons prepared to help the Negroes whom they have set out to lead. These persons are not all dishonest men and women. Many of them are sincere, and believe that they are doing the race some great good in thus holding it backward. They must be awakened and shown the error of their ways.

We have very few teachers because most of those with whom we are afflicted know nothing about the children whom they teach or about their parents who influence the pupils more than the teachers themselves. When a boy comes to school without knowing his lesson he should be studied instead of being punished. The boy who does well in the beginning of the year and lags behind near the end of the term should not always be censured or ridiculed. As a rule, such children are not responsible for their failures. Their parents and their social status account mainly for these shortcomings. The Negro teacher, then, must treat the disease rather than its symptoms.

But can you expect teachers to revolutionize the social order for the good of the community? Indeed we must expect this very thing. The educational system of a country is worthless unless it accomplishes this task. Men of scholarship and consequently of prophetic insight must show us the right way and lead us into the light which shines brighter and brighter.

In the church where we have much freedom and independence we must get rid of preachers who are not prepared to help the people whom they exploit. The public must refuse to support men of this type. Ministers who are the creations of the old educational system must be awakened, and if this is impossible they must be dethroned. Those who keep the people in ignorance and play upon their emotions must be exiled. The people have never been taught what religion is, for most of the preachers find it easier to stimulate the superstition which develops in the unenlightened mind. Religion in such hands, then, becomes something with which you take advantage of weak people. Why try to enlighten the people in such matters when superstition serves just as well for exploitation?

The ministers with the confidence of the people must above all things understand the people themselves. They must find out the past of their parishioners, whether they were brought up in Georgia, Alabama or Texas, whether they are housed under desirable circumstances, what they do to make a living, what they do with their earnings, how they react to the world about them, how they spend their leisure, or how they function along with other elements of the social order.

In our schools, and especially in schools of religion, attention should be given to the study of the Negro as he developed during the antebellum period by showing to what extent that remote culture was determined by ideas which the Negro brought with him from Africa. To take it for granted that the antebellum Negro was an ignoramus or that the native brought from Africa had not a valuable culture merely because some prejudiced writers have said so does not show the attitude of scholarship, and Negro students who direct their courses accordingly will never be able to grapple with the social problems presented today by the Negro church.

The preachers of today must learn to do as well as those of old. Richard Allen so interpreted Christianity anew to his master that he was converted, and so did Henry Evans and George Bentley for other whites in North Carolina and Tennessee. Instead of accepting and trying to carry out the theories which the exploiters of humanity have brought them for a religious program the Negroes should forget their differences and in the strength of a united church bring out a new interpretation of Christ to this unwilling world. Following the religious teachings of their traducers, the Negroes do not show any more common sense than a people would in permitting criminals to enact the laws and establish the procedure of the courts by which they are to be tried.

Negro preachers, too, must be educated to their people rather than away from them. This, of course, requires a new type of religious school. To provide for such training the Negro church must get rid of its burdensome supervisory force. If the number of bishops of the various Negro Methodist churches were reduced to about twelve or fifteen, as they should be, the amount of a hundred thousand dollars or more now being paid to support the unnecessary number could be used to maintain properly at least one accredited college; and what is now being raised here and there to support various struggling but starving institutions kept alive by ambitious bishops and preachers could be saved to the people. With this money diverted to a more practical use the race would be able to establish some other things which would serve as assets rather than as liabilities.

We say liabilities, for practically all of our denominational schools which are bleeding the people for the inadequate support which they receive are still unable to do accredited work. There are so many of them that the one impoverishes the other. Outstanding men of the church, therefore, have to acquire their advanced education by attending other schools in the beginning or by taking additional training elsewhere after learning all our denominational schools can offer. This is a loss of ground which should be regained if the church is to go forward.

By proper unification and organization the Negro churches might support one or two much needed universities of their own. With the present arrangement of two or three in the same area and sometimes as many in one city there is no chance for emerging from the trying poverty-stricken state. And even if

The New Program

these institutions could do well what they undertake they do not supply all educational needs. To qualify for certification in the professions Negroes must go to other schools, where, although they acquire the fundamentals, they learn much about their "inferiority" to discourage them in their struggle upward.

We should not close any accredited Negro colleges or universities, but we should reconstruct the whole system. We should not eliminate many of the courses now being offered, but we should secure men of vision to give them from the point of view of the people to be served. We should not spend less money for the higher education of the Negro, but should redefine higher education as preparation to think and work out a program to serve the lowly rather than to live as an aristocrat.

Such subjects of certitude as mathematics, of course, would continue and so would most of the work in practical languages and science. In theology, literature, social science, and education, however, radical reconstruction is necessary. The old worn-out theories as to man's relation to God and his fellowman, the system of thought which has permitted one man to exploit, oppress, and exterminate another and still be regarded as righteous must be discarded for the new thought of men as brethren and the idea of God as the lover of all mankind.

After Negro students have mastered the fundamentals of English, the principles of composition, and the leading facts in the development of its literature, they should not spend all of their time in advanced work on Shakespeare, Chaucer and Anglo-Saxon. They should direct their attention also to the folklore of the African, to the philosophy in his proverbs, to the development of the Negro in the use of modern language, and to the works of Negro writers.

The leading facts of the history of the world should be studied by all, but of what advantage is it to the Negro student of history to devote all of his time to courses bearing on such despots as Alexander the Great, Caesar, and Napoleon, or to the record of those nations whose outstanding achievement has been rapine, plunder, and murder for world power? Why not study the African background from the point of view of anthropology and history, and then take up sociology as it concerns the Negro peasant or proletarian who is suffering from sufficient ills to supply laboratory work for the most advanced students of the social order? Why not take up economics as reflected by the Negroes of today and work out some remedy for their lack of capital, the absence of cooperative enterprise, and the short life of their establishments. Institutions like Harvard, Yale and Columbia are not going to do these things, and educators influenced by them to the extent that they become blind to the Negro will never serve the race efficiently.

To educate the Negro we must find out exactly what his background is, what he is today, what his possibilities are, and how to begin with him as he is and make him a better individual of the kind that he is. Instead of cramming the Negro's mind with what others have shown that they can do, we should develop his latent powers that he may perform in society a part of which others are not capable.

During his life the author has seen striking examples of how people should and should not be taught. Some of these are worth relating. Probably the most interesting was that of missionary work in China. In 1903 the author crossed the Pacific Ocean with twenty-six missionaries who were going to take the Orient by storm. One Todd, from North Carolina, was orating and preaching almost every day to stimulate his coworkers to go boldly to the task before them. Dr.

De Forest, long a missionary to Japan, informed them that the work required more than enthusiasm; that they could not rush into the homes of the natives saying, "Peace be to this house." for it might turn out the other way and give somebody the opportunity to say, "Peace be to his ashes."

Dr. De Forest explained to them how he chose a decidedly different course, preferring first to study the history, the language, the manners and the customs of the people to approach them intelligently; and not until he had been in the country four years did he undertake to exhort, but after that time he had had great success and had been invited to preach before the Mikado himself. Now Todd did not take this advice, and he had not been in China five months before he and his wife had been poisoned by their native cook who had become incensed at the way they interfered with the institutions of his people.

Another striking illustration was the education of the Filipinos. Not long after the close of the Spanish-American War the United States Government started out to educate the Filipinos over night. Numbers of "highly trained" Americans were carried there to do the work They entered upon their task by teaching the Filipinos just as they had taught American children who were otherwise circumstanced. The result was failure. Men trained at institutions like Harvard, Yale, Columbia, and Chicago could not reach these people and had to be dismissed from the service. Some of these "scholarly" Americans had to be maintained by the subscription of friends until they could be returned to this country on Government transportation.

In the meantime, however, there came along an insurance man, who went to the Philippines to engage in business. He had never taught at all, and he had never studied authorities like Bagley, Judd, and Thorndike; but he understood people Seeing that others had failed, he went into the work himself. He filled the schoolroom with thousands of objects from the pupil's environment. In the beginning he did not use books very much, because those supplied were not adapted to the needs of the children. He talked about the objects around them. Everything was presented objectively. When he took up the habits of the snake he brought the reptile to the school for demonstration. When he taught the crocodile he had one there. In teaching the Filipinos music he did not sing "Come shake the Apple-Tree." They had never seen such an object. He taught them to sing "Come shake the Lomboy Tree," something which they had actually done. In reading he did not concentrate on the story of how George Washington always told the truth. They had never heard of him and could not have appreciated that myth if some one had told them about it. This real educator taught them about their own hero, José Rizal, who gave his life as a martyr for the freedom of his country. By and by they got rid of most books based on the life of American people and worked out an entirely new series dealing with the life of Filipinos. The result, then, was that this man and others who saw the situation as he did succeeded, and the work of the public schools in the Philippines is today the outstanding achievement of the Americans in that country.

We do not mean to suggest here, however, that any people should ignore the record of the progress of other races. We would not advocate any such unwise course. We say, hold on to the real facts of history as they are, but complete such knowledge by studying also the history of races and nations which have been purposely ignored. We should not underrate the achievements of Mesopotamia, Greece, and Rome; but we should give equally as much attention to the internal African kingdoms, the Songhay empire, and Ethiopia, which through Egypt decidedly influenced the civilization of the Mediterranean world. We would not ignore the rise of Christianity and the development of the Church; but we would at the same time give honorable mention to the persons of African blood who figured in these achievements, and who today are endeavoring to carry out the principles of Jesus long since repudiated by most so-called Christians. We would not underestimate the achievements of the captains of industry who in the commercial expansion of the modern world have produced the wealth necessary to ease and comfort; but we would give credit to the Negro who so largely supplied the demand for labor by which these things have been accomplished.

In our own particular history we would not dim one bit the luster of any star in our firmament. We would not learn less of George Washington, "First in War, First in Peace and First in the Hearts of his Countrymen"; but we would learn something also of the three thousand Negro soldiers of the American Revolution who helped to make this "Father of our Country" possible. We would not neglect to appreciate the unusual contribution of Thomas Jefferson to freedom and democracy; but we would invite attention also to two of his outstanding contemporaries, Phillis Wheatley, the writer of interesting verse, and Benjamin Banneker, the mathematician, astronomer, and advocate of a world peace plan set forth in 1793 with the vital principles of Woodrow Wilson's League of Nations. We would in no way detract from the fame of Perry on Lake Erie or Jackson at New Orleans in the second struggle with England; but we would remember the gallant black men who assisted in winning these memorable victories on land and sea. We would not cease to pay tribute to Abraham Lincoln as the "Savior of the Country"; but we would ascribe praise also to the one hundred and seventy-eight thousand Negroes who had to be mustered into the service of the Union before it could be preserved, and who by their heroism demonstrated that they were entitled to freedom and citizenship.

Chapter 15

Vocational Guidance

BUT how can the Negro in this new system learn to make a living, the most important task to which all people must give attention? In view of the Negro's economic plight most of the schools are now worked up over what is called "vocational guidance" in an effort to answer this very question. To what, however, are they to guide their Negro students? Most Negroes now employed are going down blind alleys, and unfortunately some schools seem to do no more than to stimulate their going in that direction.

This may seem to be a rash statement, but a study of our educational system shows that our schools are daily teaching Negroes what they can never apply in life or what is no longer profitable because of the revolution of industry by the multiplication of mechanical appliances. For example, some of our schools are still teaching individual garment making which offers no future today except in catering to the privileged and rich classes. Some of these institutions still offer instruction in shoemaking when the technique developed under their handicaps makes impossible competition with that of the modern factory based upon the invention of a Negro, Jan Matzeliger.

These facts have been known for generations, but some of these institutions apparently change not. Education, like religion, is conservative. It makes haste slowly only, and sometimes not at all. Do not change the present order of thinking and doing, many say, for you disturb too many things long since regarded as ideal. The dead past, according to this view, must be the main factor in determining the future. We should learn from the living past, but let the dead past remain dead.

A survey of employment of the Negroes in this country shows a most undesirable situation The education of the masses has not enabled them to advance very far in making a living and has not developed in the Negro the power to change this condition. It is revealed that in many establishments the Negro when a young man starts as a janitor or porter and dies in old age in the same position. Tradition fixes his status as such, and both races feel satisfied.

When this janitor or porter dies the dailies headline the passing of this Negro who knew his place and rendered satisfactory service in it. "Distinguished" white men, for whom he ran errands and cleaned cuspidors, volunteer as honorary pall-bearers and follow his remains to the final resting place. Thoughtless Negro editors, instead of expressing their regret that such a life of usefulness was not rewarded by promotion, take up the refrain as some great honor bestowed upon the race.

Among people thus satisfied in the lower pursuits of life and sending their children to school to memorize theories which they never see applied, there can be no such thing as vocational guidance. Such an effort implies an objective; and in the present plight of economic dependence there is no occupation for which the Negro may prepare himself with the assurance that he will find

Vocational Guidance

employment. Opportunities which he has today may be taken from him tomorrow; and schools changing their curricula in hit-and-miss fashion may soon find themselves on the wrong track just as they have been for generations.

Negroes do not need some one to guide them to what persons of another race have developed. They must be taught to think and develop something for themselves. It is most pathetic to see Negroes begging others for a chance as we have been doing recently. "Do not force us into starvation." we said. "Let us come into your stores and factories and do a part of what you are doing to profit by our trade." The Negro as a slave developed this fatal sort of dependency; and, restricted mainly to menial service and drudgery during nominal freedom, he has not grown out of it. Now the Negro is facing the ordeal of either learning to do for himself or to die out gradually in the bread line in the ghetto.

If the schools really mean to take a part in necessary uplift they must first supply themselves with teachers. Unfortunately we have very few such workers. The large majority of persons supposedly teaching Negroes never carry to the schoolroom any thought as to improving their condition. From the point of view of these so-called teachers they have done their duty when in automaton fashion they impart in the schoolroom the particular facts which they wrote out in the examination when they "qualified" for their respective positions. Most of them are satisfied with receiving their pay and spending it for the toys and gewgaws of life.

For example, the author is well acquainted with a Negro of this type, who is now serving as the head of one of the largest schools in the United States. From the point of view of our present system he is well educated. He holds advanced degrees from one of the leading institutions of the world; and he is known to be well informed on all the educational theories developed from the time of Socrates down to the day of Dewey. Yet this "educator" says repeatedly that in his daily operations he never has anything to do with Negroes because they are impossible. He says that he never buys anything from a Negro store, and he would not dare to put a penny in a Negro bank.

From such teachers large numbers of Negroes learn this fateful lesson. For example, not long ago a committee of Negroes in a large city went to the owner of a chain store in their neighborhood and requested that he put a Negro manager in charge. This man replied that he doubted that the Negroes themselves wanted such a thing. The Negroes urging him to make the change assured him that they were unanimously in favor of it. The manager, however, asked them to be fair enough with his firm and themselves to investigate before pressing the matter any further. They did so and discovered that one hundred thirty-seven Negro families in that neighborhood seriously objected to buying from Negroes and using articles handled by them. These Negroes, then, had to do the groundwork of uprooting the inferiority idea which had resulted from their mis-education.

To what, then, can a Negro while despising the enterprise of his fellows guide the youth of his race; and where do you figure out that the youth thus guided will be by 1950? The whites are daily informing Negroes that they need not come to them for opportunities. Can the Negro youth, mis-educated by persons who depreciate their efforts, learn to make, opportunities for themselves? This is the real problem which the Negroes must solve; and he who is not interested in it and makes no effort to solve it is worthless in the present struggle.

Our advanced teachers, like "most highly educated" Negroes, pay little attention to the things about them except when the shoe begins to pinch on one or the other side. Unless they happen to become naked they never think of the production of cotton or wool; unless they get hungry they never give any thought to the output of wheat or corn; unless their friends lose their jobs they never inquire about the outlook for coal or steel, or how these things affect the children whom they are trying to teach. In other words, they live in a world, but they are not of it. How can such persons guide the youth without knowing how these things affect the Negro community?

The Negro community, in a sense, is composed of those around you, but it functions in a different way. You cannot see it by merely looking out of the windows of the schoolroom. This community requires scientific investigation. While persons of African blood are compelled to sustain closer relation to their own people than to other elements in society, they are otherwise influenced socially and economically. The Negro community suffers for lack of delimitation because of the various ramifications of life in the United States. For example, there may be a Negro grocer in the neighborhood, but the Negro chauffeur for a rich man down town and the washerwoman for an aristocratic family in "quality row" will be more than apt to buy their food and clothing at the larger establishment with which their employers have connections, although they may be insulted there. Negroes of the District of Columbia have millions of dollars deposited in banks down town, where Negro women are not allowed in the ladies' rest rooms.

Right in the heart of the highly educated Negro section of Washington, too, is a restaurant catering through the front door exclusively to the white business men, who must live in the Negroes' section to supply them with the necessities of life, and catering at the same time through the back door to numbers of Negroes who pile into that dingy room to purchase whatever may be thrown at them. Yet less than two blocks away are several Negroes running cafés where they can be served for the same amount and under desirable circumstances. Negroes who do this, we say, do not have the proper attitude toward life and its problems, and for that reason we do not take up time with them. They do not belong to our community. The traducers of the race, however, are guiding these people the wrong way. Why do not the "educated" Negroes change their course by identifying themselves with the masses?

For similar reasons the Negro professional man may not always have a beautiful home and a fine car. His plight to the contrary may result from action like that of a poor man who recently knocked on the author's door about midnight to use his telephone to call the ambulance of the Casualty Hospital to take immediate charge of his sick wife. Although living nearer to the Freedmen's Hospital, where more sympathetic consideration would have been given this patient, he preferred to take her to the other hospital where she would have to be carried through the back yard and placed in a room over a stable. He worked there, however; and because of long association with his traducers and the sort of treatment that they have meted out to him he was willing to entrust to their hands the very delicate matter of the health of his wife. This was a part of his community.

Large numbers of Negroes live in such a community. You say that such an atmosphere is not congenial and you will not lose time with these people who are thus satisfied, but the exploiting preacher, the unprincipled politician, the notorious gambler, and the agent of vice are all there purposely misleading these

Vocational Guidance

people who have not as yet shaken from their minds the shackles of slavery. What is going to become of them? What is going to become of you?

We avoid them because we find enjoyment among others; but they are developing their own community. Their teacher lives in another community which may or may not be growing. Will his community so expand as to include theirs? If not, their community may encroach upon his. It is a sort of social dualism. What will the end be? The teacher will help to answer this question.

Such guidance, however, must not be restricted to the so-called common people. So many Negroes now engaged in business have no knowledge of its possibilities and limitations. Most of them are as unwise as a Negro business man who came to Washington recently in a ten-thousand-dollar car representing a firm with only one hundred thousand dollars invested. It is only a matter of time before his firm will be no more. He started out destroying his business at the very source. While Negroes are thus spending their means and themselves in riotous living the foreigners come to dwell among them in modest circumstances long enough to get rich and to join those who close in on these unfortunates economically until all the hopes for their redemption are lost.

If the Negroes of this country are to escape starvation and rise out of poverty unto comfort and ease, they must change their way of thinking and living. Never did the author see a more striking demonstration of such a necessity than recently when a young man came to him looking for a job. He was well bedecked with jewelry and fine clothes, and while he was in the office he smoked almost enough cigars to pay one's board for that day. A man of this type in a poverty-stricken group must suffer and die.

A young woman recently displaced in a position from which she received considerable income for a number of years approached the author not long ago to help her solve the problem of making a living. He could not feel very sympathetic toward her, however, for she had on a coat which cost enough to maintain one comfortably for at least two years. While talking with him, moreover, she was so busy telling him about what she wanted that she had little time to inform him as to what she can do to supply her needs.

A man whom the author knows is decidedly handicapped by having lost a lucrative position. He must now work for a little more than half of what he has been accustomed to earn. With his former stipend he was able to maintain two or three girls in addition to his wife, and he drank the best of bootleg stuff available. In now trying to do all of these things on a small wage he finds himself following a most tortuous course to make his ends meet, and he suffers within as well as without.

This undesirable attitude toward life results from the fact that the Negro has learned from others how to spend money much more rapidly than he has learned how to earn it. During these days, therefore, it will be very wise for Negroes to concentrate on the wise use of money and the evil results from the misuse of it. In large cities like Washington, Baltimore, Philadelphia, New York, and Chicago they earn millions and millions every year and throw these vast sums immediately away for trifles which undermine their health, vitiate their morals, and contribute to the undoing of generations of Negroes unborn.

This enlightenment as to economic possibilities in the Negro community must not only include instruction as to how enterprises can be made possible but how they should be apportioned among the various parts of the Negro community. Such knowledge is especially necessary in the case of Negroes because of the fatal tendency toward imitation not only of the white man but the imitation of others in his own group. For example, a Negro starts a restaurant on a corner and does well. Another Negro, observing this prosperity, thinks that he can do just as well by opening a similar establishment next door. The inevitable result is that by dividing the trade between himself and his forerunner he makes it impossible for either one to secure sufficient patronage to continue in business.

In undertakings of great importance this same undesirable tendency toward duplication of effort is also apparent. It has been a common thing to find two or three banks in a Negro community, each one struggling for an existence in competing for the patronage of the small group of people, all of whom would hardly be able to support one such financial institution. These banks continue their unprofitable competition and never think of merging until some crisis forces them to the point that they have to do so or go into bankruptcy. The Negro community, then, never has a strong financial institution with sufficient resources to stimulate the efforts of the business men who otherwise might succeed.

The same shortsightedness has been evident in, the case of the insurance companies organized by Negroes. One was established here and then another followed there in imitation of the first. We have been accustomed to boast that the Negroes have about fifty insurance companies in this country, marking the corners of the streets of the cities with large signs displaying what they are doing for the race. Instead of boasting of such unwise expansion we should have received such information with sorrow, for what the race actually needs is to merge all of the insurance companies now supported by Negroes and make one good one. Such a step away from duplication would be a long stride toward our much needed awakening, and it would certainly give us prestige in the business world.

This imitation and duplication are decidedly disastrous to economic enterprise as we can daily observe. A few days ago a young man in the East lamented the fact that after investing his life's earnings in the drug business and making every effort to stimulate the enterprise, he has failed. Some one took occasion, thereupon, to remind him that men have grown rich, as a rule, not by doing what thousands of others are doing but by undertaking something new. If instead of going into the retail dispensing of drugs, he had conceived and carried out the idea of the chain-drug store, he would have become an independently rich man.

There is always a chance to do this because the large majority of people do not think and, therefore, leave the field wide open for those who have something new with which to please the public. Negroes even found this possible during the days of slavery when the race supposedly had no chance at all.

About a hundred years ago Thomas Day, a North Carolina Negro, realized that the rough furniture of the people in his community did not meet the requirements of those of modern taste. He, therefore, worked out a style of ornate and beautiful furniture which attracted the attention of the most aristocratic people of the state and built up for himself a most successful business. Persons in that state are still talking about the Day furniture, and not long ago it became the subject of a magazine article. If North Carolina would turn out more Negroes of this type today, instead of the rather large number who are going to teach and preach, some of its present economic problems might thereby be solved.

During these same years another Negro was showing himself to be equally ingenious. This was Henry Boyd. After buying himself in Kentucky, he went to Cincinnati to start life as a free man. There he encountered so much prejudice against Negro labor that he could not find employment at his trade of cabinet-making. A new thought came to him, however; and in this way he solved his own problem.

Boyd became convinced that people had been sleeping long enough on straw ticks and wooden slats, and he invented the corded bed, the most comfortable bed prior to the use of springs which brought still more ease. Boyd's corded bed became popular throughout the Ohio and Mississippi Valleys, and he built up a profitable trade which required the employment of twenty-five white and black artisans. Other enterprising Negro business men like Boyd gave the Negro element of Cincinnati more of an aspect of progress before the Civil War than it has today. Has the Negro less chance today than he had a century ago?

For about thirty years the author knew an old Negro lady at Gordonsville, Virginia, who gave the world something new in frying chicken. She discovered the art of doing this thing in the way that others could not, and she made a good living selling her exceptionally prepared chicken and fried puffs at the windows of the cars when the trains stopped at the station. Well-to-do men and women of both races would leave the Pullman train with its modern diner attached and go out and supply themselves and their friends with this old lady's tastefully made up lunches.

Another woman of color living in Columbia, Missouri, recently gave the world another new idea. She had learned cooking, especially baking, but saw no exceptional opportunity in the usual application of the trade. After studying her situation and the environment in which she had to live, she hit upon the scheme of popularizing her savorous sweet potato biscuits, beaten whiter than all others by an invention of her own; and the people of both races made a well-beaten path to her home to enjoy these delicious biscuits. In this way she has made herself and her relatives independent.

This is the way fortunes are made, but Negroes, who are conscientiously doing their best to rise in the economic sphere, do not follow the noble examples of those who had less opportunity than we have today. We spend much time in slavish imitation, but our white friends strike out along new lines. Almost all of the large fortunes in America have been made in this way.

John D. Rockefeller did not set out in life to imitate Vanderbilt. Rockefeller saw his opportunity in developing the oil industry. Carnegie had better sense than to imitate Rockefeller, for that task was already well done, and he consolidated the steel interests. Henry Ford knew better than to take up what Carnegie had exploited, for there appeared a still larger possibility for industrial achievement in giving the world the facility of cheap transportation in the low-priced car.

While such guidance as the Negro needs will concern itself first with material things, however, it must not stop with these as ends in themselves. In the acquisition of these we lay the foundation for the greater things of the spirit. A poor man properly directed can write a more beautiful poem than one who is surfeited. The man in the hovel composes a more charming song than the one in the palace. The painter in the ghetto gets an inspiration for a more striking portrait than his landlord can appreciate. The ill-fed sculptor lives more abundantly than the millionaire who purchases the expression of his thought in marble and bronze. For the Negro, then, the door of opportunity is wide open. Let him prepare himself to enter this field where competition is no handicap. In such a sphere he may learn to lead the world, while keeping pace with it in the development of the material things of life.

Chapter 16
The New Type of Professional Man Required

NEGROES should study for the professions for all sane reasons that members of another race should go into these lines of endeavor and also on account of the particular call to serve the lowly of their race. In the case of the law we should cease to make exceptions because of the possibilities for failure resulting from prejudice against the Negro lawyer and thE lack of Negro business enterprises to require his services Negroes must become like English gentlemen who study the law of the land, not because they intend to practice the profession, but because every gentleman should know the law. In the interpretation of the law by the courts, too, all the rights of the Negroes in this country are involved, and a larger number of us must qualify for this important service. We may have too many lawyers of the wrong kind, but we have not our share of the right kind.

The Negro lawyer has tended to follow in the footsteps of the average white practitioner and has not developed the power which he could acquire if he knew more about the people whom he should serve and the problems they have to confront. These things are not law in themselves, but they determine largely whether or not the Negro will practice law and the success he will hare in the profession. The failure to give attention to these things has often meant the downfall of many a Negro lawyer.

There are, moreover, certain aspects of law to which the white man would hardly address himself but to which the Negro should direct special attention. Of unusual importance to the Negro is the necessity for understanding the misrepresentations in criminal records of Negroes, and race distinctions in the laws of modern nations. These matters require a systematic study of the principles of law and legal procedure and, in addition thereto, further study of legal problems as they meet the Negro lawyer in the life which he must live. This offers the Negro law school an unusual opportunity.

Because our lawyers do not give attention to these problems they often fail in a crisis. They are interested in the race and want to defend its cause. The case, however, requires not only the unselfish spirit they sometimes manifest but much more understanding of the legal principles, involved. Nothing illustrates this better than the failure of one of our attorneys to measure up in the case brought up to the United States Supreme Court from Oklahoma to test the validity of the exclusion of Negroes from Pullman cars. The same criticism may be made of the segregation case of the District of Columbia brought before this highest tribunal by another Negro attorney. In both of these cases the lawyers started wrong and therefore ended wrong. They lacked the knowledge to present their cases properly to the court.

Our lawyers must learn that the judges are not attorneys themselves, for they have to decide on the merits of what is presented to them. It is not the business of the judges to amend their pleadings or decide their cases according to their good intentions. Certainly such generosity cannot be expected from prejudiced courts which are looking for every loophole possible to escape from a frank decision on the rights of Negroes guaranteed by the constitution. These matters require advanced study and painstaking research; but our lawyers, as a rule, are not interested in this sort of mental exercise.

The Negro medical schools have had a much better opportunity than the few Negro law schools which have functioned in the professional preparation of Negroes. On account of the racial contact required of white physicians who are sometimes unwilling to sustain this relation to Negroes the Negro physicians and dentists have a better chance among their people than the Negro lawyers; and the demand for the services of the former assures a larger income than Negro lawyers are accustomed to earn. But in spite of this better opportunity Negro medical institutions and their graduates have done little more than others to solve the peculiar problems confronting the Negro race

Too many Negroes go into medicine and dentistry merely for selfish purposes, hoping thereby to increase their income and spend it in joyous living. They have the ambition to own fine automobiles, to dress handsomely, and to figure conspicuously in society. The practice of these professions among poor Negroes yields these results. Why not be a physician or dentist then?

Too many of our physicians are like the one whom the author recently visited in New York City. "When I heard you coming up the stairs," said he, "I began to feel glad, for I was sure that you were another patient from whom I might extract at least two dollars for a prescription."

Yet one would wonder how that physician could prosper in his profession, for he had no special equipment for the practice of any kind of advanced phases of medicine. About all he could do was to look at the patient's tongue, feel his pulse, ask him a few questions, write a prescription and collect the fee. The apparatus required for the modern treatment of serious maladies he did not have and seemed to have no ambition to possess.

The Negroes of today are very much in need of physicians who in their professional work will live up to what they are taught in school, and will build upon their foundation by both experience and further training. In his segregated position in the ghetto the Negro health problem presents more difficulties than that of the whites who are otherwise circumstanced. The longevity of the Negro depends in part upon the supply of Negro physicians and nurses who will address themselves unselfishly to the solution of this particular problem. Since the Negroes are forced into undesirable situations and compelled to inhabit germ-infested districts, they cannot escape ultimate extermination if our physicians do not help them to work out a community health program which will provide for the Negroes some way to survive.

Negro medical schools and their graduates must do more preaching of the necessity for improving conditions which determine health and eradicate disease. A large number of physicians and nurses must be trained, and new opportunities for them to practice must be found This can be done by turning out better products from these schools and the extension of hospitals among Negroes who have been so long neglected In this campaign, however, the Negro physicians must supply the leadership, and others must join with them in these efforts.

From medical schools, too, we must have Negroes with a program of medical research. Today the world is inclined to give attention to the health of the Negro since unsanitary conditions of the race will mean the lose of health among the whites. Philanthropists, however, hardly know how to proceed or which way to go because they have so long neglected the Negroes that they do not know how to provide wisely for them; and the Negro physicians themselves have failed to give adequate attention to these conditions. Negro medical students have not directed sufficient attention to the ante-bellum background of the Negro who, still under that influence, indulges in superstitious and religious practices which impede the progress of medicine among them. One would be surprised to know the extent to which primitive medicine is practiced Among American Negroes today. Often in the rural districts they seldom see a physician. The midwife and the herb doctor there control the situation.

The greatest problem now awaiting solution is the investigation of the differential resistance of races to disease. What are the diseases of which Negroes are more susceptible than whites? What are the diseases of which the whites are more susceptible than Negroes? The Negro escapes yellow fever and influenza, but the white man dies. The white man withstands syphilis and tuberculosis fairly well, but the Negro afflicted with these maladies easily succumbs. These questions offer an inviting field of research for Negro medical students.

While we hear much about medicine, law and the like their importance must not be unduly emphasized. Certainly men should not crowd into these spheres to make money, but all professions among Negroes except those of teaching and preaching are undermanned. All Negroes in professions constitute less than two and a half per cent of those over ten years of age who are gainfully employed. At the same time the whites find certain of their professions overcrowded, and some of their practitioners could not exist without the patronage of Negroes.

Negroes, too, should undergo systematic training for those professions in which they have shown special aptitude as in the arts. They must not wait for the Americans to approve their plunging into unknown spheres. The world is not circumscribed by the United States, and the Negro must become a pioneer in making use of a larger portion of the universe. If the people here do recognize the Negro in these spheres let him seek a hearing in the liberal circles of Europe. If he has any art Europeans will appreciate it and assure him success in forbidden fields

In Europe, it should be noted, the Negro artist is not wanted as a mere imitator Europeans will recognize him in the role of an enlightened artist portraying the life of his people. As an English abolitionist said more than a century ago, "The portrait of the Negro has seldom been drawn but by the pencil of his oppressor and the Negro has sat for it in the distorted attitude of slavery." A new method of approach, however, is now possible. There has been an awakening in Europe to the realization of the significance of African culture, and circles there want to see that life depicted by the Negro who can view it from within. There is a philosophy in it that the world must understand. From its contemplation may come a new social program Herein lies the opportunity of the Negro artist as a world reformer. Will he see it and live or continue the mere imitation of others and die?

Chapter 17
Higher Strivings in the Service of the Country

ANOTHER factor the Negro needs is a new figure in politics, one who will not concern himself so much with what others can do for him as with what he can do for himself. He will know sufficient about the system of government not to carry his trouble to the federal functionaries and thus confess himself a failure in the community in which he lives. He will know that his freedom from peonage and lynching will be determined by the extent that he can develop into a worthy citizen and impress himself upon his community.

The New Negro in politics will not be so unwise as to join the ignorant delegations from conferences and convention which stage annual pilgrimages to the White House to complain to the President because they have socially and economically failed to measure up to demands of self-preservation. The New Negro in politics will understand clearly that in the final analysis federal functionaries cannot do anything about these matters within the police powers of the states, and he will not put himself in the position of being received with coldness and treated with contempt as these ignorant misleaders of the Negro race have been from time immemorial. The New Negro in politics, then, will appeal to his own and to such friends of other races in his locality as believe in social justice. If he does something for himself others will do more for him.

The increasing vigor of the race, then, will not be frittered away in partisan strife in the interest of the oppressors of the race. It ought not to be possible for the political bosses to induce almost any Negro in the community to abandon his permanent employment to assist them and their ilk in carrying out some program for the selfish purposes of the ones engineering the scheme. It ought not to be possible for the politicians to distribute funds at the rate of fifty or a hundred dollars a head among the outstanding ministers and use them and their congregations in vicious partisan strife. It is most shameful that some ministers resort to religion as a camouflage to gain influence in the churches only to use such power for selfish political purpose.

The Negro should endeavor to be a figure in politics, not a tool for the politicians. This higher rôle can be played not by parking all of the votes of a race on one side of the fence as both blacks and whites have done in the South, but by independent action. The Negro should not censure the Republican party for forgetting him and he should not blame the Democratic party for opposing him. Neither can the South blame any one but itself for its isolation in national politics. Any people who will vote the same way for three generations without thereby obtaining results ought to be ignored and disfranchised.

As a minority element the Negro should not knock at the door of any particular political party. He should appeal to the Negroes themselves and from them should come harmony and concerted action for a new advance to that larger freedom of men. The Negro should use his vote rather than give it away to reward the dead for some favors done in the distant past. He should clamor not for the few offices earmarked as Negro jobs but for the recognition of these despised persons as men according to the provision of the Constitution of the United States.

The few state and national offices formerly set aside for Negroes have paled into insignificance when compared with the many highly lucrative positions now occupied by Negroes as a result of their development in other spheres. Sometimes a Negro prominent in education, business or professional life can earn more in a few months than the most successful politicians can earn in years. These political jobs, moreover, have diminished in recent years because the increase of race prejudice, which this policy has doubtless aided, supplies the political leaders with an excuse for not granting their Negro coworkers anything additional.

The New Negro in politics must learn something that the old "ward-heelers" have never been able to realize, namely, not only that the few offices allotted Negroes are insignificant but that even if the Negro received a proportionate share of the spoils, the race cannot hope to solve any serious problem by the changing fortunes of politics. Real politics, the science of government, is deeply rooted in the economic foundation of the social order. To figure greatly in politics the Negro must be a great figure in politics. A class of people slightly lifted above poverty, therefore, can never have much influence in political circles. The Negro must develop character and worth to make him a desirable everywhere so that he will not have to knock at the doors of political parties but will have them thrown open to him.

The New Negro in politics must not ask the party for money, he must not hire himself for a pittance to swing voters in line. He must contribute to the campaign of the party pleasing him, rather than draw upon it for an allowance to drive the wolf from the door during the three months of the political canvass. It will be considered a stroke of good fortune that a Negro of such influence and character has aligned himself with a party, and this fact will speak eloquently for the element to which he belongs.

The New Negro in politics, moreover, must not be a politician. He must be a man. He must try to give the world something rather than extract something from it. The world, as he should see it, does not owe him anything, certainly not a political office; and he should not try solely to secure one, and thus waste valuable years which might be devoted to the development of something of an enduring value. If he goes into office, it should be as a sacrifice, because his valuable time is required elsewhere. If he is needed by his country in a civil position, he may respond to the call as a matter of duty, for his usefulness is otherwise assured. From such a Negro, then, we may expect sound advice, intelligent guidance, and constructive effort fort the good of all elements of our population

When such Negroes go into office you will not find them specializing in things which peculiarly concern the Negroes, offering merely antilynching bills and measures for pensioning the freedmen. The New Negro in politics will see his opportunity not in thus restricting himself but in visioning the whole social and economic order with his race as a part of it. In thus working for the benefit of all as prompted by his liberal mindedness the New Negro will do much more to bring the elements together for common good than he will be able to do in prating only of the ills of his particular corner and extending his hand for a douceur.

Higher Strivings in the Service of Country

In suggesting herein the rise of the New Negro in politics the author does not have in mind the so-called radical Negroes who have read and misunderstood Karl Marx and his disciples and would solve the political as well as the economic problems of the race by an immediate application of these principles. History shows that although large numbers of people have actually tried to realize such pleasant dreams, they have in the final analysis come back to a social program based on competition. If no one is to enjoy the fruits of his exceptional labor any more than the individual who is not prepared to render such extraordinary service, not one of a thousand will be sufficiently humanitarian to bestir himself to achieve much of importance, and force applied in this case to stimulate such action has always broken down. If the excited whites who are bringing to the Negroes such strange doctrines are insane enough to believe them, the Negroes themselves should learn to think before it is too late

History shows that it does not matter who is in power or what revolutionary forces take over the government, those who have not learned to do for themselves and have to depend solely on others never obtain any more rights or privileges in the end than they had in the beginning. Even if the expected social upheaval comes, the Negro will be better prepared to take care of himself in the subsequent reconstruction if he develops the power to ascend to a position higher up after the radically democratic people will have recovered from their revelry in an impossible Utopia.

To say that the Negro cannot develop sufficiently in the business world to measure arms with present-day capitalists is to deny actual facts, refute history, and discredit the Negro as a capable competitor in the economic battle of life. No man knows what he can do until he tries. The Negro race has never tried to do very much for itself. The race has great possibilities. Properly awakened, the Negro can do the so-called impossible in the business world and thus help to govern rather than merely be governed.

In the failure to see this and the advocacy of the destruction of the whole economic order to right social wrong we see again the tendency of the Negro to look to some force from without to do for him what he must learn to do for himself. The Negro needs to become radical, and the race will never amount to anything until it does become so, but this radicalism should come from within. The Negro will be very foolish to resort to extreme measures in behalf of foreign movements before he learns to suffer and die to right his own wrongs. There is no movement in the world-working especially for the Negro. He must learn to do this for himself or be exterminated just as the American Indian has faced his doom in the setting sun.

Why should the Negro wait for some one from without to urge him to self-assertion when he sees himself robbed by his employer, defrauded by his merchant, and hushed up by government agents of injustice? Why wait for a spur to action when he finds his manhood insulted, his women outraged, and his fellowmen lynched for amusement? The Negroes have always had sufficient reason for being radical, and it looks silly to see them taking up the cause of others who pretend that they are interested in the Negro when they merely mean to use the race as a means to an end. When the desired purpose of these so-called friendly groups will have been served, they will have no further use for the Negro and will drop him just as the Republican machine has done

The radicals bring forward, too, the argument that the Negro, being of a minority group, will always be overpowered by others From the point of view of the selfish elements this may be true, and certainly it has worked thus for some time; but things do not always turn out according to mathematical calculations. In fact, the significant developments in history have never been thus determined. Only the temporary and the trivial can be thus forecast. The human factor is always difficult for the materialist to evaluate and the prophecies of the alarmist are often upset Why should we expect less in the case of the Negro?

Chapter 18

The Study of the Negro

The facts drawn from an experience of more than twenty years enable us to make certain deductions with respect to the study of the Negro. Only one Negro out of every ten thousand is interested in the effort to set forth what his race has thought and felt and attempted and accomplished that it may not become a negligible factor in the thought of the world By traditions and education, however, the large majority of Negroes have become interested in the history and status of other races, and they spend millions annually to promote such knowledge. Along with this sum, of course, should be considered the large amount paid for devices in trying not to be Negroes.

The chief reason why so many give such a little attention to the background of the Negro is the belief that this study is unimportant. They consider as history only such deeds as those of Mussolini who after building up an efficient war machine with the aid of other Europeans would now use it to murder unarmed and defenseless Africans who have restricted themselves exclusively to attending to their own business. If Mussolini succeeds in crushing Abyssinia he will be recorded in "history" among the Caesars, and volumes written in praise of the conqueror will find their way to the homes and libraries of thousands of miseducated Negroes. The oppressor has always indoctrinated the weak with this interpretation of the crimes of the strong.

The war lords have done good only accidentally or incidentally while seeking to do evil. The movements which have ameliorated the condition of humanity and stimulated progress have been inaugurated by men of thought in lifting their fellows out of drudgery unto ease and comfort, out of selfishness unto altruism. The Negro may well rejoice that his hands, unlike those of his oppressors, are not stained with so much blood extracted by brute force. Real history is not the record of the successes and disappointments, the vices, the follies, and the quarrels of those who engage in contention for power.

The Association for the Study of Negro Life and History is projected on the fact that there is nothing in the past of the Negro more shameful than what is found in the past of other races The Negro is as human as the other members of the family of mankind. The Negro, like others, has been up at times; and at times he has been down. With the domestication of animals, the discovery of iron, the development of stringed instruments, an advancement in fine art, and the inauguration of trial by jury to his credit, the Negro stands just as high as others in contributing to the progress of the world.

The oppressor, however, raises his voice to the contrary. He teaches the Negro that he has no worth-while past, that his race has done nothing significant since the beginning of time, and that there is no evidence that he will ever achieve anything great. The education of the Negro then must be carefully directed lest the race may waste time trying to do the impossible. Lead the Negro to believe this and thus control his thinking. If you can thereby determine what he will think, you will not need to worry about what he will do. You will not have to tell him to go to the back door. He will go without being told; and if there is no back door he will have one cut for his special benefit.

If you teach the Negro that he has accomplished as much good as any other race he will aspire to equality and justice without regard to race Such an effort would upset the program of the oppressor in Africa and America. Play up before the Negro, then, his crimes and shortcomings. Let him learn to admire the Hebrew, the Greek, the Latin and the Teuton. Lead the Negro to detest the man of African blood—to hate himself. The oppressor then may conquer exploit, oppress and even annihilate the Negro by segregation without fear or trembling. With the truth hidden there will be little expression of thought to the contrary.

The American Negro has taken over an abundance of information which others have made accessible to the oppressed, but he has not yet learned to think and plan for himself as others do for themselves. Well might this race be referred to as the most docile and tractable people on earth. This merely means that when the oppressors once start the large majority of the race in the direction of serving the purposes of their traducers, the task becomes so easy in the years following that they have little trouble with the masses thus controlled. It is a most satisfactory system, and it has become so popular that European nations of foresight are sending some of their brightest minds to the United States to observe the Negro in "inaction" in order to learn how to deal likewise with Negroes in their colonies. What the Negro in America has become satisfied with will be accepted as the measure of what should be allotted him elsewhere. Certain Europeans consider the "solution of the race problem in the United States" one of our great achievements.

The mis-educated Negro joins the opposition with the objection that the study of the Negro keeps alive questions which should be forgotten. The Negro should cease to remember that he was once held a slave, that he has been oppressed, and even that he is a Negro. The traducer, however, keeps before the public such aspects of this history as will justify the present oppression of the race. It would seem, then, that the Negro should emphasize at the same time the favorable aspects to justify action in his behalf. One cannot blame the Negro for not desiring to be reminded of being the sort of creature that the oppressor has represented the Negro to be; but this very attitude shows ignorance of the past and a slavish dependence upon the enemy to serve those whom he would destroy. The Negro can be made proud of his past only by approaching it scientifically himself and giving his own story to the world. What others have written about the Negro during the last three centuries has been mainly for the purpose of bringing him where he is today and holding him there.

The method employed by the Association for the Study of Negro Life and History, however, is not spectacular propaganda or fire-eating agitation. Nothing can be accomplished in such fashion. "Whom the gods would destroy they first make mad." The Negro, whether in Africa or America, must be directed toward a serious examination of the fundamentals of education, religion, literature, and philosophy as they have been expounded to him. He must be sufficiently enlightened to determine for himself whether these forces have come into his life to bless him or to bless his oppressor. After learning the facts in the case the Negro must develop the power of execution to deal with these matters as do people of vision. Problems of great importance cannot be worked out in a day. Questions of great moment must be met with far-reaching plans.

The Study of the Negro

The Association for the Study of Negro Life and History is teaching the Negro to exercise foresight rather than "hindsight." Liberia must not wait until she is offered to Germany before realizing that she has few friends in Europe. Abyssinia must not wait until she is invaded by Italy before she prepares for selfdefense. A scientific study of the past of modern nations would show these selfish tendencies as inevitable results from their policies in dealing with those whom they have professed to elevate. For example, much of Africa has been conquered and subjugated to save souls How expensive has been the Negro's salvation! One of the strong arguments for slavery was that it brought the Negro into the light of salvation. And yet the Negro today is all but lost.

The Association for the Study of Negro Life and History, however, has no special brand for the solution of the race problem except to learn to think. No general program of uplift for the Negroes in all parts of the world will be any more successful than such a procedure would be in the case of members of other races under different circumstances. What will help a Negro in Alabama may prove harmful to one in Maine. The African Negro may find his progress retarded by applying "methods used for the elevation of the Negro in America." A thinking man, however, learns to deal wisely with conditions as he finds them rather than to take orders from some one who knows nothing about his status and cares less. At present the Negro, both in Africa and America, is being turned first here and there experimentally by so-called friends who in the final analysis assist the Negro merely in remaining in the dark.

In the furtherance of the program of taking up these matters dispassionately the Association had made available an outline for the systematic study of the Negro as he has touched the life of others and as others have functioned in their relation to him, The African Background Outlined: A Handbook. This book is written from the point of view of history, literature, art, education, religion and economic imperialism. In seventeen chapters as Part I of the work a brief summary of the past in Africa is presented; and courses on "The Negro in Africa," "The Negro in the European Mind," "The Negro in America," "The Negro in Literature," "The Negro in Art," "The Education of the Negro," "The Religious Development of the Negro," and "Economic Imperialism," follow as Part II with ample bibliographical comment for every heading and subhead of these outlines. This facilitates the task of clubs, young peoples' societies, and special classes organized where the oppressors of the race and the Negroes cooperating with them are determined that the history and status of the Negro shall not be made a part of the curricula.

In this outline there is no animus, nothing to engender race hate. The Association does not bring out such publications. The aim of this organization is to set forth facts in scientific form, for facts properly set forth will tell their own story. No advantage can be gained by merely inflaming the Negro's mind against his traducers. In a manner they deserve to be congratulated for taking care of their own interests so well. The Negro needs to become angry with himself because he has not handled his own affairs wisely. In other words, the Negro must learn from others how to take care of himself in this trying ordeal. He must not remain content with taking over what others set aside for him and then come in the guise of friends to subject even that limited information to further misinterpretation.

Appendix

Much Ado About a Name

A PARTICIPANT who recently attended an historical meeting desired to take up the question as to what the race should be called. Africans, Negroes, colored people, or what? This is a matter of much concern to him because he hopes thereby to solve the race problem. If others will agree to call Negroes Nordics, he thinks, he will reach the desired end by taking a short cut.

This may sound all but insane, but there are a good many "highly educated" Negroes who believe that such can be accomplished by this shift in terminology; and they have spent time and energy in trying to effect a change. Many of this class suffer mentally because of the frequent use of "offensive expressions" in addressing Negroes. When dealing with them, then, one has to be very careful. For this reason our friends in other races have to seek guidance in approaching us. For example, Lady Simon, the wife of Sir John Simon of the British Cabinet, has recently asked an American Negro what his people prefer to be called, and later in England she took up the same matter with another member of this race. Being an advocate of freedom, she has written considerably to advance its cause. She would not like to use in her works, then, an expression which may hurt some one's feelings.

Although a student of social problems, this learned woman cannot fathom this peculiar psychology. Americans, too, must confess the difficulty of understanding it, unless it is that the "highly educated Negro mind" tends to concern itself with trifles rather than with the great problems of life. We have known Negroes to ask for a separate Y. M. C. A. or Y. W. C. A., a separate church or a separate school, and then object to calling the institution colored or Negro. These segregationists have compromised on principle, but they are unwilling to acknowledge their crime against justice. The name, they believe, will save them from the disgrace.

It does not matter so much what the thing is called as what the thing is. The Negro would not cease to be what he is by calling him something else; but, if he will struggle and make something of himself and contribute to modern culture, the world will learn to look upon him as an American rather than as one of an undeveloped element of the population.

The word Negro or black is used in referring to this particular element because most persons of native African descent approach this color. The term does not imply that every Negro is black; and the word white does not mean that every white man is actually white. Negroes may be colored, but many Caucasians are scientifically classified as colored. We are not all Africans, moreover, because many of us were not born in Africa; and we are not all Afro-Americans, because few of us are natives of Africa transplanted to America.

There is nothing to be gained by running away from the name. The names of practically all races and nations at times have connoted insignificance and low social status. Angles and Saxons, once the slaves of Romans, experienced this; and even the name of the Greek for a while meant no more than this to these conquerors of the world. The people who bore these names, however, have made them grand and illustrious. The Negro must learn to do the same.

It is strange, too, that while the Negro feels ashamed of his name, persons abroad do not usually think of it in this sense. One does find in Europe a number of West Indian and American Negroes of some Caucasian blood, who do not want to be known as Negroes. As a rule, however, a European of African Negro blood feels proud of this racial heritage and delights to be referred to as such. The writer saw a striking case of this in London in the granddaughter of a Zulu chief. She is so far removed from the African type that one could easily mistake her for a Spaniard; and yet she thinks only for her African connection and gets her inspiration mainly from the story of her people beyond the Pillars of Hercules.

The writer was agreeably surprised a few days later, too, when he met a prominent Parisian with the same attitude. He has produced several volumes in which he champions the cause of the Negro because he has in his veins the same blood. A well-to-do European woman, the daughter of a Dutchman and an African mother, is similarly enthusiastic over her Negro blood. The first thing she mentioned in conversing with the writer was that black mother. This young woman expressed the regret that she did not have more of that color that she, too, might say, as do members of certain tribes of Africa: "I am black and comely. I am black and beautiful. I am beautifully black."

These people surprise you when you think of the attitude of many American Negroes on this question. These race-conscious people can think, but it is seldom that the American Negro indulges in such an exercise. He has permitted other people to determine for him the attitude that he has toward his own people. This means the enslavement of his mind and eventually the enslavement of his body.

Some Europeans rather regard the word Negro as romantic. Going now along the streets of Paris, one will see advertised such places as "l'Elan Noir," and the "Café au Nègre de Toulouse." In one of these cases the writer was especially attracted by the "Choppe du Nègre" end took dinner there one day. The cuisine was excellent, the music rendered by the orchestra was charming, and a jolly crowd came to enjoy themselves. However, he was the only "Nègre" there.

Walking along a street in Geneva not long ago, the writer's attention was attracted to something of the sort, which is still more significant. It was a wholesale coffee house called "A La Case de l'Oncle Tom." He entered and asked: "Why did you give this store such a name?" The proprietress laughed and explained that her grandfather, François Prudhom, who had read "Uncle Tom's Cabin" and had been deeply impressed thereby, selected this name for the store when he established it in 1866.

The Value of Color

NOT long ago the writer saw on a street ear one of the prettiest women in the world. She was a perfectly black woman becomingly dressed in suitable gray and modest adornments which harmonized with her color. She was naturally a commanding figure without any effort to please others, for her bearing was such that she would not fail to attract attention. He could not restrain myself from gazing at her; and, looking around to see whether others were similarly concerned, he found the whites in the car admiring her also, even to the point of commenting among themselves.

This woman's common sense, manifested in knowing how to dress, had made her color an asset rather than a liability. The writer easily recalled, then, that tribe in Africa that feels unusually proud of being black. We are told that they are so anxious to be black that if they find one of the group with a tendency to depart the least from this color they go to the heart of nature and extract from it its darkest dye and paint therewith that native's face that he may continue perfectly black.

Here in America, however, we are ashamed of being black. So many of us who are actually black powder our faces and make ourselves blue. In so doing we become all but hideous by the slavish aping of those around us in keeping with our custom of imitation. We fail to take ourselves for what we are actually worth, and do not make the most of ourselves.

We show lack of taste in the selection of our dress. We long for what others wear whether it harmonizes with our color or not They have given particular attention to design with respect to their race and have written books to this effect. Thinking, however, that the Negro is not supposed to wear anything but what the poor may pick up, the artists have not thought seriously of him. Both teachers and students of nearby schools thus concerned, then, repeatedly appeal to us for help in the study of design with respect to the Negro, but we have nothing scientific to offer them. We have no staff of artists who can function in this sphere.

To be able to supply this need requires the most painstaking effort to understand colors and color schemes. It is a very difficult task because of the variation of color within the race. Sometimes in one family of ten you will hardly find two of the same shade. To dress them all alike may be economical, but the world thereby misses that much of beauty. The Negro mother, then, needs to be the real artist, and the schools now training the youth to be the parents of tomorrow should give as much attention to these things esthetic as they do to language, literature or mathematics.

In neglecting to know himself better from this point of view, then, the Negro is making a costly mistake. He should be deeply concerned with the esthetic possibilities of his situation. In this so-called Negro race we have the prettiest people in the world, when they dress in harmony with the many shades and

The Value of Color

colors with which we are so richly endowed. Why do we so away from home to find what we already have on hand?

Recently one saw in Washington a demonstration of the value of color when the Masonic conclave staged a tremendous parade in this national city. The whites were attracted to the upstanding, outstanding Negroes so becomingly bedecked in costumes of the Orient. This, however, was accidental. The color of the Negroes happened to be Oriental, and the colors of this order were originally worked out to suit the people of those parts. The dead white of the Caucasian does not harmonize with such garb. Why, then should the Negro worry about what others wear?

Carrying the imitation of others to an extreme today, we do not find ourselves far in advance of the oppressed antebellum Negroes, who, unable to dress themselves, had to take whatever others threw at them. We make a most hideous spectacle, then, when we are on dress parade in our social atmosphere. So many of us clad in unbecoming colors often look like decorated pet horses turned loose for an hour or so of freedom.

Appreciating the value of color, the artists in European cities are trying to change their hue to that of the colored people. They can understand how inexpressive the dead white is, and they are trying to make use of what we are seeking to conceal. The models in their shops are purposely colored to display to good effect the beautiful costumes which require color. Some of these Europeans frankly tell Negroes how they envy them for their color.

One is not surprised, then, to find European cafés and hotels employing American or African Negroes to supply this color which the Europeans lack. Pictures of such black men are sometimes displayed to great effect. That of Josephine Baker adorns the windows of large stores in Paris. Here in America, too, we observe that art centres are likewise getting away from the dead white to enjoy the richness of color.

The writer felt somewhat encouraged recently when he talked with a Washington lady who runs "The Pandora," a unique establishment devoted to design. Upon inquiring about her progress in the effort to teach colored people how to wear what becomes them, she reported considerable success. Sometimes customers insist on purchasing unbecoming attire, but usually she has shown them the unwisdom of so doing, and most of them now take her advice.

In this way this enterprising woman is not only conducting a pioneer business, but she is rendering a social service. She has not had any special training in this work, but on her initiative she is building upon what she has learned by studying the Negroes in her community. Others of us may do likewise, if we try to help the Negro rather than exploit him.

Notes

¹Annual Report of the Director of the Association for the [return] Study of Negro Life and History, Incorporated, July 1, 1932 to June 30, 1933. Washington, D. C. p. 4

²Annual Report, ibid., July 1, 1929 to June 30, 1930. p. 4 [return]

³Lawrence D. Reddick, "Racial Attitudes in American History [return] Books in the South." The Journal of Negro History Volume XIX No. 3, July, 1934 pp. 225-265

⁴ Thomas L. Dabney, "The Study of the Negro." The Journal [return] of Negro History ibid., pp. 265-307

⁵Horace Mann Bond, "The Curriculum and the Negro Child" [return] Journal of Negro Education Volume IV No. 2, April, 1935. p. 163 ff.

⁶ibid. [return]

⁷W. E. Burghardt DuBois "Does the Negro Need Separate [return] Schools?" Journal of Negro Education Volume IV No. 3, July, 1935. pp. 328-329

⁸ibid. p. 333 [return]

⁹ibid. p. 335 [return]

¹⁰Monroe Work, Negro Yearbook: An Annual Encyclopedia [return] of the Negro 1931-1932. Negro Yearbook Publishing Company. Tuskegee Institute Alabama, 1931. pp. 204, 205, 206.

www.ingramcontent.com/pod-product-compliance
Lightning Source LLC
Chambersburg PA
CBHW081058290526
45795CB00006B/1903